The POLITICS *of*
PUNISHMENT

The POLITICS *of* PUNISHMENT

PRISON REFORM
IN RUSSIA
1863–1917

BRUCE F. ADAMS

NORTHERN ILLINOIS UNIVERSITY PRESS
AN IMPRINT OF
CORNELL UNIVERSITY PRESS
ITHACA AND LONDON

© 1996 by Northern Illinois University Press

First paperback printing 2019

Design by Julia Fauci

ISBN 978-1-5017-4774-8 (paperback)

Library of Congress

Cataloging-in-Publication Data

Adams, Bruce Friend.

The politics of punishment : prison reform in Russia, 1863–1917 / Bruce F. Adams.

p.   cm.

Includes bibliographical references (p.   ) and index.

ISBN 0-87580-215-X

1. Prisons—Russia—History—19th century. 2. Prison administration—Russia—History—19th century. 3. Prisons—Government policy—Russia—History—19th century. I. Title.

HV9712.A63   1996

365'.7'0947—dc20   96-10422

CIP

Title page illustration from
Siberia and the Exile System (1891),
by George Kennan

CONTENTS

ACKNOWLEDGMENTS

I owe thanks to many individuals and not a few institutions for their help with this book. Grants from the International Research and Exchanges Board and the Fulbright-Hays program in 1978–1979 made the initial research possible. An IREX Preparatory Fellowship gave me the summer of 1978 to concentrate on background reading and research plans. The IREX exchange with Fulbright support then provided access to archives and libraries in Moscow and Leningrad.

My scholarly experience in post-détente Moscow was like that of many other exchange students in those years. I found service at the Central State Archives of the October Revolution (TsGAOR) in Moscow to be friendly but spotty. The papers of the Main Prison Administration, which I eventually was able to read, were long delayed in delivery but copious and well organized. I learned later from a Soviet historian in Leningrad that they had been evacuated from Moscow during World War II and had never been returned from the small Siberian town where he had had to go to read them. But while I waited for TsGAOR, I could work productively at the Lenin State Library, where the holdings were wonderful and where reading conditions and service were good.

In Leningrad I received excellent assistance at the Central State Historical Archives (TsGIA) from archivists who understood the tsarist bureaucracy better than I did and who brought me not only the materials I requested but also other files that proved to be valuable. My sincere thanks to the staff of TsGIA. Many years later I also received excellent service at the State Archive of Perm Region (GAPO). My thanks to the archivists there and to my Sister City friends in Perm, especially Viktor Khenner and Olga Bogoslovskaia, who made my stay there not only possible but also memorably pleasant.

Friends at the University of Maryland, where I completed my dissertation, have my gratitude. The inspired teaching of George Yaney and Clifford Foust helped me choose my profession. George's exacting standards and his personal example of hard work helped me understand how a scholar does his work. George Majeska gave me much-needed encouragement and advice. I owe a special debt to the late Walter Rundell Jr., who was then chairman of the Department of History. A kind and generous man, Walter befriended many graduate students. I was particularly grateful at the time for his help in finding summer jobs in Washington with which I supported my family and could afford to return to school each fall. In retrospect I am at least as grateful for his friendly, supportive personality. I am sure many graduates from College Park owe a similar debt of thanks.

I am happy to acknowledge many others for the support I have had in researching parts of this book subsequent to my dissertation. For grants I thank the Graduate Research Committee and the Arts and Sciences' Research Committee of the University of Louisville and the Southern Regional Education Board. For housing, access to an excellent library, and many a stimulating stay at the Summer Laboratory in Urbana I thank the Russian and East European Center at the University of Illinois, the Slavic Reference Room, and their excellent staffs. I would like to especially thank Ralph and Ruth Fisher for their hospitality and many kindnesses and Helen Sullivan and Larry Miller for their expert guidance to the library's resources.

For whatever problems may remain in the book I bear full responsibility.

The POLITICS *of* PUNISHMENT

INTRODUCTION

Russia's penal system has an extremely negative reputation. Soviet scholars, Russian and foreign observers, and writers and memoirists who experienced Russia's prisons and exile system have generally agreed that they were horrible. Russian practices and conditions, as they understood them, were backward and brutal. For most of the tsarist period there were good reasons for this. Russian notions of punishment were not the same as Europe's, and from a Western perspective Russia seemed "behind." All these observers wrote from such a perspective. They observed correctly that the forms of punishment Western societies had decided were cruel and unnecessary—disfigurement (such as the slitting of nostrils), branding, permanent exile, and a variety of corporal punishments—lasted longer in Russia than in most Western nations. But long after Russia had abolished most of these "anachronisms," the reputation for backwardness and brutality remained.

The image of gauntlets and salt mines still survives. And I dare say the image most Russian specialists have is not much different from the popular image. The more we have read in the memoir and secondary literature, the more likely we are to have this negative impression. For the last forty or fifty years of the tsarist regime, however, it is undeserved. After a false start in 1845 Russian statesmen and administrators began again in 1863—in the midst of the Great Reforms—to discuss the need to modernize Russia's penal practices. The discussion was protracted. Although it accomplished little in the way of prison reform before 1879 and had not ended in 1917, the discussion slowly led to substantive changes in criminal punishment and in the physical condition, population, regimes, and administration of Russia's prisons.

The abiding negative image comes from many sources. First, the memory of Russia's long history of very real violence, penal and societal, was not suddenly eradicated by the reforms of the 1860s and following decades. It takes a long time to live down a bad reputation. Repin's famous portrait of Ivan IV cradling the son he had just murdered; engravings of Peter the Great personally axing the *streltsy;* the execution and exile of Decembrists, memorialized in literature and on Herzen's masthead for *Kolokol,* which was published in London; and Dosto-evskii's *The House of the Dead* are but a few of the well-known images of Russian culture and history that may have stuck in the popular imagination. In the West, where few people knew Russian, the writings of dissident expatriates, which naturally cast Russia in a bad light, were also influential. Aleksandr Herzen and Mikhail Bakunin were probably the most important of them in the 1850s and 1860s. Especially in England and France, where the yellow press sold many an issue in the decades before the Crimean War with exaggerated accounts of Russian backwardness and oppression,[1] their views could be readily accepted.

In the decades following the Great Reforms, when significant reforms in penology were begun, political violence, popular and official, added to the impression of penal harshness. When the Polish uprising of 1863 was put down, popular sympathy in the West belonged to the Poles. When populists rose against the government in the 1870s, public sympathy at home and abroad supported the young radicals. Until the assassination of Alexander II, arrests, trials, executions, and sentences of imprisonment and exile only seemed to spur both sides to more violence and to create more sympathy for the populists. Heroes of the movement who fled Russia or were released from their exile wrote of their experiences and those of their comrades, emphasizing tales of bravery and sacrifice on the one hand and brutality, mistreatment, and injustice on the other. There were numerous incidents in the heyday of populism, 1873–1881, and famous massacres later in Siberia, which needed little dramatizing to seem horrible.

Lev Deich, Vera Zasulich, and, especially, Sergei Kravchinskii wrote colorful memoirs. So did the famous anarchist Petr Kropotkin. Kravchinskii, who had no personal experience with Russian prisons, made a career of writing, speaking, and publishing on the revolutionary movement and tsarist oppression.[2] The English Society of Friends of Russian Freedom (SFRF), which he founded, kept the issue of Russia's allegedly brutal prisons before the English public for fifteen years.[3] Other populists who had not escaped the tsarist courts—Katerina Breshkovskaia, Vera Figner, Mikhail Frolenko, Nikolai Morozov, Sofia Perovskaia, Andrei Zheliabov—later wrote voluminously about themselves and one another or were written about as heroes and martyrs of the revolutionary movement. Europeans, who had little else to read about Russia in those years, might easily believe that Russia, so recently a land of serfs and always a mysterious and frightening nation, was a vast prison house.

Most Russian radicals of this generation had grown up in relative comfort. They were not like the poorest peasants and workers who committed petty crimes when winter arrived in order to have a warm room and food in prison. Even the hardships of life in the revolutionary underground did not prepare them for prison, where they found their diet poor, their cells squalid, their isolation maddening, their guards rough and unfriendly. Exile in distant rural locations was uncomfortable and tedious for them. When they wrote about terrible conditions in Russia, they did so from a fairly parochial and privileged viewpoint. Most of their readers shared their parochialism and their revulsion.

The few expatriates of this era who experienced both Russian and European prisons agreed that European prisons were at least as bad as Russian. Petr Kropotkin, who had wide experience in Russian and French prisons, made a study of them and of imprisonment in general. From his personal experiences in French police lockups, local prisons, transport wagons, and central prisons he concluded that conditions in France were worse than in Russia. In each location he described appalling filth, cruel punishments, and/or senseless, numbing regimes. His study of other nations' prisons led him to believe that English, German, and Austrian prisons were worse in one way or another than were those of the French.[4] After Vladimir Burtsev, a populist terrorist and a member of the SFRF, spent eighteen months in two major English prisons in 1898–1899, he and Feliks Volkhovskii, Kravchinskii's assistant and then successor as leader of the SFRF, both charged that English prisons were worse than Russian prisons. Volkhovskii's article was the last the SFRF ever published on Russian prisons.[5]

The single most famous and probably the most influential book in English on Russian prisons and exile was George Kennan's *Siberia and the Exile System,* which appeared in serial form in the American *Century Magazine* in 1888–1889 and in book form in 1891.[6] Encouraged by Kravchinskii to make the study, Kennan traveled extensively through Russia and Siberia in 1885–1886 under the aegis of the Main Prison Administration, which apparently hoped he would write about the many reforms they had undertaken. Instead he spent most of his time becoming acquainted with political exiles and their life in Siberia and returned to write in negative terms about the Russian government, its prisons, and the transfer and exile systems. On his way back to New York, Kennan again visited in London with Kropotkin and Kravchinskii, who supplied him with additional information for his book. In 1894 it was they who organized his lecture tour of England.[7]

Kennan and the Russian radicals were not writing principally about Russian prisons, however; they had little interest in criminals or the prisons in which they were incarcerated. The radicals were concerned with Russia's system of government and the treatment of political prisoners—their comrades and themselves. Kennan focused on the treatment of political prisoners in Siberian exile. American and English readers likely were outraged first that young idealists, whose politics seemed closer to their own than did the Russian government's,

6 • THE POLITICS OF PUNISHMENT

were arrested at all. Then, ignorant about living and traveling conditions for the average free Russian and about the inside of prisons in their own countries, they were appalled by the conditions of imprisonment and exile. The lack of civil liberties was the more disturbing proof of Russia's backwardness and oppression, but it compounded the negative image of the Russian penal system.

The Russian government tried to blunt the sensational impact of Kravchinskii's books by discrediting him in particular and the expatriates in general as assassins and criminals.[8] After Kennan's book appeared they attempted to counter its impact by, apparently, commissioning a well-known English traveler-journalist, Harry deWindt, who had written admiringly about the administration of Siberia in a popular travel book published in 1889,[9] to write a rebuttal to Kennan. DeWindt returned to Siberia under the auspices of the government, and in 1892 he published a favorable account of the exile system.[10] It did not have the impact the Russians desired, however. His account of Siberia was too rosy, and his connections to official Russia were too apparent. The introduction to deWindt's book was written, and a large part of the book itself may have been rewritten, by Olga Novikoff, who worked in London as what we would call today a public relations and media consultant for the Russian government. Skeptical of what seemed to be a put-up job and not generally well disposed to the Russian government, reviewers found in favor of Kennan's version.[11]

The tragic history of Russia in the twentieth century has done nothing to dispel its reputation for backwardness and harshness in matters of punishment. The Revolution of 1905 was followed by severe repression that kept prisons overcrowded until 1912. In these years a hangman's noose came to be called a "Stolypin necktie" after the minister of internal affairs who directed the repression. Huge losses in World War I—up to 8 million soldiers killed, wounded, or captured, as well as unknown civilian losses—were prelude to revolutions in 1917 that culminated in a vicious civil war with horrifying atrocities and another 5 million deaths. The years of war brought on crop failure and famine in 1921 in which millions more died. And the new rulers of the country engaged in political violence on a scale far greater than did the tsars. Shortly after the October Revolution the Bolsheviks established an Extraordinary Commission for Combatting Counter-Revolution and Sabotage, the Cheka, to administer "revolutionary justice." In 1918 the Cheka managed to execute more people than the tsarist government had in the previous 300 years. They did again in 1919. The Soviet government went on to earn a well-deserved reputation for unprecedented penal harshness. The purges, show trials, the GULag with its millions of inmates and millions of deaths have all become infamous, as did the repression of political dissidents after Stalin's time in prisons, mental institutions, and a shrinking GULag. The horror of more than 20 million casualties in World War II and the revelations of recent years compound the impression of Russia as a cruel land with little regard for human life.

Most of those horrors postdate the period covered by this book and once again deal primarily with the repression of political dissidents and enemies rather than with criminal offenders. But they are not irrelevant. I believe they have a great deal to do with the preservation of the mistaken conception of Russian prisons in the late tsarist period. Our minds, colored by the knowledge of very real horrors, move from Kennan to Solzhenitsyn, and it seems as though things only went from bad to worse. The brief period in which, for better or worse, reformers did modernize Russia's prisons is buried in the much greater mass of information about the ills of the system over a much longer period.

Soviet writers have aggravated this problem. They have produced a mountain of historical scholarship, and drivel, about revolutionaries and their mistreatment. Whole periodicals and endless books have been devoted to Decembrists, populists, Bolsheviks, to everyone who suffered at the hands of the tsarist police, courts, government, and penal system for their political views. In this book I have little to say about the exile system and less about the political offenders who experienced it. Except at the height of the revolutions they never amounted to as much as 5 percent of the general prison population. Instead I focus on criminals and the penal system designed to deal with them. Scholars have paid scant attention to this subject. No Western historian has explored it previously, and the only Soviet scholar to deal with it produced a useful but highly tendentious study.

The standard work on tsarist prisons, an impressive five-volume study published in the 1950s, was written by M. N. Gernet.[12] An academic criminologist of the sociological school, Gernet had a long career. Before the revolutions he had already written several well-received studies of the etiology of crime.[13] He appears in this book as a member of the Russian Group of the International Union of Criminalists. After 1917 Gernet became a professor of jurisprudence and a prominent figure in early discussions of crime and punishment under socialism. He continued to publish extensively. His *History of Tsarist Prisons* contains a wealth of information on criminal law and on prisons; it is a valuable introduction to these subjects. It does, however, have emphases and tendencies that limit its usefulness and reliability.

A brief survey of the contents of *History of Tsarist Prisons* should make that clear. Volume 1, which surveys law and practice from the *Ulozhenie* (law code) of 1649 to about 1825, is probably least cluttered with political concerns. Gernet does, however, devote more than a quarter of it to just two prisons, the Peter and Paul and the Shlissel'burg fortresses, and to their famous political prisoners. His few interpretive, rather than descriptive, comments on criminal justice in the period are invariably negative, charging tsarist authorities with brutality, hypocrisy, and injustice. For example, he concludes his discussion of Catherine II's suggestions for criminal justice reform in her *Instruction* to the Great Legislative Commission, which were far "ahead" of contemporary practices in the direction Gernet wanted to see them evolve, by condemning her hypocrisy: "Words of humanity, although very loud, did not drown out the whistling of the knout and whips, nor the groans of the suffering victims of judicial and administrative injustice."[14]

Volume 2, which covers 1825–1870, surveys legislation governing imprisonment for those forty-five years in eighty-two pages. It includes bare mention of the law of 17 April 1863, which will play a central role in this book. That is followed by more than 400 pages on the imprisonment of Decembrists, Petra-shevtsy, Pisarev, Chernyshevskii, and others and on the prisons that held them. Only the last fifty-seven pages deal with the general criminal population and their prisons. Volume 3, covering 1870–1900, and Volume 4, 1900–1916, likewise begin with brief surveys of legislation and move quickly to lengthy de-scriptions of political prisons and prisoners. Volume 4, for example, has 45 pages of the former and 240 pages of the latter. Volume 5 is almost entirely de-voted to the mistreatment of political prisoners in the last years of tsarist Rus-sia. The only regular prison discussed in this last volume, the Orel Central, was apparently chosen because it was notorious for the severity of its regime.

Reading these five volumes leaves the same negative impression created by Kennan and Solzhenitsyn, that abusive behavior pervaded a system that changed very little. But it is a selective and misleading reading, which once again high-lights political repression and abuse. Gernet pays scant attention to the commis-sions that discussed prison systems and reforms, the Main Prison Administra-tion, which was created to establish a Russian prison system to carry out those reforms, or the reforms themselves. Those comprise the heart of my book.

I encountered unexpected difficulties in researching and writing this book, most of them concerned with the nature of my sources. First, prison reform was a minor part of the careers of most of the prominent statesmen and reformers who effected it. The men who served on the prison commissions, the ministries in which their work was discussed, the State Council through which it passed, and the Main Prison Administration itself in a few instances were involved in other issues they considered more important. Quite a few of them left memoirs or di-aries or inspired biographical studies, but few of these have much to say about their work on prisons and prison reform. Konstantin Grot, Petr Zubov, Sergei Shidlovskii, and Vladimir Kokovtsov fall in this category. So there remain many tantalizing mysteries about why certain decisions were made. I would like to know more, for example, about the transfer of the Main Prison Administration from the Ministry of Internal Affairs to the Ministry of Justice in 1895, but the statesmen involved did not discuss this in their memoirs and the official docu-ments are laconic. On the other hand, men like Mikhail Galkin-Vraskii, who spent long years in prison administration, were less likely to write or be written about. None of the directors of the Main Prison Administration, for example, left diaries or memoirs. So my knowledge of the inner workings of the administration mostly comes from more or less official reports and histories. I am aware of the need to treat such sources carefully, not to say skeptically, and trust that this is re-flected throughout the book. On the other hand, in chapter 4 I make it clear that I was impressed by the increasingly candid and critical nature of inspectoral and other internal reports, which were, after all, written for internal use only.

Another problem with sources is indicated in my last footnote. In March 1917 mobs attacked the headquarters of the Main Prison Administration, then recently renamed the Main Administration of Places of Incarceration. Among other things, they destroyed many papers. Records for the last months of the ad-ministration's operation are therefore scarce, and my story ends rather abruptly.

I did not set out to write a revisionist account. Having read Kennan, Gernet, and others before my foray into the archives, I expected to find they were largely correct. That is not what I found, however. I followed the path the prison reformers had. Starting from the movement to abolish corporal punishment in 1863, I wound my way through the commissions and bureaucracies until I found myself in 1917 with a markedly different impression. In correcting the negative image of Russia's prisons I do not try to say that they became effective correctional institutions. I am not persuaded that there were, or are, many of those anywhere. Nor do I claim that Kravchinskii, Burtsev, and Volkhovskii were correct about the relative merits of Russia's prisons. Even their experiences were rather limited. I am prepared to believe, although I think it would be difficult to prove one way or the other, that, like many other things Russian, prisons were not as clean or as orderly as were their European counterparts. What I am quite sure of, however, is that Russia, which had a smaller percentage of its population in prison than did any other European nation, gradually made its prisons cleaner, roomier, healthier places. By the end of the nineteenth century, certainly by 1917, Russia was running its prison system for the same purposes and according to the same standards in use in European nations and the United States. And that is precisely what the reformers set out to accomplish.

Their story begins in midcentury. At that time Russia had few modern prisons. As a matter of fact, compared with Europe and the United States and relative to its population, Russia had few prisons of any kind—most punishment did not involve imprisonment. Most of the prisons Russia did have were small log or wooden frame buildings, which were often not originally built to hold prisoners, and many of these were in advanced states of deterioration. The men who ran prisons, called keepers *(smotriteli)*, were usually retired military officers who typically had no training in prison administration, no knowledge of penological theory, and no sense of purpose beyond simple custodial maintenance of the buildings and their inmates. Contemporary critics claimed that most lacked even that.

Until the Great Reforms there was little need to improve this situation. A large part of the population remained legally tied to landowners and received informal trial and punishment outside the state's judicial and penal systems. For many offenses or even for legal, but troublesome, behavior, landowners and peasant communes had the power to send serfs and fellow peasants into military service or into exile in Siberia.[15] Other significant sectors of the population, such as the military and the clergy, likewise tried and punished their members independently.

Of the offenders who were processed through the state's courts only a small percentage were sent to prison. The great majority of trials ended with the release of the accused, and those who were found guilty were sentenced more often to exile, fines, or whippings than to prison.[16] When they were sentenced to imprisonment, their sentences were frequently commuted to some form of corporal punishment, either because the type of prison to which they were assigned by law did not yet exist or was already filled beyond capacity.[17] Until the reforms of the 1860s the majority of incarcerated prisoners were not convicted offenders but suspects under "preliminary arrest" who were awaiting trial.

Efforts to reform Russian criminal law and prisons earlier in the nineteenth century had been ineffective. The more ambitious efforts sometimes brought incongruous results that served more to highlight the backwardness of Russian criminal punishment than to change the system. The Prison Aid Society (*Popechitel'noe obshchestvo o tiur'makh,* or POoT), for example, was established with enthusiasm and fanfare in 1819 to enlist "social forces" in improving prison management. It soon became bureaucratized and moribund, however, a club for gentry who wanted to collect imperial medals and for merchants who were covetous of government contracts. The revision in 1845 of the Code of Criminal and Correctional Punishments, which abolished use of the knout, limited some other forms of corporal punishment, and prescribed incarceration in modern prisons, was hailed in its time as "progressive" legislation. Its drafters and Nicholas I looked to it to spur the modernization of the Russian penal system. The new code required the use of preliminary detention prisons, workhouses, "strait" houses, houses of correction, and correctional prisons.[18] Such institutions did not exist in Russia, however, and no provision had been made for their establishment. Yet the code remained the basic tool of judges and later of juries for at least four decades before modern facilities were built.

Because of this the code of 1845 did provide pressure for further reform. It caused overcrowding in prisons, which were not the complex variety of modern correctional facilities required by the code, but the simple barrackslike holding facilities that already existed. Until 1848 they grew increasingly overcrowded, too crowded for the health of the inmates or the security of the prisons. The situation made some keepers, judges, and lawmakers aware of the need to build new prisons, but support could not be found for so expensive an undertaking.

The government solved the overcrowding by less expensive, more expedient means. In 1848 many prisoners of military correctional companies were taken into active service. Many other prisoners were sent off to Siberia, and still others were formed into "work companies" to labor for the Department of Means of Communication.[19] All of the other problems, the backwardness that the Code of 1845 had hoped to drive out of Russian prisons, remained. But overcrowding was reduced, and the rest could be, for the most part, ignored. By another expedient the state assured that overcrowding would not again threaten the tottering prisons. The Code of 1845 permitted courts to substitute corporal punishment for incarceration where particular types of prisons did not exist or were overcrowded. Although a major intent of the code had been to reduce corporal punishment, this loophole was widely applied. Furthermore, judges, and later juries, because of their distrust and fear of prisons, avoided sentencing to imprisonment by acquitting some accused persons even when they knew them to be guilty.

In some ways the 1845 code did lead to further reform. The enormous difference between its aspirations and reality long embarrassed those Russian statesmen who had any interest in penology and prisons. They wrote later that they had long desired reform but that until the 1860s there were more obstacles to reform than incentives to overcome them.[20] Until the era of the Great Reforms too few people commanded the expertise or authority to bring further change to

Russia's criminal law and punishment or even to discuss it publicly. Nonetheless, the consciousness that change was desirable and the vision of what these reforms ought to be grew quietly in the 1840s and 1850s. When censorship was relaxed under Alexander II and other major reforms had already been enacted or were under discussion, proponents of reform in criminal law also reemerged.[21]

One of the first concrete problems of criminal law these reformers attacked was corporal punishment. Like many other legal problems, it had been on their minds for a long time. The ideas behind the reform, therefore, had had time to mature and sprang full blown when the lid of censorship was removed. My story begins with this discussion. In the atmosphere of the Great Reforms the effort to abolish corporal punishment led directly to the movement to reform Russian prisons.

THE

MOVEMENT

TO ABOLISH

CORPORAL

PUNISHMENT

It is possible that, on this point, the reformer may have gone ahead of the times. A certain shyness as regards Europe's opinion may not have been foreign to this particular reform; but this feeling has urged Russia into many a step in the right direction since Peter the Great, and, for states as for individuals, ambition, a care of other people's opinion, may at certain times, be good advisors. Who knows where Russia would stand now but for that very spur?

—Anatole Leroy-Beaulieu, *The Empire of the Tsar*

THE IDEA

For several hundred years before 1863 the most common form of punishment in Russia was corporal punishment. Criminals sentenced by the courts, soldiers and sailors judged by military authorities, and serfs disciplined by their masters were regularly whipped, beaten, and branded by a variety of implements. Peasant elders thrashed their fellow peasants. Yet over the previous century the severity of corporal punishments had slowly been mitigated in law, and by the middle of the nineteenth century many well-educated reformers were calling for their abolition. In 1863 they almost had their way: most remaining corporal punishments were abolished, and those that continued to be used were reduced in severity.

This occurred in the midst of the Great Reforms, when other profound changes were being made. The penal reform was part of this greater whole; it was especially closely linked to emancipation, in part caused by it. Although it preceded them, it was also closely related to the judicial reforms and, in general, to the mood of confidence and excitement generated by and producing those larger reforms. But the penal reform should not be understood simply as a necessary, but minor, part of the Great Reforms, a corollary to emancipation and court reforms. The changes made by the law of 17 April 1863 had purposely been excluded from emancipation legislation only two years before. The penal reform was not impelled by the economic urgency that stood behind emancipation or by the personal and class interests entangled in the court and zemstvo reforms. What it shared with the other Great Reforms was the old and growing desire of Russia's educated upper classes to implement a program of "liberal" reforms, as most of Europe had done much earlier. Part of that desire stemmed from their wish to consider themselves modern Europeans and to have Europeans accept them and their nation as such. Their feeling of shame at the "barbarity" of their country was a most important motivation for the penal reform.

The very old idea that corporal punishment is incompatible with the dignity of free men was resurrected in the European Enlightenment and made its way quickly to Russia. Those to whom the idea was available immediately applied its meaning to themselves and only slowly extended the same courtesy and protection to other groups in Russian society. Eventually, when the serfs were emancipated, it seemed only right to exempt them from indignities that were no longer suitable to their free condition. By that time most corporal punishments had been eliminated in other European countries.

How and where the idea originated that corporal punishment and human dignity are incompatible is unclear to me. It is not an entirely "natural" concept that arises with the first stroke of the rod or the whip, for millions of people have been punished in that way without raising that objection. In Russia, after the reform of 1863 many peasants expressed their preference for corporal punishments over fines and incarceration. Still, the idea of their indignity is old. Many great civilizations have used corporal punishments extensively and for long periods of time, but they have usually distinguished between their unprivileged masses and various privileged groups, who have been exempted from corporal punishments. In the Roman Republic, for example, where at least five forms of corporal punishment were frequently applied, they were never legally applied to a Roman citizen. In the Roman Empire corporal punishment was established only for persons of lower rank *(humiliores)*. Equality of persons before the law was a recognized principle in medieval German law, but the poor still found themselves subjected to corporal punishment much more frequently than did citizens of substance. Convicts who could not pay fines were beaten or otherwise humiliated instead. French law, which did not recognize the principle of legal equality until after the Revolution of 1789, imposed corporal punishment much more frequently on the lower classes.[1]

Severe punishment was common throughout Europe and Russia in the Middle

Ages. The use of corporal punishment, torture, and capital punishment reached its greatest heights between the thirteenth and seventeenth centuries. In the ingeniousness of devices and the ferocity and frequency of their application, the period surpassed any before or since. Only slowly did the most vicious practices disappear.

In the eighteenth-century Enlightenment the emerging intelligentsia revived and extended many old ideas they found satisfying or useful. Among them were ideas of rights and privileges that they claimed for themselves and, in some cases, for their countrymen or for all men. They propounded new ideas about the rights of man and human dignity to justify changes in civil law. These spilled over into criminal law as well and helped to cause changes in European criminal and penal practices.[2] Russia did not share in the social changes that midwifed these ideas or in the political upheavals of the "age of revolutions," but the ideas moved across its borders. Educated Russians read Locke, Montesquieu, Rousseau, Beccaria, and Bentham and were impressed by the force of their ideas and by the recent social and political changes in Europe that seemed to stem from them.

Cesare Beccaria, who had few original ideas, probably had the most direct and profound influence on European thinking about crime and punishment. In his treatise *On Crimes and Punishments,* which was first published in 1764, he compiled what the Encyclopedists, the philosophes, and his enlightened Italian friends had to say on the subject. Beccaria did not advocate the abolition of corporal punishment. On the contrary, he stated clearly that it was still needed. He was most concerned about doing away with the death penalty, with torture, which he insisted was not punishment at all because it preceded determination of guilt, and with mutilation, which he and historians of punishment have called the most barbarous form of corporal punishment.

Beyond Beccaria's intentions, however, the movement toward leniency, for which his book became gospel, produced in believers a general condemnation of all excessively harsh punishment as uncivilized and even counterproductive. Each subsequent generation of reformers reviled as cruel and unusual the forms of punishment that the previous generation had considered normal and justified. In the late eighteenth and nineteenth centuries, European reformers included one after another of the remaining forms of corporal punishments in their attacks on "barbarous" and "uncivilized" remnants of the old world. Beccaria was then used as an authority to support what he himself had not said. It is easy to read in his words general disapprobation of severe punishment, including forms he had not hoped to abolish. The following quotation conveys particularly well the spirit of this movement:

> [The] purpose of punishment is neither to torment and afflict a sensitive being, nor to undo a crime already committed. Can there, in a body politic which, far from acting on passion, is the tranquil moderator of private passions—can there be a place for this useless cruelty, for this instrument of wrath and fanaticism, or of weak tyrants? . . . Always keeping due proportions, such punishments and such method of inflicting them ought to be chosen, therefore, which will make the

strongest and most lasting impressions on the minds of men, and inflict the least torment on the body of the criminal.

Who, in reading history, can keep from cringing with horror before the spectacle of barbarous and useless torments, cold-bloodedly devised and carried through by men who called themselves wise? What man of any sensibility can keep from shuddering when he sees thousands of poor wretches driven by a misery either intended or tolerated by the laws (which have always favored the few and outraged the many)?[3]

Even in Western Europe, where the impact of Beccaria's book was immediate and strong, reform came slowly. Torture, mutilation, and the more agonizing and gory forms of capital punishment were outlawed long before abolition of whipping and caning was seriously considered. In Russia the process was slower. A major reason for this was the absence in Russia of a receptive intelligentsia.[4] Only a small educated elite could read and appreciate Beccaria and his contemporaries, and not many of them seem to have spent much time pondering criminal punishment. At any rate, few left record of it before the 1860s. Civil law, as always, received much more attention than did criminal law, which affects only a minority of any population and a distinctly unpowerful minority at that. But, as in Europe, there grew in Russia a significant body of educated people who thought of themselves as not only educated but also enlightened. As people who had seen the light, they agreed with Beccaria. Perhaps, more accurately for the first generation of this tentative new Russian intelligentsia, as men (and a very few women) who wished to seem and feel enlightened, they had to agree with Beccaria.

As a first principle, they considered humankind rational, capable of being governed by reason rather than by passion. This was a mark of the enlightened person. Corporal punishments were clearly passionate, physical, not cerebral, and, unlike imprisonment, which everywhere replaced corporal punishment, they did not give the offender time to consider his sin or guilt. What kind of "lasting impression on the minds of men" could be made by forty strokes delivered in five or ten minutes? Reasonable people who believed in due proportions could only agree with Beccaria's conclusion about the excess of punishments.

> For a punishment to attain its end, the evil which it inflicts has only to exceed the advantage derivable from the crime; in this excess of evil one should include the certainty of punishment and the loss of the good which the crime might have produced. All beyond this is superfluous and for that reason tyrannical.[5]

If an enlightened Russian had not read Beccaria, he could have found the same idea in John Locke's *Second Treatise of Government*, which had long been available in Russia: "Each transgression may be punished to that degree and with so much severity as will suffice to make it an ill bargain to the offender, give him cause to repent, and terrify others from doing the like."[6] He could also have found this concept in Empress Catherine II's *Instruction* to the Legislative Commission of 1767.[7]

A second characteristic of Enlightenment thought was that it envisioned people as creatures of the present and the future. The romantics would later grow nostalgic, but the philosophes were scornful of the past. They meant to cast aside the shadows of the past, of the dark ages, when people behaved irrationally and violently. Their vision of people as reasonable and intrinsically good (or at least as perfectible if flawed) slowly pushed aside the gloomier view earlier theologians and philosophers held of human nature. Modern people, or rather people as reason now revealed them to have always been, were violent only in a violent society. Each individual could choose to be pacific, and an enlightened person would, for it had now been shown to be in his own and society's best interest. Useless violence, including torture, mutilation, and excessive corporal punishment, was anachronistic in this new world.

Beccaria explained how such violence sustained itself once it was established:

> Men are regulated in their conduct by the repeated impression of evils they know. . . . In proportion as torments become more cruel, the spirits of men, which are like fluids that always rise to the level of surrounding objects, become callous, and the ever lively force of the passions brings it to pass that after a hundred years of cruel torments the wheel inspires no greater fear than imprisonment once did. The severity of punishment itself emboldens men to commit the very wrongs it is supposed to prevent.

He asserted in conclusion that the "countries and times most notorious for severity of penalties have always been those in which the bloodiest and most inhumane deeds were committed."[8] Montesquieu, who was popular with educated Russians, had written, "Experience shows that in countries remarkable for the lenity of penal laws, the spirit of the inhabitants is as much thereby affected, as in other countries with severer punishments."[9]

At the time the philosophes were writing, Russia was not remarkable for the lenience of its laws. More than a century earlier, Tsar Mikhail had considered exempting the Russian nobility from corporal punishment, but the idea was not widely held nor strongly supported. Terrifying physical punishments, both capital and corporal, were written into the *Ulozhenie* of 1649, and they made little allowance for rank. What class distinctions were made in punishments were of an arbitrary nature and made outside the law. Under Peter the Great no distinction was made in the army among ranks or classes when punishment was meted out. After his death in 1725, however, officers increasingly tended to be whipped or beaten with rods, and lower ranks would more likely receive the knout, which was a more painful and dangerous punishment. Still, such differences were not codified. According to Prince M. M. Shcherbatov, a marshal of the gentry and a delegate to Empress Catherine II's Legislative Commission, although there was talk from the 1730s on of treating the gentry with as much respect as they received in other European countries, nothing was said specifically about exemption from corporal punishment even twenty years later.[10] The idea began to take root early in the reign of Catherine II, which, not coincidentally, were the years that Montesquieu's and Beccaria's writings began to reach Russia.

Although historians still dispute the meaning and purposes of Catherine's acts, there is little question that she liked to think of herself and to have others think of her as enlightened. She corresponded with Voltaire, Montesquieu, and Beccaria, among others of the leading philosophical lights of the day. She not only read their books but also took serious note of them. As she prepared to convoke the Legislative Commission in 1767, she incorporated many of their basic ideas into her *Instructions* to the commission.[11] Catherine even invited Beccaria to come to Russia to help her prepare the document. A distinctly unadventuresome sort, he declined.[12] One student of the commission has called it "Catherine's wish for an advertisement to Europe of the introduction of the Enlightenment into Russia."[13] This was not the main stimulus for the commission; there were more important domestic considerations. But Catherine did use it in this way. In her correspondence with Voltaire and others she exaggerated and distorted the importance of the commission to make it seem like evidence of her own and Russia's enlightenment.

The commission did not, however, produce "enlightened" penal legislation. To the contrary, the instructions written by delegates to the commission reveal that many Russians disagreed with their empress about many of her enlightened notions, including the wisdom of making punishment less severe. Representatives of several regions protested Catherine's partial abolition of torture in 1763, claiming that "the punishment of crime had been seriously hampered." The gentry of one district felt that "soft measures" might suit more-enlightened nations but that Russia was not yet ready for them. This showed that, although they disagreed with their empress, they were at least aware of the connection the philosophes were making between lenience, civility, and civilization. Many other gentry delegations asked for the restoration of the death penalty, which had been abolished, de jure if not de facto, twenty years earlier, during the reign of Empress Elizabeth.[14]

The question of corporal punishment was relatively unimportant at the Legislative Commission. Only a minority of gentry delegations suggested in their instructions that the gentry be exempted,[15] and the way in which they presented their suggestion supports the argument that the movement to limit and finally abolish corporal punishment depended on an imported idea—that it was uncivilized and undignified. None of the delegations that requested exemption suggested it was ineffective, whereas all of them who offered specific justification for their request referred to the "dishonor" or "indignity" of corporal punishment.[16] Furthermore, none of these instructions asked for the general abolition of corporal punishment or even for the extension of exemption to other groups. It was not the punishment itself that was offensive to them but the application of that punishment to themselves as a class.

This was another characteristically "enlightened" attitude. Beccaria believed corporal punishment to be a necessary and useful weapon of justice for at least the lower classes. The literate Russian noble who had missed this point in *On Crimes and Punishments* could have found it also in *The Spirit of the Laws*.[17] Writing of modernizing punishment, Montesquieu recommended imposing fines for crimes against property. "But," he continued, "as those who have no property are generally the readiest to attack the property of others, it has been found necessary, instead of a pecuniary, to substitute a corporal punishment." Earlier, in the *Persian Letters,* and again in *The Spirit of the Laws,* he emphasized that law and punishment must conform to national customs and character:

> The imagination conforms itself to the mores of the country in which we live: eight days imprisonment, or a lighter punishment, affects the mind of a European, brought up under a mild government, as much as the loss of an arm intimidates an Asiatic.

He added that "a Frenchman shall be driven to despair at the infamy of a punishment to which he is condemned, which would not deprive a Turk of his sleep for one quarter of an hour."[18]

The commission and Catherine's *Instruction* undoubtedly spread and reinforced these Enlightenment ideas about the "softening of manners" *(smiagchenie nravov)* in advanced societies that Catherine took to be "axioms incontrovertibly recognized as true." The empress's acceptance of the ideas must have made it easier for others to accept them. Since at least 1762, when the gentry were first freed from compulsory service to the state, some leading gentry had been developing a consciousness of themselves as the bulwark of the monarchy, as they imagined Europe's aristocracy to be. In the gentry's instructions to the commission and in the years following, evidence increases that these two sets of ideas merged, that the gentry made the Enlightenment concepts of law and government part of their own self- and group identity.[19]

It was easy enough for the Russian gentry to rationalize, and possibly even to believe, that they deserved exemption from some of the rougher aspects of life but that the great majority of the population did not. The Europeans whom many of them admired and tried to emulate felt much the same. The philosophes may have been rebels against the eighteenth-century establishment, but they were aristocratic rebels who took their material comforts and social advantages for granted. They considered the peasants of their own countries their inferiors, as rude and ignorant as their ancestors of the last dark centuries. In Russia the contrast between comfortable and gracious urban or manor life and peasant squalor, ignorance, and poverty was greater than in Europe and could serve as strong evidence of the inherent superiority of the gentry as a class for those who were inclined to believe it. Russian gentry could conceive of themselves as Europeans in an Asiatic country, as polished folk of gentle manners in a rough land. Those who might have begun to feel magnanimous toward the peasants certainly felt less generous after the bloody Pugachev uprising.[20] Obviously, they could conclude, force was all those brutes understood. It was flattering, convenient, and easy to claim special treatment on the basis of progressive European thought and recently frightening Russian reality.

Like the German empress, the self-conscious gentry thought of themselves as European. They were embarrassed by what they came to consider Russia's backwardness in comparison with Europe. Just as Catherine dissembled in her correspondence with European philosophers and statesmen to put the best face on her intentions and on Russian conditions, the gentry sought to separate themselves from what was archaic and barbaric in Russia and to secure privileges and an honored place in the state, as well as a satisfying image of themselves. Catherine could take satisfaction in such an arrangement also. Not only was she an intellectual, guided in part by the images she had found in books of just and despotic rulers, but she needed educated, dedicated servitors for her military and her rapidly growing bureaucracy. In the eighteenth century only the gentry could meet these needs; only they had the funds and opportunity to educate their children for such service. That is how they happened to be enlightened. After the fright of the Pugachev uprising Catherine appreciated the vulnerability of the Russian countryside. To secure order and her own hold on the throne she turned increasingly to the gentry, eventually in 1785 with a broad program of privileges.

One of the privileges Catherine granted the gentry in the "Charter to the Nobility" was exemption from corporal punishment. Unlike the other privileges (freedom from obligatory service, the right to landed and other property, the right to engage in manufacture and trade, and freedom from personal taxes and impositions), freedom from corporal punishment brought no tangible financial advantage. It was solely a mark of respect, honoring this new conception of a European aristocracy in Russia. At the same time, Catherine freed merchants of the first two guilds from corporal punishment, thus recognizing the slowly emerging mercantile and industrial bourgeoisie as another group in the vanguard of the modern world.

Those gentry and merchants who valued European opinion could take satisfaction that the change was applauded in the West. Jeremy Bentham, to name just one of the distinguished Europeans who admired Catherine, mentioned it in his long study, *The Rationale of Punishment.* The Chinese, he said, were still backward Asians: "Nothing more completely proves the degradation of the Chinese than the whips which are constantly used by the Police. The mandarins of the first class, the princes of the blood, are subjected to the bamboo, as well as the peasant." The same had recently been true in Russia. "In the reign which preceded that of the mild and intelligent Catherine II, neither rank nor sex bestowed an exemption from the punishment of whipping."[21] Now Russia was catching up.

Emperor Paul, who followed Catherine to the throne, had little regard for the privileges of the gentry or for such niceties as their exemption from corporal punishment. At his personal insistence a law was passed in 1797 that made gentry and merchants of the first two guilds, who had by commission of a crime lost their "rights of estate," subject once more to corporal punishment.[22] Paul's son and successor, Alexander I, possessed a mind more like his grandmother's than his father's. Liberally educated largely under Catherine's influence, he soon overturned much of Paul's legislation, once more exempting these groups from corporal punishment.[23] He also extended exemption to a few small nationality groups, on the grounds that by local custom they were not subjected to corporal punishment.[24]

Under Alexander the principles that corporal punishment was an affront to civilization and to personal dignity were given wider play. In 1817 the slitting of nostrils was abolished.[25] Except for branding (*kleimenie*—actually a form of tattooing), which contemporary legislators felt was necessary for the identification of criminal exiles, this law ended mutilation in Russia. Two other laws, which made no specific abolition or limitation of corporal punishments, perhaps best symbolize the softening of manners by which enlightened Russians recognized themselves as civilized. Separate acts forbade use of the words "mercilessly" and "cruelly" when sentencing offenders in military and civilian proceedings.[26]

Other limitations were set to corporal punishment during the reigns of Alexander I and Nicholas I, but conditions at their courts did not permit consideration of its abolition. Under Alexander torture was legally ended as "a shame and reproach to mankind."[27] Its use apparently did decline, but the practice did not come to an end in this period. Several historians of the problem attribute its continuation to the influence of General Aleksei Arakcheev, Alexander's most trusted advisor in the second half of his reign.[28] Also largely because of Arakcheev, severe corporal punishment continued to be administered in the military. The number of strokes that could be meted out in a "gauntlet" was unlimited during Alexander's reign and frequently exceeded 1,000. The punishment often resulted in the offender's death. In Nicholas's reign the number of strokes was reduced to 600 during peacetime, but this was still more than enough to kill.

Beneath the surface of military harshness and strict censorship, which marked Nicholas's reign in particular, the climate of opinion continued to change, however. The Decembrist revolt of 1825 and the tremendous burst of reformist enthusiasm of the late 1850s and early 1860s testify to the changes of heart and mind that could not be clearly or openly expressed during Alexander's and Nicholas's reigns. In an anecdotal reminiscence from the 1830s that reflects this change, a general recalled how in his youth he had been beaten personally by a field marshal from whom he had swiped something. Now, in his own day as a general, he would not think of doing that. "What softies people have become," he complained. "You can't even swear at them. It used to be they would beat us and beat us with a stick, and we would not dare say a thing."[29]

THE REFORM

The accession of Alexander II to the throne immediately brought hope of reform in many areas, and Alexander buoyed the hope with speeches and pronouncements during the first months of his reign. The periodical press then felt free to print discussions of many of the burning questions of the day. Foremost among these was emancipation, but corporal punishment received a great deal of attention as well. Articles about corporal punishment appeared in newspapers and in a variety of journals, including both official ministerial publications and privately published social and political journals. Alexander Herzen, an influential liberal publicist writing from abroad who led many of these discussions with bold articles in *Kolokol,* strongly condemned corporal punishment and called for its complete abolition.[30] Soldiers and officers protested the still frequent use of corporal punishment in the military. Officers condemned fewer soldiers to such punishment and even dared to write about their wish to end its use. Soon after an article appeared in *Voennyi Sbornik* in 1861 defending corporal punishment, a protest against that article, signed by 106 officers, was printed in *Severnaia Pchela.* There was a dramatic increase in the number of cases in which soldiers in a gauntlet laid on their condemned fellow soldiers lightly.[31]

Committees studying the emancipation of serfs found they had to discuss corporal punishment. If the serfs were to be freed, what would their new status be? In what courts would they be tried if they broke laws? To what punishments would they be subject? The consensus in 1858 was that corporal punishment should remain available in the Code of Punishments. Ia. I. Rostovtsev, the chairman of the Editing Committee that later produced the emancipation legislation, wrote to Alexander II in 1858, "Concerning punishment I dare add that in any case we should not mention corporal punishment at all: first of all it would be a strain on the current legislation . . . on liberation."[32]

Rostovtsev seems to have had in mind the fear shared by many landowners and others that emancipation or even discussion of emancipation might make the serfs refractory. Should the major form of punishment also be removed, or should the peasants believe it was about to be, they might become uncontrollable. Provincial gentry committees invited to send testimony to the Editing Committee expressed this apparently widespread fear in their reports. Few favored any further limitation on the use of corporal punishment. Of those that did, some favored exempting women, and some others suggested exempting certain categories of crime. Only a minority of one gentry committee, that from Moscow, recommended complete abolition.[33]

Because sympathy seemed to be strongest for exempting women, in an 1859 circular the government asked provincial governors *(nachal'niki gubernii),* what effect they observed such punishment to have and could it be abolished "without risk of reducing the fear of legal punishment?" Practically all of them replied that witnesses to corporal punishment sympathized strongly with the "victim." Men often offered to marry women to free them from the punishment. Men and women frequently attempted to bribe the executioner. Most of the governors agreed that corporal punishment should be ended or significantly reduced for women; only two of them, from St. Petersburg and Novorossiisk provinces, wrote that corporal punishment should be abolished for men as well as for women.[34]

After 1859 a growing number of gentry deputies to the Editing Committee expressed their desire to see corporal punishment eliminated. The committee debated the matter and found itself split on the question, which was decided by its chairman. Corporal punishment was retained; between 1861 and 1863 it was widely applied. One further limitation was placed on its use, however. Peace mediators *(mirovye posredniki),* who were to implement emancipation at the local level, and gentry marshals acting as peace mediators were limited to inflicting a maximum of twenty blows with a birch,[35] a relatively mild punishment.

Rejection of the proposed reform in 1861 was a last-ditch defense. The reform of corporal punishments had almost become part of the emancipation legislation. But, although anticipation of the forthcoming emancipation had necessitated discussing the abolition of corporal punishment, fear of the peasants' reaction to emancipation persuaded the committee and the emperor that at least for a while corporal punishment must be kept available. Meanwhile, foes of corporal punishment continued to speak out against its continued existence. V. Spasovich, probably the most influential of Russia's fledgling criminalists at that time, attacked corporal punishments strongly in one of Russia's first textbooks on criminal law, published in 1863. They were worse than capital punishment, he claimed, because they not only shamed their victims but embittered and hardened them as well. No respected criminalists, he exaggerated, defended their use any longer. Most of the nations of Europe had abolished such punishments, and where they were not abolished, they were severely curtailed. "Corporal punishments can not long remain in use among educated people."[36] Herzen kept up his assault also, publishing, among other attacks on corporal punishment, an anonymous letter to the editor, whose author was outraged that the recently emancipated black American slaves had been freed from corporal punishments whereas Russian peasants had not.[37]

The opening shot in the final battle of this period to abolish corporal punishment was fired soon after the emancipation legislation. In March 1861, just a month after the "Tsar Liberator" signed the emancipation documents, Adjutant General Prince Nikolai A. Orlov wrote him and asked that the government abolish corporal punishment.[38] Orlov was son of the former chief of gendarmes A. F. Orlov, who was not known for his liberalism, but, like many sons of his generation, Nikolai Orlov had grown much more liberal than his father. He was one of the oldest friends of Grand Duke Konstantin Nikolaevich, Emperor Alexander's influential brother who was friend, inspirer, and protector to many of the reformers of the 1850s and 1860s. He was also an admired acquaintance of Grand Duchess Elena Pavlovna, who had played a similar role for reformers in the 1840s and 1850s and was not without influence in the 1860s. Orlov was a friend of E. M. Feoktistov, an outspoken liberal literary figure, who remembered Orlov as kind, rich, generous, and extremely liberal, recalling especially that he intervened with Alexander II for the Polish patriots who had rebelled against Russian rule in 1863. By education and experience Orlov was a thoroughly westernized Russian. He spent most of his adult life in Europe. When he wrote his note about corporal punishment to Alexander, he was serving as Russia's ambassador to Belgium.[39]

Orlov's note deserves close attention because in it he rehearsed all of the arguments for abolition. The strength and position he gave each argument reveals which he considered most important. As I shall show, his priorities were shared by several members of the committee that studied his proposal and were reflected in the law they produced. Their arguments clearly stem from speculative philosophy of the European Enlightenment rather than from any particular study of Russian conditions. The few points that applied solely to Russian history and conditions were not basic but supporting; they were merely assertions that what the Europeans had said about corporal punishment in general was especially true in the Russian case.

Orlov began, "In most European states corporal punishment is totally abolished or is used as a rare exception. Contrary to that in Russia and Poland, such punishments serve as the basis of the whole corrective and punitive system." The first and most compelling argument Orlov could muster for the abolition of corporal punishment was that Europe had already led the way. It was an exaggerated claim in 1861, but that only underlines the importance of the point to Orlov. Only implied here, but through repetition and more explicit explanation elsewhere, it becomes clear that Orlov considered generally superior all things and ways European. In his next sentences he went on to brand corporal punishment backward, evil, and barbaric. Because he could not say that Russia was backward, evil and barbaric, he said instead that Russia was none of those things, which was why corporal punishment did not belong there.

Corporal punishments were not native or natural to Russia, Orlov claimed. Praising the abrogation of the slitting of nostrils and the use of the knout, he execrated those practices as a "vile memorial to Tatar dominion." Later he again reviled the lash and the knout as foreign. The birch, he wrote, might be more difficult to extirpate because many Russians think of the birch as naturally and traditionally Russian, but such "lash lovers" "can be answered that corporal punishments were brought to Russia by the Tatars and made law by the bureaucracy. Where Russian man developed outside the direct influence of the Mongols and the bureaucrats, there was no corporal punishment at all." They were all "barbarian punishments, shaming the Russian name."

To a westernized Russian nothing could more satisfactorily explain the crudity and cruelty found in Russia than the "Tatar yoke." Russian historians for a long time before and after this exploited the "yoke" to explain aspects of Russian life and history they deplored. Karamzin, for example, in his famous *History of the Russian State,* lent scholarly authority to this claim. Along with other barbarities, the Mongols had introduced corporal punishment to Russia, he wrote, and had so accustomed the Russians to such cruelties that they persisted.[40] Writers who refuted Karamzin included N. D. Sergeevskii, N. S. Tagantsev, and the most thorough student of corporal punishment in Russia, N. Evreinov.[41] These scholars presented convincing evidence that corporal punishment long predated the Tatars and was quite common in early Rus history. Later writers generally accepted their view, but Orlov's idea had great appeal and, therefore, staying power. Even after corporal punishment was largely abolished and prominent students of Russian criminal law had refuted Orlov's claim, others continued to repeat it. I. Ia. Foinitskii, an influential academic criminalist, agreed with Karamzin in his 1889 massive work, *The Study of Punishment in Relation to Prison Administration.*[42] Orlov had found an excellent device with which to damn corporal punishment by making it appear outlandish in Russia.

His next argument attempted to show in another way how inappropriate corporal punishment was to Russia. Unlike the pagan Mongol hordes, Russia was a

Christian state, in which Christian "laws of mercy and meekness" must "condemn all violence and torture." Following this line of reasoning, Orlov broadened his argument against corporal punishment into a plea for equality of all before the law. It was as close as he came to a political statement in the whole note.

> There is no Christian equality, no Christian brotherhood, where side by side in one temple two men can stand who have committed the same offence but have been punished, one with brief arrest and the other with birch lashes. In a Christian state there can be no partiality, and justice of the supreme power must be like God's justice, that is equal for all.

Only after having attacked corporal punishment as something Europe had already discarded, as a barbarian leftover brought by hated pagan conquerors, and as un-Christian did Orlov move into more modern arguments. Like his previous claims, which were either exaggerated or false and for which he offered no historical, statistical, or other evidence, the following were only assertions. The arguments are interesting primarily as reflections of contemporary European thought on personality. One of the arguments also sounds a populist note that had recently emerged in Russian literature and would soon grow strong in its politics.

Corporal punishment, he wrote, was "immoral" and, at long last, "ineffective." Why? Because "it supports coarseness of manners [grubost' nravov] and strongly interferes with the correct development of human personality." Civilization is marked by gentle behavior, whereas corporal punishment coarsens people and prevents them from advancing beyond their rude, precivilized lives of rough behavior. This is no raison d'état, as were most of the principal arguments for emancipation, nor even really a clear statement of the ineffectiveness of particular punishments, but rather an argument for the development of a certain type of personality and for a new society of such individuals. Beatings and even the expectation of beatings, explained Orlov, kept simple folk "secretive" and "hypocritical" with superiors. Presumably, in the absence of such punishments all Russians would be able to speak to one another more or less as brothers.

According to Orlov, even more alarming personality defects could be produced by anachronistic punishment in the modern world. Education had spread further than many Russians realized, he believed, and educated people would recognize the shame inherent in corporal punishment. Because beatings would brutalize or demoralize men who were conscious of their human worth, "[we] are not far from the time when corporal punishments will lead to open resistance or to suicide." Orlov was probably rare in his concern for potential suicides, but many shared his fear of peasant violence. One of the compelling arguments for emancipation had been that the serfs would no longer put up with their unfree condition docilely. Others had argued against emancipation and then against the destruction of the village commune by claiming that freed serfs would soon become an uncontrollable, anarchic rural proletariat. The same conflicting fears were aired in the debate over corporal punishment. On the one hand, the danger that the peasants, now freed, would resist "shameful" physical punishments they had formerly borne patiently argued for abolition. On the other hand, the fear that without corporal punishment Russia had no effective deterrent punishment argued for its retention. Many voices in the debate continued to make this point after it had kept the penal reform out of the emancipation legislation.

Orlov conceded that corporal punishment did have a deterrent effect but concluded that its evil and ill effects far outweighed its usefulness. He believed that only complete abolition would remove the problem. Reducing the number of strokes would only reduce the effectiveness of the punishment, but the shame would remain. Orlov made it clear that dignity weighed more heavily with him than deterrence: "Freedom and the right to property are real only when those who possess them are wholly protected in their honor and personal dignity." He advocated replacing corporal punishment with fines.

Alexander II thought enough of Orlov's plea that he forwarded it in April 1861 to State Secretary Count D. N. Bludov with a request that the committee in the Second Department of His Imperial Majesty's Own Chancellery, which was then preparing a new Code of Military Punishments, study it.[43] The journal of this committee records that they first discussed Orlov's note in May 1861 but that they had discussed corporal punishment several times previously. In general they agreed with Orlov and thought that the Russian people did also. They approved of the conviction that was then "widespread among us" that "inhuman torturing, even of people who had darkened themselves with the vilest evil acts, is already extremely inconsonant with the manners of our people and the education that has spread among them."[44] A few months later E. M. Feoktistov echoed this view in a private letter to Orlov, which wound up in the Third Department's files.

> In society conversations are constantly heard about the necessity to present the government a petition with thousands of signatures in which the demands of the liberal party would be laid out. These demands comprise freedom of the press, public court proceedings, abolition of corporal punishment, and publication of the budget. The majority of the enlightened public belongs to that liberal party.[45]

The committee solicited opinions from heads of ministries and provinces. A great majority echoed the committee's own sentiment that the time had come to eliminate corporal punishment wherever possible. Grand Duke General Admiral Konstantin Nikolaevich, the naval minister, hoped Orlov's note would be given "the most attentive and immediate consideration." Corporal punishments "cause the state evil," he felt, and "may be tolerated . . . only in the most necessary cases." He thought that emancipation had made corporal punishment unsuitable for the peasants and that corporal punishment in the military undermined discipline and the feeling of solidarity of officer and soldier. Konstantin Nikolaevich recommended that whipping be entirely eliminated for numerous offenses and limited to fifty lashes in others. He hoped the committee would incorporate these changes into the Code of Military Punishments soon even if a more general reform for the whole civilian population were for any reason delayed.[46]

Here he ran into opposition from an unnamed former minister of war who served on the committee. For penalties in which corporal punishment was being used alone this ex-minister could not see that suitable alternatives were available. Soldiers did not have enough money to pay fines, he contended, and the military would not want to lock them up and keep them away from their duties. Where corporal punishment was applied in addition to other major punishments, such as penal servitude or imprisonment in a fortress, he agreed that it could be eliminated. In those cases he insisted that the primary punishment be increased substantially, in some cases by several years.

Comments from governors supported the view that eliminating what some called cruel punishments would serve to "soften the manners of the people." Some added that it would also reduce the number of crimes. An unnamed former minister of internal affairs (MVD) concurred completely. Several respondents reported that publicly performed corporal punishments had especially unfortunate results. The crowd of onlookers invariably sympathized with and tried to help the offenders, whom they saw as victims. Both the Ministry of Internal Affairs and the Ministry of Justice reported that it had become increasingly difficult to find volunteers to whip offenders. Most had been found among prisoners enticed by a State Council Opinion of 27 December 1833 that excused them from being whipped if they volunteered to whip others, but fewer were now volunteering. The committee agreed with the ministries that whipping had become extremely unpopular among the people and no longer served as a deterrent.

The committee concluded its two tasks together. From the military code they decided to delete all punishment by gauntlet and to eliminate the birch where it was used as supplementary punishment. For the general population they also recommended eliminating all corporal punishment where it was applied in addition to other punishment. As the ex-minister of war had insisted, they agreed to consider increasing terms of incarceration that would no longer be preceded by supplementary corporal punishment but made no specific recommendations about how to extend them. They hastened to add that their recommendations would not reduce respect for the law. It had not in France, they noted, when the French had similarly abolished supplementary corporal punishments in 1832, or in the decade thereafter. Nor had it in Russia, after various reductions in the severity of corporal punishment were made in the Code of 1845. The number of convicts sent into exile since then had actually decreased.

Additionally, the committee recommended ending branding as then practiced, which seemed to them the most degrading of corporal punishments because it inflicted the most enduring shame. Offenders were marked on their foreheads and both cheeks with letters identifying their crime. Thieves, for example, would be marked with the Cyrillic letters В О Р (vor—thief). Vagrants were marked with a Б for brodiaga. Exiles received marks that distinguished the various forms of exile then in use. The committee, recognizing that marked offenders faced extreme difficulty when they returned to honest lives, wanted to replace facial brands with marks on the offenders' shoulders. They urged an end to all corporal punishment for women, whom they recognized as weaker, more tender, and more sensitive. This, they wrote, "would serve the development and confirmation of respect that it is necessary people of the female sex enjoy in every educated society."

Unfortunately, the committee concluded in its report, all corporal punishment could not yet be abolished, although that final end was desirable. Like Orlov, they would like to see all corporal punishment eliminated and replaced by correctional imprisonment or fines. But, they agreed, the Russian people did not have enough money to pay such fines, and the state did not have enough jails, let alone modern correctional facilities. Temporarily, then, birches would still have to be used. The lash could be replaced by the birch, which was a milder instrument, and all birching should be done privately.

Count Bludov presented this report to the emperor just a few months after the committee took up its work. Alexander ordered that copies of the report and of Orlov's note be sent to all ministers and directors (heads of "main administrations"—*glavnye upravleniia*) for their comments. In an unusually short time all of these administrators replied.[47] Most approved at least the spirit of the committee's recommendations, but many discovered factors that would make practical application of the proposals difficult.

MVD P. A. Valuev, who responded first, was one of only a few who raised no objections. Not known then as a liberal or reformer and remembered as a policeman, he wrote that he could "only express his full sympathy with the philanthropic effort" of the committee.[48] Valuev's explanation reveals once more how importantly emancipation figured in this question. He thought that the abolition of corporal punishments used supplementary to other punishments would help to equalize Russians before the criminal law, as emancipation had done in civil law. Furthermore, the changes that freedom had brought to peasants' lives made it unnecessary to increase the remaining part of such compound punishments. Now that peasants had so much more to lose in property and rights, exile had become a much more serious punishment.

Valuev commented on two other recommendations. He called branding unfair because it made it so much more difficult for ex-offenders to make their way in society. Even those who behaved well and worked hard were deterred from returning to normal life. He also concurred that women should not be beaten, not because they were weaker or more sensitive but because they deserved greater respect. The dignity and rights of women must be protected, and men and women would better recognize what these were if they stopped beating and accepting the beating of women.

Several others supported the proposals with no reservations. Minister of War D. A. Miliutin contributed a brief note in which he expressed "thorough" approval. The minister of education, the head of the Postal Department, and an admiral from the Naval Ministry did likewise. Grand Duke Konstantin Nikolaevich, whose opinion was already known to the committee, sent a long response in which he reiterated many of his own and the committee's opinions. His first line of attack was once more the assertion that corporal punishment was "extremely outdated. . . . All educated people understand that corporal punishment is evil . . . , a remnant from times of rough ignorance."[49]

Apparently the administrator-respondents believed that they were expected to agree with the proposals. It might have been that as civilized men they felt constrained to approve progressive European reforms. To disapprove would put them outside respectable, cultured, capital-city society. Or it might have been that Alexander II wanted this reform and that they knew of his attitude. In any case, with the exception of three undiplomatic respondents, even the ministers and directors who disagreed with the committee's proposals prefaced their objections with circumspect insincerities of agreement. M. N. Murav'ev, the recently retired minister of state domains, agreed fully with the committee's "generous sentiments." However, he demurred, most of the worthy proposals were premature. Because the manners of the Russian people were still rough and their "understanding of the law little developed," reducing punishment would only reduce its deterrent value. About women he disagreed more strongly. They were often tougher and more stubborn than were men and should not be exempted, at least not until the committee could suggest suitable alternative punishment. His full agreement reduced to approval of only the proposal that corporal punishments not be administered publicly.[50]

The minister of the imperial court also approved, except that he feared that ending branding would make escape easier and recapture more difficult. And, like Murav'ev, he did not want the law to make exceptions for women. The minister of justice (MIu) agreed that "forms of punishment must correspond to the degree of development of national education and conception of honor" and then proceeded to disagree with the committee's proposals in great detail. V. A. Dolgorukov, director of the Third Department, Russia's secret police, agreed with the committee; the minister of finance agreed completely. Yet they raised objections that would block various penal reforms until 1879 and slow them considerably after that.

Those few who made no pretense of agreement used arguments that probably had little influence on their fellow administrators or on the committee. Not only were they diplomatically maladroit, but they were out of step with their times. Most committee members were too modern to credit imprecise and old-fashioned thinking or, apparently, to be swayed by religious arguments. The age had grown secular and would become increasingly so. The reformers accepted the criminology of their time, which explained that men behaved reprehensibly because they were oppressed by their environment or by unjust and archaic laws. Yahoos and zealots who still believed in "evil will" did not speak their language.

The Great Reforms discomfited the state controller. As he put it, everything else had recently changed in Russia, and this had created turmoil. Europe was also experiencing unspecified unrest. It was not a good time for further change. Even mentioning the committee's proposals would be dangerous, he thought, because that "would weaken the fear of punishment and further shake authority," possibly paralyze it.[51] The director of the means of communications and public buildings believed that many criminals were so evil that they had "lost all human feeling and fear of God and the state's law." They needed to be beaten.

He conceded only that they be birched rather than whipped and that the beatings be carried out in prison, before other criminals, instead of publicly.[52]

The ober-procurator of the Holy Synod reported to the committee the opinions of Metropolitan Filaret, the head of the Russian Orthodox Church. Filaret drew a line between the functions of church and state. Christ, he said, had founded a church, not a state. The state's job was to protect order for its citizens. To do so it must punish. The mercy, meekness, and forgiveness required of Christians somehow did not apply to the state in carrying out this function. Concerning the form punishment might take, Filaret pointed out that "the Savior, not the Criminal Code, corrects." The state need merely punish and Biblical chastisement was perfectly suitable. If God had thought corporal punishment harmful to social morality, he would not have commanded Moses to beat offenders (Deuteronomy 25:3). Filaret further argued that corporal punishment did not destroy the feeling of honor in criminals, for they had already lost that when they decided to commit a crime. He supported this with citations from Acts 5:41 and 2 Corinthians 11:25, with which he hoped to show that the apostles had not considered corporal punishments dishonorable.[53]

The most complete and practical comments came from D. N. Zamiatin, the MIu.[54] At every step he cited the pertinent articles of the codes and explained for what offenses various forms of corporal punishment were then applied. He took care to couch his objections in conciliatory language, in some cases holding out hope of further future reform and in others offering immediate concessions. As I have already shown, he began by agreeing with the well-established idea that "punishment must correspond to the degree of development of national education and the concept of honor." For this to be so, he wrote, change from more to less severe punishment must be gradual. Were it more rapid than the development of education and the maturation of the concept of honor, it would disturb the fear of punishment. The minister pointed to the history of gradually expanding exemption from corporal punishment in Russia as proof of his contention.

Zamiatin took this idea further in a direction that could not have pleased the reformers. As MIu he was not unaware that punishment ought to be equal for all. This was another idea that had grown firm roots since Catherine's time. But, he continued, different degrees of development of individual education required different forms of punishment. Having all made that point about education to assault corporal punishment, it would be difficult for the reformers to refute Zamiatin's logic. As the most physical punishment, corporal punishment was needed for the least cerebral offenders, to whom it was completely comprehensible. To them its abolition would signal the end of all punishment. Later, when discussing exile and supplementary corporal punishments, he reinforced this thought. It was easier for "homeless simple folks" to bear a few years of exile than it was for people unused to physical labor. For the latter exile was sufficient punishment, but for the former only the additional lashes could "terrify [them] and impart full understanding of judicial retribution for crime."[55]

The minister interpreted the evidence others had used against public corporal punishments in his own way also. Here he had no Enlightenment maxim to logically manipulate, so he approached it head on with a cleverly explained counterassertion. "Corporal punishment, serving as the retribution of justice for crime, serves as an example for spectators," he began. This had for centuries been the thought behind public executions and whippings, but this only made the practice vulnerable to attack now as archaic. No appeal to fear inspired by grisly spectacle would do. Indeed, that justification had been specifically rejected in European campaigns against public executions. Instead, Zamiatin supplied the thought with a new interpretation. The sympathy the people sometimes feel and express for the criminal is

> nothing more than the condolence [*soboleznovanie*] shown identically to a mali-cious murderer by those who must witness [his] execution. . . . Condolence is a Christian feeling that causes everyone to shudder at the pronouncement of a death sentence, even though the form of death is not considered painful.[56]

By employing this new word, "condolence," he could redefine the feeling. Instead of the ghoulish titillation that some spectators were thought to experience and that reformers believed brutalized them, the public execution of corporal punishment inspired a noble Christian sentiment. In Zamiatin's opinion, because even executions instilled condolence, corporal punishments could surely not threaten the development of finer feelings. Zamiatin concluded that the obvious involvement and feelings of condolence of observers showed that people understood the severity of the punishment and that, therefore, public corporal punishment was effective as a deterrent. He objected to his predecessor's claim that the difficulty in finding whippers indicated their repulsion to beating. More likely, he averred, it reflected the fact that executioners had to live in virtual isolation in prison. Neither he nor anyone else discussed fear of reprisals by other prisoners, especially by those who had been beaten, but this is apparently why executioners were kept apart. Volunteer executioners of corporal punishments were caught between the Scylla of retribution and the Charybdis of isolation. The reluctance of prisoners to volunteer was easily understandable in these terms and was not a strong factor in the campaign against corporal punishment.

Zamiatin concluded that corporal punishment should not be abolished, but in the last two-thirds of his paper he diplomatically offered concessions to the reformers. Branding on the face, for instance, might be replaced by branding on the shoulder. Various forms of beating could be reduced in severity. The gauntlet, which was used among civilians only on men who committed serious crimes while in exile, was already applied only rarely. It might be permitted to disappear. Where judges had latitude in sentencing, they usually chose the lowest, least severe sentence on the so-called ladder of punishments. Zamiatin suggested that the whole ladder could be modified to lessen the severity of punishments and made specific recommendations to that end.

On women Zamiatin again disagreed with the committee but offered a compromise. He did not consider women necessarily weaker or more sensitive than men. Even were that so in general, he added, it was not in particular. If all women were to be exempted, then exemptions should be given to weaker men as well. Nor did he accept that women be exempted because of the shame of baring their bodies for punishment. Women's crimes were more often "shameful" to begin with—he seems to have had prostitution, adultery, and other sex crimes in mind—proving that women do not have a more developed sense of shame. Nonetheless, he recommended they receive one-half the number of strokes a man would and that they never be whipped publicly.

An unsolicited comment came from a gentry landowner who wrote personally to Count Bludov. The committee could not have been pleased with his opinion, but they dutifully included it in their collection of documents for the State Council's consideration.[57] Emancipation had been introduced in the district where this gentleman resided. A peace mediator sent there to assist with the negotiations required by emancipation had acted on his own to forbid corporal punishments. Soon, however, he was asked by the peasant elders to reinstate them, because they were losing control of the younger men, who refused to pay the fines that were levied in lieu of corporal punishments. The gentleman complained that the peasants had recently been granted so many new advantages that they expected more decrees to expand them endlessly. Now was a bad time to encourage such thinking, he concluded. Note, in this single unofficial comment, that some peasants were unhappy at the prospect of eliminating corporal punishments and that others were displeased with the alternatives. As I shall demonstrate, many peasants would regret the passing of corporal punishments.

A few of the ministers, whose comments I have already examined, and two other officials made observations concerning the development of alternative punishments. Over the next several decades, as the Russian government struggled to deal with the so-called crime problem, it would often seem that the consequences of the loss of corporal punishment had not been well anticipated, so it is instructive to note that they were pointed out. The desire to abolish outmoded forms of punishment were obviously stronger at the time than were the real fears of some statesmen that good alternatives did not yet exist and would be difficult to establish.

Zamiatin believed that both fines and imprisonment would be harder than corporal punishment on the peasants, who did not have money to spare or extra hands they could afford to lose to time in prison. He also noted that until modern prisons could be built, imprisonment could not have the desired result—"correction of morals by punishment."[58] Dolgorukov of the Third Department concurred that the people considered even short-term arrest more onerous than whipping, but for him this affirmed the superiority of imprisonment even as it then was practiced.[59] The Ministry of Finance made the same point that it would almost always make: Russia did not have the money to build modern prison facilities.[60]

Valuev, who perhaps hoped to build a new bureaucratic empire, a prison system in the MVD, was more optimistic. He understood that the variety of correctional facilities called for by the Code of 1845 did not yet exist and asked that, because this alternative was not available, corporal punishments continue to be available as a substitute for imprisonment. If all of his statements—even the apparently contradictory statements—were sincere, Valuev must have come to this conclusion reluctantly. He disliked corporal punishments and deemed them ineffective. Criminals, he wrote, often act out of desperation and poverty. They are "abnormal, not in a physical sense, but in a moral sense." Corrections, therefore, must be moral rather than physical. Corporal punishment degrades the offender and turns him morally against those who punish him, who cannot thereafter correct him. The future could be rosier, though. Valuev looked forward, quite unrealistically, to saving the cost of executioners and all their tools and to spending that money to build needed correctional facilities.[61]

Ober-procurator of the General Assembly of the Moscow Department of the Governing Senate, N. A. Butskovskii, also thought that the purpose of punishment was to correct. Like Valuev, he feared that corporal punishment had the opposite effect, to "harden the criminal's heart." Moreover, it sapped his physical strength, which left him unfit for labor. Butskovskii believed in the corrective power of honest toil. Russia had a great deal of "social work" that could be done by prisoner brigades—building roads, draining swamps, clearing fields, and so forth.[62] Labor as a tool of corrections and prisoner labor attracted a great deal of attention by criminologists and penologists in the next half century.

Moscow's Provincial Procurator D. A. Rovinskii agreed that corporal punishment should be abolished. The alternative already existed, he felt. Prisons were sufficiently frightening, so much so that prison terms could be reduced and still have a beneficial effect. By reducing terms, space could be made in prisons and more offenders could be imprisoned. Overcrowding would be approached in this way several times in tsarist Russia (and continues to be in many countries in the contemporary world).

There is no record of how frequently the committee met to discuss these many opinions. Nor is it known how heatedly they debated their internal disagreements, or with what degree of unanimity they came to their conclusions. It is known that in the spring of 1862 Baron M. A. Korf, who had become the chairman of the committee and chief of the Second Department of the Imperial Chancellery, passed the committee's report and collected papers to Alexander II and on to the State Council. In its final report the committee reviewed the opinions they had received, dividing them into three categories as opposed completely to abolition, in favor of some lightening of severity, or in agreement with the committee. Their own recommendations and justifications remained essentially the same, with the addition only of the suggestion that the State Council empower the MVD to study ways to increase prison space and improve prison administration.[63]

On 18 April 1862 the Joint Department of Laws and Civil Affairs of the State Council voted eight to one in favor of the proposals in general. Only Count V. N. Panin dissented, insisting that it is crime that is shameful and that "punishment is shameful only in the sense that it is the consequence of crime." In a full meeting of the State Council on 18 July 1862 the committee's proposals were carried, twenty-three to three.[64] The law that resulted could conceivably have been published within days. Alexander obviously favored it, and the law differed little from the committee's final report. Yet it did not become law for another nine months. It was most probably delayed to permit unrest caused by emancipation to subside. It might also have been delayed in an attempt to identify the further reduction of corporal punishments with the emperor. The new law was enacted on Alexander II's name day, 17 April 1863.

The title of the new law, "On Several Changes in the Existing System of Criminal and Correctional Punishments," was carefully chosen to contain no reference to the abolition of corporal punishment. Apparently the State Council shared the fear that abolition of most corporal punishment would be perceived by the people as the abolition of all punishment. The law eliminated most remaining instruments and forms of corporal punishment. Branding, use of the rod, public whipping, and the whipping of women except for exiles all were ended. *Volost'* (county) courts could still sentence peasants to up to twenty strokes with a birch. Criminal courts could give male offenders for whom there was as yet no space in prisons from three to one hundred strokes with a birch. Soldiers, sailors, and exiles who committed further offenses were still subject to birching, but to fewer strokes than previously.[65]

AN EXPLANATION

Why was corporal punishment so strongly and successfully attacked in Russia during this period? Emancipation of the peasants is, of course, an obvious part of the explanation. It changed the legal and social status of the peasants, making them more nearly equal to the empire's other free subjects. Reformers frequently referred to the peasants' new status to justify the reform. But emancipation should not be seen as either a necessary or a sufficient cause of the penal reform. On the one hand, the peasants' emancipation was not complete—the continued existence of the village commune and various forms of collective responsibility made that clear. On the other hand, the government had attempted to eliminate corporal punishments as early as 1845. Passage of this reform in 1863 did not depend on the freedom of the peasants. The law of 17 April was passed two years after the serfs were emancipated but three years before the state peasants were freed. Nor were previously unfree peasants the only people who were affected by the penal reform. Although they were by far the largest legal group touched by the reform, everyone not previously exempted from corporal punishment by birth or education was equally affected. The most that can be said of emancipation is that it restarted discussion of this reform and helped to create pressure for its passage.

What else propelled the movement for abolition? Russian historians have not answered this question. Some texts and monographs that examine the Great Reforms have mentioned penal reform, but most pass over it in silence. Those historians who did write about penal reform at length did so in Russian before

1917, and most of them were in the camp of prerevolutionary Russian liberalism. They shared the attitudes and sympathies of the abolitionists and, therefore, did not examine carefully the sources of the reformers' ideas or the accuracy of their claims. These works are valuable sources of information but not of explanation.

Nor do explanations provided by other historians for similar movements elsewhere hold up in the Russian case. Myra Glenn argues that the primary forces for the abolition of flogging and whipping in the United States in these same years were the weakening of orthodox Calvinism and the growing strength of the ideologies of democracy and free labor.[66] Secularization certainly played a role in Russia's Great Reforms, but neither democracy nor free labor was as developed in Russia as in the United States, either in practice or in ideology; nor were urbanization and commercial capitalism, to which Glenn ascribes the ideological changes in the United States. David Cooper believes that most severe punishments, including public executions, were ended in England in this period because fear of crime and of "the dangerous classes" had diminished.[67] I am not convinced that he is correct about England, and I believe strongly that this argument would not hold up in the Russian case. The reform was not passed in 1861 because of fear of peasant disturbances and was passed in 1863 over repeated objections that it might undermine order and respect for law. No one argued in the Russian case that corporal punishments could be done away with because criminality had diminished.

Pieter Spierenburg contends that the European nation-states that had developed by the eighteenth and nineteenth centuries could afford to abolish the "spectacle" of extraordinary suffering because they were more powerful and stable than earlier governments.[68] This idea is appealing, but it has its weaknesses. One might wonder what the abolition of torture in France between 1780 and 1788, just a year before the revolution began, had to do with power and stability. Was the Russian state more stable or the authority of its government less questioned in the wake of the Crimean War and in the midst of the Great Reforms than it had been, say, in 1815 under Nicholas I, or a hundred years earlier under Peter I? I do not think so. The fate of capital punishment in Russia between 1917 and 1922 shows that governments undertake such reforms sometimes out of strength and sometimes out of weakness.[69]

An important part of the explanation of the mitigation of corporal punishments in Russia, as John Langbein says of the earlier abolition of torture in Europe,[70] is that by the middle of the nineteenth century an acceptable alternative to it, in this case correctional imprisonment, existed. The American and European experiments with correctional imprisonment had begun more than half a century earlier, and (as I shall show) Russian reformers had viewed them with admiration for a long time. A movement for prison reform had been building for several decades. Although it had had to be abandoned because Russia did not have such prisons then or the money to build them, Russia's Criminal Code of 1845 had prescribed correctional imprisonment in place of corporal punishments. The problems that had scuttled the 1845 reform were still present in 1863, but in the midst of the Great Reforms the optimism and determination that something positive could be done returned redoubled. The presence of an acceptable, and preferable, alternative punishment was necessary to the reform. I shall discuss in the following chapters why prisons were an acceptable alternative, but I must first demonstrate how corporal punishments had become unacceptable, earlier in the West and then in Russia.

In recent years a few historians have helped to explain how hostility to corporal punishment spread among Russia's educated elite. Their work was done in the context of child rearing, however, not in the punishment of criminals. What they have learned is that in the first half of the nineteenth century Russia's educated middle class increasingly rejected the notion that children should be beaten or even spanked. They found most of their evidence for this in family-advice literature—some of it written by Russians, more of it translated from French, German, or English—and in the popular romantic and sentimental fiction of the time—which also followed Western European models.[71] Although these historians trace clearly the sources and growth of this attitude, they are less successful in explaining why Russian readers would be receptive to the idea. They believe that this middle class gradually developed a consciousness separate from the estates of imperial Russia, defined to a great extent by the traits and attitudes of its European counterparts. I think they are entirely correct in this, which leaves me to wonder how these ideas arose in Western Europe.

Here the writings of Pieter Spierenburg and James Turner are most important. Spierenburg found that through the eighteenth century Europe's upper classes became increasingly sensitized to pain and suffering. He writes that grisly public punishments were abolished in large part because the ruling classes could no longer bear either to watch them or to inflict them. James Turner's writing on animal cruelty suggests the origin of this sensitivity. Turner thinks that, as urbanization removed men from contact with the blood and brutality of nature and of farms, they came to think of many forms of bloodletting as cruel and unnecessary. They hunted less or not at all; they butchered no animals and saw fewer butchered; they no longer participated in or witnessed blood sports. The longer and farther they removed themselves from the countryside, the less they saw of the blood and death that is normal on farms and in villages and the more they came to think of these things as uncivilized.[72]

The process of urbanization that produced these ideas and attitudes in Western Europe came later in Russia. But when it occurred, the people who were part of it changed not only because they went through the same process their western neighbors had a century or so earlier but also because they found ready models for behavior and thought in Western Europe that accelerated their mental transformation. The well-educated, city-dwelling elite, including the bureaucrats and reformers who wrote Russia's Great Reforms, found physical punishment repugnant, barbarous, and anachronistic, not because it was so per se but because their perceptions of it had changed. Even though the conditions that had created the new sensibilities in the West did not exist to as great a degree in Russia, Russia's urban elite "knew" what was "civilized" and what was not. The reformers' increased sensibility came in large part from their education and their desire that their country, like themselves, be as modern and enlightened as they believed Europe to be.[73]

THE AFTERMATH

The 1863 law satisfied most opponents of corporal punishments for several decades, but it did not entirely abolish corporal punishments. There remained a few of the mildest varieties, which were extensively used in the countryside, and against which later reformers did crusade. In the 1890s, and even more in the tumultuous first decade of the twentieth century, much new literature appeared demanding its complete abolition. An even stronger crusade in the same years demanded abrogation of the death penalty.[74] The movement against remaining corporal punishments can be seen as a fringe of this more vital issue. At that time, decades after 1863 and almost a century and a half after Beccaria's treatise appeared, exactly the same arguments were employed again. A. G. Timofeev, for example, writing in 1897 (the book was revised, expanded, and reprinted in 1904, presumably because of its popularity) had this to say:

> The lightest corporal punishment, which represents no danger to either the life or the health of the punished [offender] is attended *in civilized countries* by such shame, is so degrading and distressing in a moral sense, that it may not be commensurate even with, for example, extended imprisonment.[75]

By this time Russian criminologists had established themselves at home and in international societies. European sociologists had hooted Lombroso and the anthropological criminalists from the international stage, and the Russians had followed their lead. For decades they had tried to buttress their arguments with "criminal statistics," to be scientific, not merely moralistic. What evidence did they marshal against corporal punishment? In most cases, none. They just did not like it. Anyone who dared to act like a sociologist on this question would have found ample evidence that "the people" missed corporal punishment and much preferred it to modernity.

An educated Russian contemplating making such a study might have been warned away by the experience of counterparts in Germany. Most corporal punishments had been eliminated in the German states during the crises of 1848, and few were reinstituted during the subsequent reaction. The All-German Criminal Code abolished most corporal punishments in 1871, leaving only male natives of German colonies subject to any corporal punishment. Germany had also begun to modernize its prisons in the 1850s. By the mid-1870s some critics of the new prisons had already begun to wonder whether corporal punishment had not been more effective after all. The prisons failed to do the job they were intended to do, especially for juveniles. They seemed to harden prisoners and to make better criminals of them. And they were hugely expensive. Yet Germany did not return to corporal punishments. According to Timofeev, the most

telling defense against reinstatement of corporal punishment by Germany's leading criminologists condemned it as "a barbarous punitive measure intolerable in
cultured states."[76]

What of the evidence in Russia? Reports remain from some prison administrators about their prisoners' attitudes and of a governmental commission that
asked "the people," among many other things, how they felt about corporal
punishment. In October 1869 a priest in a naval correctional prison responded
to an MVD project for a new correctional prison:

> The philanthropic measures of punishment applied by the government since the
> abolition of corporal punishments have noticeably not yet entered the understand-
> ing of the lower classes of the Russian people, and, not surprisingly, these measures
> are not received by the people with the gratitude they deserve.

Many prisoners stated that they did not deserve imprisonment and that they
would prefer corporal punishment. How could this be? The priest believed, "It is
apparent that the sense of human dignity which is so deeply injured by corporal
punishment does not have even the smallest place in human souls so complected." Because he could not reject the enlightened dogma that corporal punishment was an offense to human dignity, he had to reject that prisoners who
denied being offended by it possessed human dignity. The priest detected a
"deeply hidden antipathy to prison and attempts at correction" in his charges
and feared that such people would not benefit from prison. He thought it might
improve matters somewhat if the warden—or, even better, the priest—explained to inmates why they were imprisoned.[77]

The Commission on the Reform of the *Volost'* Court found the peasants just as
unenlightened in 1872. They believed that the reform had complicated their lives
unnecessarily, and many of them wished that more general use of corporal punishment could be restored. Arrest (imprisonment for up to seven days) and fines,
which had replaced flogging for most minor offenses, punished not just the offender but his whole family, by removing the breadwinner's earning power or his
earnings, and at times they caused serious hardship. Corporal punishment, on the
other hand, punished only the offender. It had long been and in their minds it remained an effective punishment and deterrent. In some places where it had been
little used since 1863 the peasants noticed a slackening of discipline and feared
the consequences if the reform were taken further: "If corporal punishment were
abandoned the peasant would not listen to the head of the community or be
afraid of the township court. It would not be bad to permit as many as fifty
lashes." In another locale, they reported, "flogging is seldom imposed but always
feared." Peasants from a Moscow province township said it clearly: "The *muzhik*
[peasant] prefers flogging; it is a disaster neither to him nor the community."[78]

But, said a commentator on the commission's reports in the liberal journal
Vestnik Evropy, abolition of corporal punishment in *volost'* courts was important, and judges would just have to find suitable alternatives. Taking into account the season of the year and the financial condition of the offender, they
should sometimes fine, sometimes imprison, and when neither was suitable,

consider alternative sentences such as "social labor." The commentator attempted to debunk all of the findings of the commission that were incompatible with liberals' aspirations. First, charged the commentator, the commission's interviewers raced through the countryside, spending only a week in a *guberniia* and two or three hours in a *volost'*. Moreover, the peasants were not likely to tell the interviewers that they were dissatisfied with things because their elders were standing by, any more than a soldier at an inspection would in the presence of his lieutenant. What the commission did hear and report was that peasants and judges preferred corporal punishment. Judges claimed that it was the only reliable way of deterring drunkenness and theft, among other crimes. The commentator dismissed this, saying that the judges did only as they were told by village elders and court clerks.

As far as the people were concerned, they were not the ones to ask about corporal punishment—not if one wanted to disapprove of it, that is.

> The people's voice can hardly be considered competent. Ask the mass of people how one should deal with disrespectful sons, unfaithful wives, horse thieves, and even with fast breakers, and compile a criminal code on the basis of the people's conceptions!

Indeed! The whole *volost'* court, he continued, was a remnant of "patrimonial justice" that "no longer befits modern Russia." There was no such thing as customary law and therefore no justification for continuing a special court based on a myth. "Legislation must stand above peasants who think that justice need be meted out with fist and whip and say 'no' to such 'custom.'"[79]

If it were not yet widely true in Russia that manners had been "softened" by the advance of culture, perhaps "softer" punishments as a concomitant of civilization would serve to gentle manners. It was frequently true that some vanguard sought to put a European cart before a Russian nag and exhort the nag to catch up. The law of 17 April 1863 was just such a cart and grandstand. Its aim was to reduce the severity of punishments in general, wherever possible by substituting more civilized forms of punishment for archaic corporal punishments. There never was a movement to return to corporal punishments. Once discarded as archaic, with never so much as a single study to demonstrate their ineffectiveness, they could not be adopted again.

Fines were considered an acceptable substitute in the case of minor infractions; imprisonment was the only acceptable alternative for more serious crimes. The most optimistic reformers hoped to build modern correctional facilities, to incarcerate offenders for terms commensurate with their crimes, and to release them reformed or corrected. In 1863 Russia was far from that goal.

The direct connection between the reform of corporal punishment and the movement toward prison reform is seen most clearly in the final recommendations of Baron Korf's committee. As part of its work, the committee had attempted to study the feasibility of imprisoning offenders who were exempted from corporal punishment. They were aware, of course, that most corporal punishment was then administered under the temporary rules of 23 November 1853 amending the Code of 1845 to permit corporal punishments to be substituted for forms of imprisonment prescribed in 1845 but still unavailable.[80] The committee gathered what material it could on prisons and prisoners as of 1861. They had to rely on the MVD, which had more information than did anyone else, but the ministry had information on only thirty-four provinces and had to admit that even that was incomplete. The ministry and the committee had no good way of estimating the number of prisoners who entered the system every year or the length of sentences being served by prisoners.[81] In short, they had no way of estimating the number of spaces that would be needed.

They were also aware that making new spaces would be prohibitively expensive. In 1845, having enacted the new Code of Punishments, Nicholas ordered MVD L. A. Perovskii to study the costs of constructing isolation prisons in Russia along the lines of Pentonville Prison in England. Perovskii embraced the idea wholeheartedly less than a year later in an official report *(vsepoddanneishei doklad)* in which he estimated a onetime immediate cost of about 23 million rubles. He had calculated a need to house 40,000 prisoners, 520 in each of seventy-five new isolation prisons, each of which would cost 300,000 rubles to build.

Nicholas established a commission under Perovskii to study these plans and to find means to finance them. The commission endorsed its chairman's findings and recommended that the prisons be built with a loan, which they proposed to pay back over thirty-seven years from a "special collection from tax-paying souls and merchant capital" that had been established in 1834 to collect money for building prisons and offices. The government did not approve the loan, but it did allocate some money to the commission. In 1848, its first year of operation, it began construction in several cities with a fund of 500,000 rubles. Work slowed after this modest beginning, but several facilities were built. The commission, though less active, continued to operate on a small budget until Alexander II, consulting with Count Bludov, decided that the whole question deserved another look. He abolished the commission on 8 June 1862.[82]

By then the MVD had begun to study the prisons under its control. Minister Valuev may have volunteered his good offices to make the study more thorough. As an appendage to its conclusions Korf's committee asked the State Council if it would not find it useful "to empower the Ministers of Internal Affairs and Justice to search for means to immediately increase the number and improve the organization of strait houses, workhouses, and prisons." The council did find the thought useful and incorporated it as an order in the law of 17 April. The council also agreed with the committee's recommendation

> to concentrate in the Ministry of Internal Affairs the management of all civilian places of imprisonment, not excluding correctional arrest companies, the reorganization of which the Ministry of Internal Affairs will plan with the cooperation of the Ministry of Justice to make them serve their purposes better.[83]

CHAPTER TWO

PRISON

ADMINISTRATION

IN THE MINISTRY

OF INTERNAL

AFFAIRS

THE RUSSIAN PRISON AID SOCIETY

> I was in prison and ye came unto me. . . . And the King shall say unto them . . . inasmuch as ye have done it unto one of the least of them my brethren, ye have done it unto me.[1]

Like many other institutional and attitudinal innovations, the inspiration to establish prison-aid societies came to Russia from western Europe. In this case the Englishmen who carried the idea to Russia had found their inspiration in America. Like the prison-reform movement, of which they were a small but integral part, prison-aid societies had various and disparate roots. The European Enlightenment, as I discussed in connection with corporal punishment, played an important role. The societies also derived in large part from Quaker attitudes of nonviolence, toleration for deviance, and sympathy for the unfortunate. These forces converged in Philadelphia, where both the first penitentiary and the first prison-aid society were established.

The Philadelphia Society for Assisting Distressed Prisoners had the bad luck to be founded in 1776, only nineteen months before the British occupied Philadelphia, which put an end to its work. Its sole purpose had been to improve the physical comfort of prisoners. When it was reestablished in 1787 as the Philadelphia Society for Alleviating the Miseries of Public Prisons, it quickly adopted a much wider agenda. Composed of Quakers and Episcopalians and presided over by the bishop of the Protestant Episcopal Church of Philadelphia, the society recommended many changes in local prisons concerning food, hygiene, alcohol, the separation of prisoners, and labor. High on its list of priorities was the religious edification of prisoners. The first sermon given at the Walnut Street jail was delivered by a member of the society in 1787. He stood beside a loaded cannon that was aimed at the prisoners by a soldier holding a lighted match.[2]

American Quakers and Englishmen who had visited Philadelphia soon carried this idea to England, where John Howard, author of several famous volumes on the condition of prisons, had already begun his crusade for prison reform. Howard, who was not a Quaker, twice visited Russia and inspected prisons there. He died in Kherson in 1790 and is buried there. His belief in the need to reform prisons is said to have persuaded numerous Russians that reform was needed in Russia, but his visit led to no concrete results.[3] That awaited the visit of several Quakers in the 1810s.

Emperor Alexander was well disposed toward the Quakers, whose industry he had admired on a visit to England in 1814. He invited several of them to work in agriculture and various industries in Russia, where he permitted them to proselytize. Other Friends regularly visited Russia on business. Among those who took their business and ministry to Russia, a few were active in prison reform. Stephen Grellet, for example, had become active in prison visiting in Philadelphia. When he traveled to England "in the ministry" in 1812–1813, he was particularly disturbed by conditions at the women's section of Newgate Prison, where he set fellow Quaker Elizabeth Fry on her career as the "Angel of the Prisons." Grellet lived for a time in Russia, where he associated with other Friends from England, but it is unclear what, if any, role he played in the founding of Russia's first prison-aid society.[4]

The English Quaker who was instrumental in that development was Walter Venning, who had helped his father trade in Russia since 1799 and was well connected there by the time he made his fourth trip in 1817.[5] Venning arrived on 18 May 1817 accompanied by Reverend and Mrs. Edward Stallybrass, who were on a mission to the Mongolian tribes of Siberia. He had been deeply religious and committed to prison work since his experience with Elizabeth Fry's male relatives in their Society for the Reformation of Prison Discipline, which was founded in London in 1816.[6] In St. Petersburg Venning expressed to Prince A. N. Golitsyn, then minister of spiritual affairs and national education, his hope to organize a prison-aid society in Russia. Golitsyn, who was sympathetic to the idea, took Venning with him to Moscow when the imperial court moved there for a season in February 1818. There Venning presented his ideas to Governor General Count Miloradovich and Princess Meshcherskaia, both of whom were receptive and supportive. In July 1818 Golitsyn wrote the emperor of plans submitted to him by Venning to establish a prison-aid society in Moscow. Alexander approved the plans and by a law of 19 July 1819 established Russia's first *Popechitel'noe Obshchestvo o Tiur'makh* (POoT) (Prison Aid Society) in St. Petersburg.[7]

Not surprisingly, considering its origins, this POoT emphasized religious instruction. Its members, who were all well-to-do, Orthodox Russians, believed firmly that crime, the product of sin and evil, will and should be dealt with by requiring criminals to recognize their sins and come to repentance. That attitude is apparent in Venning's plans, in which he stated:

> Criminals are usually people held in thrall to passions, who do not believe in religion and do not understand their responsibility to God. . . . They must be taught that the all-seeing eye of God is always trained on them, and they are frightened by the . . . righteous anger of God towards them, sinners who violate God's law, but at the same time we must inform them and persuade them that God is always ready to forgive those who come to him in sincere repentance.[8]

Russian Orthodoxy encouraged a similar view. Prince Golitsyn, whom Alexander appointed the society's first president, said much the same in his inaugural address.

> Ladies and gentlemen, let us go into these gloomy abodes, where sin, appearing in all its ruinous consequences, is only deprived of the power of multiplying the deeds proceeding from a corrupted will;—where crimes, the progeny of violent passions, and dissolute habits, have only lost the opportunity of darting their venom;—where . . . above all forgetfulness of God, and dislike of his commandments, assume their various shapes of temptation and transgression.

According to Prince Golitsyn, the state's only responsibility was to provide justice, which it did by putting criminals in prison. The society, he hoped, could do more; its members would show mercy and thereby win sinners for Christ.[9] Such were corrections in the early part of the century.

The members of the society, divided into men's and women's committees, were limited in their activities from the start. Although their charter gave them fairly wide responsibilities for prisoners' welfare, it also made it clear that they had no authority in the prisons but were solely a philanthropical organization. Only about a dozen members had access to the prisons, and most of those, being highly placed officials, were too busy to do much visiting. Princess Meshcherskaia regularly visited female prisoners to read them edifying religious texts and to bring them work. She had English Bible tracts translated into Russian and printed for distribution to prisoners, but few others did such things. The new society soon discovered that it lacked the money it needed to accomplish its aims in the prisons; it had only its members' donations. In 1820 they were given control of other donated money, the so-called *kruzhechnye den'gi,* but even that left them with little money and with no control over other funds disbursed by the state for prisons. It was not until 1825, 1827, 1829, and 1837 that laws gave them control of treasury funds for heating, cleaning, and provisioning the prisons.[10]

The most prominent and highly placed of the POoT's official leaders were not always sympathetic to its original purposes. In 1822 Prince Golitsyn was replaced as chairman by Baron Baltazar Kampengauzen, who apparently found his colleagues' sensitivity misplaced and annoying. He wrote to Count Arakcheev in September 1822,

> Now I have new worries from the prison society, not because their work is so hard, but because it is difficult to reach agreement with this colorful assemblage of grandiloquent philosophers, sensitive philanthropists, enlightened ladies and ingenuous people. Sometimes you agree, if only to avoid falling out altogether, and wind up signing something horrible.[11]

The Moscow committee of the POoT was established on 24 January 1828 at the request and insistence of Governor General D. V. Golitsyn. At its first meeting, on 29 December 1828, he expressed his hope that some prisoners would justify the members' care and prove "that great truth, that even the most evil of criminals is never hopelessly beyond reformation." Because the governor general and Metropolitan Filaret, who served as the committee's first vice presidents, were too busy to handle its daily affairs, they were entrusted to Doctor F. P. Gaaz, who became one of Russia's most celebrated philanthropists. According to A. F. Koni, who wrote a laudatory biography, Gaaz devoted most of the rest of his life to caring for the poor and the imprisoned. In the twenty-five years before he died in poverty in 1853, Gaaz missed only one of the Moscow committee's 293 meetings.[12]

For most of these years, Gaaz visited various Moscow prisons four times a week to care for the sick and to insist on better care for all of their inmates. From early on he paid particular attention to "transfer" prisoners who passed through Moscow on their way east into exile, often to penal servitude. Almost half of the country's exiles passed through Moscow. For several years in the late 1820s he fought to have the heavy, inflexible leg irons *(prut'ia)*, which frequently caused injuries, replaced with lighter leg irons *(kandaly)*, joined by a chain. This change was made in 1831–1832. He also often ordered longer layovers in Moscow for prisoners who were not up to the long walk into exile.

To win his few signal successes Doctor Gaaz often had to work against the inertia and even active resistance of the bureaucracy. MVD A. A. Zakrevskii and General P. M. Kaptsevich, commander of the military corps of prison guards, were particularly hostile to his work. When Governor General Golitsyn intervened for Gaaz on the question of leg irons, Zakrevskii reprimanded him for interfering in matters that did not concern only Moscow. Kaptsevich, who frequently complained about the "flimsy" excuses for which Gaaz ordered prisoner layovers, used his power as head of the staging *(etapnye)* prisons to try to prevent the replacement of the heavier leg irons. In a circular to the keepers of these prisons he asked whether the *prut'ia* caused injuries and, if they did, why he had not been informed of the situation earlier. Naturally, most of the keepers replied that they caused no discomfort, and it was only with difficulty that Gaaz was able to prove their dangers.[13]

Few of the other committee members worked actively at prison affairs, and even Metropolitan Filaret grew impatient with Doctor Gaaz's persistence. D. A. Rovinskii, Moscow provincial clerk *(striapchii),* witnessed frequent clashes between the two men at committee meetings. In 1842 the committee had created the position of intercessor *(khodatai)* for prison affairs, of which Gaaz made use in order to buy the freedom of debtors and to have wrongly convicted prisoners released. At one meeting in the 1840s Filaret, tired of Gaaz's petitions to the committee about innocently convicted prisoners, informed him that there was no such thing as an innocent prisoner. If they were convicted, they were guilty. Gaaz leaped up and yelled, "Sir, you have forgotten about Christ." A deep, embarrassed silence ensued. Finally the abashed Metropolitan excused himself for his hasty words, blessed everyone, and left the meeting.[14]

It is extremely difficult to judge whether the POoT committees did much good, particularly outside the capital cities, because there is little information about their activities. But a study of the St. Petersburg Committee's annual reports makes it clear that for at least the first two decades the idea of prison philanthropy attracted many upper- and middle-class members. In its first seven years the POoT opened an average of one new provincial committee per year. Between 1826 and 1837 another thirty-eight provincial committees were founded. By 1844, the twenty-fifth year of its existence, the POoT comprised 49 provincial and 217 county *(uezd)* committees.[15] According to a few commentators, the committees, particularly those of St. Petersburg and Moscow, did much in the late 1820s and the 1830s to improve the physical condition of prisons and to ease the lot of prisoners.[16] Most students of the societies are much more critical, however, and suggest that they never were very effective.[17]

All sources agree that by the 1840s the prison-aid societies became and remained moribund. Even as sympathetic a commentator as Dmitrii Krainskii describes an atrophying of "the philanthropical impulse." According to Krainskii, apathy and lethargy set in everywhere and, in places, abandonment of responsibility.[18] This decay is associated with changes in the administration of the POoT, which Krainskii sees as a healthy attempt by the government to overcome apathy. Other commentators blame this intrusion of bureaucracy into voluntary or "social" activism for causing the apathy.[19]

In 1841 Nicholas I appointed Chief of Gendarmes Count A. Kh. Benkendorf chairman of the POoT. Benkendorf immediately set about giving them more formal structure and attempted to create county committees where they did not yet exist by requiring the cooperation of county marshals of the gentry and other local officials. In his first three years, more than 100 county committees were established, but most of these were apparently never very active. Soon, despite all the prodding of Benkendorf and the leaders of the provincial committees, a limit seemed to have been reached in the number of county committees. When Benkendorf died in 1844, the new chief of gendarmes and POoT chairman, Count A. F. Orlov, continued that effort but to no avail. In county after county, merchants, clergy, and citizens of substance refused the call to form prison committees. And in existing committees, attendance and participation dropped, and dues fell into arrears. Some provincial committees turned to the police and courts to collect dues, which had been pledged on an annual basis and in some instances had never been paid. Not surprisingly, this did not encourage greater participation either.[20]

Meanwhile, the POoT had been given increased responsibilities for prisons and control of funds for those purposes. By 1844 the committees were responsible for provisioning prisons throughout the empire. But the tsarist government, which had never entrusted much to "social forces" or private initiative, took with one hand as it gave with the other. As we have seen, through the chairman of the St. Petersburg Committee, who not just coincidentally was chief of gendarmes, it began to pressure "volunteers" to donate their time and money to POoT committees and their activities. When the POoT was given a new charter on 7 November 1851, the obligatory nature of participation was made complete. Certain officials at the provincial and county levels were required to join and to donate a set amount annually, committee directors were appointed from above rather than elected locally, and the free participation of interested nonpaying volunteers was ended. In 1855 the POoT was made part of the MVD, and the minister became president of the society.[21]

From that time on reformers agree almost unanimously on the causes of the failure of the POoT and on their solutions. First, they believed that too many POoT officials at all levels were already busy with other duties for which they bore more direct responsibility and to which, consequently, they gave most of their energy. As they saw it, once the first creative burst of energy of the 1820s and 1830s had passed, the committees became glutted with dilettantes interested in "earning" medals for their sham service or in making connections in the way of business—to sell food and other supplies purchased by the committees for the prisons, for example. They sought to solve both of these problems by establishing a central prison administration with local functionaries who were responsible only for prison affairs. Some of the reformers were also concerned, on the other hand, by the loss of "free and creative initiative," for which "chancellery routine and formality" were an inadequate replacement. No one believed that a bureaucracy could harness those forces, and (as will be demonstrated) the several offices that handled prison affairs would try to avoid, ignore, or destroy the POoT. "Social forces" would not be called on in prison affairs for several decades and would reemerge only at the end of the century in the *patronatstvo* movement.[22]

By the time the law of 17 April 1863 restricting the use of corporal punishment was passed, almost everyone agreed that the POoT committees were not doing the job for which they were intended. Prisons were obviously in poor condition, and much of the blame was laid on the POoT. When the emperor called on the MVD to do something about the deplorable condition of Russian prisons, it was not to the POoT but to the MVD Department of Executive Police (DPI) that the minister turned.

REORGANIZATION AND REFORMS TO 1867

From its work for the committee on corporal punishment the MVD had learned how little they knew of prison conditions. In 1861 the MVD had ordered governors *(nachal'niki gubernii)* to report in general terms on prison conditions, prison regime, and the reliability of prison "keepers." A ministerial circular of 12 April 1862 required them to respond to specific questions about prisons in their provinces on forms printed for that purpose.[23]

The fact that this activity began after Count Bludov's (later Baron Korf's) committee had commenced its work suggests that, from the beginning, consideration of the abolition of corporal punishment was linked to the development of modern prisons. Minister Valuev issued the detailed circular of April 1862 the same week that Baron Korf sent his committee's final report to the emperor and to the State Council. Less than two months later Alexander II abolished the Perovskii Commission, which had begun to build a few modern prisons. The slow progress that would be made toward developing a prison system in the next seventeen years gainsays the conclusion, but it would seem that during the tenure of the Bludov-Korf committee—in the excitement of the Great Reforms—there was enthusiasm and optimism about making a new start in building a modern prison system. Valuev's approval of the committee's work may have stemmed from his hope of building that system within his ministry.

The first reports revealed serious shortcomings. Overcrowding was the most frequently mentioned and probably the most serious. The problems of sanitation and hygiene caused by overcrowding were not mentioned in the MVD's summary of its reports, but they must have been great. It is apparent that whoever compiled the summary had knowledge of western penological theory, for the remainder of his comments reflect concerns of that science in Europe in the 1860s. Prisoners were rarely separated into groups or categories but were forced together. This permitted the worst of the lot to "infect" the less hardened criminals. In many places prisoners were not even segregated by age or sex. Everywhere prisoners languished in "idleness [which] bred depravity."[24]

The cause of many of these problems, the MVD editor postulated, was that various keeps *(tiuremnye zamki)*, workhouses, and strait houses "were built at different times and under the influence of different theories and conditions, without a plan and system." He wrote of system once more to point out a last major problem. Because administration of these miscellaneous prisons was divided among too many departments, there was no unity, or system.[25] The solution he hinted at, by mentioning that it had been successfully adopted throughout western Europe in the previous few decades, was the creation of a central prison administration. Probably not coincidentally, this very much suited the style of the Russian government of the 1860s and of the MVD, Valuev.

Responses to the circular of 12 April 1862 also supplied more detailed information, which the MVD needed to justify reorganization and reform. The circular asked governors for precise data for the years 1857, 1858, and 1859 on, among other things, the number of places available for prisoners, the actual

number of prisoners, the cost of administration and maintenance, and the estimated cost of needed repairs. It also asked for descriptions of shortcomings and
problems, including causes of the problems and suggestions for overcoming
them.[26] The governors replied quickly but with enormously varying degrees of
punctiliousness. Some reports ran to only four or five pages, reflecting the absence of records or concern, or both. A few others covered from forty to eighty
pages. The report from Orenburg province filled fifty pages but had little to say
that might give the MVD guidance. Orenburg officials saw little wrong with
their prisons but thought that reform would be nice, too.[27] Moscow's was by far
the most detailed and carefully considered report, full not only of statistical
compilations but also of descriptions of all Moscow province's prisons and the
sorts of recommendations for improvement the MVD wanted to hear. Because
other provinces' reports, where they were useful, duplicate the information of
Moscow's (except generally to say that conditions were even worse) Moscow's
report can be used to sketch a picture of Russian prisons in 1857–1859.

After detailing the location, number, and type of prisons in the province and
supplying the statistical information asked for, the Moscow report went on to
describe individual prisons and to make generalizations about their condition.
The larger prisons and the county lockups alike were "old, dilapidated buildings." Some had walls or floors so rotten one could push through them with a
hand or foot. Others had roofs that seemed ready to collapse, threatening the
safety of the prisoners and administrators as well as prison security. Whereas basic security was sometimes provided, proper placement of prisoners never was.
"Not in one prison of Moscow province is the proper disposition of prisoners
observed." Lack of space was the most frequently cited reason, but badly constructed rooms, inept administration, and corruption were frankly acknowledged. Much of the corruption was attributed to poor pay. The report claimed
that guards, who were enlisted soldiers, often received less money in pay than
prisoners did in charity. Consequently, "the soldiers often became servants to
prisoners" to carry messages, bring them forbidden goods, and relax multitudi-
nous other rules. Beyond these serious faults, the report's author believed that
the prisons' greatest problem was idleness. Not only did they fail to provide
minimal custodial care, they were also doing harm. Many prisoners who had begun their sentences in good health and accustomed to hard work left prison
weakened physically and habituated to sloth and vice.[28]

All of these characteristics had persisted for several generations. By themselves
they did not make the prisons suddenly unacceptable. What made contemporary
conditions unacceptable was that attitudes to prisons had changed.

> Turning now to the question of the degree of satisfactoriness of the aforemen-
> tioned places of imprisonment in Moscow, it would seem that they are generally
> unsatisfactory. The reasons for this are rather complex. They can be found partly
> in the decrepitude of the buildings, partly in the crowding and discomfort of the
> cells, but most of all in the difference of contemporary views of imprisonment in
> general as compared with the views of the past. As a result of that it can be said
> that in general the whole former prison administration is now unsound.[29]

Part of the solution, wrote the Moscow respondent, was to centralize administration.

> Generally it is necessary as far as possible to subordinate to a single office prison administration, which is now divided among various offices and requires redundant supervision and accounting. The result of all this is complete chaos, costing the state an extraordinarily great amount of money without any advantage to the populace.

The report asked rhetorically whether guards, bookkeepers, and clerks did not outnumber prisoners in the existing system.[30]

At the same time and somewhat contradictorily, the report also suggested that the POoT, which had begun as a public body but had become ensnarled in government bureaucracy, "be released from officialdom to a slight degree." A new class of "active" members should be accepted, who should not have to pay dues. Those who continued to buy a position on a society's board should be called honorary members.[31]

Taken together, the material sent in response to the circular painted a wretched picture of Russian prisons. Most were old, small, dilapidated wooden structures that could barely provide for the security of prisoners. They could not begin to provide "correctional" care in the modern sense because they did not have the space for isolating individual prisoners, for segregating categories of prisoners, or for using workshops. For the most part the men who ran them did not have the knowledge or the desire to modernize. The prisons were riddled with vice, incompetence, and corruption. Another major problem that the reports did not address, because it was not as apparent in 1862 as it would soon become, was that Russia had few prisons relative to the size of its population. When most corporal punishments were ended, there would not be sufficient prison cells to accommodate the sudden influx of new prisoners.

Not long after 17 April 1863 a small commission was created at the initiative of the MVD to study this material and to consider how best to implement the new law's directives to improve prison conditions. The group comprised Count D. A. Tolstoi, head of the MVD Department of Executive Police; Baron Korf, past chairman of the committee on corporal punishment, now attached to the MIu; and Major General Marchenko of the Main Administration of Communications and Public Buildings.[32] They delayed beginning their discussions until the responses from the provinces had arrived and until two other reports on foreign prisons were received. In 1862–1863, again apparently in anticipation of centralizing and reforming prison administration in the MVD, the ministry had sent two young men abroad to study European prisons and report back.[33] What the commission did once the material became available can only be surmised. It seems that they quailed before the enormity of the work and decided to do nothing.

While this commission was supposedly sitting, another group in the MVD was independently trying to draft recommendations for the creation of a prison system using the same materials. They, too, retreated before some combination of the already overwhelming task and events that seemed to run too fast before them. As the MVD group explained it, the reform of corporal punishment and the Polish revolt in 1863 had created such a sudden, large demand for prison space that they had to turn their energies to finding or making that space. Various government departments met their requests for vacant government buildings that could be used at least temporarily for prisons.

The domain of Russia's prison administrators quickly expanded, but with no semblance of plan or system. The rapidly growing prison population complicated all efforts to bring order. Unable to undertake more ambitious plans, the MVD group contented itself in 1865 by publishing the collected documents on prison conditions. "Any reform," it wrote, "must have as its starting point the real facts." Then "the experts," on the basis of "existing means and materials," could "decide in a practical way the question of what sort of prison system we can achieve at the present time without disrupting state finances and without being awed by unsound theories."[34]

The group may not have been entirely candid in its explanation. The explosion of the prison population certainly did create problems of scale. But thornier problems, which may have been the true cause of the defeat of the 1863–1865 commission and the MVD group, lay cryptically exposed in that last sentence. There were now "experts" to be consulted and "theories" to be observed. Wrapped as they were in a modern, western, and scientific mantle, the theories appealed strongly to reformers, but the experts, even the foreign experts, did not agree among themselves, and traditionalists viewed their solutions as "unsound theory." At first glance it still might seem strange that the reformers did not seize the opportunity. Korf's commission, the State Council, and the emperor had been apprised of the consequences of abolishing corporal punishment, yet they had embraced that reform with apparent enthusiasm. How could conservatives stand in the way of the next logical step so soon thereafter? As it transpired, they did not lack imagination, but conservatives did not need much imagination to sabotage prison reform. The greatest constant obstacle to reform reverberates in the innocent phrase "without disrupting state finances." Sweeping prison reform could not be accomplished without such a disruption. All efforts to introduce major changes, if they were not defeated on other grounds, foundered on the shoals of the Ministry of Finance (MF). Change, therefore, came piecemeal and slowly.

Until 1872, when the next commission on prison affairs was appointed, the only organized efforts to improve the condition of Russian prisons originated in this same Second Department of the Department of Executive Police. An internal reform of the DPI in 1862 had concentrated in the Second Department responsibilities for several types of prisons that had been scattered in various offices of the MVD. The personnel of this department felt so overwhelmed by current duties, however, that they were unable to propose reforms in the next few years. In addition to prison affairs, the Second Department was charged with "suppression of all arbitrariness" in personal rights and property; handling complaints of inaction on the part of provincial police; supervision of police investigations in criminal cases; exile of suspicious foreigners; discovery of thieves, swindlers, and the like; investigation of false and forged documents; suppressing circulation of "harmful books"; and more.[35] Quite a job for a handful of men!

Even after the 1862 reorganization the Second Department did not have anything like full control of prisons. The responsibilities of the POoT, governors and vice governors, provincial boards (gubernskie pravleniia), and other ministries overlapped. Within the DPI both the First and Third Departments also had duties that would have required their cooperation in any reform. The First Department held responsibility for all government "places" in the provinces, counties, and cities and for all transactions concerning them and abuses in them. The Third Department was charged with seeing that courts' sentences were carried out. In 1868 they were also given control of moneys earmarked for prison repair and construction.[36]

Despite the myriad difficulties the Second Department did accomplish some major changes in the prisons. Some were pressed on the department by forces beyond its control, but others it consciously designed and put into effect. One little-noticed change was made by a law of 3 May 1865 that removed military guards from inside prisons and replaced them with freely hired guards. Prison administrators and military leaders, who did not want their men tied down in such jobs, had long agreed on the desirability of this change, but money could not be found earlier to hire other guards. Guards remained poorly paid and a source of corruption in prisons for many years, but in this one way, at least, prison administrators began to take control of their own institutions.[37]

The change to freely hired labor was characteristic of the spirit of the Great Reforms. A major argument for emancipation had been that free labor worked more productively than did unfree labor. The truth of this assertion soon made itself felt in prison affairs. Many Russian criminals had been sentenced to penal servitude (katorga) in exile, where they labored to support themselves and to hold costs down on state projects. Many worked at state-owned factories in the Ural Mountains and in Siberia. In competition with free labor, however, compulsory labor in penal servitude quickly proved unprofitable. Government factories began to lose money, and in the 1860s most were sold to private owners who did not employ prisoners.[38] One immediate consequence was "idleness" in katorga barracks and prisons, the very condition most frequently blamed for breeding "depravity" among convicts. This lent further urgency to the search for improved forms of imprisonment and for ways to develop corrective labor in prisons.

Free labor undermined the exile system as well. In Western Siberia, especially, exile had already fulfilled one of its intended purposes, the settlement of sparsely populated territory. Many areas that had been heavily settled by exiles had grown to sufficiency and respectability and no longer welcomed convicts. The collapse of government factories and the easy availability of nonconvict labor left little for exiles to do to support themselves. They turned in large numbers to vagrancy and theft. Complaints about the criminal activity of exiles predated emancipation but grew rapidly more numerous and incessant in the years following it. In 1867 the governor general of Western Siberia formally asked for an end to exile in his provinces. The MVD cooperated by sending more exiles to Eastern Siberia, where large projects on Sakhalin Island and mining at Nerchinsk were begun in order to accommodate and use exiled convicts.[39] A more remote result of these changes was a movement to replace exile and *katorga* with correctional imprisonment. As usual, consideration of the possibility long preceded its realization.

In 1867 the Second Department displayed enormous new energy. It began to implement one significant reform and issued a much more significant reform project, it absorbed new responsibilities transferred from elsewhere in the government, and it reorganized internally to handle the new duties it had created or inherited. Apparently, funds were found to hire additional personnel, for over the next five years the Second Department expanded to six desks, and its staff doubled several times.[40]

One reform not forced on the Second Department by emancipation or by changes in other ministries was improvement of the system of transferring prisoners and exiles. Until 1867, Russian prisoners had trekked from the place of their sentencing to the place of their incarceration or exile. For reasons akin to the arguments against corporal punishment, this form of transportation became undesirable and finally unacceptable. The sight of ragged, weak, and often sickly prisoners straggling through the streets of towns and into the countryside toward a distant prison or exile evoked strong sympathy. Villagers often turned out to offer the prisoners, whom they called the unfortunates *(neschastnye)*, food, drink, and alms. Some who wished to eliminate the spectacle feared that the outpouring of sympathy would encourage prisoners to believe they were being unjustly or excessively punished. Others claimed that the system was unjust, that the march was greater punishment than that which awaited the prisoners at their destinations. Exposure and inadequate dietary and medical care along the routes did claim many victims. Additionally, the system was expensive and, according to contemporary theory, penologically unsound. Because prisoners could not walk far each day, the MVD had to maintain many small, overnight lockups along the routes. The costs of running numerous small prisons, the staging stations, considerably exceeded the expense of running fewer larger prisons. The military was also unhappy with the system because of the expense and inconvenience of supplying convoy guards between stations. The soldiers had to be paid and fed but performed no military function. Also, at the prisons and on the marches prisoners were indiscriminately mixed, which permitted, as the experts now knew, criminal "infection."[41]

In 1867 the DPI ordered that prisoners be transferred by train and boat where possible and that they not be transported in winter and began the orderly dismantling of the old system. Replacing the old system required a great deal of planning and significant new money for larger winter layover and transfer prisons. To accomplish the change the DPI further expanded its staff, opening the Transfer Desk. A second new desk was established in 1867 to administer correctional and *katorga* prisons.[42]

THE MVD'S REFORM PROJECT OF 1867

The effort by the MVD to seize control of prison affairs by creating a central administration in the DPI met immediate and continuous resistance. Some agencies were happy to unburden themselves of extraneous responsibilities; others did not find prison affairs extraneous or for other reasons did not want to relinquish them. Every major change and even rather minor changes suggested by the department brought confrontations with other departments and ministries that were jealous of intrusion into their bailiwicks. Sides were quickly drawn, and battle was joined in one commission after another. Struggles territorial merged with battles philosophical until the antagonists must have thought they knew what they were fighting about. Many of the lines of disagreement became obvious in discussions of the MVD's first comprehensive proposal for prison reform.

The reform project developed by the MVD in 1867 had its roots in western penological science. Although it was considerably longer and more thorough, the project seems to have been based on the reports of A. Passek, one of the two men sent abroad by the MVD in 1862–1863 to study European prisons. Passek died abroad; but his report had been submitted, and in 1867 it was published in St. Petersburg under the title *A Project for the Reform of Prisons.*[43] N. Orlov, who was quite probably Nikolai Orlov, author of the 1861 broadside against corporal punishment, wrote an introduction to the book in which he acknowledged the support of Valuev and the MVD for his own and Passek's interest in prisons.[44]

Passek began his report by discussing the foreign prison systems he had observed and studied. He had been most impressed by the Irish system, which at the time was considered Europe's most progressive, but he dutifully described his other impressions as well. He cited the work of Europe's outstanding criminological and penological theorists writing in Italian, French, German, and, especially, English. He then summarized quite succinctly the general principles he could derive from his investigation. They were exactly the principles a mainline English or Irish penologist would have outlined.[45]

His first principle was to "separate pretrial and term-serving prisoners." As I have stated, Russian prisoners were generally lumped together indiscriminately. So were western European prisoners, until England and the United States led the way in prison reform during the first decades of the nineteenth century. It was now penological gospel that prisoners not yet sentenced should not be mixed with sitting convicts. Beyond the obvious danger of "contamination," it was considered juridically unjust. Pretrial, or preliminary, prisoners were not yet being punished but only bound over for trial. If they were to be confined at all, they should be kept in separate preliminary prisons, which would naturally have a milder regime.

The second principle was particularly un-Russian. In the individualistic, capitalistic West it practically went without saying, but in Russia, only a year after emancipation of the state peasants, it might still seem ironic that a purpose of imprisonment was to "strengthen a prisoner's willpower by supporting individuality, supporting belief in self and one's own strengths; and to create belief in a potentially better future." If the policy had been adopted and made effective, Russian prisons would have become more "progressive" than freedom where, at least for the peasants, legal and fiscal forms of collective responsibility continued to shape their lives.

Passek's third point stated that incarceration should "begin with isolation, sufficiently long as an introductory stage to the remainder of the term of imprisonment." The Europeans had worked backward to this principle through a long and costly experiment with longer and more thorough forms of isolation. Great enthusiasm had greeted the American experiments at Auburn and Philadelphia early in the nineteenth century. These two isolation systems had been widely replicated and then hotly debated in the United States and Europe. Eventually a consensus had emerged that isolation was powerful medicine, useful for intimidating the unruly and certain to prevent "contamination," but that too much isolation bred listlessness and madness. Several compromises had been reached. Nighttime separation after a day's work with other prisoners was commonly practiced; preliminary isolation at the start of a term had more recently gained favor.[46]

Principles four, five, and six were related to principle two. Four asked that "general incarceration" be "organized so that the individual is not lost in the mass, so that he retains interest in self-improvement," and six urged "continuous preparation of the prisoner for freedom." There was no longer any doubt that the overriding purpose of punishment was correction. Through some failure of personality or environment the prisoner had strayed, but he could be rehabilitated and returned healthy to society. To encourage him to develop interest in himself and to evince his readiness for freedom, the fifth principle held out the enticement of parole, or the conditional early release of prisoners, as "the greatest encouragement to correction."

Parole already had a long history in the United States, where it began. English prisons had offered parole for more than forty years, and continental administrators were still enthusiastic about it after twenty or fewer years of experience. Russian advocates of modern correctional systems were well aware of this and repeatedly recommended its adoption in Russia. They succeeded after another forty years.

Passek's seventh and eighth points pertained to discharged prisoners. Police were to be charged with surveillance of parolees, and charitable assistance was to be organized to aid discharged prisoners. Both of these became matters of deep concern to the corrections movement. Both also became deeply involved in the ongoing debate in Russian society over the relative merits of government action and private initiative.

Passek's last principle seemed to bow deeply once more to European experience, but it was clearly mindful of Russian circumstances. He called for "organization of a special prison administration that could guide and unite these efforts." All of the advanced western European nations had developed central prison administrations. Some, like England, had begun to reform prisons at the local level and worked up to centralization; others, like France, had begun from the center. Passek noted that the English organization, which he particularly admired, was "of course subordinated to the minister of internal affairs."

He recommended that Russia's central administration be organized as a "council" in the MVD and that its president be appointed by the minister. The officials or directors of the administration would be called inspectors, each in charge of a branch of prison work—internal economy *(khoziaistvo)*, new construction, remodeling and repairs, corrections, juveniles, statistics, and so forth. They would travel extensively to inspect Russia's prisons while their assistants and staffs carried on at the ministry. Passek emphasized that the selection of the inspectors was vitally important. They must be able, experienced, and devoted to prison work. Interestingly, in describing this council Passek called it by the two different names Russia's central prison administration actually bore from 1879 to 1917 and from May to November 1917.[47]

State Councilor Galkin, the other young man sent abroad in 1862–1863, had returned to the MVD and remained active in prison affairs. With the chief of the DPI, Kholodkovskii, he wrote a "note on the reform of prison affairs in Russia," which, like Passek's paper, included a report on prison affairs abroad. A letter dated 15 February 1867, probably from Kholodkovskii's office, forwarded the note to Minister Valuev.[48]

In mid-February and early March 1867 Valuev wrote to MIu D. N. Zamiatin and to V. N. Panin, director of the Second Department of the Imperial Chancellery, asking that they appoint representatives to a special committee *(soveshchanie)* to study this note and issue a project for correctional prisons. Zamiatin soon replied, appointing his assistant, K. I. Fon-der-Palen (hereafter called Palen); Panin appointed E. A. Peretts; and Valuev made other appointments to complete the committee. Prominent among them was Galkin, who was variously identified in the letter of appointment as chief of department of the Chancellery of the Committee of Ministers and as a member of the staff of the president of the POoT, who was Valuev himself in one of his roles as minister. Other members included a vice president of the St. Petersburg POoT committee, vice director of the MVD's Medical Department, a member of the MVD's Technical-Building Committee, a Professor L'vov, and an unnamed academic from the Academy of Arts.[49]

Count Palen assumed leadership of the committee and set its first meeting for 14 October 1867. This first delay probably reflected turmoil in the MIu, from which Zamiatin had departed on 18 April. The interim ministry of S. N. Urusov ended on 15 October, when Palen became minister, a day after he had planned to convene the committee. The committee did meet later in October and November but left no record of its work until 11 May 1868, when Palen sent its journal to the new MVD, A. E. Timashev. According to a working paper dated 22 April 1869, further considerable delay resulted because of the appointment of the director of the DPI, Baron Belio, to other duties and because of the serious illness of his vice director. Neither Baron Belio nor his assistant were members of the committee, so the comment that their indisposition held up the project suggests that much of it was actually prepared in the DPI's Second Department. The "Project Charter for Correctional Prisons," which the committee completed in April 1869, did not differ greatly from Galkin's note.[50]

This project did not encompass discharged prisoners but otherwise contained most of the principles found in Passek's note. Its primary emphasis had been his last—to establish a prison administration that could design and carry out the reform outlined in his preceding principles. "Correctional prisons," it began (having posted in neat outline form that this was a "general principle"), "are established to hold civilians sentenced to corrective imprisonment by court sentences with the purpose of accustoming them to labor and inculcating in them religious and moral principles." The twin requirements that prison reform a man's habits and his soul were characteristic of this period in Russia. Thirty years earlier activists had cared only for prisoners' souls; before the end of the century administrators would tend almost exclusively to their work habits.[51]

A "comment" following this general principle stated that, until the Code of Punishments was reviewed, persons who were sentenced to prison, workhouses, and strait houses could be sent to correctional prisons, whereas those who were sentenced to arrest companies would go to the companies. This attempted to account for the confusion of types of prisons created on paper by the Code of 1845 but never in reality. It also reflected the tacit understanding in government offices dealing with prisons that attempts to comply with the letter of the code were still on hold and would remain so until the code was reviewed. I shall offer explicit evidence for this later. The experts wanted to eliminate the confusing variety of prisons and to create a simpler, more modern system. "General principles" two and three revealed just how simple. There would be separate men's and women's correctional prisons, and for men these would be of two types: long-term, for sentences of more than one year, and short-term, for sentences of a year or less. Arrest companies were to be used for minor offenders sentenced to incarceration for a few days or weeks. There were too few women prisoners to justify the expense of building separate types of facilities. They would be separated within women's prisons.

This completed the general principles. The next forty-two points (the project contains eighty-one altogether) concerned the administration of correctional prisons. Starting at the top, the project proposed the organization of a central prison administration. "Central administration of correctional prisons is [to be] centered in the Ministry of Internal Affairs, in the Main Prison Committee." There it was. The MVD volunteered to take under its wing this new organization that promised to grow large and expensive. This point would be a major bone of contention. The MVD would win the bone in 1879 but have it taken away in 1895.

The Main Prison Committee (GTK) would be composed of top MVD officials; directors of the Departments of Executive Police, Economy, and Medicine; the chairman of the Technical-Building Committee; and main prison inspectors, who would be appointed by imperial order at the recommendation of the MVD. The assistant MVD would chair the GTK. Representatives of the Ministries of War, Finance, and Justice would "participate in the committee as members." The wording is imprecise but seems to indicate a subordinate position for these outside members, who in any case would be outnumbered by MVD members and appointees. The business *(deloproizvodstvo)* of the committee was to be carried out by special clerks under the direction of the vice director of the DPI. They were most likely the staff of the Second Department, who probably helped to write the document.

The GTK would have large responsibilities. They were first "to apply measures worked out in the project," which meant to create a network of modern correctional prisons. In these prisons they were to "decide all questions relating to administration and economy . . . that exceed the powers of the governors." That is, they were to set policy. Beyond the scope of this already ambitious project, they were to search for means "to gradually improve the functioning of correctional prisons" and "to organize correctional shelters for juvenile criminals." Additionally, the GTK must collect data on recidivism by prisoners released from correctional prisons. That, of course, would reveal just how effectively prisons were rehabilitating their inmates. Small matter that in a country as vast and populous as Russia, especially now that the state had abjured branding, keeping track of prior offenders was next to impossible. Several commissions would confront that dilemma without solving it.

At the provincial level, administration of correctional prisons became more complex. Final administrative authority for all prisons in a province lay "in the person of the chief of the province," that is, in the governor general, governor, military governor, or other official in charge of a region, all of whom were responsible to the MVD. But this titular authority aside, prisons were to be run "by the provincial board *(gubernskoe pravlenie)* through one of the councilors, who is to be called the main prison inspector." The provincial board was a collegial body composed of up to seven councilors, each in charge of a different function of government. Each of them was responsible through the board to the governor and through various other chains of command to the ministry whose work they oversaw. The fiscal administrator, for example, was paid by and reported to the MF. The *prokuror* was on the staff of the MIu. Although they were called by the same name, provincial inspectors were not the same as the main prison inspectors on the GTK. These inspectors/councilors were to oversee the condition of prisons in a province by inspecting them and reporting to the provincial board. The project emphasized that they were not to give any orders on the spot as they inspected but were to report back to the board and, through the board, back to the GTK. Lines of authority were quite unclear and would be worked over repeatedly in future deliberations.

The project went on to detail administration within correctional prisons and included as an appendix three recommended tables of staff for prisons holding more than 500, 250–500, and fewer than 250 inmates.[52] Clearly in charge in each prison was the warden, who is here called by the name wardens would have until the revolution *(nachal'nik tiur'my,* not *smotritel').* He and his assistant would be appointed by a governor, to whom they would be directly responsible. That stipulation would further call into question the roles of the provincial inspector and the provincial board.

The staff of each prison would include a priest, appointed by the local bishop; a doctor and teacher, appointed by the governor; a secretary, chosen by the warden; and an "economist," whose provenance was left unstipulated. Together with gentry, ecclesiastics, merchants who might be invited to participate, and representatives from the local city and land board *(zemskaia uprava)*, who must be invited, these "higher employees" constituted an "economic board" *(khoziaistvennoe pravlenie)*, which had wide responsibilities. They were to oversee the prison's day-to-day functioning, to find work and conclude contracts for prisoner labor, to distribute the income from that labor, to accept donations, and to provision the prison. The board would choose one of its members to be chairman for a term of three years. "Lower employees," all of whom the warden hired, included senior and junior guards, medical assistants, hospital orderlies, and a turnkey or matron. Women's prisons required also a part-time midwife.

Inattention to the matter of financing the reform constituted a major flaw of the project. Two brief articles stipulated that the State Treasury would bear all costs and that the treasury would find money for the purpose from several sources, including income from prisoner labor. Despite this, the committee made no effort to estimate any of the costs of the project. Eight more articles suggested regulations to govern miscellaneous petty financial matters. For example, donations to individual prisoners were not to be permitted; also, prisons were forbidden from displaying a collection plate for donations. Such collections had long been used to supplement the food rations of prisoners.

Prison regime received close attention in twenty-six articles. In general, the "special committee" adopted a hybrid of the Pennsylvania and Auburn systems. Prisoners would work six days a week in common rooms, but in silence, and would spend nights in individual cells. Prisoners would be appointed by the warden to either internal housekeeping work or to contract work. The former produced no income but saved the prison the expense of hiring outsiders to perform kitchen, cleaning, laundering, and maintenance chores. Contract work was rewarded, 10 percent of its income being kept by the prison for expenses, 60 percent going to the treasury, and 30 percent to the prisoners. Ten percent of that 30 percent would be distributed among prisoners doing housekeeping work. Prisoners not fit to work would not be admitted to correctional prisons.

Work played an important role in the project's conception of corrections, but by itself it could not reform the criminal. All inmates were also to be taught "God's law," that is, Orthodox catechism. Long-termers would also receive some regular education. It was expected that free time would be spent reading edifying books, studying, or praying.

For those who behaved well there would be rewards. They could receive visitors on holidays, and, much more important, they could gain an early release. Good behavior alone could reduce a sentence by one-quarter. Prisoners who also helped to teach others a trade, literacy, or good behavior might reduce their term by one-third. Those who did not work well or obey regulations faced a variety of punishments at the discretion of the warden. They might have their pay docked, be put in isolation, or even have sentences extended for short periods.

With the project in its hands, the MVD took over. Under its circular of 17 June 1869, the DPI sent copies of the project to ninety-three chiefs of administrative regions asking for responses no later than October, "because the present project is intended to be sent for review to the State Council during the next legislative session." A letter from Timashev, dated 20 June, accompanied copies sent to the ministers of Justice, War, Finance, and Education; the state controller; the ober-procurator of the Holy Synod; the directors of the Second and Third departments of the Imperial Chancellery; and the directors of MVD departments. Fifty-nine additional copies were posted with copies of the same letter to "interested specialists." The DPI proposed to Timashev that when the replies had been gathered, the councils of the minister and of the POoT (also chaired by the MVD) discuss them.[53]

Among the first responses, all of which were requests for additional copies, came a brief note from the MF asking for a rough estimate of annual costs and for information on where and how many correctional prisons the MVD planned to build.[54] Effusive enthusiasm greeted the project from many directions, but this grain of fiscal realism soon fouled the legislative gears and brought the project to a full halt. The DPI replied to the MF on 20 October 1869 that it did not yet know when it might build the prisons, "nor is there any possibility of even approximately estimating the annual costs of maintaining the administration of such prisons." It did not know enough about the size of the prison population or the size of the prisons to begin to make an estimate. "Much work," it gloomily confessed, "remained to be done."[55]

Timashev had already written to several directors and ministers, asking that they hasten their replies,[56] when the MF responded again on 29 November. His ministry, he wrote, "must be concerned with the cost of prison reform." It would be senseless to begin such an undertaking even if the project and, therefore, its costs were to be spread out over many years without first determining whether there was sufficient money to allocate for it. He advised that the MVD could base estimates on several years of experience with the few new experimental prisons that were already functioning. Someone, quite possibly Timashev, to whom the letter was addressed, penned the word "true" in the margin. The MF concluded that until the MVD could say where and how many or how expensive these facilities would be, "I do not find it possible to inform Your Excellency of the conclusion demanded of me on the project on correctional prisons." He advised not sending the project any farther into the legislative process until costs were well worked out and recommended that the MVD ask, instead, for a small allocation to build several more such prisons as an experiment. Another marginal note beside the MF's refusal to provide a conclusion conceded, "Entirely rational."[57]

The marginal notes conceding the truth of the MF's objections may have been as placid as they appear. Timashev and the DPI knew full well that financial problems facing prison reform were yet to be surmounted. Some funding for prison construction had been assigned by the State Council decision of 22 April 1868, but MVD officials realized that this could at best meet only a small part of their needs.

An interdepartmental note from this time reveals how little was being done and how constrained expectations were in the DPI. On 1 June 1868, shortly after the special committee had sent its journal to Timashev, the Second Department wrote to the Third Department, which controlled this new fund for construction. They had received inquiries from governors about remodeling old prisons or constructing new modern facilities. Nothing had been done, however, because the money had not been available. Now, the Second Department wondered, might there be enough money in the fund to consider building a single new prison? They included plans for the construction they had in mind.

The Second Department hoped that DPI money would suffice, for Timashev had been refusing all requests from them for money for new construction "except in cases of extreme necessity." That meant, the note explained, cases in which extreme decrepitude made detention of prisoners impossible, costs of repair had been shown to exceed costs of new construction, and suitable structures were not available for temporary rental. Timashev was reluctant to spend any extra money right then because "the question of a new prison system was currently being worked out" in the MVD (notice that they did not say in an interministerial special committee), and the minister did not want to begin construction until that system had been approved and he could know what sorts of prisons had been approved.[58]

Responses to the project from other ministers and departments posed no insuperable problems. Among the first came one from the director of the Medical Department in the MVD, who had been a director of the St. Petersburg POoT committees for six years and had studied foreign prisons as well. He had long seen the need for such reform and fully approved the plans. The director attached to his own reply a note from one of his medical inspectors, a Doctor Kholomskii. Like his superior, he had the highest praise for the project, calling it "mature," "well thought out," and "fitting in with the other great reforms of Alexander II's reign." He noted approvingly that the project was based on "western science and experience."[59]

The ober-procurator replied laconically on 6 October 1869 that he had no objections. He then offered a separate, unofficial piece of advice that prisoners be permitted to elect two or three of their number weekly to observe the delivery, preparation, and distribution of food. A correctional arrest company in Tver had done that and found that it eliminated suspicions that the prison staff were pilfering goods and shortchanging the prisoners.[60]

The Third Department of the Imperial Chancellery, Russia's secret police, did not reply until 5 January 1870. Their most serious objection to the plan suggested that, if there were to be special division of prisoners, it should be by the prisoners' age rather than by the length of their sentences. The same problem of "contamination" that prompted the separation by sentence length was offered in explanation but without elaboration to explain why separation by age would be superior. The Third Department made many other comments on individual articles. None was particularly important, but their number presaged the struggle ahead in commissions and councils that would discuss each project article by article.[61]

The minister of war, or whoever on his staff drafted his reply of 25 February, admired the Irish progressive system. He resurrected a proposal from Passek's project that all new prisoners be subjected to preliminary isolation imprisonment. The special committee's project had retained isolation only as a punishment for misdeeds committed in prison. He further suggested that during the last four to six weeks of incarceration prisoners be used for small errands outside prison, be permitted to work outside without guards, and be allowed to visit their homes. The Irish system incorporated such activities to accustom prisoners to trusting their own willpower and to freedom. The only major theoretical problem broached by the minister of war concerned the length of imprisonment. Advocates of the Auburn system in the United States, which he called the "foundation of the treatment of civilian prisoners," had based its minimum sentence on what it took to be experimental evidence that rehabilitation could not be affected in less than one year's detention. The minister wondered whether the demarcation time for short- and long-term prisoners had not been set too low.[62]

In a much longer response received in March, the state controller pointed out the same problems of finance that the MF had raised in earlier correspondence.[63] No one annotated this report, however.

Later in March, Timashev wrote Palen and Urusov to remind them that he needed their replies as soon as possible. Hearing nothing from them, he addressed the same message to the directors of their chancelleries on 5 September 1870. There is no record that Justice ever replied and no evidence in later comments that it did not. The Second Department wrote on 13 December 1871 to say that it would not reply officially until another commission, the Frish Commission, which was then studying reform of the Code of Punishments, had met and reported. Timashev, with considerable patience, agreed in a letter of 14 January 1872 that the Frish Commission was working on a similar project but insisted that most of the DPI project could be considered independently. Two and a half years after circulating the project the MVD still needed the Second Department's response "as soon as possible."[64]

Governors apparently invited or delegated a wide variety of officials to respond to the project. Replies from the provinces came from judges, procurators, POoT directors, provincial-board councilors, and others, as well as from governors and vice governors. Some were extremely brief, indicating approval or at least lack of objection, but most were considerably longer than were the notes from ministries and departments and had substantive points to make about local administration.

In general, response from the provinces was positive. Many respondents disagreed with small parts of the plan but embraced it on the whole. Everyone agreed that Russian prisons were in dreadful condition and required organization and reformation. The POoT of Lifland province commented mildly that "contemporary prisons suffer from great deficiencies," and the governor concurred.[65] The procurator of the Odessa Court Chamber (palata) called them "horrible" and "unable to fulfill their purpose."[66] Others, like the senior councilor of Kazan's provincial board, felt even more strongly. Contemporary prisons made "more and better criminals," he said.[67] Kaluga's governor knew them to make prisoners "more vicious."[68] The governor of Vladimir wrote that just to establish correctional prisons would not be enough. If preliminary prisons were not also overhauled, correctional prisons would fail. People "just begun on the path of crime" would mix with the "rabble of all professions" and become hardened criminals themselves. "The correction of depraved people is in general not an easy matter. When they will have passed through the school of today's preliminary prisons, it will become thoroughly impossible."[69]

Few of the respondents mentioned the western roots of the theories of penological reform, but everyone who did expressed assurance that these origins proved that at least the theory of the project was sound. A POoT director from Bessarabia praised the project as "based on scientific principles tested in practice."[70] One of the "interested specialists," B. A. Neidgart, who had studied the field as a scholar and had inspected the famous European prisons, found the project "well thought out."[71] Although the procurator of the Moscow *okrug* court had many reservations concerning the reform in Russia because of Russian conditions, he was convinced of the desirability of corrections and correctional prisons.[72] The governor of Arkhangelsk—who had worked out his reply with the chairman of the court chamber, the chairman of the commercial court, and the provincial procurator—stated his faith in western science most boldly. Considering that the project was "based on the best of science and experience of the western nations," he "would not think to quarrel with the theoretical side of the problem." Because Russia had no real experience in such matters, it would have to rely on European and American "science and experience."[73]

That times were changing and that at least this elite yearned to make Russia more western can be seen also in comments concerning moral corrections. Remember that the project's first general principle allowed for the dual reformation of secular habits and of the soul by "accustoming [prisoners] to labor and by inculcating in them religious and moral principles." Yet in more than 1,300 folio pages of responses, many of them double sided, only one respondent spent part of four pages to support the idea of religious suasion. The priest of a naval corrections prison argued that many criminals felt guilty at their criminal acts and could be persuaded to repent. Their repentance could lead to a spiritual rebirth that would constitute correction. The priest did not discuss labor at all.[74] An intermediary position was held by the respondents from Astrakhan, who suggested that religious instruction be carried out by priests—not monks, who were too far removed from the real world. In a somewhat sociological comment, the report added that priests could better understand the environment from which most prisoners came.[75] Kazan's officials wanted to know what special treatment or regulations might be needed for Moslem prisoners but said nothing specifically about religious instruction.[76]

On the other hand, many respondents had a great deal to say, all of it positive, about the corrective influence of steady work. The Bessarabian governor and two POoT directors thought that habituation to labor would help convicts to return to society as "better people."[77] Kaluga's report emphasized its authors' "firm belief" in the corrective power of labor and discussed at great length the proper organization of productive work and distribution of earnings.[78] The *ober-politseimeister* (chief of police) of Moscow concurred in similar words.[79] European experience had shown that it was labor that corrected prisoners, added the procurator of Odessa's court chamber.[80]

The *ober-politseimeister* of St. Petersburg, in supporting the use of labor, lodged a specific objection to the idea that moral instruction corrected anyone. The first general principle would have to be reworded to remove its philanthropic character, he wrote. The articles about compulsory labor, "which are the real basis of correctional prisons, already settle the question of moral education."[81] For him, a man's attitude to work was his moral condition. This was indeed a secular man. Professional prison administrators, as they gradually emerged, would much more resemble him than the pious priest.

Neither respondents from the ministries and departments nor those from the provinces had anything specific to say about a central prison administration. Only a few bothered to mention in passing that they considered such organization necessary. Only the MF spoke against the plan. Reports from the provinces, however, had quite a bit to say about the nuts and bolts of local administration. The role of the provincial inspector and his place on the provincial board drew the greatest amount of attention, and opinions were mixed.

Two points of view on the inspectors' position dominated debate about them for the next two decades. The project itself, as I have shown, would have had a provincial inspector attached to each provincial board as a councilor. He would have no authority to issue orders but would investigate, inspect, and report back to the board and to the GTK. The project did not specify who would appoint inspectors. A director of the Moscow POoT, I. Ia. Davydov, stipulated that the GTK should appoint provincial inspectors and should require that they have completed special university courses to prepare them for their work. He insisted that they receive extra money to support an independent chancellery and to reimburse them for their travels. Otherwise, he concurred with the project's view of their relationship to boards and governors.[82]

Other respondents feared that the collegial structure of the board would hamstring the inspectors. They recommended that inspectors and their staffs be placed directly under governors. The governor of Penza felt that way,[83] and so did B. A. Neidgart.[84] Advocates of an even more independent role for the inspectors, as regional representatives of a central administration, believed that they would be powerless until the central body had become more of a reality.

To some MVD officials, the provincial inspectors seemed to be the heart of the new organization. Without representatives throughout the far-flung empire, the central organization would be as blind as the DPI now was to the condition of prisons and also to the effects of their future orders. The MF wrote that until the new prison buildings were ready (and he wrote in the same note that money for construction was not forthcoming), there would be no need for a central administration or for inspectors. Timashev, or whoever annotated this report, penned in the margin, "To abandon the Main Committee there is some justification, but the inspectors, never." When the MF advised that the DPI could rely on regular inspection tours or specially assigned briefer inspections, the annotator wrote, "It would be interesting to know how much money is spent on these largely fruitless inspection tours."[85] The inspectorate system would prove to be expensive, as the MF feared, but extremely valuable, as the MVD hoped. It became a major force for the professionalization of the prison system.

Considering that many of the respondents were themselves members of POoT committees, it is surprising that so little controversy arose from the project's silent dismissal of the society. The Arkhangelsk governor noted with approval that the project assigned the society no specific role. The POoT, he agreed fully, "should be excluded from any part of the administration of correctional prisons."[86] Moscow's *ober-politseimeister* disagreed. He, too, noted the project's omission of a role for the POoT, but he said without any elaboration that it could be useful in "moral edification" and "material assistance."[87] I. Ia. Davydov, who submitted a thoughtful and detailed report, commented on the inability of POoT committees and the disinterest of POoT directors without suggesting that the society be offered a role in correctional prisons.[88]

The dearth of comments implies strongly the truth of a complaint heard frequently at that time, that the POoT had become largely inert and marginally useful. Although many respondents were POoT directors, most were not. In a few cases, society directors who were asked to comment on the project failed to do so. The governor of Perm, for example, wrote the DPI that he had asked for reports from a few directors whom he considered well qualified. One wrote back that, "perceiving from the explanatory notes to the project that the Ministry of Internal Affairs had worked this out with particular thoroughness and detail on the basis of a huge amount of previously collected information," he felt inadequate even to comment.[89] Mogilev's governor had appointed a three-member committee of POoT directors to study the project and draft a reply. They never began it, however, and two had subsequently left the area. Mogilev was one of the few provinces that never sent in a report.[90] Governors turned more frequently to judges and procurators, whose ties to prisons were less direct, for reports on the project.

Still, asked the Arkhangelsk governor, what should he do with an organization of five thousand directors and 2 million rubles' capital? His own inclination was to reorganize it. True, it had many faults, but it was large and already in place. Given a direction and new goals, it could be made useful. Once again, the best new direction had been indicated by "science and the experience of the European nations." POoT committees should be transformed into charitable *patronaty*—organizations to help discharged prisoners reenter normal society.[91] A marginal note beside this paragraph expressed the MVD's approval. The governor added that the committees could work with juveniles also.

Several other respondents urged the creation of *patronaty*. Two POoT directors from Bessarabia were enthusiastic about them. They did not say how they might be created, however, so I cannot know if they envisioned them as part of the POoT's work or as independent from it.[92] The governor of Vladimir, who had been so concerned about preliminary prisons, saw *patronaty* at the other end of the prison system as completing the work of corrections, assisting in the readjustment and reintegration of ex-convicts. "Without improvement in preliminary and after-prison care, prison reform by itself will mean little." Russia needed a whole reform.[93]

The MVD had fewer problems gathering in the large number of replies from the provinces than it had in convincing other ministries in St. Petersburg to answer them. Some responses arrived in August 1869, a few in September, and the majority of them in October, as the DPI circular had requested. A few straggled in as late as November, and some others probably never arrived, but, unlike the silence of the Second Department of the Imperial Chancellery and of the MIu, these lacunae did not seriously disturb the MVD. Timashev waited until 22 September 1871 to write to twenty-one governors from whom he had not heard and did not trouble to do so again.[94] Early in 1872 the question of future reform was removed from the MVD and placed in a commission that, it was hoped, might be able to bring together and reconcile the many departments interested in prison reform.

CHAPTER THREE

THE

COMMISSIONS

DISCUSS

PRISON REFORM

I
THE SOLLOGUB COMMISSION

n February 1872 events finally overtook the DPI. Perhaps tiring of the stand-off among the ministries in St. Petersburg, the emperor turned to an energetic Muscovite to chair the next commission on prison affairs. V. A. Sollogub had been interested in prisons and corrections since before 1866, when he published a small book, *On the Organization of Prison Labor in Russia.* At that time he had been warden of a house of correction in Moscow that I. Ia. Foinitskii called a model prison.[1] Unlike many wardens and keepers criticized in contemporary reports, he seems to have been neither venal nor apathetic. Sollogub had made it his business to study theoretical penology and took an active interest in the condition of Russian prisons and in the progress of efforts to improve them.

In 1866, returning to Moscow from a trip to St. Petersburg, Sollogub toured prisons along the way. He wrote M. N. Pokhvisnev, director of the DPI, that, although he had seen the same terrible conditions before in other prisons, he still found them appalling. He visited one county *(uezd)* prison in which prisoners had no new shoes, shirts, or jackets for four years. "And by the way," he noted, "there is a [POoT] committee in town." Prisoners there were not separated, as law and scientific theory required, even though the prison was a large stone building with one floor completely vacant. The head guard, who was temporarily acting warden, kept his pig in the prison courtyard, "from which you could just suffocate." "For God's sake," he implored his correspondent, "do not take the sin on yourself; do not defend our disgraceful prison administration. . . . [It is] offensive to God."[2]

Sollogub wrote in this letter that he was studying prison affairs daily and that "it is all becoming clearer." Just what was clearer would be difficult to say, for Sollogub was obviously torn. On the one hand, he recognized that prison administration needed reorganization, and he had concrete suggestions to that end. He sympathized with a warden he met in Orel who complained about the POoT and wished that there were "just one chief in the prison." Sollogub too had little use for the POoT. Although he was himself a director of the Moscow POoT, he had never been invited to a meeting. He thought they might be useful as "charitable philanthropic" organizations but wanted them to withdraw from meddling in administrative affairs.

Prison administration might be reorganized along the lines of the gendarme administration, he speculated, with a central administration and subordinate provincial organs. Something would have to be done, he thought, because as things were "now we do not have a prison administration, and there are no prisons that are morally influential." He thought it might help to learn how prisons were run abroad and volunteered to go to Belgium, where all prisons were part of a modern, centralized correctional system, to study their organization "for the minister."[3]

On the other hand, Sollogub had serious doubts about bureaucracy, the usefulness of issuing enlightened laws, and even about corrections, at least in Russia. He had been to St. Petersburg to submit a manuscript of his book "for Petr Aleksandrovich to censor." Petr Aleksandrovich was the MVD Valuev, who was a longtime acquaintance of Sollogub. In his letter Sollogub described his book as an exposé of "the whole, naked, irrefutable truth" and confessed that it was quixotic. He would not abandon his idealizing, however, unless Petr Aleksandrovich would put himself above his work and Pokhvisnev would "put the state's interests before his comfort." But he feared that neither of them would. Although he found his St. Petersburg friends to be "not only statesmen but also men of high civic honesty," they were nonetheless, "excuse me, drowning in waves of paper."

And what good was the paper? "Even with the very best laws prison administration in Russia will not be any good—its foundation is rotten." That is, the people in it were not up to the challenge. Prisoners could not be corrected by guards who fetched liquor for drinkers and cards for gamblers. Moreover, in Russia, prisoners were not the same class of people found in Belgian prisons. "How can we expect some wild man raised in ignorance and left to solitary masturbation to be transformed in prison?" Despite his doubts, however, Sollogub held to one contemporary hope—the corrective power of habitual labor. "You are entrusting me with prisoners," he wrote as he returned to Moscow to begin work as a warden. "I will try to make out of them not virtuous people but good workers."

Sollogub kept in contact with Pokhvisnev, with Galkin-Vraskii (then a top assistant to Valuev in prison affairs), and with Valuev, but his career did not advance as he would have liked. He hoped to become a governor but was passed over on several occasions, possibly because of ill health. At least twice he threatened to retire. In July 1867, when the DPI project was written and the Palen Committee was put together to study it, Sollogub was once more left out. He wrote Galkin-Vraskii that he wished "the whole prison question might be removed from the Department of Executive Police and given to me" in a position directly subordinate to the minister.[4]

Under Valuev nothing of the sort happened. When Sollogub was appointed chairman of the next prison commission in 1872, Valuev had been removed and A. E. Timashev had been MVD for four years. Sollogub came from a wealthy, prominent family and moved in high circles. It is possible he was also acquainted with Timashev or that his book had attracted the new minister's attention. If not, he brought himself to Timashev's attention in 1869 by writing the longest and most comprehensive reply to the special committee's project that was received by the DPI. The governor of Moscow wrote in his reply that he had asked for Sollogub's comments, using Sollogub's surname as if he expected it to be known to the director and minister. The reply itself was more fully annotated with marginal notes than was any other except that from the MF.[5]

Sollogub's report contained many of the points raised in his earlier letter, along with more detailed explanations revealing how he wished to set about reforming prisons. He began with large, general objections. First, the project was incomplete and premature. Of the four rungs on the so-called ladder of punishments stipulated by the Code of 1845—preliminary prisons, strait houses, correctional prisons, and punitive prisons—this plan accounted for only the middle two. Leaving out the first (as the governor of Vladimir also pointed out) would defeat the purpose of the plan. The initial reform should be for preliminary prisoners, who were thrown into general prisons that were "overcrowded," "unclean," "stinking," and "full of lice and brutality," where prisoners were "underfed, underclothed, and treated rudely and roughly."[6] The other reforms were needed too, but this first step must not be skipped. The reforms must be gradual and orderly.

The project was also "much too ambitious financially." The government did not give prisons enough money to keep themselves in basic repair. To try to remodel or to build new short- and long-term prisons would be much too expensive. Once again, he cautioned against haste and recommended gradualness, proceeding with the building program "using money only as it is available." He buttressed his argument for deliberation with a point he had made in his book and in his letter: Russia did not have the trained men to reform all of its prisons at once. A deliberate pace would permit men to be prepared, along with the facilities.[7]

Sollogub found the project overly ambitious in another way. Thinking probably of the failure to implement the requirements of the 1845 Code of Punishments, he remarked that there had "long been a great gap in prison affairs between the indications of law and practice." He feared that the project could give rise to further such discrepancies. Moreover, the project was not sufficiently clear. For example, experience had shown that correction could not be achieved quickly. Therefore, special conditions must be specified for short-term prisons. They required different architecture, maintenance, discipline, and regimes of study and work—in short, a whole separate project. The same was true for intermediate-term (he preferred to call penal servitude "long-term," and what the project called "long-term" he renamed "intermediate"), long-term, preliminary, women's, and juvenile facilities. They were all different and would require separate sets of regulations.[8] He went on to discuss at some length the additional complication that, by applying ameliorating or extenuating circumstances, judges could choose among optional punishments and sentence prisoners to one of several types of prison. Until the Code of Punishments was revised or at least the ladder of punishments overhauled, he foresaw much confusion arising from the project's imprecise categories.[9] This, of course, implied the need for another huge task that would, if undertaken, further delay prison reform.

Before he moved on to more specific comments about the project, Sollogub discussed one more point that had been omitted from the project. Like the governor of Vladimir, who hoped the DPI would devise a "whole reform," Sollogub was concerned with the project's failure to discuss discharged prisoners. He spoke especially of the need to help those whom village societies refused to reaccept. It was their privilege to turn away ex-convicts, who would then be sent away into exile. Sollogub called this double punishment and unjust. No one who was discharged from the correctional system should be exiled without a court sentence, he insisted. It destroyed in prisoners the impulse to reform and be reintegrated. Those who earned attestation to their industriousness in prison should be permitted to choose their place of residence on discharge and live there under the surveillance of the police or of reformed POoT committees. Recidivists, he distinguished, should be exiled immediately and not taken into the correctional system.[10] As logical as this idea may seem, it ignores the fact that the whole system of exile was also under attack.

Sollogub briefly expanded his comment on the POoT. It could be made useful as a charitable organization assisting in prison work but not involved in its administration. Citing English experience, he particularly encouraged work with discharged prisoners, with prisoners' families, and in organizing shelters for prisoners' children.[11]

Sollogub agreed with many detractors of the existing system that Russian prisons suffered from having too many chiefs. Recall his sympathy for the warden in Orel. The project, he complained, would create that problem anew. Unclear and overlapping authority of the provisioning committee, wardens, provincial inspectors and boards, governors, the GTK, and the minister would cause business to be conducted as slowly as it currently was. No one would be directly responsible, and all would hesitate to act: "Once more there will be no directly responsible individuals in a business that requires military precision and commercial accuracy."[12]

He found the provisioning committee expendable: "For an honest warden the complex control is unnecessary; for an unreliable warden such control will only serve as a shield for abuses and free [him] from any direct responsibility." With the warden directly in command, the prison staff, assisted by a representative from the zemstvo and one from the local Duma, could handle provisioning. Sollogub suggested, as had the ober-procurator, that prisoner representatives participate in receiving, preparing, and apportioning food in order to avoid complaints of peculation.[13]

The honest and competent warden was, of course, a major problem. Sollogub, as we have seen, was appalled at the general level of present wardens and pessimistic of finding enough good men. A fellow director of the Moscow POoT Committee, I. Ia. Davydov, shared his views: "In our prisons," he wrote in his response to the project, "wardens are appointed from among police ranks. To meet among them an upright man with noble impulses is a rare exception." Davydov warned that "worthy, honest, and fully trained" men must be found, but he did not say how.[14] Sollogub insisted that new wardens be selected at the recommendation of the minister of war from among officers who were used to military discipline and economy. To these he would give much more authority than present wardens enjoyed or the project offered.[15]

The best of these, as they gained experience in prison affairs, would move up to become provincial and regional (okrug) inspectors. Unlike the inspectors in the project, Sollogub's would have the power to give orders on the spot as they conducted inspections. Russian distances required that, he insisted. Without such authority, inspectors would be indifferent to their work, and local prisons would remain unreached by the "constant, special, responsible supervision" of the GTK. The provincial inspectors would provide a "responsible link" between local and central levels. Timashev, if it was he who annotated the reports, heartily endorsed this point with an emphatic "Just so!" and added that governors' inspection tours could not provide that.[16]

By calling the inspectors the responsible link between St. Petersburg and the countryside, Sollogub implied that he did not like their position on the provincial boards and possibly also their subordination to the governors. He had earlier said, "My opinion is that prison affairs are purely a police [matter] and require no complex conferential and collegial discussion once the rules and instructions are given to those who execute them." The organization he prescribed to ensure that rules were carried out consisted of a simple pyramid of inspectors that did not include either provincial boards or governors. In keeping with his advice to proceed step by step, he recommended trying that system on a small scale experimentally.[17]

Prisoner labor played a large role in Sollogub's vision of reformed prisons. He largely agreed with the project in this area and contented himself with elaborating on what types of work and remuneration could be arranged. Prisoners, he thought, would be grateful to earn money and would work well if they were treated honestly. And the work, he was sure, would rehabilitate them so slowly that they would not notice the change.[18] The income earned from prisoner labor should be saved, he urged, for it would be most important to the convicts after their release. Without it, they would be forced once more into poverty and fall back into crime. Moreover, if they learned to save while in prison, the habit would remain useful to them after their release.[19] Parole, which he mentioned only briefly, he saw as a reward for good work, which both caused and gave evidence of correction.

Sollogub's observations on labor appear in a section of his report that he introduced as a discussion of "total moralization." Recall the phrase from his 1866 letter that he would endeavor to make "not virtuous people but good workers" of prisoners in his charge. The only other subject in the section was drink, which he deplored. Sollogub clearly equated work as a way of life with a moral life. Good workers would be virtuous people by definition, and workers who saved what they earned would be twice blessed. Three years later, a few months after he became chairman of the commission on prison reform, he reported at an international prison congress in London:

> The cause of crime in my country arises from a certain oriental fatalism, which enters profoundly into the character of the people. This fatalism, which is associated with a profound religious faith, inspires frequently a singular indifference to life and death, to the enjoyments and privations of life, sometimes even to moral good and evil. The result is a spirit of indolence, which, however, is often roused by the temptation to drunkenness and the excitements aroused by it.[20]

Sollogub seems to have hoped that work and temperance would at once make Russians decent, law-abiding, self-supporting, and European.

Sollogub dissented from the project's use of isolation and spoke out against rules of silence in prisons. He doubted that either had any corrective effect, and as punishment he found them excessive. Monastic separation from women and general loneliness were sufficient punishment. Silence and isolation on top of this would breed only resentment, anger, and possibly madness. All of these were worse than the harm that might be done by prisoners conversing. Work alone would be enough to accomplish correction.[21]

In conclusion, Sollogub reiterated his belief in deliberation and his caveat that abuses of the system would require extirpation regardless of the rules that might be written. Most of his principles were incorporated into the projects produced by the commission he would soon chair.

Sometime in 1871 Sollogub made an official trip to inspect Siberian prisons. Along with the other work that had made him eminent in the field, the emotional report he wrote about this tour came to the emperor's attention.[22] Shortly thereafter he was named to chair the Imperially Established Commission for the Composition of a General Systematic Project of Prison Reform. The commission met first on 29 February 1872, apparently at Sollogub's residence in Moscow. In addition to its chairman, members included three representatives from the MVD; three from the MIu, including E. V. Frish, who would chair one commission and serve on later ones that deliberated prison reform; two from the Second Department of the Imperial Chancellery; one from the Third Department; one from the MF; and a secretary. As its name and composition suggest, the commission was meant to take a wide view of prison problems and reform. The commission members spent this first meeting trying to decide just how wide.

The first major problem they identified, its members agreed, was too large and too specialized for the commission to handle, but they joined the consensus among men working for prison reform that it was a problem that must be solved before prison reform could proceed. Laws governing the handling of prisons and prisoners were "hodge-podge collections . . . accumulated over time according to the circumstances prevailing at the time each law was added." The collections— the Charter on Persons Held under Guard *(Ustav o soderzhashchikhsia pod strazhei)* and the Charter on Exiles *(Ustav o ssylnykh),* which together made up the Code of Punishments and included the ladder of punishments—therefore reflected no consistent theory of punishment or corrections. They contained contradictions and confusions, which would have to be eliminated, and, having no theoretical basis, lacked "system," which would have to be supplied.[23] While this commission deliberated its other work in the next two years, a second commission, chaired by E. V. Frish, would be working simultaneously to overhaul the "ladder."

Having agreed not to attempt to rewrite the charters, the commission defined a broad range of other problems to discuss. Its members recognized, for example, that laws were already on the books whose purpose they concurred with, but whose strictures were being disregarded. For example, prisoners in pretrial detention were not being held apart from convicts, because of general inattention or lack of space. For the same reasons, prisoners were not being segregated by established categories. The POoT came under heavy criticism again. Its charter and operation the commission termed a "confusion of governmental and private charitable purposes and responsibilities." As the society now functioned, there were no clear expectations of its responsibilities, so it often did its work poorly and sometimes actually contributed to the poor condition of prisons.

The commission identified several problems with the categories of prisons established by the Code of 1845. Strait houses and workhouses, the few that were operable, held prisoners for between two months and two years. Because the commissioners believed that a mere two months could not serve "correctional purposes," the houses' regime, which was meant to be correctional, could not serve the needs of all of their inmates. They would have to be recategorized, and other short-term punishments would have to be devised. At the same time, the commission found disturbing similarities between the two types of "houses" and the correctional arrest units *(ispravitel'nye arestantskie otdeleniia).* The commission wondered whether redundant functions and purposes could not be eliminated and new functional boundaries drawn. The report does not mention it here, but at least some of the members, including Frish, must have been aware that such recategorization would require changes in the "ladders," which the commission had decided not to undertake.

One aspect of the houses' operation especially upset some members. Village societies, because they had the power to exile their undesirable elements, also had been given the right to send them to the houses. Therefore, prisoners who were sentenced by courts and those who were merely expelled by fellow villagers were commingled. This was clearly an anachronism in an era of enthusiasm for the new courts; customary law retained a function that ought to belong to legal institutions. It also violated an old and basic principle of criminal law: that there be no punishment except where crime has been proven *(nulla poena sine crimine)*. The theoretically troublesome institution—the preliminary or investigatory prison where suspects were held before their trials—was created to make a similar distinction between persons who had been accused of crime and convicts who had been sentenced by courts.

The commission's members intended also to take up the matter of work in prisons. The systems of exile and penal servitude and the labor implied in each seemed ineffectively organized and in need of attention. Some prisoners were made to work; many more languished in idleness. A general regulation was needed to govern prisoners' labor. The commission members also criticized the administration of the experimental correctional prison in St. Petersburg. A special charter had been drawn up to regulate its operation, but it had not been made mandatory and was not being applied. This specific item, along with general problems concerning guards and escapes, was also put on the agenda.[24]

Unlike its predecessor, this commission did not solicit opinions from around the country, but several interested parties volunteered materials for the commission to consider. The MVD signaled its temporary withdrawal from efforts to directly control prison reform by forwarding its project to Sollogub, along with notes and comments on the project and two manuscript volumes on prison reform, which had been given the minister by an Italian diplomat in St. Petersburg.[25]

The MIu, who had never responded to the MVD's project, wrote to Timashev on 22 March 1872 that he, too, had passed his copy of the MVD project on to Sollogub.[26] Much later the Second Department explained that in response to the Timashev letter of 12 January 1872 it had begun a review of the project, but when Sollogub's commission had begun its work, the department had stopped. By 3 September 1873, the Frish Commission had begun to review the ladder of punishments, and a "final commission" was envisioned to reconcile all that work, so the Second Department planned to leave everything to that commission.[27] Galkin-Vraskii, by then governor of Saratov, sent through the ministry a plan offered him by a local landowner to build a correctional prison on land he owned and would donate.[28]

The commission set quickly to work and completed its first project in early summer. Significant disagreement within the group caused many points to be presented with majority or minority reports or to be stated only tentatively. In the first part of the report, which dealt with classification of places of imprisonment, Chairman Sollogub's hand is recognizable. The commission's categories are those he had recommended in response to the DPI's project in 1869. Suspects held over for trial would be detained in special prisons apart from term-serving convicts. With this stipulation the commission took one more step toward confronting the modern dilemma of individuals' civil rights and public safety. The commission members recognized that prisoners who had not yet been tried ought not to be treated the same as convicted offenders but that, because they might be guilty or dangerous, they could not be left at liberty. Preliminary detention should be carried out carefully, they wrote, and it should not be considered punishment. This must have been a relief to preliminary prisoners. The commission appears not to have considered that most detainees awaiting trial ought not to be imprisoned at all. It remained clearly on the public safety side of the nascent dilemma. As they put it, preliminary detention was based not on rights but on "fear and necessity."[29]

The categories of prisons for serving court sentences were Sollogub's, too, but they also incorporated features derived from the DPI project. The special committee had been omitted from the project but included in its "explanatory note" several recommendations that Sollogub adopted. Two of these were that exile to Siberia for life or to special exile colonies for specified terms be abolished and be replaced by sentences to central prisons in which heavy labor, such as was done in penal servitude, be organized.[30] On the copy sent to Sollogub by Shidlovskii and Iuferov, Sollogub penciled "Excellent" in the margin beside these recommendations.[31] In his response to the project in 1869, he had called penal servitude "long-term" imprisonment. In his own commission's project these features were amalgamated. Long-term prisons were to be established to replace penal servitude as it was then practiced.

The commission strongly attacked the exile system, especially as organized on Sakhalin, and recommended that exile for life be replaced by penal servitude and that exile to colonies be preceded by penal servitude. They offered the rationalization that exile to distant places offered no benefit to the nation as a whole and was so far removed from the general population that it was invisible punishment; it was costly, wasteful, and had no deterrent force. Prisoners in penal servitude, with those who would previously have been exiled added to their numbers, comprised a significant workforce that could be harnessed in large, well-organized central prisons. After serving a portion of their terms in these prisons and acquiring skills and good habits of work, these prisoners would be released to exile colonies for the larger part of their terms.[32]

The commission could not bring themselves to abolish penal colonies. Even after incarceration in the new *katorga* prisons, they believed, some prisoners would not be prepared to be reintegrated into decent society. The commissioners also turned aside criticism of the *katorga* system as a whole, contending that the category was needed even if its performance in the past had been faulty. The cruelty and arbitrariness that were then its hallmark and that were under attack in liberal society could be rooted out. Better locations could be selected for the new prisons, not for punishment's sake but to bring prisoners to where they could perform useful labor. If, while they were in penal servitude, prisoners would be made to work hard and productively, both the prisoners and the state would benefit. As work in correctional prisons must prepare prisoners to live in freedom, so work in penal servitude would be organized to prepare them to live in penal colonies. The only major disagreement on *katorga* among the members concerned a form of parole. A majority preferred that the only reward for good work be increased pay. Sollogub, with two other members, wanted shortened sentences to be awarded to outstanding prisoner workers.[33]

As Sollogub had in 1869, his commission's project designated correctional prisons as intermediate and emphasized the importance of labor in them. The explanatory note to the DPI project had made clear the special committee's opinion on the etiology of crime and the reformative power of labor. The general purpose of "deprivation of freedom," they wrote, is correction, which is best effected through compulsory labor, because the "major causes of crimes are idleness, laziness, and inability to earn a living by labor. . . . Term imprisonment without labor is senseless." Sollogub's red pencil wrote large in the margin "Right" and "The whole secret is in the organization of labor."[34]

The commission did not push far beyond the special committee in divining the "whole secret," but they did establish categories of labor that were long used by others who tried to organize prison labor. "Black" labor was the name for unskilled physical work. All new prisoners would perform black labor ten hours a day for no pay. Older and weaker prisoners would move on to unskilled mechanical tasks, such as making mops and brooms. For such "gray" labor they would receive one-third of the earnings they produced. Able-bodied but unskilled prisoners would be apprenticed to prisoner masters who performed more highly skilled tasks, such as tailoring, cobbling, or carpentry. They would work eight hours a day learning this skill and two more hours assisting newcomers at black labor. They would not be paid. Their incentive to learn their master's trade was the knowledge that they could then graduate to his status, train apprentices, and keep two-thirds of the income they produced together.[35]

Not all of the commission members shared their chairman's deep aversion to isolation. Everyone agreed that it was a stronger punishment than simple incarceration, but a majority preferred to use its strengths as an additional tool of correction. All prisoners sent to a house of corrections, said the majority, should begin their terms in isolation. Solitude permitted a prisoner to settle into his new environment without distractions, to look within himself and reflect on why he was in prison. It also gave prison personnel a chance to observe the prisoner to learn what sort of person he was and how to treat him. The priest, teacher, and administrators could speak with him in private in isolation. Even in a mild regime institution, isolation would give each prisoner a "taste of harshness" to remind him of the burden of his crime, and it might make those who were disinclined to work eager for some movement and activity. They argued that time spent in preliminary detention could not do any of this because the prisoner's mind would be focused on the hope that he would escape a court sentence.[36]

Sollogub and three others contended that preliminary detention, which in the new system would be carried out in isolation, would serve most of these purposes. Any time spent in isolation in houses of correction, on the other hand, would be time lost from learning a trade, learning to read, and the other useful activities the houses were supposed to administer. Because sentences ranged from only one year to four years, there was no time to be lost. Furthermore, handling two types of incarceration, isolation and general, would be burdensome to administrators and confusing for the prisoners. Isolation as an additional punishment during general imprisonment *(kartser)* would still be available in any case.[37]

Different factions disagreed about the same issue as applied in strait houses. Realistically, the commission faced the problem that if some facilities could be built to be used as strait houses, not all would incorporate the costly isolation cells the Code of 1845 called for; others might, however, so they tried to account for both situations. Prisoners serving their term in general incarceration would serve their full sentence. A majority of members agreed that those sitting in isolation should have their terms reduced by one-third. A minority led by Chairman Sollogub dissented. "Cellular" imprisonment, they felt, should reduce a prisoner's term by two-thirds. The maximum sentence in that institution was sixteen months. The maximum period spent in isolation would then be five months and ten days. This more generous reduction would still provide "memorable" punishment, which was the primary object of the strait house. Beating with a rod, they offered as an analogy, was "brief but memorable" punishment, and effective. Isolation for longer periods, the minority argued, had been known to cause suicide and madness. They branded the majority's position "not just cruel, but inhuman." The shortened terms they advocated would have an added benefit. More prisoners, twice as many, could be moved through the system in the same time, cutting in half the costs of constructing new isolation cells.[38]

Unanimously the commission joined its chairman in echoing the special committee's doubts about the POoT. The explanatory note to the earlier project had attacked the society from several directions and at considerable length. The MVD had not had much success to date in administering prisons, the attack began, "largely because responsibilities are not defined."

> The primary obstacle in the way of consistent and energetic action by the minister of internal affairs in the field of good prison management is the indefiniteness of its relation with the POoT and the absence of definite demarcation of the areas of prison management between the administration and those institutions that are basically philanthropic.

The resulting confusion of too many chiefs paralyzed the wardens, who received contradictory orders and could not know which of their numerous superiors to obey. POoT committees tended to attract people not trained for prison work who were interested primarily in the prestige of belonging. Some directors were too busy to do much for the committees; others were simply disinterested. The project characterized them as "unpaid," "unresponsible," and "uninterested." Even those exceptional directors who tried to work for prisons found themselves bound by a collegiality that did not suit the type of work they needed to do. As a parting shot, the project described a recent state controller's report of widespread financial carelessness and abuse in the POoT.[39]

Without going into detailed justification for its conclusions, Sollogub's commission made clear that it agreed that the society should be excluded from prison administration. The society's work should be limited to charitable functions, such as building and decorating places of worship in prisons, speaking with prisoners, organizing shelters for prisoners' children, and assisting discharged prisoners. The closest they might approach administration would be to suggest improvements to wardens.[40]

Sollogub concluded from this sorry recitation of the woes of prison administration that Russia needed a central prison administration. He wrote at the end of the earlier project's assault on the POoT, "After this superlative argument how [can we] explain the delay of the creation of the Main Prison Committee, and with it of the provincial prison committees?"[41] His commission concurred, but in an indecisive fashion. They recommended creating a main prison administration in "one of the higher government offices" that had provincial organs. That, of course, could apply to either the MVD or the MIu. The organization they then sketched out resembled that described in the earlier project.[42]

Copies of this project went to the emperor and to the heads of the ministries and departments that had participated in the commission's work. Having quickly reviewed it, on 18 July 1872 the ministers and directors responded to Sollogub. Adjutant General P. A. Shuvalov, chief of the Third Department of the Imperial Chancellery, wrote on behalf of the group that it had concluded that prison reform should be carried out as an experiment in the ten provinces of the Moscow Court Chamber. They asked that the commission submit "for our joint consideration":

1. Plans for what should be done in these provinces, including a timetable and an estimate of goals, and a recommendation on how to involve prisoners in the construction of the new prisons;
2. Plans, including a budget, for one *katorga* prison somewhere in that region at a location of the commission's choosing;
3. Plans for reforming the transfer system in these provinces, with an estimate of costs;
4. Personnel tables for prisons and a central administration and a plan for subordination of the prison administration to "higher government institutions"; and
5. Annual budgets for the postreform period in that region.[43]

Work on the second project was delayed by the coming of summer. Tsarist administrators often took a large part of the summer off. In any case, Chairman Sollogub was abroad for more than a month at the International Prison Congress in London.[44] K. Golovin, who was a member of the commission, recalled that "[our] wandering colleagues met rarely," but in August 1872 they were summoned to Sollogub's autumn residence and thereafter met regularly. The only extant account of these meetings was written by Golovin, who apparently did not sympathize with or understand the commission's work. He was sure that the "engineers and architects" who "arrived there one after another from various provinces" had plans "to rob the treasury," but the impression he created is of busyness and hard work.[45]

By May 1873 the second project was ready. It was sent to the MVD, the

MIu, the MF, and the directors of the Second and Third Departments of the Imperial Chancellery. These five men constituted themselves as a special conference and quickly reviewed the report once more. This time they presented the journal of their comments to the emperor. Alexander II deigned on 19 May to confirm their opinion that the commission had produced "extensive and entirely conscientious work . . . that can serve as a solid foundation for the further discussion of this matter."[46] He ordered that a special committee be established for that purpose and may have signaled his impatience with this ten-year-old problem by calling it the Imperially Established Committee for the Final Discussion of the Project of Prison Reform in the Empire.

Assuming that Sollogub was the conscientious man he seems to have been, he learned something of the difficulties of prison reform in Russia in these four years. Recall that he had found the DPI's project premature and overly ambitious in several ways. It had called for an expensive building program, assumed that qualified men could be found to implement their modern programs, and proposed many new regulations that Sollogub doubted would or could be observed. When Sollogub had marked up the copy of the DPI's project sent him in 1872, he editorially subtitled its explanatory note "Or the Discord of Chancellery Theory and Real Life."[47] Yet the project his own commission produced later that same year borrowed a great deal from the earlier work and even expanded on it. To do the job correctly, it said inferentially, we must be even more ambitious. We must have separate preliminary prisons with isolation cells. We must have strait houses and workhouses with separate sets of regulations and regimes and more expensive isolation cells. Additionally, we need huge new prisons for thousands of prisoners formerly sent to *katorga* colonies and into exile. And a central administration, and inspectors, and wardens, and guards. . . . He had chided the 1869 work for imprecision. It had spoken of the need for short- and long-term prisons but produced only one set of regulations. His own described a greater variety of prisons and offered no detailed sets of regulations. His commission approved the DPI's notion of a central administration with an inspector corps and largely reproduced it, but could not say in what ministry to organize it. The problems were many, and much work remained.

THE FRISH COMMISSION

One piece of work that had been completed by this time—although, like everything else, it would have to be redone—was a study and revision of the ladder of punishments. Sitting from 1871 to 1873, a special commission under the chairmanship of E. V. Frish examined the second chapter, first division *(razdel)* of the Code of 1845, the ladder, to excise those portions made obsolete by emancipation and the reform of corporal punishment and to make recommendations for other changes and rearrangements it found desirable. Frish, who was then ober-procurator of the Criminal Cassational Department of the Senate and had been a member of Sollogub's commission from the MIu, sent his commission's work to the MIu on 28 February. Palen submitted it to the State Council on 2 March 1873. There it languished until 4 October, when discussion of it began and was cut short by a strenuous attack on it by MF Reitern.[48]

Frish's work faced other serious difficulties. He lived and worked in a legal world distant from the realities of prison administration. In the Criminal Cassational Department he was concerned with interpreting which laws took precedence over others if two or more seemed to conflict and with questions of procedure, jurisdiction, and appeal. Although he had been on Sollogub's commission and must have been aware of the directions prison reform might take, he did not attempt to coordinate his commission's work with Sollogub's. A prominent contemporary criminalist, who followed closely the work of all of these commissions, conferences, and committees, observed at the time that the work of the Sollogub and Frish Commissions "despite the close connection of their purposes . . . do not have the desired unity." The State Council, which would have to consider the proposals of both "will inescapably be put in serious difficulty by the variance of demands and principles in their conclusions." They worked separately and from different points of view. Sollogub paid little attention to existing law, whereas Frish ignored prison practices and experience in Russia.[49]

The MIu, which attempted to defend Frish's work, replied to the MF's objections in May 1874 and was to have received a hearing of its proposals in a joint session of the departments of the State Council on 30 November of that year. The State Council, however, found the financial objections too great:

> In establishing a new system of punishments, it is necessary to keep in mind not only its theoretical correctness but also the full feasibility of the suggested punitive measures, primarily from the financial point of view. Only by observing the last conditions can we be certain that the newly established ladder of punishments will be useful and not just remain a dead letter of the law.

By themselves, financial difficulties would likely have killed Frish's project, but the State Council had further justification for postponing consideration of the project. The ladder was essentially a summary in outline form of the types of prison facilities and the lengths of prison terms to be served in them. Because yet another commission had been established to study the reform of prison administration, its work would have to be coordinated with the Frish Commission's, as Sollogub's project had not. The council decided to postpone further study until it had in hand the conclusions of the Committee for the Final Discussion of the Project of Prison Reform in the Empire.[50]

THE ZUBOV COMMITTEE

Alexander II ordered on 19 May 1873 that the new committee include Sollogub and the members of the special committee, who could each appoint one additional member from their ministry or department, and that it be chaired by

P. A. Zubov. At the time, Zubov was on the staff of the State Council. Born in 1819, he had graduated in 1841 from the Imperial School of Jurisprudence and had worked as a lawyer in several Senate departments, the MIu, the procuracy, and the State Council. During the 1860s Zubov held important posts in the Imperial Chancellery and the State Council as well as on several of the committees working on the court reforms, in which he played a prominent role. He had been made a senator on 1 January 1865 and served in the Criminal Cassational Department, along with Frish, from 1866 to 1871. When it was found necessary in 1872 to increase the staff of the State Council with lawyers because of changes created by the 1864 court reform, Zubov was among the first added.

His committee's task was to study Sollogub's second project and review his estimates of costs, choice of sites for new prisons, and timetable for implementing the experimental reform in the ten provinces around Moscow. It was also to determine what temporary measures might be taken to ameliorate the serious condition of Russian prisons before a "full general reform" could be accomplished. This last assignment probably acknowledged a point that Sollogub had made in his 1869 response and that had been emphasized in the conclusions to his commission's second project: temporary measures must be taken before a general reform to alleviate the overcrowding of prisons.[51] The MVD had recently made the same point in an internal paper, complaining that even temporary improvements were being held up because the Sollogub Commission was expected to produce a grand and final reform.[52]

By 11 June the committee had been constituted and its members officially appointed. In addition to Sollogub, it included several men who had served on his commission: Frish, from the MIu; Iuferov, of the MVD; Shmidt, from the Third Department; V. A. Zheleznikov, from the Second Department of the Imperial Chancellery; and two representatives from the MF, D. O. Koleko and N. V. Grave. Ministers and directors did not actively participate but were represented by their assistants. These included M. P. Shidlovskii, now the assistant MVD and a member of the Suite of His Highness the Emperor; S. A. Grieg, the assistant MF; O. V. Essen, the assistant MIu; and Count N. V. Levashov, from the Ministry of State Domains. Chairman Zubov selected Ia. I. Utin from the Statistical Department of the MIu to serve as secretary to the committee.[53]

Many of the committee members were, of course, well acquainted with the Sollogub projects. The others took the next ten days to familiarize themselves with the problems and the proposals they would be dealing with. They all seemed to share two fundamental premises about prison reform that by 1873 had become axiomatic. Russian prisons were in horrible condition and required urgent and radical reform; and too many offices shared imprecisely defined responsibility for their care and, therefore, collectively paralyzed prison administration. Gripped by these certainties, the committee did not need to begin by discussing the condition of prisons. They only mentioned in passing that prison affairs were "daily sinking into a sadder state," which could mean either that they perceived actual further deterioration or, more likely, that the longer they lived with the situation, the greater a problem it seemed to be. Nor did they consider exhorting, threatening, or increasing the pay of the many people engaged in prison-related work in hopes that the existing organizations could solve the problem. At their first meeting on 22 June they immediately turned to discussion of the Sollogub Commission's insistence that a special organ for prison administration was needed.[54]

First they reviewed what Russian law said about administrative responsibility in prisons and what recent experience had shown to happen in practice. Articles 15 and 16 of the Charter on Persons Held under Guard assigned primary care (*glavnoe popechenie*) of prisons to the POoT, and their superintendence (*zavedyvanie*) jointly to the MVD and MIu. Article 16 did not distinguish the roles of the two ministries in any way. According to articles 17 and 18, supervision (*nabliudenie*) also belonged to governors, provincial boards, city and other police officials, procurators, and wardens and their staffs. Again, the law made no delineation of duties. The committee noted that for a long while and for a variety of reasons the POot had not been effective in its role and that neither had the two ministries, although there were significant differences between their efforts. The MIu had no special office for prison affairs. Its influence in the field was limited to the activity of the procuracy whose duty it was to see that prisoners were properly (that is, legally) "maintained." The existence of the Second Department of the MVD's DPI was noted but not commented on immediately. This slight, as I shall show, reflected the domination of the committee by individuals loyal to the MIu.

Although there would be significant disagreement over even major aspects of the committee's conclusions regarding the central administration, the committee could agree that it was needed. Not only did they recognize, in agreement with the recommendations of the previous prison commission, the urgent need for the radical reform of existing prison administration, they also had become firmly convinced that the successful implementation of prison reform would be impossible without the prior and immediate establishment of a special prison administration.[55]

But where could they establish such an organization? They seem first to have considered expanding the Second Department of the DPI. The committee's report does not record how the whole membership felt about that possibility but quotes Assistant MVD Shidlovskii as saying:

> Leaving prison affairs in the DPI is positively impossible, not only because of the immensity of the forthcoming reform effort but also because of its peculiar nature and the special knowledge required to direct these affairs correctly, which cannot be expected from an organization occupied at the same time with affairs of higher police.

Shidlovskii, as soon became apparent, did not mean to reject the idea of directing prison affairs from within the MVD. He had in mind establishing a separate department in the ministry. The committee agreed that a specialized and separate prison administration would be needed, but it did not have a ready plan for its structure or administrative placement. To expedite this decision and the "immediate establishment of a special prison administration," the committee decided to submit a separate proposal to the State Council and appointed a special subcommittee of three to prepare a preliminary report.

Shidlovskii was chosen chairman of the subcommittee, which was to draft plans for the central and local administration of prisons. Between June and August it met four times, and late in August it submitted its reports to the full committee. Two members of the subcommittee expressed their preference for establishing the prison administration in the MVD. They suggested that the MIu should help write regulations for administering prisons and maintaining prisoners and should retain a large role, through the procuracy, in the supervision of these regulations. This sop (if that is what the two meant it to be) did not satisfy the third member of the subcommittee. The minority of one submitted an opinion that the MVD and the MIu share equally in the administration of prisons.[56]

The full committee debated the question again and wound up disregarding both reports. The majority of the full committee granted the minority, who favored keeping prison affairs in the MVD, that the historical development of prison administration in Russia did show a gradual concentration of that work in the MVD. But they did not observe that improvement in prison conditions had paralleled this development.

> The present condition of the system in the empire hardly testifies to the benefit of the removal of prison affairs from the direct participation of the Ministry of Justice, but on the contrary, discloses the unconditional need for the widest possible involvement of that ministry in the administration of prison affairs in the empire.[57]

The conclusion was hardly fair, for none of the concentration that had occurred in the DPI had come at the expense of the MIu. The Ministry of Justice had never been deeply involved in prison affairs except through the procuracy. It also ignored the fact that the DPI had taken the initiative in prison reform. The department had proposed making many of the changes and improvements that the committee would recommend but, because they had not been funded, had not been able to follow through. This was not so much condemnation of what the DPI had done or failed to do or, even less, admiration for the MIu's accomplishments in the field. The majority acted on principle to wrest prison affairs from a ministry of policemen and to ensconce it in a bastion of law. This skirmish was part of a larger philosophical struggle to determine whether Russia would evolve toward legal order and constitutional law or remain dominated by administrative fiat and justice.

Almost from the moment of their creation in 1864, Russia's new courts and lawyers were bitterly criticized by "conservative" forces, both within and outside the government. Criticism took many forms, and critics found many different aspects of the new systems to assault, but they had in common the fear that the impersonal power of law would displace the traditional networks of paternalistic and authoritarian administrators that had long ruled Russia. These forces were somewhat disorganized and demoralized by the enthusiasm that swept through the government and educated society in the years of the Great Reforms, but they soon regrouped. Within the government, the MVD was the stronghold of these forces.[58]

The MIu and "liberal" supporters, naturally, defended the court reforms, both for their own sake and also to ensure that the philosophy guiding them would come to inform the activities of other governmental organizations as well. They saw the business of prisons as an extension of the actions of courts, and the failures of prisons as the failure of the police spirit that dominated them. Prisoners had long been subject to abuse by their jailers, abuse that was arbitrary, often cruel, and in contravention of laws already in the charters. Like corporal punishment before, this arbitrary brutish treatment had become intolerable to contemporary sensibilities. As in the effort to abolish corporal punishment, however, it was not enough for advocates of prison reform to say that their sensibilities were offended by current practices. Quite probably they did not understand this to be a cause of the problem. They simply believed in what they were doing and had to explain, in more or less scientific terms, why the changes they advocated were necessary improvements.

Supporters of the MIu's point of view in the Zubov Committee had ready arguments to legitimize the MIu's interest in prisoners and had precedents for their desire to administer prisons. Seizing the established belief that prisons suffered from having too many administrators, they reasoned that putting the MIu in charge would minimize that number. They could reasonably claim that among government organizations the MIu was most legitimately interested in preliminary prisoners. Held in custody before and during their trials, they were as yet unsentenced and might not even be guilty. They were more wards of the courts than prisoners. The committee contended that if the MIu were given direct responsibility for preliminary prisons, the ministry would find it in its interest to speed the trial process in order to reduce the time these prisoners spent under preliminary arrest. Not only would speedy trials be more just, they would also reduce operating costs. Given control of the variety of term prisons, the MIu could also supervise the proper application of court sentences. A majority of the committee liked the idea of a single ministry handling prisoners from their arrest through the time of their release.

The idea least attractive to the committee members was that of the subcommittee's minority report, that the MVD and MIu share equally in the administration of prisons. Disagreements, "quite possible between two independent offices," would harm prison affairs. No European state had arranged its prison administration that way. In Prussia the MIu administered preliminary prisons, and the MVD had charge of term prisons. In all other European nations, all prisons came under either one or the other ministry. The committee's journals enumerated which ministry had charge in which countries. Their final report listed only those six countries in which the MIu administered all prisons. As if to clinch the argument for the majority's preference, reference was also made to up-to-the-minute European opinion. A French commission meeting at the same time was receiving recommendations from "specialists" overwhelmingly in favor of entrusting prison reform and administration in France to the MIu. The Zubov Committee concluded that prison administration would cost the same in either ministry and that the MVD was already overburdened. It recommended that all prison affairs be transferred to the MIu.[59]

A second subcommittee, this one under Assistant MIu O. V. Essen, was appointed to work out a project along these new lines. Once again the members of the subcommittee, and subsequently the whole committee, were unable to agree. Their final report submitted to the State Council included "considerations" that indicated majority and minority positions and in some cases the names of the members supporting each point of view.

The greatest difference between Zubov's and Sollogub's reports concerning the administration of prison affairs in Russia came at the top. Zubov's committee recommended that administration of all civilian prisons be entrusted to an office in the MIu to be called the Main Prison Administration (*Glavnoe tiuremnoe upravlenie* [GTU]), which would be comprised of a director, his assistant, main prison inspectors, and staff. These points squeaked through the committee by a seven-to-six vote, but the report did not explain the minority's objections or counterproposals. The subcommittee had recommended establishing two departments within the GTU, organizational and executive, but the whole committee cut out the organizational department. Instead of establishing a permanent council on prison affairs (such as was later organized), the committee preferred to let ad hoc groups be formed as required to discuss theoretical problems as they arose.

The GTU was to be given a wide range of authority. It was to administer all prisons, which meant not only to supervise the application of sentences but also to run all prison facilities and to decide all matters of policy. It was also to be given charge of the anticipated reform. Main prison inspectors would be sent by the GTU to conduct inspection tours in the provinces, where they could issue orders on the spot to provincial inspectors and wardens. Only afterward did they have to inform the region's governor.

Provincial prison inspectors enjoyed no such unambiguous authority. A major point on which the committee could agree was itself a great victory for the paper edifice of the GTU—there should be an inspector in each province. But they also agreed that governors could not be stripped of the title they held as "chief of prison affairs in the province." Beyond this, unanimity broke down. A majority of seven members insisted that the best way to coordinate prison affairs with other administrative work in each province would be to make the provincial inspector and his staff (the inspectorate) part of the provincial board. A minority of five preferred to give the inspectorate greater independence by organizing it outside the board, directly under the governor's office. In this function, as they worded it, the provincial inspector became "special assistant and executor of orders of the governor in prison affairs," and the governor acted as "chief of prison affairs" through the inspector. The governor in this role was responsible to the MIu through its provincial office. MVD representatives on the committee voted with the majority to put the inspectorate in the MVD-dominated provincial boards. Representatives of the MIu split their vote. Chairman Zubov and Count Sollogub both voted with the minority. The final project had to reflect the view of the majority, but it made clear that the provincial inspector was the real linchpin of prison affairs in the provinces.[60] The committee estimated an annual budget of 56,000 rubles for the GTU and annual salaries of 4,300 rubles for each provincial inspectorate.[61]

Chairman Zubov sent this project to D. M. Sol'skii, as head of the State Council, on 28 February 1874 and sent him an additional one hundred copies for distribution on 2 March. Sol'skii forwarded copies to the MVD, MIu, and MF on 8 March.[62] The MVD responded first on 11 April, its reply coming from the DPI and cosigned by Timashev. Not surprising, its tone was highly defensive. Several pages were devoted to a narration of the recent history of prison affairs in the DPI, written to emphasize its "natural" growth. As the War Ministry and other offices chose to divest themselves of irrelevant functions, they turned to the DPI as the best-organized and most logical place to transplant those functions. The DPI and MVD, their reply reminded the State Council, had begun several major changes in prison affairs and had recommended others. If its performance had been unsatisfactory in recent years, it was because practically all projects had been repeatedly postponed in expectation of more sweeping reforms from each of the commissions and because the money allotted for prison buildings barely covered their maintenance. The report denied the Zubov Committee's statement that the MIu had been left out of prison affairs. On the contrary, it averred, the MVD had invited the MIu to work with it on numerous problems in prison administration. It also pointed out that the MIu had participated in all the commissions and committees.[63]

Coolly the MVD next faced the great threat posed by the project: the removal of prison affairs to the MIu. Timashev asserted at the outset his disagreement with the principle on which the decision had been taken. "I believe that the foundation of [prison affairs] as an executive function is police authority." He agreed with his predecessor, Valuev, that the state's interest was better served by ministerial bureaucracy than by judicial process. And this was not his opinion alone, he carefully pointed out. To support placing the GTU in the MIu, the Zubov Committee had argued that many European states had done so and had listed Belgium prominently among them. Timashev pointed out that the Belgian prison system, which had been highly praised also by Sollogub and many other contemporary criminologists, was entrusted "to that department of the Ministry of Justice which administers security, i.e., the police section." He also took advantage of the committee's mention of the Prussian system to reemphasize that in Prussia all but preliminary prisons were administered by the MVD.

There was great uncertainty about administrative placement, he hastened to agree. The French parliament, which had received recommendations from a French counterpart of the Zubov Committee, was even then arguing the question indecisively. And, of course, the most telling proof of uncertainty lay in the records of the Zubov Committee itself. When the question first arose in the "special section" appointed to decide the matter, "all but one" member of the section favored leaving prison administration in the MVD. Timashev managed to avoid mentioning that this subcommittee was headed by Assistant MVD Shidlovskii and that it consisted of only three men. He went on to show that only five days separated votes taken in the whole committee that decided, first, that prison administration belonged jointly in the MVD and MIu and then, on 26 September, that it belonged in the MIu alone.

Not that he especially wanted the GTU in the MVD. He agreed with the committee, whose report cited Shidlovskii on this point, that the GTU should be separate from the DPI, but he was "entirely indifferent" to which ministry was chosen. He merely wanted to point out some inconsistencies and problems in the committee report. As a matter of fact, there were other functions now overseen by several departments in his ministry, such as the transfer of prisoners, which should also be made part of the GTU. Leaving them separate would create "interoffice disagreements" and unnecessary expense.

It is difficult to assess how "indifferent" Timashev was at this point. He was not known as an empire builder. Later, however, he did act more aggressively to retain the GTU, and on the question of local administration of prison affairs he supported the majority opinion of the committee that provincial inspectorates should be organized within provincial boards. This, he explained most reasonably, was not because he wanted to bind the inspectors to the MVD-dominated board but because having all the offices in the boards would create "a unity of affairs in the province, including especially financial unity," which would yield savings. The inspectorate could share with the other offices their building, chancellery, archive, print shop, and administrative section. Governors, he added, should have final inspectoral *(revizionnyi)* authority over the inspectorate, as they had over the other offices of the board.[64]

The MF offered the objections everyone must have expected. Russia did not have enough money to fund the project. In his reply of 28 May 1874, the MF expanded the committee's estimate to show just how expensive the new administration would be. Multiplying the committee's figure of 4,300 rubles per year per provincial inspectorate by the number of geographical administrative areas (which the committee had probably quite purposely not done), the MF discovered an annual cost of 322,500 rubles. Adding that to the estimated annual cost of running the central offices of the GTU gave a total annual cost of 378,000 rubles. The MF observed that travel expenses of provincial and central prison inspectors would add considerably more but did not attempt to estimate how much.

As if this were not enough to halt the project, the MF reminded the State Council of another, even greater expense and offered a damning opinion along with it. The failure of prisons to function properly was probably due more to their poor physical condition than to faulty administration, he asserted. To repair, remodel, or build anew would cost many times the estimated annual costs of administration. The MF cited a memorandum he had before him from the director *(upravliaiushchii)* of the MVD, dated 17 April 1873, which estimated that it would cost 553,000 rubles beyond the 184,000 already allocated to accomplish basic repairs in Russia's prisons. He and the state controller had already agreed that they would limit the allocation for that purpose for 1874 to 300,000 rubles. That would only repair some old buildings, he reiterated, not remodel any to modern penitentiary uses.

"In view of all that," the more than 400,000 rubles that Zubov asked for administration must be seen as "extremely burdensome" for the treasury. The creation of the GTU could be permitted from a fiscal point of view only if its expenses could be covered, or mostly covered, from savings in the DPI, the provincial boards, and other offices whose burdens were lightened and staffs decreased by the transfer of duties to the GTU. (I shall discuss how reluctant the MVD was to relinquish any of its funds when prison affairs were transferred in 1895 from the MVD to the MIu.) The MF concluded that if savings could not be found to pay for the GTU, then the new administration would have to be made less expensive. The only partial solution he had to offer was seriously considered later on. The number of regional inspectors could be reduced by organizing *okrug* inspectorates connected with court chambers that were regional offices subordinate to the MIu, rather than an inspectorate in each province.[65]

The MIu took much longer to respond, although, not surprisingly, he had much less to object to. He offered no objections to the first part of the plan. The MIu would accept the responsibilities of organizing the GTU. He also approved the creation of inspectorates and the role of governors at the head of prison affairs in each province "with his subordination in this relation to the minister of justice." He did not, however, like the committee's plan to organize inspectorates in provincial boards; he agreed with the minority's opinion. The inspectors needed latitude, a certain degree of independence, to accomplish the tasks they would be given. The minister also hoped to involve the procuracy more actively in prison administration.

The MF must have blanched when he read Palen's response. The MIu, Palen reported, had no objections to the staff and pay scale provided by Zubov for the central GTU. As the committee had written, it was a temporary table and could be adjusted as experience suggested. However, he believed that the inspectorates were too stingily supported. The independent inspectorates he preferred would cost slightly more than would inspectorates attached to provincial boards because they could not share certain facilities and functions. He would add a secretary to each, at 700 rubles a year, and would pay certain other expenses. Inspectors should be paid 2,800 rubles. Chancellery expenses would run approximately 1,000 rubles. His total added an average of 400 rubles per year per province.[66]

Zubov officially learned of the ministries' reaction when Acting State Secretary K. K. Rennenkampf sent him copies of their replies on 21 July and answered the ministries' objections in a note to Rennenkampf dated 24 September.[67] He responded first and most thoroughly to Timashev's objections. First, he retorted, the MIu had not been so deeply involved in prison affairs as Timashev tried to show. All of the paperwork of prison administration was concentrated in the Second Department of the DPI; all moral and economic *(khoziaistvennyi)* work, in the POoT, whose chairman was the MVD. None of the current mess could be blamed on the MIu. More important, insisted Zubov, his committee had argued that prison affairs were "by their nature" closer to the MIu than to the MVD.

Timashev had tried to exploit the divisions in the committee, claiming that their vacillation in deciding on the proper home for the GTU showed that it could be equally well housed in either ministry. That was a perilous concession, and Zubov leaped on Timashev's seeming uncertainty to claim the GTU exclusively for the MIu. His committee's change of mind did not reveal uncertainty, he wrote, as much as the extreme care with which they had worked to arrive at a final and correct solution of the problem. He now claimed that their preference for the MIu was a well-considered and firm decision.[68]

On one last point concerning the central administration Zubov ducked Timashev's objection. The MVD had found the word "main" in GTU an "exaggeration." He envisioned a separate organ for prison administration but did not wish to give it the independence that the words "main" (*glavnoe*) and "administration" (*upravlenie*) usually connoted in the Russian ministerial structure. Zubov did, but he fibbed in his reply that "main" was meant only to distinguish central from local administration. And where he might have offered to substitute "central" for "main" and "council" or "department" for "administration," he kept silent.[69]

Zubov strayed farthest from his committee's view when he countered Timashev's support for the committee's majority with his own opinion on local administration. Where Timashev insisted, as had his ministry's representatives on the committee, that provincial inspectors be organized within provincial boards, Zubov asserted that being part of a collegial body would unnecessarily and dangerously slow the inspectorates' efforts to carry out prison reform. He did not explain why the cooperation and coordination the majority of his committee and Timashev thought the affiliation would enhance were not necessary or how they might be secured by independent inspectorates. Without clarifying how, he asserted that his plan—that is, the minority plan—left a place for the inspectors on provincial boards that would give them some influence with the boards while leaving them the necessary independence.[70]

Zubov's reaction to the MF's devastating report was even more craftily wrought. To Timashev, however indirectly, he had responded point by point. He could not dispute the MF's calculations, however, so he took two other approaches to negate them instead. Without even mentioning the size of the expenditures, he reminded the officials who would read his report that it was they who had asked him to solve an urgent problem. His Majesty the emperor had called attention to the horrible condition of prisons on several occasions, and the State Council had, too, most recently by asking his committee to conduct the "final discussion of the project of prison reform in the empire." The council need not be reminded, he reminded them, that in their present state Russian prisons represented a grave threat to "security and order, etc."

Then, most optimistically and without supporting figures, he took up a thought from the MF's report. Money now budgeted in the DPI and the provincial boards for prison affairs would be freed for the GTU and would cover a large part of its expenses. The greater expense identified by the MF had been the cost of seventy-five regional inspectorates. Zubov wrote that the committee had not yet decided that the reform would immediately and simultaneously be introduced into all seventy-five geopolitical units. They would probably recommend introducing it more slowly, which would cut down at least on the initial expense. He became no more specific, but the State Council might recall that the committee had evolved directly from consideration of Sollogub's second project, which envisioned an experimental reform in only ten provinces. Zubov then plunged ahead with his most outrageous assertion. By the time the GTU was ready to expand its operations, the labor of prisoners in reformed areas ("it went without saying," he said) would be producing more than enough income to cover additional expenses. If that fiction could be firmly rooted, the larger reform could grow from it. Having shown money to be no problem, he rejected the MF's idea to effect savings by establishing *okrug* rather than provincial inspectorates.[71] The MIu's response required no reply from Zubov. He noted the minister's support, which he welcomed, in two short paragraphs.[72]

Meanwhile, the committee had turned out other projects. The first of these Zubov sent to the State Council on 18 July 1874. Sollogub's first project had made some recommendations for changes in hiring and organizing prison guards and for reforming transfer operations for prisoners being sent to distant places. The Zubov Committee's Project on Prison Guards and Transfer Operations tried to systematize the needed changes and to fit them into the proposed new administrative structure of a GTU within the MIu. The Zubov Committee would have preferred to hire civilian guards for civil prisons but in the end felt compelled to adopt the approach recommended by Sollogub. "Because of the definite impossibility of finding a sufficient number of civilians even the least bit prepared for prison service and accustomed to strict discipline," guards should be recruited from among former military personnel. Discipline was the key word here. Military personnel would have no more experience with prisons than would civilians, but they would have become used to a more orderly, disciplined way of life. The dirt, disorder, and corruption perpetuated in contemporary prisons by the laxity and venality of the guards would, the committee hoped, be abhorrent to veterans. The committee recommended putting the new guards into uniform, paying them better than their predecessors, and organizing them like a military unit. As a group, they would be subordinated to the military or, preferably, to the chief of gendarmes.

All transfer duties, which were then spread among several departments, would be consolidated in the GTU. The chief of gendarmes would retain inspectoral responsibilities only. These two projects were combined because the transfer project encompassed only the reorganization of the transfer guards. Building special transfer prisons would have to wait. As far as they went, however, the committee planned thoroughly. The main project laid out in standard form the size of the corps of guards envisioned, their organizational structure, and their duties. Appendixes covered ranks, pay and pensions, and, separately, uniforms and arms and their costs.[73]

Zubov sent ninety copies of these papers to Acting Secretary of State Rennenkampf in mid-July. Rennenkampf forwarded them for comment to the appropriate ministries a week later, on 27 July 1874. Replies came back late in the year, probably a reflection of how little work was usually accomplished in the capital during the summer.[74]

The MVD–DPI responded first, but not hastily. It obviously had its guard up higher than in March and April, when Zubov had stunned it with the proposal to organize the GTU in the MIu. Despite agreement with most of the proposals in the guards and transfer project, Timashev cautiously wrote that he was "unable to come to an identical conclusion." In fact, in all essentials he did come to an identical conclusion, but now apparently he did not want to seem to. Timashev laid out more than twenty pages of charts enumerating the men and costs of internal, external, and convoy guards. His tables showed where the men were administratively attached and how the several departments then shared responsibilities and expenses. Impressive in their clarity and completeness, they displayed the structure Zubov proposed to dismantle. Timashev agreed that the old structure should be razed and rebuilt and approved Zubov's plans for the replacement organization. He had simply taken advantage of the opportunity to respond to the project in a way that would display his ministry's greater familiarity with the complexities of the problems.[75]

The Third Department responded laconically on 29 November. The head of the department, who was chief of gendarmes, had no objection to being put in charge of guarding prisoners. He agreed with the whole plan in one page. The War Ministry agreed, too, but at much greater length. For many years the ministry had asked to be relieved of the unmilitary functions of guarding prisons and prisoner convoys. To make certain that the State Council understood the rightness and importance of the committee's proposals, the ministry provided charts and explanations, as Timashev had, to show how inappropriate and burdensome their duties had been. Something was missing from all of this paperwork, however—the stated willingness to transfer the money previously expended in this unmilitary sector to the MIu or to the chief of gendarmes. The ministry said only, implying its intent to keep this money, that so many officers, noncommissioned officers, and soldiers would be freed to return to full-time military duty to serve their country, as their emperor meant them to.[76] Who would argue with that?

The MF recorded its reaction to the project on the last day of the year, but ringing out the old was not on its mind. Predictably, the MF found the project too expensive. Advocates of the reform could not have gainsaid the evidence that the new system would cost considerably more than the old system did, especially if the cost of new transfer prisons were added in. They might not have expected, however, the MF's statement that the existing system was satisfactory. Until everything else was accomplished, he wrote, it made no sense to change the system of guards. Without new prisons, without the new administration, they could do no good.[77]

Money and its jealous guardians really were the catch. The MF had now said that reform of the central administration was too expensive and would be meaningless without modern prison facilities; modern prison facilities were much too expensive and could not be run properly in Russia anyway, where there were not enough trained men to run them; the proposal to find disciplined guards who could help make prisons more orderly was too expensive and could not be effective anyway until the other reforms were in place. And, most emphatically, Russia was much too poor to undertake everything at once. On top of this all, of course, lay the philosophical and interministerial struggles to control the meaning prison reform would contain and convey. The "final discussion" threatened to become interminable.

The committee continued to meet until 14 February 1875, in all, thirty-eight times. Having completed its work on administration and guards, it tackled the other problems it had been convoked to study. The product of this third period of activity defined the types of prisons that might be established in Russia. Zubov sent the "Project Charter on Civilian Places of Imprisonment," along with its extensive explanatory notes, to the secretary of state on 28 April 1875. At the same time, he forwarded a personal opinion, which he titled "Project on Prison Administration."[78]

The more startling of these projects was Zubov's short personal opinion. He began with a lengthy preamble, in which he described the purpose and place in a prison system of the various types of prisons that already existed or that would be established in Russia. He did not make entirely clear why he bothered, but his point seems to have been that the system was larger and more complex than the reformers, including himself, had thought. Their projects covered only preliminary prisons, strait houses, houses of correction, and *katorga* prisons. In addition to those, left untouched by any commission's considerations, there were jails at police stations, lockups for incorrigible debtors, facilities for people who were arrested by justices of the peace, correctional shelters for juveniles, and transfer prisons. Somehow, he intimated, this fact now led him to reverse his previous opinions. The GTU, he wrote, should remain in the MVD, and provincial inspectorates should be made part of provincial boards!

Zubov claimed that leaving the GTU in the MVD would result in significant savings. Keeping transfer operations as they already were, shared by the MVD and the War Ministry, would yield further savings. In his previous report, written only nine months earlier, Zubov had taken the extremely optimistic position that basic expenses of these activities could be met by transferring funds from the DPI and the War Ministry, where staff and budget reductions would be made, to the MIu. Now, suddenly, he eschewed that view and espoused the opposite one. He may have come to fear that lack of cooperation from the DPI–MVD would kill the chance of establishing a central administration. The MVD had played on the MF's objections in its last response to the committee's work. If that were so, he might have chosen to abandon his philosophical preference for the MIu's leadership in the field to achieve the primary objective—creation of the GTU. On the other hand, for unexplained reasons he may have come to prefer the MVD's tutelage. He did not specifically reject his previous opinion that funds could be transferred, nor did he explain very well why keeping the GTU in the MVD would be significantly less expensive. Zubov offered his new opinion as if he had never thought otherwise. None of the other participants have left any records that shed light on his turnabout.

Zubov suffered an incapacitating stroke the day after these papers were submitted to the State Council. The strain of the last years had obviously taken a toll. It is tempting to speculate that the about-face, which forced Zubov to place practical politics above his principles, may have been the greatest strain, but there simply is no evidence one way or the other.[79]

With the third project the committee completed its work. On 24 May Ia. I. Utin, the committee's secretary, sent the State Chancellery 100 copies of an essay on exile and prisons, which the committee had commissioned, and 40 copies of the committee's 38 journals. Three days later the secretary of state sent copies of all these documents, including Zubov's personal project, to the MVD, the MIu, the MF, and the directors of the Second and Third Departments of the Imperial Chancellery.[80]

Only the Third Department responded soon. Less than three weeks later, on 13 June 1875, P. A. Shuvalov wrote a single careless page to say that he "completely shared" Zubov's opinions. He did not bother to make it clear with which of the chairman's contradictory opinions he concurred, but he apparently meant the latest.[81]

The other ministries took much greater care and much more time to fashion their replies. Of the remaining few, the MIu worked fastest. Responding only to the third project and not to Zubov's personal opinion, the MIu threw his full support behind the reforms it envisioned. Moreover, said the MIu, the changes proposed by the third project corresponded with the changes recommended in the Frish Commission's review of the ladder of punishments. Thus the MIu declared the Zubov projects to have cleared a high hurdle at which the Sollogub Commission had balked.[82]

The minister proceeded to comment on the committee's second project, on exile and transfer, to which he had not previously responded. He approved these plans also and included with his remarks a copy of a note sent him by Lobanov-Rostovskii, director of the MVD, in July 1875. The MVD had received requests from administrators in Western Siberia to stop sending exiles, even those of privileged estates, to certain areas because of an imbalance of free and unfree populations. Lobanov-Rostovskii asked how the ministries could cooperate to curtail or stop the flow of exiles to the region. Palen wanted the State Council to know that the project answered a need that was widely felt.[83]

The MF's response of 8 December 1875 was, as usual, most damaging to the committee's proposals. This time the MF began with words of praise for the committee's work, maybe a sign that pressure for prison reform was growing stronger. Because prisons were in such horrible condition and the project was needed, the MF found it laudable, but at the same time he noted that it was hugely expensive. Like the Perovskii Commission, which had met in 1845, the Zubov Committee had tried to estimate the total cost of a comprehensive building program that would replace all old structures with new, modern facilities. Using statistics from western European experience and their own knowledge of construction costs in Russia, it estimated that space for each prisoner would cost an average of 600 rubles. For the approximately 70,000 prisoners who would have to be accommodated the bill would total around 42,000,000 rubles. The committee did not propose spending all of that. In fact, it stated plainly that no government could afford to. Instead, it proposed a plan of gradual improvement, outlining which types of prisons should be built first, and set out a tentative schedule of costs. Again the MF agreed, up to a point.[84]

Work on prison reform had evolved considerably since the corporal punishment reform had led the DPI to work out its first project. In 1867 the more alert respondents to the special committee's work had pointed out that its project began and ended in *medias res;* that is, it proposed reforming corrections but skipped entirely over the problems of preliminary prisons, *katorga,* and exile. Sollogub had been among the perspicacious then, and he made certain a few years later that his commission began at the beginning with preliminary prisons. His comments on exile and penal servitude and his redefinition of the latter as long-term imprisonment helped make *katorga* a permanent part of the prison-reform agenda also. Now, in 1875, a consensus held that exile must ultimately be abolished and that penal servitude be in prisons, where correction might take place. Zubov's remarks in his 31 July 1874 letter to Rennenkampf that a gradual reform could be carried out on the proceeds of prisoner labor probably reflected debate in his committee on how to organize *katorga* prisons and labor in them. The committee's third project, which presented the results of that debate, put *katorga* into first position.

There were several good reasons for beginning at the "end." Although Russia's prisons were shabby and seriously overcrowded, they did accommodate their prisoners and could be left as they were for a while longer. This was, however, left unsaid. But Russia had no penal servitude prisons and suffered from the recently discovered need for them. More persuasive might have been a second argument. *Katorga* demanded the most severe regime of labor. It would potentially be the most financially productive form of imprisonment. Preliminary imprisonment, on the other hand, would be the least productive, and without doubt a drain on the treasury rather than a source of income. Regulations for the new experimental preliminary prison in St. Petersburg, for example, stipulated that adult detainees could choose to work if they so desired but that they did not have to. Timashev and Palen had signed these regulations only days after receiving the committee's third project.[85] If the reform program began by constructing *katorga* prisons, they would absorb the most dangerous class of criminals, who were now living idly in relatively insecure settlements. The convicts would be set to work and, if things went well, the first prisons would help to pay for those to follow. The project suggested that *katorga* prisoners could build the prisons that would house them, from the first to the last.

The MF liked this concept. He noted that his ministry "had not been ungenerous" in allocating money to the MVD to improve the organization of *katorga* and added that it would continue to give what it could to that end. As far as preliminary prisons, strait houses, and houses of correction were concerned, they required such huge amounts that it would be difficult to say how many years it would take to find the money. The first allocation could not be made before 1877.[86] A committee had finally scored a point with the Ministry of Finance, albeit a small one. Prisons that could return the investment made in them could be financed. The MF did not evince much faith in the idea of corrections, which, were it valid, would produce savings in less perspicuous ways. Unless *katorga* could be made to yield enormous profits, development of the rest of the system of preliminary and correctional prisons still seemed a long way off.

The MF's other remarks were important. Indeed, the whole struggle to capture or retain the administration of prisons may have been decided by them. They seem superficially to have been based solely on financial considerations, but some facts allow for the possibility that the MF took a side in the philosophical interministerial struggles.

Unlike the MIu, who chose to ignore Zubov's personal note when he responded to the committee's last project, the MF paid close attention to it. Where the MF had previously registered only qualifying objections to the committee's first plan for establishing a GTU in the MIu, he now called it "quite impossible." He found Zubov's plan less expensive and realizable if (and he placed the same qualification on this plan that he had earlier applied to the other) "sufficient money can be released from the DPI to pay for the larger part" of the central administration. He went farther. The MF could and would take on the treasury the "reduced additional expense" needed to establish the GTU in the MVD, but only if it were agreed that, at least at first, only that part of the reform were implemented. New prison facilities would again have to be deferred. Much more work needed to be done, the MF wrote, on estimating the costs of remodeling or constructing the prisons before that work could begin.[87] The GTU now had a blinking amber light at its most hazardous intersection.

The MVD, who was so recently "indifferent," found new enthusiasm. Restrainedly he left his comments on Zubov's plan to the last 10 pages of his 112-page response. The caution, which had been the hallmark of his prior response (to the guards and transfer project), was replaced by confidence. He seemed to consider the battle won. In November 1874, when he largely agreed with the second project, he wrote he was "unable to come to an identical conclusion." On 21 December 1875, responding to all the projects and raising many objections along the way, he stated at the outset his agreement in general "with the needs and the proposals" set forth by the committee.[88]

Timashev began with the committee's third project, on places of imprisonment. In general, he agreed that preliminary prisoners should be kept under a much lighter regime than term prisoners. The regulations he and Palen had recently signed for the new St. Petersburg "house of preliminary detention" offered a lenient regime. For that reason, he objected strongly to the committee's plan to keep these prisoners in isolation cells. Citing the project itself, which gave Sollogub as its source, Timashev explained that the average length of preliminary detention was one and a half years. It would be most unfair, he wrote, to make preliminary prisoners suffer "one of the most severe forms of punishments" for a longer period than most convicts.[89]

Timashev objected as well to several smaller matters, this time suggesting that the committee may not have considered the negative aspects of some privileges. For the prisoners' comfort, the project proposed allowing them to supply their own beds, furniture, books, and writing materials and to smoke at will. Timashev pointed out that a roomful of furniture might hinder observation of the prisoner by guards. He did not object particularly to books but feared that writing materials could be misused. One of the strongest reasons for holding preliminary prisoners in isolation, or in prison at all, was to prevent them from communicating with accomplices and friends to establish an alibi. Smoking presented other dangers. First, smoking presupposed matches and, as everyone knew, lucifers were hazardous. Somewhat more surprising, perhaps, was his statement in 1875 that smoking, at least as some practiced it, was also harmful: "In addition to that, some [prisoners] smoke tobacco of the very lowest quality, and if its use is permitted, the smoke, penetrating through the cracks and crevices, could spread through the whole prison and harm nonsmokers."

Timashev paid special attention to the projects' comments on prison labor. Sollogub's categories of black, gray, and white (skilled) labor and the ten-hour workday, which the committee had adopted, met his approval. He did object, however, to the article that would reward prisoners in houses of correction with two-thirds of the income produced by their labor. Not only was this excessive, it was also "hardly punitive." Because prisoners paid nothing for room, board, or clothing, they would be "much better off than free tradesmen." Timashev proposed to reduce their share to 20 percent up to 100 rubles, 15 percent for the second 100 rubles, and 5 percent above that. He also disagreed that prisoners should be allowed to choose their line of work and their foremen.[90]

Another objection Timashev raised made clear the philosophical difference between him and the MIu-dominated committee. Currently strait houses and houses of correction held not only people sentenced by courts but also several categories of "criminals" identified by extra-judicial means. Children turned over by their parents as "vicious" or "disobedient," people turned over by village societies as indebted as a result of a "depraved" way of life, and people identified by police as leading "vicious" lives needing "correction" all wound up in them. The Zubov Committee would permit only people sentenced by the courts to be incarcerated. But what, asked Timashev, should be done with the others? The committee had not said but apparently believed that nothing could be done with them until they had been convicted of crime—*nulla poena sine crimine*. Timashev would lock them up.[91] For the near future Timashev prevailed, but the separate issues of juvenile offenders, administrative justice, and customary village justice would all become targets of criminological and judicial reformers in the following decades.

Timashev raised several other, similar questions that had not been addressed by the committee. For example, what would be done with persons who were sentenced to certain forms of imprisonment if there were no room in that type of facility? He offered no answer either, but the point was well taken. Thirty years had passed since the Code of Punishments of 1845 had prescribed incarceration in strait houses and houses of correction that remained unbuilt. Again rhetorically, he asked what might be done with discharged prisoners who were not accepted back into their village societies? He agreed with Sollogub that it was unfair to exile them after they had been punished and were theoretically "corrected." But what could be done with them?[92]

The MVD devoted a great deal of space in his report to financial aspects of the committee's plans. Money for repairs to prison structures, for their maintenance, for the supplies and provisions needed by prisoners, and for personnel and administrators still came from a confusing variety of sources. The committee had not discussed them all and had included an article in its project that stated that the treasury would cover all expenses. Timashev hastened to disagree. His reply described the support that had been provided by cities, the POoT, and the treasury and held out hope that the income from prisoner labor would also contribute heavily to the support of prisons. The committee's project, he concluded, contained financial holes that would require further patching.[93]

When he turned to Zubov's personal paper, he also emphasized financial concerns. Zubov's plan, he made clear, was superior to the committee's first project. It was based on more information and on intelligent consideration of several ministries' objections to the earlier proposals. Prominently among these, Timashev mentioned the MF's refusal to "burden the treasury" with the expenditures required to implement the first project. Cleverly, Timashev did not mention his own first response, which had fashioned an even more expensive GTU. Nor did he try to show how Zubov's project could actually save money. His careful expounding of the faults of the committee's third project makes the carelessness of these omissions seem artful. Because Zubov had concluded that it made good fiscal sense to leave prison affairs in the MVD, Timashev meant to make Zubov's project appear intelligent and prudent. His only objection to the plan was that he would prefer to name the office simply Prison Administration, not Main Prison Administration.[94]

His indifference of the previous year had vanished. Zubov's project provided the means of legitimizing his claim to the GTU. To underscore his ministry's experience in the field, if the State Council had failed to get that message from the thoroughness of his replies of 9 November 1874 and 21 December 1875, Timashev appended to the latter an eleven-point note enumerating the accomplishments of the DPI–MVD in prison affairs since 1868.[95]

When the Second Department of the Imperial Chancellery filed its report on 28 May 1876, the package was complete. The Second Department concerned itself with legal codification, and its report indicated which articles of various Russian codes would be affected by the changes recommended in the several projects. Its comments were legalistic and would not significantly influence the State Council, which sat to examine the merits of the major arguments about prison reform. For the council's convenience a "collection of comments" on the project was compiled, and the whole body of material was made ready for examination.[96]

The MVD may have gained much confidence by Zubov's defection but was still obviously not sanguine that it would soon take charge of the larger prison reform. On 14 July 1876 it submitted to the State Council a project to increase the rank, salary, and pension rating of prison workers. Its stated intent was to enable the DPI to recruit and retain a better class of employees, primarily for posts as wardens in provincial and county prisons and in county strait houses and workhouses. The State Council considered this project at a meeting of its combined departments on 16 October 1876, five months after the Zubov Committee's materials had been submitted and three months before the council began to discuss them formally. It approved the plan with the comment that it was urgently needed and could "not wait for the realization of the forthcoming general prison reform."[97] The council may have already anticipated further delays in the general reform.

The combined departments of the State Council met in joint session on 22 January 1877 to review and discuss together the projects of the Zubov Committee and the Frish Commission. The members took seriously the problem of prison reform in Russia. They recorded in the journal of the meeting their "often expressed conviction . . . that our penal institutions including preliminary prisons cannot remain in the condition they are now in without significant injury to the welfare and internal security of the state." This urgency did not, however, translate into haste. The State Council recalled that the major problem with previous reform efforts (they cited especially the Code of Punishments of 1845) was "the failure to handle the matter practically." They feared to "rush ahead" now, even when things appeared theoretically sound. Moreover, the bulk of the materials confronting them made deliberation of the problems by the whole State Council difficult. Not only were there the projects themselves, but also the responses from the affected departments who raised "many and very important considerations."

Taken together, the projects and responses did not constitute a plan that could be made law and carried out, and preparing such a plan went beyond the duties of the State Council.

> The projects being reviewed by the State Council draw a picture of that order which can be established only when Russia is covered with the projected places of imprisonment of the improved type. . . . But, as the compilers of the projects have themselves admitted, that time, because of a lack of money and men, is very far off, and past experience has shown what difficulties legislation meets that tries to establish norms for such a future.

What was needed was a review of all of the work of the last four years and the working out of a specific plan from it. Because the problem was urgent, they agreed that it would be better not to farm that work out to any other office but to create a small commission within the State Council for the purpose. The upshot of this first meeting was a request to the emperor that he create such a commission, because it was not within the power of the State Council to establish one itself.[98]

THE GROT COMMISSION

Another month passed before Alexander's permission was received and the ground rules and membership of the new group worked out. On 28 February 1877 Grand Duke Konstantin delivered to the State Council a "list" that effectively created the Commission on Prison Reform. Konstantin Karlovich Grot was named chairman. Members were A. Zablotskii-Desiatovskii, Prince D. Obolenskii, N. Stoianovskii, K. Pobedonostsev, and Count Palen.[99]

Other than Count Palen who, as MIu since 15 October 1867, had been involved peripherally in the earlier prison-reform commissions, Grot was the only member with experience in prison affairs. His interest may have begun more than thirty years earlier, when he began to work with public charity organizations that cared primarily for the blind but that also administered the few workhouses and strait houses.[100] Grot explained in a short autobiographical note written in 1896 that he became more deeply interested in penology in 1872, when he began to work in the Department of Laws of the State Council. He studied foreign criminal law and traveled in Europe to inspect the more famous prisons and the systems practiced in them. He met and corresponded with prominent European penologists and regularly received new publications in the field from a German book dealer. When the Russian government sent several young men abroad in 1878 to study foreign prisons, they carried with them letters of introduction to penologists and prison wardens from Grot, who knew them personally.

When the question of prison reform finally rose to the State Council in 1876, it was Grot who suggested to his superior—the chairman of the Department of Law, Prince Urusov—that another committee would have to work through the Zubov Commission's proposals to make certain that they dovetailed with the Frish Commission's reform of the ladder of punishments. Theory and practice, which he identified respectively with the MIu and the MVD, would remain divided until the two reforms were worked out simultaneously.[101] His experience since 1872 and his position in the State Council placed him ideally to be selected chairman of this next "last" commission. Zubov was also a member of the council, but he was seriously ill by this time and could not undertake further work.

There were probably other political considerations in the choice of Grot as chairman. He was identified with the party of reformers, including A. A. Abaza, M. T. Loris-Melikov, and others who worked their way to the pinnacle of ministerial power in 1878. Grand Duke Konstantin Nikolaevich, the chairman of the State Council and a supporter of that group, may have helped gain the appointment for Grot.

The Grot Commission, as it came to be called, was charged broadly with studying the materials of the Zubov Committee and the Frish Commission and the problems of prison reform in general. It was to prepare and submit plans in a form the State Council could handle. Its charter specifically required that minority reports be included, so a place was provided in which the struggle to control a new central administration could continue. All of the ministers and directors who had participated in the Zubov committee were invited to participate with voting rights. They could choose, instead, to send deputies, who would not be permitted to vote. The commission was empowered to call other officials and experts to testify.[102]

The commission set to work in the spring of 1877 and, with the usual long summer breaks, continued its deliberations for a year and a half. The seven journals and several appendices it ultimately produced are organized topically rather than chronologically, so they do not permit analysis of evolving or shifting opinions, as the Zubov journals do. They do, however, record the dates on which the commission met, and it is apparent that no matter how urgent the problem was thought to be, it did not stir the bureaucrats to give up their long breaks. They met twice in April 1877, four times in May, and then not again until 27 October, more than five months later. Through the winter they met regularly, but then only once in May, once in July, and, after another summer recess, concluded with two meetings in November. They completed the first half of their work, review and revision of the ladder of punishments, on 10 February 1878 and turned immediately to their second major task, organization of a central prison administration, on 15 February. That project was completed on 3 November. The meeting of 24 November 1878 was held to approve the final version of these two major projects.[103]

All of the commission members and its regular participants were prominent men, busy with other affairs. For some of them this commission was obviously a minor part of their work. Grot, however, threw himself energetically into the work. When the commission was not in session, he continued to study and investigate the subject firsthand. In the summer of 1877 he made an extended tour of European Russia to see for himself the condition of Russian prisons. He included the model prisons the MVD had constructed within the last decade and much older prisons built long before penology pretended to be a science. Beginning in Moscow, he toured through Nizhnii Novgorod, Kiev, Kharkov, Warsaw, Riga, Mitau, and Pskov.

That same summer he began to plan part of his next summer's activities. The Swedish ambassador to Russia asked Grot to intercede with his government to ensure that official Russian delegates be sent to the International Prison Congress to be held in Stockholm the following summer and invited Grot to participate personally. The ambassador had learned that the Russian government intended to refuse the official invitation. Grot investigated the MVD's intentions and then wrote to Timashev on 26 August. The ministry had meant to turn down the invitation on the grounds that prison reform was under discussion in Russia and that before its resolution Russian delegates would have nothing firm or final to report. Grot pointed out that this had been true in 1872 also, but the government had sent Sollogub as official delegate to the London Congress that year. He agreed it would be disappointing that Russia's delegates would have little to report but suggested that their absence would be noted. He added that he probably would attend the congress on his own in an unofficial capacity. Timashev wrote on 1 September that he had already replied in the negative to the invitation of the Swedish government. The ambassador persisted, however, and prevailed. Timashev appointed Grot Russia's official representative on 28 May 1878.[104]

Before either of these eventful summers, Grot and the commission set to work at their first task—to determine what kinds of prisons Russia would have in the reformed era and to revise the ladder of punishments to make clear what sentences would be served in each type of facility. Approaching this part of their work in an orderly fashion, they thoroughly discussed each rung of the ladder.

Beginning near the top of the ladder, the commission first took up the issue of *katorga,* which still largely meant exile to penal servitude in Siberia. *Katorga,* which had become increasingly more important to each commission, occupied seven meetings before the members could agree on their conclusions. In addition to the chairman and members, three top representatives from the MIu and one each from the MVD, the MF, and the Second Department of the Imperial Chancellery participated. The commission called on the governors general of Eastern Siberia and Western Siberia, the governor of Zabaikal region *(oblast'),* and the former Iakutsk governor to share their thoughts on the strengths and weaknesses of the *katorga* system. They heard also from mining engineers; from the chief of the DPI, who supplied statistics; and from Professor I. Ia. Foinitskii of St. Petersburg University, who spoke of theory and practice abroad.

The Grot Commission reversed the decision reached by the Zubov Commission. Where the latter wanted to do away with exile and to have penal servitude served in special *katorga* prisons, the Grot Commission preferred to have the system made to work as it had long been meant to work. The commission recognized the difficulties in this approach, especially as revealed in the recent history of *katorga.* The first pages of the first journal reviewed the collapse of the old system and the efforts that had been made since the early 1860s to organize penal servitude at Nerchinsk and Sakhalin and in central prisons.

The experience of the last decade or so had shown, the commission thought, that the efforts in Eastern Siberia were more successful than were the experiments with hard-labor prisons. Traditional *katorga* permitted families to accompany prisoners. Usually after a short term spent in close confinement, prisoners were permitted to live outside the prison or compound, and many built houses, raised their families, and remained in Siberia after completing their sentences. Where imprisonment was long-term and strict, it usually destroyed already existing marriages and families. Moreover, the regimes at Nerchinsk and Sakhalin were judged to satisfy "the penal objective of punishment," while the organization of hard labor within prisons continued to prove difficult for administrators.[105]

In the mid-1870s about 2,500 offenders were sentenced each year to penal servitude. Approximately 12,000 were then in *katorga,* including about 1,000 women. Since the effort to curtail exile and organize *katorga* prisons had been launched in the late 1860s, it had become standard practice that men and women offenders who had families that were willing to accompany them were sent immediately to Siberia. Others sat in prisons in European Russia until they achieved, through time served and good behavior, the category of "correcting" prisoners. Then they were transferred to places of exile. According to its admin-istrators, there had been some notable successes in the reorganized system. The Algachinskii silver and lead mines in Nerchinsk region and the mines on Sakhalin were functioning fairly well, they claimed. Only 150 men worked at the former, however, and 1,400 on Sakhalin. Another 200 men worked at two ironworks, 529 in three salt mines, and 3,000 explored for gold on three rivers and in several mines in Eastern Siberia.

But the problems and failures were greater than the successes. Of the 12,000 prisoners sentenced to *katorga,* only about 1,500 served as they were intended. The DPI considered only the silver mining and the work on Sakhalin "hard la-bor," as *katorga* was meant to be. Another 3,700 were usefully employed under more relaxed regimes. The other 7,000 were supposed to be hard at work in *ka-torga* prisons. However, there was room for only 4,645 in special prisons built since 1867, and these prisons had proved disappointing. It had been difficult to find work for the prisoners, and health, morale, and security had all suffered. The remaining 2,355 prisoners in this category, who did not fit in the new pris-ons, served their time in prisons not designed for hard labor, and many did not work at all. In 1875 in the Zabaikal region 3,571 prisoners were in penal servi-tude. On the average day 354, or about 10 percent, were in hospitals. Another 624, about 17 percent, were declared unfit for work, and 878 were suited only for light work. In other words, on any given day fewer than half could perform the tasks they were meant to do, when and if their administrators organized the work. Each year about a tenth of the prisoners escaped.[106]

The commission faced difficult choices because so little of the current system worked satisfactorily, but it determined to find forms of work that would make the system useful. It quickly discarded the idea of reorganizing government facto-ries. These had failed and in the early 1860s had been sold to private en-trepreneurs. Mines, they felt, offered the best opportunity for exploitation, but not all types of mines, they learned, would be suitable. Hard coal, for example, if it were extracted faster than it could be used, would deteriorate in contact with air. Because transportation was bad in Siberia, the commission foresaw that either coal would be wasted or the labor of prisoners would have to be made discontinu-ous. Metal mines were therefore preferable. Committee members then discussed at some length the location, security, and type of work available at mines through-out the country and recommended that mining operations by *katorga* prisoners be undertaken at several isolated spots in the Ural Mountains and Siberia.[107]

In addition to these specific recommendations, the commission made two ba-sic observations on exile to penal servitude. First, it should be developed along its traditional lines, not in new prisons. It did settle sparsely populated parts of the country, and it did help to develop the national economy. Traditional *ka-torga* also gave a prisoner a chance to start over, "to reconcile himself to God and his conscience, to begin a new life in a different environment, and to make good by his labor in a distant place." Those benefits would be worth the government's effort. Also in its favor, exile to penal servitude, if it were properly organized, would provide severe punishment. The long, heavy labor was meant to repress "the rough inhuman urges" of the toughest criminals; "life settlement" accompanied by the loss of all rights, which followed *katorga,* amounted to "civil death." The commission recommended that it be sparingly applied, much less than currently, "and only to the worst criminals, whom it would be dangerous to leave in the midst of society." They urged that penal servitude be applied instead of the death penalty and that capital punishment thereby be avoided altogether.[108]

When the commission turned its attention to other forms of exile, it showed the same resolve to reduce the severity of punishment. After exile to penal servitude, the next most severe form of exile was exile for life *(na zhit'e)* in Siberia and other distant provinces. The commission recommended that this be entirely abolished. Likewise, it asked that exile to settlement *(na poselenie)* in the Caucasus be done away with. It would have preferred to abolish exile altogether, but, realizing the poor condition of the rest of the penal system, it feared that alternatives were unavailable. So, instead of recommending the abolition of exile to settlement in Siberia, it suggested many changes that would make exile less harsh for the offenders and more useful for the state. First, it asked that the use of exile to settlement be restricted. One of the applications heretofore widely used, which it wanted to end or restrict to the greatest possible extent, was the right of peasant and artisan *(meshchanskii)* societies to turn over their "depraved" members to the government for exile. The commission asked that this right be removed, at least in areas where the court reforms of 1864 had been introduced.

One of the most important benefits of the exile system—and a powerful argument for retaining it whenever it came under attack—was that it settled and Russified thinly populated regions. The commission argued that the organizers of the exile system could pay attention to the demography of Siberia and the needs of the people exiled there and still further this purpose. It agreed that some areas to which exiled settlers had been sent had been overused but believed that other areas still needed to be filled and tamed. It specifically named the regions *(oblasti)* of Amur, Primor'e, Semirechensk, Akmolinsk, and Semipalatinsk. Not that they intended exiled settlers to be dumped in the wilderness. It stipulated that the judicial sentence should name the region of exile but that the individual offender could choose his place of residence within the region. It also suggested that administrators who selected the areas to be settled by exiles consider the size of the native Russian population, the amount of available useful land, and the development of industry, trade, and other economic conditions that would permit settlers to earn their living.

The commission asked that existing prohibitions making exiled settlers' lives difficult be abolished or made less restrictive. Currently exiled settlers had to reside continuously in a single district *(volost')* for ten years before they could join the peasant estate. The commission advised reducing this period in Siberia to six years or, with the permission of provincial authorities for exiled settlers who had behaved well and worked hard, to four years. It asked that the same privileges apply to those who chose to join the artisan estate.

Once a settler had been accepted into one of these estates, the commission recommended that he be permitted to live wherever he wished in Siberia. The commission also sought to abolish the prohibition against settlers' owning immovable property outside the district in which they lived, the prohibition against marrying within five years of beginning a sentence, and the practice of pursuing settlers as for flight if they were absent from their residence for more than seven days. All of these practices interfered with the settlers' ability to conduct business and with their desire to settle honestly and permanently.[109]

Judging from the changes recommended, the commission was concerned about reducing the harshness of this punishment and, thereby, the rate of recidivism and flight associated with exile. Complaints about these failures two decades earlier had finally led to the cessation of exile to Western Siberia. The commission intended to avoid creating the same problems farther east and at the same time to develop the region and make it a more productive part of the empire. Attitudes toward Siberia and toward punishment had evolved. No one referred to any form of exile as corrective punishment. The commission and the criminalists all hoped that the exiles were not beyond redemption; they had, after all, recommended an end to the death penalty. But they did not ask that settlers be invited or even permitted back to European Russia after serving their terms in exile. As they had said in regard to exile to penal servitude, they hoped the exile could "begin a new life in a different environment and make good by his labor in a distant place." Eastern Siberia was still something of a dumping ground, but the government meant to profit by its past mistakes and to manage its use and development more wisely. The frontier had been pushed back, but clearly it had not yet reached beyond Baikal.

A humanitarian concern is also apparent in the recommended changes. Commission members extended to Siberia—and to the exiles with whom they planned to people it—the "softening of manners" characteristic of civilization. The same process of widening the compass of "civilization" that slowly spread exemption from corporal punishment to additional groups and classes now worked to mitigate all the so-called special punishments. For the first time since the days of Empress Elizabeth (1741–1762) an official body suggested that capital punishment was undesirable and unneeded. The harshest forms of exile were also to be abolished or reorganized in order to reduce senseless and unproductive suffering. Exile to penal servitude, the most severe form, could not be abolished altogether because there were some vicious criminals who still required "spirit-numbing" labor. But the commission did assume that there were many fewer of these types than were currently being sent into exile to penal servitude and asked that the penalty be much less frequently applied. The next most severe form, exile for life, was to be abolished, and, as I have just demonstrated, many of the prohibitions that made exile to settlement counterproductively harsh were removed.

At meetings in December 1877 and January 1878 the commission systematized its tendency toward lenience in regard to special punishments. A historical problem with special punishments, it explained, was that they had never been put in any particular order, like a ladder, and it was therefore impossible except by traditional usage to know when to apply them. Their application was consequently arbitrary. If there were anything law must not be, it had been thought in the last several decades, it was arbitrary. That smacked of illegal and extralegal administrative justice, that is, of injustice. The pendulum would swing again later in the century, when the most up-to-date criminalists would demand individualization of treatment for offenders. Then they would ask that judges and penal authorities be given more latitude, but not that they be able to act in an arbitrary manner. Now the commission desired to impose order and banish arbitrariness.

Because there was no ladder, there could be no direct correspondence between more or less severe special punishments and the ladder of general punishments, which itself was now condemned as rickety. This required that different groups within the population, some of which for one reason or another were ineligible for general punishments, receive different punishments for similar offenses. One such class of injustice stemmed from the exemptions various groups had been granted from corporal punishment. As I have shown, corporal punishment was not entirely eliminated in 1863, but before that date several nationality and other groups had been entirely exempted. An irony of these "privileges" was that it also made these groups ineligible for regular, correctional punishments in which corporal punishment was still used. They had, therefore, to be subjected to special punishments that were usually much more severe. For example, exile for life in Siberia had often been substituted for a sentence of just two or three years in a correctional arrest unit.

The commission agreed that special punishments still were needed for special groups and for especially horrible or shameful crimes. It mentioned treason as an example. But it emphasized that "special" implied "exceptional" and urged that as many offenders as possible be subjected to general, correctional punishment. It constructed a ladder of special punishments and then carefully explained the correspondence between special and general so that courts could assign the latter whenever the law permitted or when there were mitigating circumstances that would justify the substitution.

Execution remained at the top of the special ladder. The movement to abolish capital punishment did not become strong and coordinated until the 1890s. Without a movement like the one that led to the reform of corporal punishment and without proof that exile to penal servitude and correctional prisons could be made effective punishment and rehabilitation, the commission could not remove execution from the top rung. It could only urge that execution be used sparingly and offer a respectfully dreadful alternative. The death penalty was made to correspond to exile to penal servitude without a definite term. That meant a long period of hard labor in a distant and secure place, which could be remitted only by the permission of several layers of officialdom after the prisoner had proved his contrition and rehabilitation. It could become a life sentence for the recalcitrant and incorrigible.

With exile for life to be abolished, exile to settlement in Siberia would be the next rung in the reformed ladder of special punishments. It could be assigned in two degrees: with or without loss of all rights of condition (sostoianie). The more severe of these corresponded to exile to penal servitude for a fixed term. The next lower step on the special ladder was incarceration in a fortress (krepost').

This punishment was theoretically designed and traditionally used for classes of offenders who did not require correction—for example, political prisoners, duelists, and a few other categories of offenders who could distinguish right from wrong but who acted against the law anyway on principle. Exile to settlement without loss of rights and incarceration in a fortress for a term of not less than eighteen months corresponded to incarceration in a house of corrections. A sentence to a fortress for less than eighteen months corresponded to incarceration in a prison. Deportation for foreigners, the fifth and lowest rung of the special ladder, was not made to correspond to anything on the general ladder.

The commission's work on correctional punishment was its most difficult, controversial, and significant. It was, after all, the Commission on Prison Reform, and this was the portion of its work that dealt with prisons. It required only three meetings to complete discussion of correctional punishments, but a great deal of work had been done in advance—by previous commissions and for this body by the MIu. MVD representatives participated in these meetings, but the MIu dominated the meetings in terms of numbers of representatives present and took the initiative in presenting projects for consideration. The MIu set a professional and legalistic tone for the proceedings and frequently referred to recent theory and European experience.

The commission began by reviewing the current status of correctional punishment in Russia. The existing ladder, as it had been established in 1845 and amended several times since, included seven steps. The most severe was assignment to a civilian correctional arrest unit *(ispravitel'noe arestantskoe otdelenie grazhdanskogo vedomstva)*. The units received this name when they were transferred from the Ministry of Communication to the MVD in 1870. They had begun in 1827 as civilian arrest companies *(roty)*. These, in turn, had been modeled on military arrest companies that had been organized four years earlier. From 1827 to 1845 they had served as a general dumping place for a great variety of offenders who were fit to work but not for military service. Prisoners comprised a grab bag of old and young criminals sentenced for a wide variety of crimes to terms ranging from relatively short terms of imprisonment to life. The revision of 1845 had produced a more orderly ladder that meant to eliminate the breadth of variation in sentences, but the less severe alternatives projected in 1845 were not realized. Mixing of old and young, experienced and inexperienced criminals, and the "infection" of one group by the other continued in prisons at the lower end of the ladder and in the "units" at the upper end.

By the mid-1870s only men not exempt from corporal punishment, aged seventeen to sixty, could be sentenced to the units. Offenders who were exempt from corporal punishment were sent to exile for life in Siberia. Women were sentenced, instead, to a workhouse or prison. Sentences in the units ranged from one to four years and were meant to be spent at work. Well-behaved, hard-working prisoners could earn a form of parole. All prisoners began their terms in a probationary *(ispytaemyi)* group and could earn their way into a "correcting" *(ispravliaemyi)* group. In the latter, each ten months counted as twelve, so terms could be shortened by one-sixth.[110]

Below the units on the existing ladder came workhouses. Punitive workhouses *(rabochie doma)* had existed since the time of Peter the Great, as had charitable workhouses for the unemployed, homeless poor *(rabotnye doma)*. There had never been many, however, and they had never served the purposes of the legislation that created them, at least not on a large scale. The Code of 1845 placed them in this position on the ladder of correctional punishments with the express intent of habituating lazy offenders to work. Most of the crimes for which offenders could be sentenced to workhouses were designated "crimes against property motivated by greed." Prisoners could be sentenced to terms of between two months and two years, during which time they would learn and practice a trade. For two years after their release they would remain under police surveillance.

The strait houses also carried a term ranging from two months to two years. The regime within the strait houses was considerably milder than in the workhouses, however. A wider range of offenders were supposed to be assigned fairly light work according to their condition, sex, and age.

Imprisonment in a regular prison was considered even lighter punishment. Sentences ranged from one to sixteen months. Prisoners could usually choose whether they would work, but peasants and artisans could be made to perform work that had been assigned by the government. On the basis of this regulation, work had been made compulsory in the new experimental correctional prisons constructed by the MVD in Moscow and St. Petersburg in the late 1860s. The fifth, sixth, and seventh steps of the ladder were arrest, which ranged from one day to three months and involved no labor, monetary fines for which arrest could be substituted, and reprimands by the court.[111]

The MIu proposed a revised ladder that reflected clearly what Russian criminalists had learned since 1845. From the embarrassing failure to implement the ambitious and complex ladder of 1845 and from the repeated assertions of the MF that Russia did not have the money to implement a sweeping reform, the MIu had learned to simplify. Its project included fewer steps, fewer types of facilities, and regimes based partly on theory and partly on financial prudence. From European criminology it had learned that more severe punishment did not necessarily correct or deter more effectively than milder punishment did. The language of the commission's documents makes clear that it took pride in the mildness of the regimes it proposed as proof of its own and the nation's "civilization."[112]

In the MIu's proposal there were no correctional arrest units. Houses of correction replaced the units and, in part, workhouses and prisons. Every feature of the house of correction, as the MIu designed it, was in 1878 a logical end point to the evolution of thinking in the previous commissions. The range of terms that offenders could serve in them—from one and a half to five years—met several theoretical and practical demands. First, the terms were long enough for correction or reformation to occur. Recall the responses to the 1867 MVD project and to the Sollogub project, which objected that incarceration for less than a year could not achieve correction. No one claimed in any of the commissions' documents to have witnessed correction in Russia in either more or less time, but western European penologists had concluded that at least a year was needed, and Russian experts "knew" this to be so.

The range of terms also permitted this single institution to replace the three that had previously served as correctional facilities. Within this one institution a longer or shorter term served in the single regime would serve the purposes of three different regimes of three different facilities. This would obviate the training of wardens, guards, and others to three regimes and would at least blunt the earlier criticism that Russia could not find enough trained men to carry out modern prison reform. Raising the upper limit of the term from four years, as it had been in the correctional arrest units, to five years seems at first to contradict the trend toward milder punishment. It was made clear later in the commission's discussions, however, that the MIu hoped that many offenders relegated to more severe, noncorrectional punishment, such as exile and penal servitude, could be subjected to correctional punishment instead. The commission could justify that mitigation only by increasing the length of the less harsh form of punishment.

Features of the proposed correctional regime likewise reflect the evolution of ideas and practical criticism of earlier proposals. Incarceration in the house of correction could begin with a time in isolation. This introduction could range from two weeks to eight months and would depend on many factors. Prison administrators were to keep an eye on prisoners in isolation; their sex, health, mental condition, and evidence of corrigibility would determine the length of time they spent in isolation. Isolation was meant to produce docility quickly, but it was recognized to be potentially dangerous, and individual offenders' reactions to isolation were known to vary greatly. In modern theory the individual, not the form of punishment, had to be studied to know when the personality change called "correction" had occurred.

Prisoners would be isolated at night throughout the period of imprisonment. During the day they would work in general shops in which silence would not be enforced. The struggle between the potential harmfulness of isolation and the recognized evils, "infection" and "vice," of general incarceration had reached this compromise of nighttime separation half a century earlier in the United States and Europe. What the commission saw as peculiarly Russian features reinforced the inclination to adopt this system. The MIu said no more about work in its brief proposal, but the idea that labor, more than anything else, effected correction made this stipulation almost wholly noncontroversial by that time.

The MIu's proposal included the strait houses. In their revised form the strait houses retained their most prominent features in ways that reflected modern theory. Although they were included in the correctional ladder, they had been meant to deter rather than to correct. The largely forgotten etymology of "deter" and of the Russian word *ustrashat'* convey the difference well. The harshness of the strait-house regime would terrorize its inmates. Again as etymology intimates, the regime was planned to "straiten" offenders the way a strait jacket did the insane. It would provide a force against which it was useless to struggle, requiring the prisoner to become calm and tractable. Offenders whom the state did not want to incarcerate long enough to reform had still to be kept from recidivism. They might not be changed in the same ways as properly reformed ex-inmates of a house of corrections, but they would not want to return to the strait house. The MIu reduced the range of terms in the strait house, from two months to two years, to one day to eight months. The whole term was to be served in full isolation at compulsory labor.

The shorter range indicates recognition of the hardships of isolation and follows the general trend of shortening terms of imprisonment. If all true correction were to take place in the houses of correction and if strait houses were used only for deterrence, a term of less than a year—the period in which correction might theoretically begin to be achieved—seemed reasonable. The MIu was also concerned about expense in the construction of facilities and the maintenance of prisoners and realized that more offenders could be processed through the system in a given time if each served, on the average, a shorter term. Modern theory and statistical planning combined to urge the more humanitarian, shorter range of terms.

The same held true at the third rung of the MIu's revised ladder. Arrest, or "simple deprivation of freedom," was reduced from a range of one day to three months, to a range of one day to one month. It involved no work or isolation.

Monetary fines were not reduced. In a society that was becoming increasingly westernized in many ways, money was becoming more important. Previously, failure to pay a fine sentenced by a court led to incarceration in an arrest facility for a period assigned by a court and supposedly judged comparable with the size of the fine. Now the MIu proposed that fines could be assigned either separately or in combination with other penalties. Failure to pay a fine would result in imprisonment, as before, but in the new proposal the substitution could be much more severe. Arrest of up to one month replaced fines of up to 100 rubles; incarceration in a strait house for up to a month substituted for fines of from 100 to 300 rubles; and for failure to pay fines of more than 300 rubles an offender could be sent to a house of corrections for up to nine months. Reprimands "pronounced in public session of the court" remained the bottom rung of the MIu's foreshortened ladder.

As for earlier projects, other departments were invited to comment in writing on the proposals laid before the commission. Only the Second Department of the Imperial Chancellery and the MVD availed themselves of the opportunity. Most dissent was made orally at the sessions of the commission. The Second Department asked in a written comment that the minimum term for the house of correction be reduced from eighteen months to six months. This would permit one of the largest groups of criminals, offenders committing unaggravated theft and other crimes against property, to be sentenced to the houses. These crimes usually brought a sentence of from four to six months. Under the existing ladder those sentences would have been served in workhouses had workhouses actually existed in sufficient numbers. In the MIu's proposal they could only be served in strait houses. The Second Department's recommendation amounted to a plan that Russia try to rehabilitate its thieves. It violated the principle that correction could not be achieved in under a year but clung to the assumption that thieves committed their crimes against property from laziness and could be reformed by habituation to labor in prison. Clearly this pointed to a major problem in the MIu's proposal. The commission would have to decide which groups of offenders would best be treated by "terror" and which by "correction." The MIu had not done this when it devised ranges of terms for its simplified list of penal facilities.

The MVD had more objections, but they were not as fundamentally damaging to the MIu's proposal. It asked that the preliminary period of isolation in the house of corrections be set at one-twelfth the prisoner's sentence. This would narrow the range set by the MIu, from two weeks to eight months, to eight weeks to five months. The MVD was still fighting the battle to reduce arbitrariness in administration. The MIu, having fought this battle in earlier decades, had begun to think it had been too thoroughly won. Government officials, they would continue to agree, had no right to be "arbitrary." There were legal means to settle civil complaints as well as criminal ones, which provided just and standard procedure. But to the MIu's way of thinking, court officials by definition were not arbitrary; they were judicial.

The feeling had grown among legalists and criminalists in Russia, once more following a trend that had first grown in western Europe, that courts and penal administrators were too strictly bound by the Code of Punishments and current prison regulations to treat individual offenders as they ought to be treated. The difference (or their argument that there was a difference) between judicial and penal authorities on the one hand and other tsarist administrators on the other was that the former were now professional. These authorities were trained in law or in science and were thus endowed with understanding not available to the uninitiated. They were thereby qualified to judge the defects and strengths of others, to prescribe treatment, and to pronounce cures. The greater range proposed by the MIu provided the latitude needed by trained professional observers to remove quickly offenders who were soon straitened by isolation or who showed signs of unhealthy mental strain. They could likewise keep tough cases who resisted its purposes in isolation longer. The MVD's shorter range guaranteed that everyone had at least an eight-week dose but that no one could be kept in isolation "too long," here defined at five months. This removed from wardens, guards, and others the opportunity to be bribed to reduce or increase the term arbitrarily. All of the commissions and ministries had agreed up to this time that there were not enough trained men to administer modern prisons. The MIu assumed they could be found or trained. The MVD trusted instead to regulation.

The MVD disagreed also with the MIu's reduction of arrest to a maximum of one month. It would keep it at three months and add compulsory labor, offering that inmates could choose in which types of work they would engage. With arrest reestablished at three months, they would make it the only substitution for failure to pay monetary fines. It seems fair to speculate that the MVD still had its feet more firmly planted in traditional Russia and could more easily forgive debts than the MIu.[113]

The commission had these papers when it began its deliberations on the correctional ladder on 30 November 1877. First it agreed on the principles of correctional punishment. Over the objection of a few members, the majority stipulated that all punishment serve "punitive purposes, which are a necessary aim of punishment in general." The most modern criminalists wanted to eliminate the concept of retribution or revenge and to provide, instead, treatment leading to reformation. The commission was not ready to go that far, however. Corrective punishment, it wrote, must provide some sort of "deprivation that will serve as retribution for the evil committed in the crime." This was not an argument over treatment, which would remain precisely the same. Although it was not expressed as such, this was an argument about the existence of evil and of free will. The older view held that men possessed will and chose to commit evil. The newer views, more anthropological and sociological, credited men with less free will and believed that heredity, evolution, and environment made men what they were. They might be restrained or reconditioned, but it did no particular good to censure them. That argument would be made more clearly, frequently, and forcefully in later years. In 1877 it was more implicit than open, and it was easily overridden.

If commission members could not agree completely on the reasons for punishment, they could agree unanimously on its purposes. The point was not just to remove criminals from society but to return them to society changed, so that they were not potential recidivists. The way they expressed this, however, once more showed they doubted that criminals could be truly reformed. Punishment, they wrote, would serve as a "warning against recommitting" crimes. In other words, the ex-convict would return to free society the same person as when he left it, but he would carry the memory of his time in prison and would therefore avoid behavior that would return him to prison. That is a good definition of deterrence, but it is not what the theorists meant by correction. They would have to be content that the commission was willing to supply the machinery and forgo the benediction. The commission added a second principle, that the deprivation be just and in proportion to the crime. Now they had only to agree on what was just and what was proportional.[114]

The commission began by agreeing on acceptable names for the several steps of the reformed ladder. It accepted the MIu's suggestion that the highest stage of correctional punishment be called the house of corrections. Apparently, civilian correctional arrest units were sometimes called houses of correction already. It accepted also the name arrest for the lowest stage of incarceration. The name strait house, however, it did not like and suggested that, instead, these facilities be simply called prisons. The people, it felt, were used to that name and would accept it more readily.[115]

Commission members found it easier to agree on the names than on their precise meaning. At each step of the ladder they debated the range of sentences, use of isolation, labor, and correspondence between the old ladder and the new one. The top step, the house of corrections, engendered the most controversy. Count Palen defended his ministry's position that more criminals who were then punished by exile and *katorga* be subjected to correctional punishment. To encourage judges to sentence offenders to the house of corrections instead, the ministry had proposed a longer range of initial isolation, which would make the house a stiffer penalty and a fitter substitute for *katorga*.[116]

This caused disagreement in the commission. Seven members, a majority, agreed with Palen that correctional punishment in the house of corrections was preferable to *katorga* and that somehow the former should be toughened to make it a suitable replacement for the latter. Lengthening isolation could not serve that purpose, however, because of the difficulty of implementing longer isolation. Once again the reality of finances struck down a part of the reform that almost everyone involved would have liked to implement. Russia would have to build whole new prisons like Pentonville in London or remodel all the facilities now used as correctional arrest units, and that would be too expensive.

Some of these seven and others in the commission opposed Palen's plan for theoretical reasons as well. Close examination, they explained, had shown that preliminary isolation as now used had not produced results that were positive enough to justify huge expenditures for it. Isolation would be theoretically acceptable only if work could be organized in prisoners' cells, but these men were certain that their government could not find enough men "theoretically or practically prepared" to organize such work. Without work, "that complicated system of imprisonment leads inescapably to physical exhaustion and mental disorder." Once more they pointed to the brief experience at the St. Petersburg house of preliminary detention, where prisoners "left to their own thoughts" had gone mad and committed suicide. And once more they added, with a discomforting sense of Russia's inferiority to Europe, that isolation might be effective in the West but that it could not work in Russia. European prisons and systems of isolation were well organized; their inmates were better educated than were Russian prisoners and were able to pass time in thought. Most of the Russian prisoners, on the other hand, were illiterate and were used to working together and living in large families.[117]

The major purpose of preliminary isolation was to "straiten" incoming prisoners who might be unruly. Palen apparently thought that perpetrators of more serious crimes, whom he wished to correct rather than abandon to exile and penal servitude, might require this more severe treatment. The seven commissioners, who for various reasons could not accept isolation, seem to have agreed but chose to achieve that goal by different means. Most purposes of isolation, they contended, such as observation of prisoners by their jailers, could be served by imprisonment in small groups that avoided the risks associated with isolation. If isolation were judged necessary at all, it could be applied for days, even for a few weeks, but not for months. The strict compulsory-labor regime and an increase of the maximum term from five to six years, which they proposed instead of isolation, would be sufficient punishment to allow houses of correction to replace *katorga*. They further stipulated that judges not be given authority to assign preliminary isolation but that corrections administrators apply preliminary isolation as they saw fit for a flexible period of time not to exceed four weeks.

They further disagreed with the MIu on the role of isolation in general. The original idea of isolation, which was retained in the ministry's plan, derived from the practices of monastic seclusion and Christian contemplation. The offender was meant to stay inactive, to ponder his infraction along with his life, and to become penitent—as in penitentiary. These commissioners discarded that notion. They were probably aware of isolation's history, but as modern bureaucratic administrators they were too time- and work-oriented to be impressed with the rigors and benefits of seclusion.

Although they did not articulate this, it is consistent with contemporary Russian criminology. By the 1870s it was acceptable to think of criminals as products of either their heredity or their environment. Neither etiology could be overcome by contemplation; the modern criminal would have to be rehabituated. Before Pavlovians or behavioralists had come on the scene, penologists had begun to act as if men were creatures of habit and that their habits could be broken, remolded, and reestablished.

Two other reasons could have led this majority to reject isolation in general and isolation in idleness in particular: their intense admiration for ways European and their pragmatism. Recent experience at the St. Petersburg house of preliminary detention was always pointed to, not as independent and conclusive evidence but as substantiating the reports of European and American experts. Some leading criminologists had been writing for several decades by then that isolation was not only ineffective but also dangerous.[118] Combined with its enormous cost, this was more than enough to deter would-be reformers from the risk of experimentation. These seven agreed that short-term inactivity could be useful in creating a desire for work, but they insisted nonetheless that, even in short-term isolation, work be available for inmates who desired it. Work was increasingly seen as rehabilitative, whereas isolation was left only deterrent powers.

The seven agreed completely with the ministry's project that prisoners be separated at night and at all other times when work was not scheduled. This separation was not as complete as isolation and could be achieved at a lower cost. Its chief value, according to the commissioners, was to prevent prisoners from communicating with one another. Russian commissions had long ago abandoned the rule of silence, as practiced in the Auburn system in the United States and elsewhere, as antisocial and cruel. They did not aim to stifle all conversation, but they did hope to eliminate the nightlong sessions of storytelling and bragging about criminal deeds by which experienced and more serious offenders could contaminate tyros. By preventing communication among prisoners away from their guards, they also hoped to reduce the chances of prisoners' coordinating plans and thereby to reduce prison disorders. High also on their list of priorities was the opportunity to reduce "the disgusting vices that are so widespread in prisons having general sleeping quarters." Masturbation was another serious concern but not so easily attacked.

"One of the best means of rehabilitation" was their characterization of work in prison. What the other good means were they did not say, but of the beneficial effects of habitual labor they were firmly convinced. Compulsory work would impart skills and habits that would be useful in freedom. In addition, it would help to maintain discipline and order. These commissioners faced reality squarely on the issue of labor, as they had in discussing isolation. Because external work—that is, work outside the prison walls—would be more difficult to enforce and would entail greater risk of escape, they prefered that prisoners work inside the houses of correction. But because they thought that not enough internal work could be found or organized, they suggested that external work be permitted as being preferable to no work at all. Work was so vital to correction that it could not be abandoned even in the face of significant risk.[119]

Having suggested raising the maximum term in the house of corrections to six years, the seven recommended a way to shorten that term. They wanted to establish in the houses, as already existed in the correctional arrest units, a category of "correcting" prisoners. Those who stood out by their good behavior and hard work, including progress in schoolwork, could earn their way into this category. Time would then pass more quickly for them. For the "correcting" groups in the arrest units, each ten months counted as twelve.[120]

The bloc of seven commissioners had obviously coordinated their thoughts before the commission met the final time to discuss the ladder of punishments on 14 December 1877. Not only did they agree to disagree with the MIu's plan, but they agreed with one another in all particulars. To complete their version of the house of corrections they had even researched the number of prisoners in various categories who would be assigned to the new house of corrections. The MF might eventually halt its plans, claiming that Russia did not have the money to implement them, but it could not discard this plan with the criticism that the cost was unknown. The seven calculated that, altogether, approximately 11,500 prisoners were sent annually to correctional arrest units, *katorga*, exile, and the workhouse for categories of crimes that would in their plan be subsumed in the new houses of correction. Because the average term ran three years—that is, because the population of these prisoners would turn over every three years—they computed a need for about 35,000 spaces in the new houses. Further research revealed to them that existing correctional arrest units had only 7,000 places, that strait houses and workhouses provided only 450, and that the new *katorga* prisons in European Russia had only another 1,000 or so. From this they knew how many spaces would have to be provided through renovation and how many by new construction.[121]

These men who felt so strongly about isolation when discussing the houses of correction were not consistent opponents of isolation when they argued the regime of prisons, the second rung of the reformed ladder of correctional punishments. More offenders would be sentenced to prisons than to the houses of correction. About 60,000 would be assigned there each year. How many cells or spaces would be required to hold these offenders would depend on whether they were put in isolation and on the average length of their sentence. The commission debated, apparently intensely, several alternatives.[122]

First they had to establish principles. Prisons would be run, they decided, not so much to correct as to punish. This distinction derived naturally from the belief that at least a year's time was required to reform a criminal. Simple, noncorrectional punishment existed simply to deter offenders by memory of their punishment and others by knowledge of it. But prisons had a dreadful reputation as cradles of vice and schools of criminality. Administrators had to take care that imprisonment did not cause more harm than good. They would have to segregate inmates carefully to avoid their mutual corruption.

Separation could, of course, be achieved by isolation, but, as I have stated, the majority of this commission had serious objections to isolation. The alternative was to separate prisoners into various categories so that prisoners similar by some system of classification and therefore less able to "infect" one another were lodged together. The commissioners examined this possibility but rejected it. They knew of attempts to categorize offenders by the nature and severity of their crime, the degree of their corruption, length of sentence, age, and work skills. They concluded that none of these systems kept experienced and inexperienced malefactors apart. Nor could they devise a system that would, to their satisfaction. Likewise, they rejected the enforcement of silence that they considered unenforceable—which brought them back to isolation.

Having rejected the use of general isolation and limited the use of preliminary isolation in houses of correction, they now endorsed the MIu's plan for isolation in prisons. They recommended that inmates of preliminary prisons be isolated as well. In the first case, as they explained it, their fear and abhorrence of the ill effects of isolation had overcome their desire to observe the principle that prisoners ought to be separated to avoid mutual contamination. In these cases, because of that principle, they accepted the need to isolate prisoners.

Several apparent contradictions present themselves here. Not only did the majority of the commission approve the use of isolation, but where they had reduced the time the MIu's plan would have applied in the house of corrections, for the prisons they increased its use. The MIu had recommended from one day to eight months in isolation. The commission increased that to between two weeks and a year.

They did not treat this as a contradiction. Because they did not explain why they so strongly opposed isolation in one case and recommended it in the other, any explanation must be inferred from the recommendations themselves. First, as I have shown, isolation had lost part of its theoretical hold. The commissioners did not believe that contemplation could correct a criminal. They much preferred to put their faith in habituation to an orderly life of work. Because they believed that Russian prisoners and jailers were inferior to European ones, they had convinced themselves that even if isolation worked in Europe it could not be used as a correctional tool in Russia. Moreover, they knew that even some European experts had doubts about it. In Europe and in Russia, however, isolation had shown itself to be a frightening experience. In houses of correction it could be used for a flexible period to "straiten" newcomers before beginning more specifically correctional treatment. In prisons, where inmates were only to be deterred, isolation would be entirely appropriate.

Having agreed on principles through compromise with Russian reality, they then faced the hardest reality of all, Russia's heretofore niggardly finances. Government and society, they argued, would more willingly part with money for isolation cells if they realized that use of isolation would reduce the length of terms and thereby reduce costs. The commission would recommend that time in isolation count as time and a half; that is, that a year in isolation equal a year and a half in regular confinement. Therefore, a given number of prisoners would pass through an isolation prison in only two-thirds the time those same prisoners would have to be held in group confinement. Fewer isolation cells, as if for fewer prisoners, would be needed by that same factor.

They did not claim that isolation cells would cost less than would regular cells for half again as many prisoners. The truth of the matter is that they would cost more. The commission could only claim that fewer spaces would be needed in isolation than in group incarceration. They could and did claim, however, that maintenance costs for prisoners would also be reduced; and they noted that isolation prisons built recently in Europe had been built at less expense than had earlier facilities by applying cost-cutting "simplifications."

The commissioners were practical men. Russia, they well knew, could not afford to build isolation facilities for all its offenders. So these men lowered their sights and compromised with the expected opposition of the MF. They offered some savings by reducing the use of isolation in houses of correction and pointed out less-than-obvious savings in its use in prisons. They did not want to come away empty-handed.

The increases in minimum and maximum terms of imprisonment suggested by the commissioners, which seem at first glance to contravene their intent to reduce costs and minimize the dangers of isolation, were proposed, probably reluctantly, in the interest of writing a coherent program. The MIu's plan called for a maximum prison term of eight months and a minimum correctional term of eighteen months. The majority of the commissioners, for reasons I explained above, agreed that the eighteen-month minimum had to be retained, but they could not leave that gap of ten months. If punishment were to fit the crime, judges must have a graduated set of punishments to apply against a hugely various set of crimes. They agreed with the MIu that sentences ought to be as short as possible (to return breadwinners to their families as quickly as possible), but they reasoned that some offenders would fall into the gap left by the MIu. Isolation would serve the purpose of shortening sentences, an eighteen-month prison sentence to a year and all others proportionally.

The third and fourth categories of punishment engendered much less controversy. The commissioners accepted the MIu's proposals on arrest and added only a few conditions. Most important, they insisted that work must be offered to prisoners who did not want to remain idle. Second, the question of facilities, and therefore cost, had to be addressed. The commissioners proposed that arrest be served in prisons or at police lockups, thereby obviating the need to build and staff additional facilities or another type of facility. For the gentry they proposed to make arrest easier. Gentry could serve their sentences apart from hoi polloi at military guardhouses or even at their own residences or places of business.[123]

On fines the commissioners essentially agreed with the MIu. They did, however, emphasize even more the seriousness of failure to pay judicial fines. Failure to pay, depending on the size of the fine, could result in the substitution of arrest for up to a year.[124] They left the last category essentially unchanged. Reprimands could be either strict or simple and would be read to the offender by the court in public session.[125]

According to the Zubov and Grot commissioners, previous commissions and committees had failed to enact prison reform because they had never approached the problem in a comprehensive manner. They had, like Sollogub, only addressed themselves to administration or, like Frish, studied only the laws involved in the ladder of punishments.[126] The Grot Commission meant to be the final commission and had, therefore, to present the State Council with firm, comprehensive, and realistic proposals ready to be adopted as law. Having overhauled the ladder of punishments, they turned to the question of prison administration.[127]

The Grot Commission preceded its written considerations and conclusions on prison administration with a summary history of the problem it was trying to solve. This was standard practice for tsarist commissions. The commission had similarly prefaced its previous journals. Like many other histories of prison administration written in the last decade, the summary emphasized dispersal of authority and absence of clear lines of responsibility for prison affairs. It was not meant to be only informative, however, but was tendentious history and didactic, written to help persuade its audience, the State Council, of the need for a central prison administration.[128]

The Grot Commission understood the problems of prison administration exactly as had its predecessors. As the Grot commissioners saw it, many problems of administration at several levels still needed to be solved. First, the decision had to be made to reform prison administration at central and local levels or—as some reformers, including the Zubov Commission, had proposed—only at first at the top. The Grot Commission had also to face the failure of the POoT. Should they simply abolish it and have another agency assume its functions, or would it be more useful if it were revamped in some way? The greatest problem of all, of course, whatever the theoretical considerations, was the cost of realizing any proposal. This factor remained foremost in the commissioners' minds and clearly helped to determine the path they chose.[129]

The desire to write a practical reform that both the State Council and the MF could accept had set the guidelines of simplicity and economy that the commissioners employed in rewriting the ladder of punishments. They applied the same criteria to their hopes for reform of prison administration. As they put it, "instead of putting before the government the choice of a hugely expensive reform or none at all, it would be better to make a modest proposal." Previous commissions, they knew, had failed at that juncture of theory and finance. The most recent recommendations, those of the Zubov Commission, would similarly fail, they noted, if not tempered by "modesty."[130]

This made the basic decision easy. They would recommend the creation of a central prison administration and postpone all other reforms. They did not wish to jeopardize their major goal by loading their proposal with unrealizable riders. For example, the commission expressly denied the need to write regulations for each form of incarceration before carrying out the reforms. Without rules to guide wardens in performance of their duties at the "new" prisons, the reform would be incomplete. To wait once again, however, while each set of regulations was drafted, circulated, commented on, revised, rejected, and redone would entail a delay of years. The commission embraced simplicity and economy from a sense of urgency. It decided to sacrifice scale and detail in order to implement the most basic part of the program.

To explain away the need for comprehensiveness the commissioners turned an old argument against previous reform proposals to their advantage. It made no sense to devise complete prison regulations in Russia, they wrote, where only two prisons (the Moscow house of corrections and the St. Petersburg prison) met even the basic correctional requirements, and elsewhere "neither physical structure nor personnel are able to fulfill detailed regulations."[131] The reformed ladder offered sufficient guidance in that case. Although they could not have intended such a conclusion to be drawn, they admitted with these words that even the simple reform they proposed would be stillborn. The reformed ladder could no more be adhered to than the existing ladder. I shall demonstrate below that they did say this in other words but insisted that their skeleton proposal was the proper beginning for the eventual realization of a comprehensive reform. They reiterated one other old argument to buttress their recommendation against drafting prison regulations. "Even many countries that are far richer than Russia in money and in people, and that modernized their prison systems long ago . . . do not have [such] regulations."[132] Grot's program, like Zubov's, like Sollogub's, was modeled on the enviable and superior conditions in the West. Regulations might be desirable, but they were not necessary. If some western nations managed without them, surely Russia could.

They approached the Prison Aid Society similarly. The POoT deserved a quick demise, but now was not the time to tangle with its influential membership or to wrangle out more compromise or reform. That, too, would be a long process, which would unnecessarily and detrimentally delay the beginning of basic prison reforms. Because it could not all happen at once, it would just be left for now. They may also have been thinking that the central prison administration they hoped to establish would be a better platform from which to assault the POoT than would their temporary commission. As they put it, the new central organ "would be responsible for and in an excellent position to work out the future development of penal law and prison reform."[133]

Grot's determination to start with this beginning came in large part from his personal exposure to foreign systems and foreign attitudes. At the International Prison Congress in Stockholm, which Grot chaired as president *honoris causa*, it was agreed that, to be run well, prison systems required a single central administration. Soon after returning from Stockholm, Grot wrote an official report of the proceedings for Alexander II, in which he emphasized this point.[134] As he diplomatically explained in a brief introduction to the report, he did not try to cover every subject discussed by the congress. He did not want to burden the emperor with a long report, but he felt obliged to mention briefly those aspects of its deliberations that might be useful "to the prison reform being undertaken here."[135]

Most important of these was the first question taken up by the congress, that of central administration. The congress resolved that "it is not only useful, but necessary . . . that there be one central organ for the administration and inspection of all places of imprisonment without exception."[136] Grot emphasized that this resolution was adopted unanimously by administrators as well as scholars. He added that "practically all countries" (seventeen nations, including all of continental Europe and the United States, were represented at the congress) already had central administrations and that those like Prussia, which still worked in the "abnormal situation" of a mixed administration, were thinking seriously of "reforming." He then briefly reviewed the sorry state of Russian prisons and the many organizations that shared confusedly and ineffectually their management. Such a situation, he concluded,

> shows clearly the necessity first of all to give our prison administration greater unity and independence, and to create for that purpose a special central organ which would administer all civilian punitive institutions, direct the activity of local organs, take upon itself all responsibility for the correct management of [these] matters, and be subordinate to only one ministry.

He mentioned that the imperially established Commission on Prison Reform, which he referred to by name without mentioning his position as its chairman, had already worked out such a plan, which it hoped to submit soon to the State Council.[137]

This report was nicely timed to bring the matter to Alexander II's attention just two months before the Grot Commission reported to the State Council. With it, Grot probably won valuable support for his primary project. Alexander II jotted on the report on 28 September, "I have read this with great interest. I sincerely hope it will have practical results in Russia."[138]

Having decided to ask for the establishment only of a new central administration, the commission discussed the problems such an organ would have to overcome. Foremost was the dispersal of authority cited by Grot in his recent report and by every other previous commission. Leadership must be concentrated in a single ministry. But which one? Sollogub had leaned toward the MVD, and Zubov had preferred the MIu before he changed his mind. The Grot Commission without hesitation chose the MVD. In the briefest of explanations the commissioners explained their choice by saying that the MVD already had a department performing similar functions.[139]

We have seen how rattled Timashev and the DPI had been by Zubov's initial preference for the MIu. There is strong evidence that Timashev was much better prepared to deal with Grot. As I stated earlier, they were personal friends. It can also be shown that, in the interval between Timashev's initial refusal to send Grot as Russia's official representative to the International Prison Congress in Stockholm and his reversing his decision, Grot informed Timashev of his commission's decision to attach the central prison administration to the MVD. Grot sent a preliminary project with this proposal to Timashev on 8 April 1878. The MVD replied over the minister's signature on 4 May. On 28 May Grot was given permission to go to Stockholm in August.[140]

Although there is no particular evidence to suggest that Grot and Timashev had made a deal to achieve this happy conclusion, there is excellent evidence that Grot did make a deal with Timashev's successor, L. S. Makov. Makov was appointed as revolutionary terrorism began to seriously worry the tsarist government. The Russo-Turkish War was going badly. Vera Zasulich had recently been acquitted by a Russian jury of attempted murder in a terroristic assassination attempt against a high tsarist police official, and there was every reason to believe that the terrorists intended further attacks. Makov's appointment reflected a shift at the highest levels of government away from further development of the liberal legal reforms of the 1860s. Faced with terrorism, which respected liberalism no more than autocracy, the emperor and many close to him increasingly felt the need to fall back on administrative and police powers.[141] Makov was the sort of man who perceived prisons and corrections as part of the police function. State Secretary E. A. Peretts, writing in 1880, recalled that Makov, Grot, and others (including himself) planned to have Grot appointed head of a new central prison administration in the MVD.[142]

Grot did not receive this appointment under Makov. Had he received it, I would have had to ask why the conservative Makov should have chosen a man so closely identified with reformers such as A. A. Abaza and E. A. Peretts. Peretts wrote in his diary that Makov deceived Grot. There is no further evidence to substantiate the nature of the plans or the deception, but it seems that Makov may have deceived Grot in order to guarantee his support for subordinating the prison administration to the MVD and abandoned him when that end had been achieved.

It is tempting to speculate further that changes at the top of the MIu contributed to this turnabout. On 30 May 1878 D. N. Nabokov replaced K. I. Palen as minister. That was about two months after Grot had informed Timashev of his preliminary decision in favor of the MVD, but half a year before he submitted his commission's final reports. It may be that Nabokov was selected at least in part because he was willing to acquiesce in this decision. It is also possible that, by the time Nabokov had settled into his job, it was too late for him to exert his influence on the Grot Commission. They met only three times after his appointment to discuss the question of central prison administration. For one reason or another, Nabokov played a much less active role in Grot's commission than Palen had in Zubov's.

Grot and his commission retained the proposal made in their preliminary project of 8 April recommending that the central prison administration be made more independent of its bureaucratic parent than MVD officials liked. They feared to have too many departments even of the same ministry involved in prison affairs, because they believed that would inevitably cause bureaucratic delays. To achieve that independence, they proposed the creation of a single organization within the MVD, to be called the Main Prison Administration. It would have authority over all nonmilitary places of imprisonment, over all organizations involved in prison administration, over transfer of prisoners, and over expenditures for all of the above. It would also be responsible for future reforms in these areas. The head of the GTU, its director (*nachal'nik*), would have authority over all civilian prison affairs, and, unlike heads of other departments in the MVD, he would personally handle those matters that required cooperation with other departments, directorates, or ministries or with the emperor, the Senate, and other high government bodies as "representative" of the minister.[143]

Except for relatively greater autonomy, the commission asked little for the new administration. Its composition reflected the prudent austerity of the rest of the reform proposal. In addition to the director, it would consist only of an assistant director, seven prison inspectors, and a small chancellery.[144] The commission required that the people to fill these positions be found in the "prison department" of the DPI and the chancellery of the president of the POoT. The former was, of course, the Second Department, where prison affairs had been concentrating for the last decade. Because the president of the POoT was the MVD, almost the entire staff of this new MVD administration would be drawn from within the MVD.[145]

The commission seems to have pursued two goals with this stipulation. Most obviously, it would save money. The commissioners also proposed that 19,332 rubles allocated to prison affairs in the DPI be transferred to the GTU, along with the personnel. This represented almost one-third of the 61,000 rubles asked by the commission as the annual allocation for the GTU.[146] Secondarily, by guaranteeing places for all MVD personnel then employed in prison affairs, they may have sought to defuse resistance and delays the DPI might otherwise have organized. The commission knew from the memorandum of 4 May that the MVD would disapprove of its proposal to create a "main administration" rather than a more dependent "department."[147] By requiring that the GTU staff come almost entirely from within the MVD, the commissioners may have tried to sweeten their proposal, to make it more palatable to MVD officials at several levels.

In addition to the GTU, the commission proposed the establishment of a Council on Prison Affairs *(Sovet po tiuremnym delam),* also to be attached to the MVD. This council would be composed of seven members, one of whom would be the director of the GTU; the MVD would serve as chairman. The commission intended this council to replace the Council of the President of the POoT, which would be abolished. Once again, as they took from the MVD with one hand, they gave back to it with the other. The MVD thereby remained as the chairman of the only council in his ministry that dealt with prison affairs, and this council clearly received a wider mandate. Councilors would discuss all prison affairs outside daily routine. Repairs, construction, and reform all came under their purview. No matter that required higher approval could pass from the GTU without receiving the council's approval.[148]

It was in the council that the reformers seem to have placed their hopes. In the commission's considerations they expressed the hope that the council would be staffed by specialists. The director and his staff would be kept busy with other responsibilities, they anticipated, and would need the advice of specialists, especially when they came to consider reforms. Prison administration had become a profession in the West; in Russia it was slowly being professionalized. The commission could not staff the GTU with specialists, much as some of its members might have wanted, because of the cost of starting de novo and the fear of antagonizing the DPI and the MVD. They could, however, with a council staffed by lawyers, criminalists, and penologists, guarantee that professional reform proposals be raised and that unworthy proposals be shelved. But where could they find these specialists if cost were a major consideration in not appointing them to the GTU itself? The commission thought that there were enough professionals already occupying high posts in various departments or living independently of service who would be willing to donate their time in unsalaried positions because of their interest in improving Russian prisons. They therefore stipulated that membership in the council not depend on government service and that council members receive no pay.[149]

Creation of the council would not remove responsibility from the director of the GTU. The GTU could not forward proposals for change without the council's approval. On the other hand, the council did not have executive powers. It could make suggestions and block acts of the GTU it considered mistaken, but it would have to work closely with the GTU. Furthermore, the commission provided that in the absence of the MVD the director would act as chairman of the council.[150] Considering the responsibilities owned by the minister, it could be assumed that the director would often have the opportunity to replace him. As I shall show, how effective a leader the director could be would depend a great deal on his relationship with the minister.

The Grot Commission completed its work and signed its journals on 24 November 1878. Just three weeks later, on 16 December, the State Council met in combined departments to consider the commission's last journal, its proposals on prison administration. It should be remembered that Grot and his commissioners had been appointed from within the State Council to rework the Zubov Commission's proposals. They were aware of the council's objections to Zubov's work and had tailored their own conclusions to produce not an ideal project but an acceptable one. The State Council embraced the plan in precisely those terms.

The council first thanked the Grot Commission "for the successful completion of its work," which it described as "thorough" and "thoughtful." The Zubov Commission, the councilors recalled, had also worked out thorough plans, including a complete set of prison regulations. Its work had without doubt been more comprehensive than that of the Grot Commission, but that was its greatest weakness. Because it was "too ambitious," the Zubov project "would unavoidably face insurmountable problems . . . too few people properly trained for prison administration and insufficiency of funds needed for the simultaneous reformation of all our penal institutions." The greatest merit of the Grot Commission's proposal was that it was "practicable."[151] With few changes, all of them minor, the council approved the commission's proposals. The project became law on 27 February 1879.[152]

THE MAIN

PRISON

ADMINISTRATION

THE FIRST YEARS

Several problems delayed the start of work in the Main Prison Administration. Political and personal considerations complicated the choice of men to staff the GTU and the Council on Prison Affairs. Grot expected to be named chairman of the council and from there to direct prison affairs and reforms. So firm was his conviction that he began to select assistants to work with him.[1] Makov, however, quashed his expectations. Grot's biographer is either circumspect or ignorant about how this happened. It was unclear to him how Grot happened to be passed over, but he was aware that disagreements arose over appointments to the GTU.[2] Grot managed to have some of his choices appointed. One of the original prison inspectors was V. N. Kokovtsov, a protégé of Grot who had accompanied him on his tour of prisons in the summer of 1877.[3] Kokovtsov later became MF and chairman of the Council of Ministers. D. A. Obolenskii, who was chosen for the position Grot had wanted for himself, was also close to Grot. On the other hand, Grot was highly displeased by the other appointments.[4]

The position of director lay vacant for some two months after the law creating the GTU was affirmed. On 23 April 1879 Mikhail Nikolaevich Galkin-Vraskii was appointed director.[5] Galkin-Vraskii had most recently served as governor of Saratov province and before that of Estland province.[6] He had long been interested in prison affairs: recall that he had been one of the two young men whom the MVD sent abroad to study foreign prisons in 1862–1863, and in 1867 he had coauthored the "Note on the Reform of Prison Affairs in Russia," had written an additional note on prison affairs abroad, and had served on the small commission appointed to study the proposal. At that time he held the rank of state councilor and had several positions close to Valuev in the MVD. He was head of a department of the MVD's council and was also on the staff of the president of the POoT.[7] In 1872, while the Sollogub Commission was meeting, Galkin-Vraskii, then Saratov governor, forwarded to the MVD a reform proposal that a Saratov landowner had sent to him.[8]

Further delay was caused by a backlog of paperwork in the lame-duck Second Department of the DPI. The GTU officially began its work on 16 June 1879.[9] But even then it could not begin on the reforms intended by the project on the ladder of punishments because that project was not reviewed by the State Council until February 1879, and then it met with objections. It was not issued as an "opinion" of the council until 11 December. In revised form it became law on the last day of 1879.[10] By that time populist terrorists had further shaken the confidence of the autocracy. The government hastened to conciliate the liberal gentry while still attempting to suppress the terrorists. These efforts disrupted the GTU once more.

The GTU began its work by organizing its staff on paper. The table of organization gives a fair idea of the magnitude of the job with which it had been entrusted. The first bureau *(deloproizvodstvo)* was to handle all correspondence about the GTU staff and about all private organizations, such as the POoT, all correspondence of the minister as president of the POoT, and all personal correspondence of the director. This bureau was also responsible for political prisoners and their special accommodations; for maintaining copies of all laws, orders, and circulars on prison affairs; and for compiling the annual report on GTU activities. The second bureau handled special places of incarceration. It directed the operation of central transfer prisons, special-investigation prisons, including the St. Petersburg "house of preliminary detention," and police lockups. It also took care of correspondence about private and state juvenile correction shelters and about places of arrest for those who had been sentenced by justices of the peace.

The third bureau was given charge of exile and *katorga,* including central *katorga* prisons. It also handled correspondence about administrative exile imposed by villages, the return of exiles, and all miscellaneous correspondence that arose as a consequence of punishment. The fourth bureau had responsibility for running "all regular prisons, strait houses and workhouses, correctional prisons, and correctional units and companies." This phrasing shows that the GTU did not anticipate converting all places of imprisonment quickly to conform with the new ladder of punishments. The fifth bureau managed the GTU's finances. The sixth was responsible for the transfer of prisoners, for their transportation and staging (providing secure places along the route of transfer for stopping overnight or longer), and for inspection of that process.[11]

Galkin-Vraskii and his staff spent their first summer organizing and familiarizing themselves with their new work. Although many of them and most of their work derived directly from the prison section of the DPI, there were new tasks and new men who knew little about prison administration. Kokovtsov, for example, had his first and only exposure to prisons and prison administration only two years earlier, when he accompanied Grot on a tour of prisons in nine cities of European Russia. That summer of 1879 the GTU inspectors fanned out across Russia to familiarize themselves with the extent and condition of the network of prisons and the exile system. Galkin-Vraskii personally inspected prisons of the central provinces of European Russia in the autumn, with a special eye to studying the construction and repair of prisons.[12]

The GTU had to know how many prisons there were in Russia and how many prisoners they held. The records of the old Second Department, which the GTU inherited from the Executive Police along with its staff, proved to be well kept. From them the GTU learned both the number and the types of places of incarceration it was to administer. The records did not, however, contain current information on the number of prisoners. Nor could the GTU obtain those statistics from any part of their parent organization, the MVD. Galkin-Vraskii had to write to the MIu, whose procurators gathered such statistics annually. N. A. Manasein, who was then a department director in the Ministry of Justice, quickly replied to Galkin-Vraskii's requests and supplied statistics on the numbers sentenced to various categories of punishment over the past three years and on those imprisoned while under investigation and trial for the same years.[13]

The completed survey showed that Russia had approximately 700 prisons of various sorts, not counting police lockups. There were 84 provincial prisons, 510 county prisons, and 32 other prisons. Calculations based on a GTU circular of 25 September 1879, which defined a recommended minimum of space for each prisoner, showed that these prisons had room for 54,253 inmates. They then held 70,488. The GTU counted 33 correctional prisons and correctional arrest units that together held 9,609 prisoners. These, too, were overfilled. They properly had space for only 7,136 inmates. The new *katorga* prisons had not yet entirely replaced *katorga* at places of exile and hard labor. Seven in European Russia had room for 2,745 but held only 2,525. Five more in Siberia with space for 2,800 held 2,721. Altogether, including preliminary and transfer prisons and a few other small facilities, the GTU had charge of about 100,000 prisoners in prisons that it calculated should have held no more than 80,000.[14]

Overcrowding had been a serious problem before the GTU existed. The first systematic survey of Russian prisons had revealed severe overcrowding in 1865. That was only two years after the corporal-punishment reform had required most Russian criminals to be jailed. The prison section within the MVD had been enlarged and reorganized to deal with this problem, but obviously it had not yet in 1865. Nor could it ever. As it frequently complained, especially when one or another commission seemed about to give its job to someone else, it did not receive the money it requested from the government. The construction and remodeling projects simply could not keep pace with the growth of the prison population.

All through the 1870s the tsarist government allocated much less for repair and construction than officials requested, and as the prison commissioners seemed to be nearing completion of their work, the government became more reluctant to part with money for what it came to call partial prison reform. It could thus rationalize that, if the reforms called for sweeping changes, it would have thrown good money after bad. In 1875, when provincial authorities reported they needed 506,313 rubles to repair prison facilities, the government allocated 300,000 rubles. In 1876, 1877, and 1878, as the reported need rose from 522,490, to 598,940, to 603,070 rubles, the annual allocation fell to 246,505 rubles. The year the GTU was established, 1879, the treasury showed even greater reluctance to maintain old prisons. Responsible officials asked for 737,000 rubles but received only 177,505.[15]

By 1878 the problem had been largely solved, but only by using inadequate, temporary buildings that had not been designed to serve as prisons. Then, in 1878 and 1879, overcrowding once again became a critical problem. Revolutionary acts were frequent and violent in 1878–1879, and the government responded by arresting more terrorists and political offenders than ever before. Criminal activity also increased in these years. Unprecedented numbers of political and criminal offenders strained the capacity and security of Russia's dilapidated prisons. Escapes and acts of violence against prison personnel also increased.[16] Even before the GTU could officially begin its work, it began to address this problem in an ad hoc fashion. In an effort to preserve the proper operation of more up-to-date facilities, administrators of overcrowded correctional arrest units could, by a law of 4 May 1879, transfer convicts to regular prisons. This law and another, of 29 November, compounded the problem in the regular prisons, however, by sending more prisoners to those already overcrowded facilities. Moreover, these laws lengthened the terms of prisoners who were transferred out of the strict-regime units by one-half, thereby increasing even further the number of inmates in regular prisons. The GTU acknowledged that the system could not bear the burden imposed by strict adherence to theory in another law, of 11 April 1880, which freed these transferred prisoners at the end of their "simple, not [their] increased terms of imprisonment."[17]

A major purpose of the recent tours of inspection had been to determine which prison facilities required immediate new construction or repair. Because there were not enough regular prisons, many prisoners were incarcerated in rented houses or government buildings that had been converted to hold prisoners. Many of these buildings, and the prisons also, were dangerously run down. The GTU would have preferred to construct new penitentiaries and correctional prisons, but it understood that it would not soon have the money to realize this dream. Instead, the GTU began to search for other structures already owned by the government that could have been converted. It asked provincial governors to supply lists of available buildings.[18]

Overcrowding pressured the GTU to do whatever it could as quickly as it could, and it seems to have gone about that task energetically. Frequently, however, its efforts were frustrated by other agencies of government that refused to cooperate. In Riga, for example, severe overcrowding in the main municipal prison had contributed to the outbreak of an "epidemic disease." The GTU sent an inspector to Riga to locate a suitable building to which to transfer enough prisoners to relieve the overcrowding. In all of Lifland province he could find only one such building, a vacant army barrack. After long correspondence, however, the war minister maintained his refusal to release the barrack. The GTU drew up a project to build an additional new prison in Riga and, meanwhile, transferred some prisoners from there to other locations.[19]

A similar problem occurred in Moscow, where the GTU saw the need for a new prison. Galkin-Vraskii wrote the governor general of Moscow, V. A. Dolgorukov, on 18 September 1879 that the GTU "thought it desirable to begin [prison] reforms in Moscow." He asked that Dolgorukov undertake to find suitable buildings to convert to, or land on which to construct, two new prisons. The governor general acted quickly to appoint a committee under his own chairmanship to investigate the matter. That was in early October. On 11 December, when the committee first met, it wrote to Galkin-Vraskii to tell him that it had made some progress. In April 1880, however, it turned out that the head of the City Duma, who had picked out one of the sites, had chosen a privately owned plot in a swampy area for which the owner wanted 20,000 rubles. The committee soon found another plot belonging to the city, which it thought would be better. The GTU wrote to members of the committee twice in December to ask them to speed up their work, but nine months later the City Duma had still not agreed to release the land chosen for the prison.[20]

Several bureaus of the GTU ran into similar problems that first year. Prison affairs had not yet been fully centralized into the GTU, and at every turn the administration's officials stumbled into other departments' territories and sensibilities. The second and sixth bureaus, which oversaw the operation of transfer prisons, reported that the whole operation had benefited from reforms made by the DPI in the 1860s. Although they had to cope with some dilapidated buildings and with overcrowding, on the whole they were satisfied that the system served its function. But when they recommended improvements, they ran into interministerial jealousies. In its first in-house annual report, the GTU recommended that the position of chief inspector of the transfer-prison system, which was attached to the War Ministry, be abolished and that the GTU take over its functions. The war minister preferred to keep that function, however, and the suggestion was excised from the next draft of the GTU's official annual report. The report on inefficiencies and irregularities in prisoner convoys, which were also managed by the War Ministry, fell under the same red pencil.[21]

The second bureau encountered more obstructionism in another project. In 1875 a house of preliminary detention had been built in St. Petersburg. It was established by a command (povelenie) of Alexander II as a model institution, and a special committee of notables was appointed to administer it. When the GTU inspected it in 1879, however, it found the house poorly run. The GTU concluded that the members of the special committee were too busy with other obligations to give the house the attention it needed and asked to take it over. By a command of 14 December 1879, the GTU received "all rights and responsibilities" for the prison. The municipal governor did not want to relinquish his authority over the prison, however, and the GTU wound up limited to studying its operation and recommending ways to improve it.[22]

Money proved to be a prime limiting factor for the GTU's ambitions, as it knew it would. Not only was little new construction undertaken, but only the most desperately dilapidated prison facilities could be repaired. Continuing an effort that had been begun by the Second Department of the DPI, the GTU tried to persuade the MF to allocate more money to increase the number of prison guards and their pay. Because of the rapid growth of the prison population, the ratio of guards to prisoners had decreased significantly. Escapes and acts of violence in prisons had increased correspondingly. The MF agreed that the problem was serious and authorized hiring new guards to reestablish the former ratio of one guard for each twenty prisoners. It did not, however, agree to support an increase in pay.[23]

On the other hand, centralization of financial planning disclosed some waste, and the GTU was able to save some money in several areas during 1879 and laid plans to save more. In later years it would be able to make much-needed improvements with money it would not have had if the funds had not been saved or produced by changes begun in 1879. The budget for 1880, prepared in 1879, marked the first time Russia had centralized its prison finances. Despite the shortness of time for preparation, the GTU was able to go far beyond what the old Second Department had done. By categorizing expenditures by type of prisons and the type of expenses within them, it discovered huge variations in the requests from individual prison administrators. When it made this known, requests from the provinces dropped. The Second Department had anticipated an increase, but the GTU's closer look apparently closed some avenues of corruption.[24] Later budgets became more detailed and probably produced further savings of this sort.

The fourth bureau found a similar inconsistency in the costs of provisioning individual prisons. Correctional arrest units, for example, were provisioned by provincial boards, which usually hired a tradesman to handle the whole operation and to make whatever profit he could from the money allocated for food. In only a few units did the administrators purchase and the prisoners prepare the inmates' food. The savings were great in these units, but, as the bureau's report put it, "because it requires a great deal of work, it is rarely seen." In prisons the situation was even worse. The POoT committees and branches had responsibility for food supplies in prisons, but in many places they did not fulfill their responsibilities. In others the variation of expenses from one area to another, even allowing for regional differences, was enough to suggest that many were not handling the funds entrusted to them honestly.[25] By tabulating these variations the GTU began to discover unusually loose spending. In later years it was able to regularize this function and realize significant savings.

In his first year as director Galkin-Vraskii concentrated, among other activities, on forging ties between the GTU and the community of professional and academic criminalists, both in Russia and abroad. He met with Russian criminalists and with administrators of various facilities within the GTU's far-flung system.[26] Throughout 1879 he corresponded with directors of prison administrations and prison societies abroad. He informed them of the establishment of the GTU and of his desire to join and work with international organizations. His letters received warm replies of congratulations and in some instances immediate invitations to join the international groups.[27]

Galkin-Vraskii and his staff did not soon solve the problem of overcrowding. Nor did they make much progress during that first year on several reforms they hoped eventually to carry out. In addition to the shortage of funds, several other obstacles stood in their way. Not only was the GTU deluged with routine work during its first year (it was hard-pressed just to cope with the rapid increase in the number of prisoners) but political circumstances also conspired against vigorous reformation. The MVD, Makov, was not a reformer. This might not have mattered much had Galkin-Vraskii aggressively promoted reform, but he did not. It is possible that he was selected, rather than Grot, for just that reason. The Council on Prison Affairs, from which Grot had hoped to manage prison reform, met only twice in 1879, and then it discussed only the GTU budget for 1880. In 1880 it met eight times.[28] Galkin-Vraskii was slow, deliberate, and patient over the next seventeen years as director of the GTU.

The unsettled political atmosphere of those first years may have inhibited the urge to experiment, that is, to reform. I. Ia. Foinitskii—a leading Russian criminologist, whom I already discussed as the author of some of the commissions' "expert" commentary—had been enthusiastic over prison reform, but in 1879 he suddenly found many reasons for the GTU to proceed cautiously. He cited the usual problems with money and with finding suitable personnel to staff reformed institutions, and he concluded, rather vaguely, that this was an "extremely awkward" time for reform.[29] By mid-1880 Makov's hold on the MVD was threatened, and Galkin-Vraskii's position was probably thereby weakened. When M. T. Loris-Melikov replaced Makov on 9 August 1880, uncertainty about policy and individuals' careers likely disrupted the GTU even further.

Soon after he became MVD, Loris-Melikov began planning to supplant Galkin-Vraskii with Grot, whom he had just met in August through A. A. Abaza and M. S. Kakhanov. These men were all reformers, believers in decentralization, who wished to give department heads greater autonomy and to relieve ministers from some routine chores so they were more free to concentrate on matters of higher administration. After replacing Makov as MVD, Loris-Melikov had asked him to stay on as head of the new Ministry of Posts and Telegraphs, which he separated out from the MVD. Likewise, he wished to make Grot head of a more independent GTU.[30] These plans were well advanced by 8 November 1880, when State Secretary E. A. Peretts dissuaded a colleague from appointing Grot to another position because "Loris wants to ask Grot to undertake administration of the prison section." They were finalized with the emperor's approval by 18 December.[31]

Loris-Melikov proposed this change in a note to the Committee of Ministers on 22 January 1881.[32] The committee took the matter up on 27 January and recommended confirmation.[33] Because no other documents shed light on this appointment, at the risk of reading too much into his words, I must let Loris-Melikov explain. The GTU was given responsibility, he wrote, not only for a "police-type administration of prisons" but also for implementing a "very complicated general reform of prisons."[34] As he saw it, there existed a difference between policing prisons and running reformed prisons, and he apparently identified

Makov and Galkin-Vraskii with the policemen. Grot would be his reformer. Loris-Melikov was not the complete reformer some earlier scholars have portrayed him; he was neither a constitutionalist nor an enemy of administrative justice. He was, however, willing to accept useful criticism of the existing order and to embrace beneficial change. As one recent student of Loris-Melikov put it, quoting him, he "advocated a 'softening of the methods and manner' of administrative behavior."[35] In prison affairs that meant accepting the criticism frequently leveled at Russian prisons and working as the academic criminalists advised to clean them up and make them decent and useful.

Because this reform procedure was "multifaceted" and "enormous," Loris-Melikov suggested that someone "fully familiar with prison affairs" be appointed to begin the main parts of the reform. Diplomatically he recommended that the task be undertaken by "the man to whom Your Majesty, the emperor, entrusted preparation of the reform in committee, State Secretary Grot." He proposed to transfer to Grot his powers as MVD in prison affairs: to be president of the POoT and to direct the GTU. Loris-Melikov asked to retain only the right to approve GTU papers, which had to be passed on to higher government organs.[36] The Committee of Ministers gave their approval, and the document was made law on 30 January 1881.[37] On the same day Grot was also named chairman of the Council on Prison Affairs to replace D. A. Obolenskii, who had died on 22 January.[38]

Grot assumed his new positions on 17 February 1881, by which time he had effectively taken upon himself "the direct leadership of basically all activities" of the GTU.[39] This must have brought him into conflict with Galkin-Vraskii. According to Grot's biographer, Galkin-Vraskii and Grot "never had bad relations,"[40] but this does not ring true. Once again there are few documents that illuminate this relationship, but those that do infer an uncomfortable and uncertain struggle. Grot's appointment had made him Galkin-Vraskii's superior and had made impossible "independent actions and orders from the director." On the other hand, Galkin-Vraskii's presence may have made it difficult for Grot to take over completely and to give his whole attention to his work. Sometime soon after Grot's appointment, Loris-Melikov attempted to remove Galkin-Vraskii, gently but completely, from his position as director.[41] He asked Alexander II "to help Galkin-Vraskii in this uncomfortable situation" by appointing him to the Senate, "with dismissal from his present position." Alexander II was assassinated before he could act on this request, however, and his son and successor Alexander III was unwilling to give Loris-Melikov an immediate, unequivocal reply. He recommended instead that Loris-Melikov confer with MIu D. N. Nabokov. Loris-Melikov complied and asked that Nabokov help him effect Galkin-Vraskii's appointment to the Senate as soon as possible, in order "to give State Secretary Grot the opportunity" to begin to work on the prison reform.

What happened after that remains even less clear. Galkin-Vraskii was not soon appointed to the Senate, nor was he removed from his post as director of the GTU. Grot remained in his temporary, superior position. Apparently, the whole problem was left to simmer on a back burner while a much larger issue occupied the most powerful figures of the tsarist government. Alexander III had to sort out in his first months as emperor what direction he would take and which advisors he would heed as he tried to guide Russia through a period of crisis. He had before him Loris-Melikov's extensive plans to reform and reorganize Russia's ministerial government. His father had been about to implement them, but Alexander III's favored advisors disapproved of them. As Pobedonostsev, Timashev, Delianov, and, to a lesser degree, Valuev and Makov won the battle for Alexander III's mind, they increased their pressure on him to scrap the plan and to dismiss Loris-Melikov. By mid-March Loris-Melikov's star was in decline. On 29 April he resigned.[42]

Why Grot remained when Loris-Melikov departed poses another mystery. He did remain, however, and so did Galkin-Vraskii. In July they reached a compromise over their shared problem. On 4 July 1881, Galkin-Vraskii left on a year-long tour of Siberia to study the exile and *katorga* systems.[43] Only then, apparently, was Grot able to turn his mind to the prison reforms he had advocated in 1878–1879.

Grot believed strongly in modern corrections. His minimal recommendations as chairman of the last commission were indeed only tactical. Once in charge he meant to proceed as quickly as he could to modernize as much as the GTU's limited finances would allow. He was especially interested in building more isolation cells and in training wardens to operate prisons as they were being run in Europe.[44] Russia already had a few "modern" correctional prisons, but in Grot's opinion even they were poorly run. He was particularly dissatisfied with the prisons of St. Petersburg, which were supposed to be exemplary. The wardens and officials of St. Petersburg's only correctional prison, according to Grot, "did not understand their duties or the purposes of punishment and a correctional regime."[45]

Contemporary Russian criminalists agreed. I. Ia. Foinitskii wrote in 1879:

It was easy for the old prisons to find people. All they needed were supervisors of cleanliness and order. New prisons will be able to justify their cost . . . [only] when their personnel will obtain the required levels [of training in] pedagogy and psychology. To find such people is not an easy task. A special difficulty is that such people must be found not among today's prison workers but in a completely different sphere.[46]

Foinitskii had in mind Russia's universities, which were beginning to train criminalists and just beginning to think about training penologists. He himself had taught the first course in penology in a Russian university in 1874, at the University of St. Petersburg.[47]

One of the major achievements of the GTU, from the perspective of 1881, was the eventual establishment of a large cadre of professionally trained wardens. They were, however, far from that goal in 1881, and there were many obstacles that they had not yet imagined. For example, Grot found and appointed several acceptable wardens to St. Petersburg prisons, only to discover that they could not work the way they wished in the institutions they ostensibly headed. Even after the establishment of the GTU, there were still many organizations that had overlapping rights and responsibilities in prison administration, and Grot had to fight, as had Galkin-Vraskii, to ease them out of "his" prisons.

This was a problem almost everywhere, but the obstacles were particularly formidable in St. Petersburg, where a modest effort by Grot proved to be his undoing. On 3 October 1881 Grot pushed through the Council on Prison Affairs a plan to remove the mayor *(gradonachal'nik)*, the city police, and the POoT committees from administration, leaving them only the right to enter and inspect city prisons.[48] The new MVD, N. P. Ignat'ev, approved the council's journal on 20 October. The GTU's council then prepared a complete project for the State Council's consideration, which by the GTU's charter also had to pass through the minister's office. Grot sent the project to Ignat'ev early in February 1882.[49] By this time, however, relations between the two men had soured. The cause of their estrangement can only be surmised. Grot has been described by friends as stubborn and independent, which may have made him difficult to work with.[50] More likely, Ignat'ev, who was generally hostile to reform efforts,[51] had been persuaded by conservative colleagues to rid himself of the "liberal" Grot. In any case, Ignat'ev sat on the project and did not forward it to the State Council.[52]

Grot had encountered this sort of resistance from Ignat'ev before but had ascribed it to Ignat'ev's heavy workload and his ambition. Peretts recorded in his diary on 18 January 1882 that

> K. K. Grot . . . frequently complains about Count Ignat'ev. According to him, the latter, not having time to delve into the heart of important matters presented to him, only laughs and jokes and, like an eel, slips away from serious deliberation. Then he asks that the case be left with him, and finally he sends it on but not at all as intended by its originator; that is, Grot. "Human ambition is to blame for it all," he has repeated to me several times. I do not think that Grot will remain in that strange, ambiguous position. He is a man of character.[53]

Grot tried to find out why Ignat'ev obstructed the project and tried to persuade him to forward it. Ignat'ev did not, however, and, as Peretts had predicted, Grot resigned. On 8 April 1882 Ignat'ev sent the emperor a note indicating Grot's desire to resign. On 28 April he was officially relieved of his duties.[54] Galkin-Vraskii soon returned to resume his duties as director.[55]

THE REFORMS

Interministerial and larger policy politics disrupted the GTU only once more before the revolutions of 1917. That occurred in 1895, when the GTU was transferred from the MVD to the MIu. Until then and after then the GTU slowly transformed Russian prisons from an inchoate collection of miscellaneous and mostly shabby facilities into a professionally run system of prisons that more closely accorded with its conception of modern correctional institutions. It accomplished much that it had set out to do and gained the respect of Europe's professionals in the process. That is not to say that it succeeded in deterring crime or correcting criminals or in stilling criticism of Russian prisons. The maddening aspect of this "progress" must have been the realization by many criminalists that for all their good intentions, for all their years of hard work, and for all the money the state had put into it, the modern Russian prison system did not noticeably deter or correct.

To upgrade and modernize Russia's prisons and to make them into a coherent system, the GTU began to make changes in several areas simultaneously. It continuously strove to improve the physical condition of prison facilities, usually under the constraint of a small budget. Where it could, it converted old prisons to conform to new theories or even built anew. Elsewhere it made necessary repairs to keep old facilities at least functional. To save money, to raise money, and to achieve correction in prisoners as contemporary theory told it was most effective, it worked to introduce compulsory labor into all of its prisons. Solid buildings and effective regimes would have been meaningless, however, without properly trained personnel to carry out the program. The GTU continually tried to recruit interested and educated men and to train those whom it already employed. It also frequently attempted to raise the pay scale of its employees with an eye to attracting better men. The crown of the Russian prisons system was to be a network of inspectors who would ensure that the GTU's programs were being carried out in all of the far-flung empire. The GTU's effort to establish this linchpin of its operations struggled against small budgets and hostile politics through almost its entire existence.

Construction and Repairs

Construction and repair always took up a large part of the GTU's annual budgets. This was at once the most urgent and the most straightforward task facing the administration. It had to decide which facilities to repair first, which to convert to meet the requirements of correctional incarceration, and which to abandon as too badly deteriorated. It had also to decide which rented properties to renew leases on, which to purchase, and which to let go. As more money became available, it also faced the choice of building new prisons or further repairing and converting existing structures. Using the reports of GTU inspectors as well as reports coming in from governors, POoT committees, and individual prison administrators about the physical condition of each facility, the GTU identified the prisons in most urgent need of repair. At the same time, it identified the areas suffering from the worst overcrowding and made plans to provide additional spaces there first.

Once the GTU was actually established, the treasury became less niggardly in its appropriations for prison construction and repair. In its first four years of operation, 1880–1883, the GTU had available 688,848, 702,589, 2,474,721, and 1,162,073 rubles for that line of its budget. Of this, it spent 3,589,626 rubles to repair and expand old buildings and to purchase previously rented space. The remaining 1,438,605 rubles were used for new construction. By 1882, 10,000 additional spaces had been provided to relieve overcrowding.[56]

In 1884, when the initial emergency of revolutionary activity and subsequent prison overcrowding had passed, the GTU worked out its first detailed plan to begin replacing the older buildings with new facilities that were designed to meet the requirements of the new ladder of punishments. Compared with the comprehensive recommendations of the early prison commissions, it was a modest plan. Galkin-Vraskii understood that the State Council's intention in establishing the GTU was to have a central administrative unit to plan and carry out a gradual reformation of Russian prisons as finances allowed. This plan was meant to be the first of a series of three-year plans that only over many years could provide the correctional facilities that contemporary theorists insisted were needed. The Council on Prison Affairs and the MVD, D. A. Tolstoi, approved the plan and passed it on to the Department of State Economy of the State Council, which was then studying allocations for 1885. The State Council reported that it could not guarantee appropriations three years thence, but it did offer a minimum of 1 million rubles annually, half for new construction and half for repairs. That basic appropriation meant that the GTU could count on steady, sizable allocations for construction and repair, but it also meant that they would have to progress even more slowly toward their goal than they had hoped. Provincial officials submitted requests to the GTU in 1884 for new construction costing a total of 12,175,000 rubles, and none of these plans included isolation prisons that would satisfy the law of 11 December 1879.[57]

The GTU drafted alternative plans to discover better and less expensive ways to realize its goals. The first of these, dated 15 February 1885, proposed to repair, convert, and expand many smaller county prisons, which housed all local prisoners except those assigned to long terms. That is, they held pretrial, short-term, and transfer prisoners. New laws required that some of these be held in isolation, but a large county prison built to hold one hundred prisoners in general or group cells might yield only forty to fifty isolation cells upon conversion. On closer inspection, conversions in many cases turned out to be technically impossible and in others to be prohibitively expensive. The GTU, still conscious of the shortage of trained men to run its prisons, realized that this plan would also require more than six hundred wardens "capable of handling the more complex requirements" of isolation prisons. It, therefore, scrapped this plan in favor of plans to build fewer, larger central prisons to provide administratively more demanding forms of incarceration.[58]

Like the plan for county prisons, the new plan for central prisons was general. It provided no schedule for building new "isolation centrals," only guidelines to help determine where and when they might be constructed. For example, the plan stipulated that where new prisons were required in distant locations poorly served by means of transportation, especially railroads, only "simple" prisons would be built. Expansion and repairs in such places would be limited to maintaining prisons "of the general type." The plan also provided that all buildings purchased from private owners or inherited from other government agencies would be converted into prisons "of the general type" only. This would maximize the funds left available for construction of large, modern correctional facilities, which would be built only in "large, administrative, trade-industrial, or transportation centers." Furthermore, new construction in one of these areas would begin only when "absence, overcrowding, or disrepair of existing facilities" required it.[59]

It took several more years to develop architectural plans, to convince the treasury and other offices of the necessity of the first large projects, and to carry them out. Between 1879 and 1895 the GTU built twenty-eight new prisons, but only three of them were large central prisons. Two of these were constructed in St. Petersburg. The huge St. Petersburg isolation prison, completed in 1892, had space for 1,150 prisoners and cost 1,480,000 rubles. The St. Petersburg central transfer prison, which could hold 700 prisoners, opened in 1894. The only large project completed outside St. Petersburg, where the government's concern that the capital be a model city lent special urgency, was an isolation prison for 681 prisoners that opened in Odessa in 1894.[60]

The transfer of the GTU from the Ministry of Internal Affairs to the Ministry of Justice in 1895 deprived the GTU of significant sums of money that the MVD managed to hang on to despite direct orders to transfer all budget lines associated with prison affairs, but the building program was well under way and was not seriously disrupted. Had the prison population grown only at the rate of the population as a whole, the GTU could have concentrated on replacing aged facilities by constructing modern correctional facilities. Overcrowding was not a serious problem after 1890 and had been completely overcome before 1900.

Between 1879, when the GTU was established, and 1905, when the revolutionary situation led once more to severe overcrowding, the condition of Russia's prisons improved considerably. By relieving overcrowding the GTU improved hygienic conditions and freed additional space that wardens could use to separate prisoners into smaller groups and into categories as required by prison regulations. The building program provided fifty new prisons by 1905, remodeled about thirty other arsenals, barracks, and monasteries, and purchased and converted about twenty other buildings from private owners, at a total cost of more than 12 million rubles. Legal capacity increased by more than 21,000 spaces. Repairs costing almost 12 million rubles more kept in operation many other prisons that had fallen into disrepair. Numerous older prisons that had been damaged by fire or otherwise declared unfit were closed or razed.[61]

After 1905, however, overcrowding quickly became a more serious problem than ever before. Arrests stemming from the Revolution of 1905 doubled the number of inmates in Russian prisons between 1906 and 1908. The GTU once again set about renting barracks and other unused buildings to incarcerate its thousands of new prisoners. From 1906 to 1912 the situation continued to worsen. In 1906 the GTU had room for about 104,000 prisoners and was called on to maintain approximately 110,000. By 1909 the gap had widened: more than 170,000 prisoners crowded into space that was intended for 129,000. In 1912, the peak year, almost 184,000 prisoners were squeezed into cells for about 130,000. Only the manpower demands of World War I eventually relieved this overcrowding. In 1916, the last year for which GTU statistics were compiled, 142,000 prisoners remained in tsarist prisons.[62]

Corrections

The GTU's efforts to implement an effective program of corrections were not as successful as its building and repair efforts. In 1879 most Russian criminalists were confident that labor and/or a judiciously applied regime of isolation would rehabilitate all but the most hardened criminals. For a variety of reasons, however, it was much more difficult to implement these regimes than it was just to construct the buildings. Because the necessity to provide the legally required space for prisoners took precedence and because isolation cells cost many times more per prisoner than did general cells, the GTU did not at first concentrate on building isolation cells. Many of the administrators would have liked to, and they continued to make plans to construct more as finances allowed, but by 1895, when construction caught up with the prison population, they had built only about 2,500 isolation cells.[63]

In 1898 the GTU reestimated its needs on a much less ambitious basis, in line with the revised ladder of punishments. Estimating a continuing need to keep 15,000 people in correctional arrest units, it calculated the cost of increasing the number of isolation cells in them to about 2,300 and of building "nighttime separation cells" for the rest of the inmates. Nighttime separation cells were a compromise form of isolation adopted long before in the West as a way to relieve the mental strain of complete isolation yet retain some of the benefits. They were meant to eliminate homosexual sex and all-night confabs, which were thought to be a major source of criminal education and "contamination." And they were doubly attractive as an economy measure. The GTU estimated that it needed an additional 1,269 isolation cells—it already had 1,025 in correctional arrest units. Cutting some corners, it estimated that it could build them for only 520,000 rubles, or only slightly more than 400 rubles each. The 12,188 nighttime separation cells would run only about 70–75 rubles each, or another 900,000 rubles.

Isolation in prisons would be more costly, because three-fourths of the estimated 28,000 prison inmates were supposed to be kept in solitary confinement. New Russian prisons already had 5,683 isolation cells. The additional 15,300—some of which could be built into existing prisons, others in additions, and only 640 in one wholly new building—would cost an estimated 7,368,000 rubles. For a total cost of 8.8 million rubles, the GTU calculated, it could make Russian prisons conform with the requirements of Russian law.[64]

Three years earlier, when the GTU was still part of the MVD, Minister of Internal Affairs I. N. Durnovo had asked for an annual appropriation of 1.9 million rubles for construction and repairs, 1 million of which was to be designated for new construction. The MF rejected his request as "desirable but not possible."[65] Since the transfer of the GTU to the MIu in 1895, money had grown even tighter. Sufficient funds never were found. Ten years after this estimate was submitted, only 270 more isolation cells had been built in correctional arrest units, and 361 of the total 1,294 were being used for nighttime separation. More than 85 percent of the 18,891 prisoners in the units remained in general incarceration.[66]

Had the Russian treasury had the money, more Russian prisons would have been transformed into solitary or modified solitary prisons (nighttime separation, for example). But Russia did not have the money. An alternative method of correction was already available in the idea of prison labor, however, and it was in this idea that the GTU officials increasingly placed most of their hope. Russian theorists also largely abandoned hope for solitary confinement and embraced the thought that a strict regime of labor in prisons would habituate criminals to work and produce law-abiding, industrious ex-convicts. It is tempting to think that the lack of money for pet reforms pressed administrators and theorists to discard one theory and embrace another. Isolation had lost its theoretical hold in the West long before it did in Russia, but it had taken several decades for disillusionment to set in strongly enough to cause theorists to declare isolation more dangerous than useful and to turn to other ideas. Russian criminalists, who began their experiment with correctional prisons much later than the West did, may have had to go through a somewhat telescoped period of disenchantment before they gave up so beguiling an idea. I doubt that they would have done so as quickly if they had had the money to spend.

Another episode demonstrates how inadequate finances forced the GTU and academic criminalists to postpone another part of reform and to adopt alternative solutions to sustain their hope for prisoner rehabilitation. Since the early nineteenth century, most Russian criminalists and some statesmen had wanted to end the Russian exile system.[67] In the first half of the century the system was attacked almost exclusively for the danger it posed to the law-abiding citizens of the regions to which exiles were sent, primarily western Siberia. When the idea of corrections seized the imagination of Russian criminalists after mid-century, they began to assault the system as harmful to the exiles as well. Expelling people from the society that had produced them and sending them out into sparsely populated, "wild" areas, they believed, proclaimed that those men were eternally lost to society, that they were incorrigible. The thought that men might be incorrigible could not be accepted by criminalists who were then brimming with hope for the power of orderly, professional corrections.[68]

The same thought that drove Russian reformers in many other areas, including the movement to abolish corporal punishment and to modernize prisons, gave additional impetus here. European countries had ended their use of exile, and their professional criminalists, academic and bureaucratic, now regarded its use as barbaric. When MIu N. V. Murav'ev addressed the State Council a few months before the exile system was almost entirely abolished, he called exile "that aged and obsolete remnant" and asked that it be replaced by "all the means of sensible punitive policy available to us." He rehearsed the standard arguments against the exile system and clinched his argument by saying that "penal administrators of all cultured countries and civilized peoples of the world, including our society, agree" that exile had failed. He then went on at some length to recount which European nations had stopped exiling criminals and when, and he pointed out that the International Prison Congresses had condemned the practice as early as 1872 and 1878.[69]

That was in 1900. The last sustained effort to abolish exile, for which the minister's speech was merely a capstone, began in 1886, after the GTU had begun to work its way out of the overcrowding crisis. On 28 December 1886 Galkin-Vraskii sent to MVD Tolstoi a "detailed note," produced by the GTU's third bureau, which proposed that the approximately 3,000 people who were sent into exile to penal servitude each year be sentenced instead to correctional imprisonment for terms of about three years. That was not a new suggestion, but all previous efforts to replace exile with imprisonment had quickly foundered on the shortage of prison space for criminals already sentenced to prisons and on the expense of providing sufficient spaces. Never before, however, had the suggestion come from an office that administered prison affairs. The GTU reported that 9,000 additional spaces would have to be found— 3,000 prisoners times three years. But if criminals formerly exiled were to be imprisoned, transfer prisons would no longer be needed. The GTU had 3,500 spaces available in four large transfer prisons. Officials thought they could make 1,500 more spaces by expanding those prisons and would, therefore, have to construct only 4,000 new places. The total bill came to around 4 million rubles.

In a fairly rare example of cooperation, the MVD and MIu sent a lengthy joint proposal supporting this reform to the State Council on 26 February 1888. In it they detailed precisely where all of the space could be found for the new category of prisoners and reestimated costs. The new total came to nearly 5 million rubles, but they were able to show that significant savings would result from closing down the exile and transfer system and that the government would have to find only 2.5 million rubles over the next four years to pay for the change. The State Council discussed the matter in April and May and expressed its regret that it could not come up with so much money "in this time so difficult for state finances." A "general meeting" of the State Council on 30 May declared the plan to abolish exile "premature." Because money could not be allocated to build new spaces, it feared that abolishing exile would harm the rest of the prison system by burdening it with additional prisoners.

All of the reasons for limiting or abolishing exile remained the same, however, and voices were frequently raised to urge that measure. The question became part of the complex debate over a new criminal code that continued through the 1890s. Not until eleven years later did a different MIu and emperor lend their support to a similar project that reached the State Council. The cost had increased slightly, to 6.6 million rubles, by then, but with the support of the emperor the legislation was approved and the money provided. Offenders previously sentenced to exile and *katorga* would henceforth be incarcerated in large central prisons in general, not solitary, cells. The GTU did not propose to convert older prisons, nor did it ask for extra money to build its new "*katorga* centrals" as isolation prisons. To have done so would have increased their estimated cost by at least half again. Had the GTU asked for that additional outlay of funds, it might have received nothing. It looked to the new prisons to rehabilitate prisoners formerly not subjected to a correctional regime, yet it hoped to achieve correction without isolation. Labor would serve in them as the primary corrective agent. By 1900 administrators and theorists alike were comfortable with that idea.[70]

The several groups that were working on the new criminal code must have been pleased that this reform had been implemented. Their work had long been held up because many of the other changes they wished to suggest would cost too much to be carried out. They hesitated to pass laws that they knew would remain, like the Code of 1845 and the ladder of punishments of 1879, unfulfilled expressions of their fond hopes. They were still certain there were ways to rehabilitate prisoners but knew them to be too expensive. Only about a year before Nicholas had lent his influence to gain passage of the law of 12 June 1900 and to squeeze 6 million rubles out of the treasury, the State Council had met to debate whether it made sense to pass the new criminal code if it could not be implemented. The council had to listen to V. N. Kokovtsov, former prison inspector in the GTU and now assistant MF, tell them that the Ministry of Finance could not possibly give the GTU a large enough one-time allocation and that even gradual reform would be costly and funding uncertain. A majority thought the law ought to be passed anyway, to serve as a distant goal toward which officialdom should strive. The council ordered the minister of justice, who was nominal head of prison affairs now that the GTU was in the MIu, to take measures to reform prisons as required by the new law.[71]

Nicholas II appointed a "special board" in the State Council on 6 October 1901 to examine how the code might be implemented. At a meeting on 3 May 1902, presided over by ex-MIu K. I. Palen, MIu N. V. Murav'ev presented the project of costs and alternatives worked out by the GTU. Construction costs alone would run 23,440,000 rubles. For repairs, which were diplomatically not mentioned in the report, the GTU would need more than another 7 million rubles. The GTU and the MIu knew that they had no chance of receiving these sums. They devoted the greater part of their report to subjects that had not specifically been within the purview of the special board: suggestions on how to decrease the costs of construction required by the reformed code. All of the suggestions were ideas already in use in the West, and all had been discussed in print by professional criminalists in Russia. Here they clearly received a boost from the administrators because they could reduce costs and thereby assist the GTU to reach another goal, namely prisoner rehabilitation. The GTU and the MIu wished to subtract time served in preliminary detention from judicial sentences, to expand the system of colonies for juvenile offenders, to improve the reintegration of released offenders into society, to introduce the use of probation and parole, and to require mandatory "social work" of the indigent as prophylaxis.[72]

Prisoner Labor

All of these measures were still wishes and suggestions in 1902, whereas prisoner labor had received increasing attention from the GTU since 1879. Like other "luxuries," however, implementation of a program of prison labor had to wait until the congenital problem of overcrowding had been dealt with.

Efforts to organize labor in Russian prisons long predate the establishment of the GTU. V. A. Sollogub, for example, had emphasized the need to make work available even before his commission sat in 1872. In 1866 he had written a prophetic little pamphlet, which the MVD published, to attack the idea of isolation and to support instead the use of labor. He criticized the use of isolation on several grounds; some concerned Russian problems and characteristics but others were based on American and European experience. The latter, he wrote, had shown that "isolation does not prevent recidivism, but it does sometimes drive prisoners mad." All of the special buildings and the enormous expenditure of energy and money required for isolation seemed to him so much evidence "of the cruelty sometimes caused by speculative philanthropy." Labor, on the other hand, was a useful, sensible, and easily justifiable alternative. Imprisonment was a double drain on a nation's resources, which lost the labor of the men taken from it and paid to keep them incarcerated. Because society did not want to imprison men but was forced to do so by their behavior, society was entitled to make prisoners pay for their imprisonment.[73]

In Sollogub's conception, prisoner labor was at least as important as an economic measure as it was a means of rehabilitation. In a prison system so bedeviled by lack of money the economic side of convict labor remained prominent, but from the beginnings of the GTU's efforts it was not paramount. Even in 1866 the publisher of Sollogub's pamphlet felt the need to comment editorially that "the corrective effects of labor are more important than the economic."[74] Historians seeking economic motivations for human behavior may prefer to believe that fiscal considerations provided the basic motivation for organizing convict labor, but they would find no evidence to support such a claim in this case. Economic considerations may well have given rise to and/or reinforced other justifications for prison labor. It may be that it was less acceptable to talk about making prisoners work for their keep than about the hope that work rehabilitated them. All such conclusions, however, would be entirely speculative. All the evidence—from monographs on penology to memoranda, circulars, and prison-inspectors' reports not intended for public eyes—indicates that economic considerations were important but that the effort to effect corrections was of prime importance.

The GTU's self-appointed, semi-official historian, N. F. Luchinskii, who was himself a strong proponent of convict labor after 1900, wrote that convict labor was an immediate concern of the GTU in 1879 but that concentrated work on designing and implementing a program of mandatory, productive, and corrective labor could not be undertaken until the overcrowding crisis was under control.[75] By 1885 the GTU could devote sufficient attention to the matter to draft a plan that was intended to make work available to all prisoners who either wanted to work or who were required to by their sentence. That plan became law on 6 January 1886.[76] The GTU sent copies to all their wardens, along with a circular dated 25 April 1886, which explained the importance of the law to Russian prisons and the GTU's strong desire that wardens do all they could to fulfill the law. Other circulars of 3 March 1888, 14 December 1888, and 25

June 1889 repeated this concern and offered some suggestions about how labor might be organized.[77]

It took many years to implement work programs, even in the larger prisons, where it was easier. The GTU had to continually press wardens, inspectors, and other local employees to make an extra effort to find useful work for their inmates. Finally, in 1902, a special section in the GTU was organized to further spread and improve the organization of convict labor.[78] The effort had two immediately discernable results. Inspection reports, which up to 1886 had emphasized overcrowding and the physical condition of prisons, regularly reported on the lack of prisoner labor or, with increasing frequency and detail, on its organization and results. Second, annual reports showed an almost continual growth of income from prisoner labor.

Before 1886 most reports sent to the GTU came from provincial POoT committees. Most had little to say about prisoner labor. The report from Penza province in 1884, for example, stated briefly what sorts of jobs were being performed by some prisoners. It did not analyze what percentage of the prison population labored, describe earnings, or explain what efforts might have been under way to improve the situation. The report from Tver province was even skimpier. Simbirsk's report painted a fuller and more hopeful picture. All the housekeeping work of the prisons (which usually meant cleaning, food preparation, and laundering) was done by prisoners. Some other prisoners cleaned streets, and at two prisons convicts broke rocks. No attempt was made to summarize earnings or explain how income was shared among the prison, the prisoners, and the GTU.[79]

In the 1890s and thereafter, the GTU continued to receive reports from POoT committees, but by then they also had a corps of central and provincial inspectors who knew what most interested the GTU and who filed much more comprehensive reports. The major purpose of one GTU inspector's report, of 16 October 1893, was to report on the operation of the new provincial inspectorate that had been established in Kazan province in June 1891. While he was in Kazan, he also inspected prison facilities and wrote a thorough report on each. On the Kazan city prison, for example, he spent three pages describing the prison staff and their salaries, the number of prisoners, the budget, and the physical condition of the buildings. Then he spent three more pages discussing the organization of labor. For the correctional arrest unit he spent proportionally more space on physical problems. One wing of the wooden structure was "approaching complete dilapidation, so that in the near future, despite annual repairs, it will be useless and due for demolition." Nonetheless, he still devoted more space to convict labor, which, despite the condition of the facilities, he found to be well organized. Most prisoners were involved in one or another handicraft, and all but a few of the rest were kept busy with the housekeeping work of the prison.[80] The provincial-prison inspector of Saratov, where an inspectorate had been established in 1890, showed a similar emphasis in his report on the operation of the Saratov correctional arrest unit for 1892. He spent one page summarizing prison population changes, three pages on finances, one page on "measures of moral correction," which concerned religious and educational activities, and eight pages on prisoner labor. The last was a detailed report on how many people spent how many working days producing specified items.[81] A report on Moscow's prisons filed by a GTU inspector on 21 July 1893 contained similarly detailed information.[82] Thorough and candid reports became the rule by the mid-1890s. The reports from the Kharkov, Kiev, and Ekaterinoslav provincial inspectors in 1896 contained, among much other information, precise data on the numbers of prisoners working and descriptions of the sorts of tasks they performed.[83]

By the late 1890s the GTU had increased severalfold the number of prisoners engaged in productive work and likewise the value of their labor. That is not to say that the GTU ever completed this task. It encountered difficulties everywhere. Local businessmen and workers frequently complained of unwanted and unfair competition from prisons and in some instances had certain types of work stopped. Until the late 1880s, overcrowding took up room that would later be used as workshops. Then, after 1895, because the GTU was transferred to the MIu, the GTU had less money to budget for nonessential items, such as starting up work programs. Not long after that situation had been normalized, the Revolution of 1905 again overloaded the prison system. Throughout the entire period programs of external work, which took prisoners outside prison walls to places where they might work, were severely limited by the inadequacy of money in the GTU budget to hire additional guards.

Nonetheless, belief in the efficacy of work programs continued to grow. By the turn of the century labor had undoubtedly displaced isolation as the greatest hope criminalists and administrators had for corrections. S. K. Gogel', a prominent academic criminalist who frequently wrote about means of rehabilitation, strongly advocated work programs. In a book-length essay written in 1897, which was reprinted twice and frequently quoted, Gogel' described various measures for corrections and examined how well they had been applied in Russia. His conclusions were gloomy: "Our places of imprisonment doubtless serve only one purpose: keeping the criminal from committing another crime during his imprisonment; they do not achieve the purposes of deterrence or rehabilitation." The reasons were many. Russian prisons had only rudimentary libraries and schools or none at all. Discipline in them was "more than kindhearted" and "unsystematic," which meant that it could have "no real effect." The prisoners' usual regime of sleeping, resting, playing chess, smoking smuggled tobacco, and bragging about their crimes could "hardly deter, much less correct." Another major cause of the failure of the regime, in Gogel's opinion, was the lack of isolation—but isolation could only deter, whereas work could correct. If Russian prisons had none of the other positive qualities—education, discipline, and isolation—"but only had labor, occupations, work, then our prisons would cease to be what they remain—nurseries of vice and crime, sources of moral infection."[84]

Russian criminalists believed as strongly as they did in the corrective power of labor, as usual, in large part because foreign criminalists were writing that this was what worked best in Europe. Their certainty preceded Russian experience. Russian academics were learned men, who were usually fluent in two or three European languages and were familiar with the theories of Italian, French, Belgian, German, English, and American penologists. Many read the originals; others read the major works, which were soon translated. All of the writings of the foremost criminalists were thoroughly discussed in reviews and review articles in several professional journals, some of which were published by the government. These intellectual contacts were reinforced by many personal meetings between Russian academic and administrative professionals and their foreign counterparts. The Russians traveled abroad to tour the facilities of Europe, and many also attended the international congresses and conferences that met regularly after 1872. The question of convict labor was extensively discussed at international congresses, including one held in St. Petersburg 3–12 June 1890.[85]

Gogel' cited many foreign experts in his article on convict labor and quoted not only their writings but also conversations held with them at the St. Petersburg Congress. Herbette, the director of French prisons; Illing, a Prussian criminalist; de Renzi, an Italian delegate to the Congress; and an Austrian lawyer agreed on the need to organize labor in prisons. An English prison administrator, who was active in organizing the international meetings, told him, "I have deep faith in the rehabilitative influence of productive labor. . . . Labor is the very life of every good prison." Gogel' took away from this contact the firm belief that "in practically all foreign states convict labor [is organized] completely successfully, even magnificently. . . . The example of western Europe shows there are no insurmountable barriers to organizing work in prisons." Like his foreign peers, he believed just as firmly that, although the income from convict labor was a welcome by-product of the process, it was "not the most important condition of the organization of labor." Most important was, of course, rehabilitation.[86]

Another important proponent of this idea was N. V. Murav'ev, Russia's MIu between 1894 and 1905. Opening the First Congress of Russian Prison Administrators on 11 March 1902, he devoted almost his entire speech to the necessity of improving the organization of convict labor. All of the points he made could have been found in the writings of Russian criminalists, who must have been thrilled to find their ideas championed by the administrative head of Russian prisons. "A scientific rationalization of prison labor is hardly needed," he began,

> its necessity springs directly from the essence of human nature, from the demands of social life, and from everyday common sense. Nobody doubts now the tremendous rehabilitative and educational [vospitatel'noe] influence of labor on infirm will, on fallen morality.

Prison labor, he went on, is unquestionably the best means of combating "parasitism" and "idleness," "those greatest causes of crime." It is the "most hopeful weapon for the return [of prisoners] to an honorable and regular life." He recited the other benefits of such labor: that it brings order and discipline, which are needed in prisons; and that it relieves the treasury of many expenses, thereby freeing a great deal of money to be more productively spent. For Murav'ev, as for Gogel' and others, this last point was important but secondary.[87]

Others, including other administrators, waxed more eloquent about the power of labor to reform prisoners. N. F. Luchinskii, perhaps the most prolific writer among Russia's penologists and a longtime member of the GTU's inner circle, wrote in 1904 that work should occupy the same place in correctional arrest units "that prayer does in a monastery, filling the day, the life, the consciousness of its occupants with the meaning it requires." In his study of Russian prisoners, Luchinskii was struck by his finding that more than 70 percent were either charged with or convicted of crimes against property. Most of the other 30 percent fell into political or other categories that were not required to work in prison. Luchinskii reasoned that people who stole other people's property, the "fruits of others' labor," had little respect for the labor that had earned the property. Most of them, he wrote, had a fear of work, an "inclination to idleness." They were "bad workers" who needed to be taught the habits of good workers.

In qualifying that generalization, Luchinskii revealed what lay at the base of much of the support for this form of correction. Not all offenders against property harbored such an aversion to labor. Some industrious men fell into crime accidentally or "innocently," through dire need. He offered the examples of peasants who stole an ax to be able to chop wood or hay to feed a hungry horse. Like the characters of L. N. Tolstoi's novel *Resurrection,* who were exiled or imprisoned for minor infractions yet who were otherwise noble, these offenders "are no lower than their fellow citizens . . . from the point of view of general morality."[88] In rapidly industrializing, bourgeois Russia, work and morality were increasingly linked. Laziness, idleness, and immorality were likewise becoming synonymous. The "strayed children," as Luchinskii referred to Russia's prisoners, had not strayed from the earlier, more religious society that believed prisoners might be cured by prayer and contemplation. Religious activities in prisons received little attention from academic or government penologists, who now accepted that offenders had strayed from a secular, bourgeois society whose ethic was disciplined, orderly work.

In 1886, the year in which the GTU issued its first general law and circular to spread and regularize the organization of convict labor, Russian prisoners produced 345,000 rubles' worth of goods. In 1887 that sum rose to about 538,000; by 1895 it exceeded 1 million rubles. After a decline during the revolutionary crisis of 1905, the program quickly recovered. Almost 2.5 million rubles were generated by prisoners' labor in 1909. In 1910 that figure exceeded 3 million, and in 1911 it passed 4 million. During World War I, Russian prisoners produced much-needed boots, clothing, and other items for the military.[89]

Almost all of this labor value was produced in reformed prisons. None of it was produced by political prisoners and only a small part by other exiles. As I pointed out in the introduction, the image Europe had of tsarist Russia as a land filled with laboring prisoners chained to wheelbarrows or stooped in Siberian mines is mistaken. Some political prisoners were undoubtedly beaten or otherwise abused in violation of prison regulations and the law. On the other hand, the evidence is unambiguous that legally and, for the most part, in fact, Russian political prisoners were handled with a milder regime than were criminal prisoners. Among other differences, they were not required to labor. Neither in prison, where, space permitting, they were held apart from criminal inmates, nor in exile did they contribute to labor-output statistics. As a matter of fact, in exile their sentences often permitted them to travel within large areas of Siberia; and because of the laxity of this punishment, they frequently escaped. Nonpolitical exiles did perform some labor in Siberia, but even before the law of 12 June 1900, exiles were only a small part of Russia's convict population. After 1900 the flow of exiles slowed to a trickle, and few of these wound up in mines. Russian prisoners were used to help build the Trans-Siberian Railroad. They helped on the Ussuri and Arkhangelsk lines, too. In 1895, for example, 3,355 prisoners worked on the railroad. Only a few hundred worked in lead and silver mines in the late 1890s.

Other prisoners were made useful cleaning cities of snow and mud, disposing of sewage from jails and other government buildings, loading and unloading trains and ships, chopping wood, hauling water, digging pits, graves, and canals, and performing other external work. At thirty-two prisons, inmates worked in brick factories—though, apparently, not efficiently. In most prisons some small part of the prisoners took care of the housekeeping work; a smaller percentage worked at many different crafts; and some assisted in repairing the prisons themselves. When Gogel' surveyed the organization of labor in Russia's prisons in 1906, he collected data on all 32 correctional arrest units, 85 of the 95 provincial prisons, and 442 of the 522 county prisons. In the arrest units, where everybody was supposed to be working, he found 54 percent at work, fully one-third of them occupied in housekeeping chores. Only 28 percent of the inmates of provincial prisons were productively employed, and only 21 percent of those in the county prisons. That compared poorly with the 76 percent said to be working in English prisons and the 77 percent claimed for Belgium.[90] When Gogel' updated his study in 1913, he found few changes in the majority of Russia's prisons.[91] Until World War I, Russian penologists were consistently frustrated in their desire and efforts to bring to Russian prisons the degree of discipline and mandatory labor they observed and read about in Europe. On the average, Russian prison discipline was far more relaxed and many fewer prisoners were made to labor, hard or otherwise.

Personnel

Another problem the GTU faced for a long while after 1879 was the shortage of trained personnel to run reformed prisons. Several commissions had expressed their fear that reform efforts would fail for lack of men to carry them out, and the MF had used that deficiency, among others, to justify its refusal to fund prison reforms. The fear was real. Lacking modern facilities in most prisons, the GTU had for many years to rely solely on its wardens and other workers to set an improved tone in prisons. It wanted them to separate prisoners by legal

categories, to oversee the maintenance of order, discipline, and cleanliness, to organize useful labor for the inmates, and in general to create an atmosphere in
which rehabilitation might occur. When the GTU was established, few active
wardens were much concerned with corrections; educated men who were concerned with such things usually would not consider working as wardens.

Like other improvements the GTU wished to implement, finding and hiring
trained wardens or training competent men had to be considered less urgent
than the overcrowding emergency. Unlike other programs, which would require
a great deal of money, however, the search for better personnel could begin immediately, with decisions to hire or not to hire candidates as they presented
themselves. That proved to be a sufficiently large obstacle in the first years, for
few men whom the GTU considered qualified put themselves forward for consideration. Galkin-Vraskii included among his first tasks responding to petition-
ers and interviewing men seeking administrative positions in the GTU.[92]

Personnel problems did not seem as urgent as some other problems for another reason, too. Most positions in the prison system when it became the GTU
were already filled. Prisons already had wardens; they were not the men the reformers envisioned in that position, but they could function while the executives
dealt with other problems. The DPI's Second Department became the GTU
staff, so there was not an extensive recruitment to fill the desks in St. Petersburg.
Only the Council on Prison Affairs, whose members were prominent men serving without pay, and some prison inspectors had to be appointed immediately.
Most of the inspectors were either found within the DPI or were already known
to the men who were putting the GTU together, like Grot's protégé Kokovtsov.

Because of overlapping authority and responsibilities for hiring and paying
prison personnel, the GTU did not hire and pay wardens until 1882. By a law of
9 February 1882 it assigned wardens to 51 provincial prisons and 5 workhouses.
At that time the GTU employed 107 senior wardens and 892 junior wardens,
who were paid, respectively, 240 and 180 rubles per year.[93] After 1882 the central administration's concern became more pronounced, or at least more visible.
A large part of Galkin-Vraskii's correspondence between 1883 and 1886 was
taken up with the search for better-qualified men. In 1883, for example, he
wrote to the governor of Vitebsk province to ask about the warden of the
Vitebsk provincial prison. The warden had been recommended to Galkin-
Vraskii as a candidate for assistant warden of one of the large "model" prisons of
St. Petersburg and had been described as "energetic and efficient" and "very familiar with prison administration." The director wanted to know whether the
governor concurred. The governor replied that the man was young and would
need a good superior but that he would be an excellent assistant. Both letters
were formal and businesslike; neither contained a hint of patronage or fa-
voritism. The same was true of the other letters from these years.[94]

Few documents from the 1890s exist to explain how the effort to find better
personnel progressed, but those from the early 1900s attest to the fact that a
great deal of progress had been made. Sometime in the 1890s a school to retrain
wardens in new methods was opened at the "model solitary prison on the Vy-

borg side" in St. Petersburg. In the first years of the new century, wardens went regularly on temporary assignment to the "prison lyceum," where they studied theoretical and practical sides of prison administration and took short courses in criminology and the history of prisons and punishment. N. F. Luchinskii, who was on the GTU staff when he wrote of the school in 1904, said that its most important function was to inculcate in the student-wardens "respect for the law, unbribable honesty, bravery, and firmness of character."[95] After 1905, for which period the documentation is better, the GTU clearly had more candidates for administrative positions than it could use and began to turn down men it would have been happy to hire two decades earlier.

In 1907 several new provincial inspectorates were scheduled to be opened, and applications for positions of inspector and assistant inspector poured in. The GTU had its pick of many well-qualified individuals and was forced to refuse others. Most of the candidates recommended themselves and sent along with their applications letters of reference from various provincial officials; others came recommended by governors. Many of them had had administrative experience; some had served as the councilor in charge of prison affairs in provincial boards, the very position the new inspectors would supplant. The GTU rejected many of the candidates immediately, usually for lack of experience, and wrote to the former employees of others to learn more about them. The candidate selected for inspector in Kostroma province, for example, had been a land captain, an appointed official working with the peasantry. He was thought to have had useful experience in both administrative and judicial affairs, which is what the GTU was looking for, and he received excellent recommendations from all of his references.[96] Another candidate for inspector had good qualifications, but because the GTU judged others to have more experience, it could offer him only the position of secretary to the inspector. He accepted. Others with similar qualifications had to be rejected.[97]

The GTU was loath to lose some candidates, to whom it could not immediately offer jobs, and entered them into a register for future consideration. One well-qualified young man from Voronezh was told that he was being made a "candidate assistant inspector" but that the GTU feared there might not be an opening soon. It told him that the "candidate list" was long and that when an opening did occur the GTU gave preference to those "who by their former service have acquired experience in administrative and judicial affairs." (Recall that after 1895 the GTU was part of the MIu.) It preferred ex-procurators, land captains, and military men with administrative experience who were "used to dealing with mobs." The latter quality they found especially important "in these troublous times." The young man replied that he was still interested and added information about his experience as a land captain and some legal training he had received. Nonetheless, about a year later he was dropped from consideration when the list had grown even longer with qualified candidates and there seemed to be no chance that he might be offered a job.[98]

The search for qualified wardens was also successful. The GTU apparently fired few of the wardens it inherited in 1879, but over twenty-some years it had the opportunity to replace many of them. By 1907 it was rejecting most of the candidates who applied. By that time the GTU had worked up a form letter, which it sent, stamped "confidential," to former employees of applicants asking for "detailed information with full frankness about the service and moral qualities" of the candidates.[99] When a lighthouse keeper wrote and asked for a job in prison service, for example, the GTU wrote back to the "director of lighthouses and pilots of the Black and Azov seas" for the man's service record and the director's opinion. The director gave him a strong recommendation, but the GTU judged him less qualified than other candidates and rejected his application.[100]

Several times in 1907 high-ranking officials wrote A. M. Maksimovskii, then director of the GTU, to ask that he find positions for favorites. Early in February the chairman of the Council of Ministers recommended to Maksimovskii a "thoroughly reliable" man then serving as director (smotritel') of Kovno municipal hospital. The chairman was concerned that the man could not afford to educate his three children on the salary the hospital paid him and asked Maksimovskii to appoint him a prison warden. Maksimovskii refused on 10 February, explaining that "only people with long experience in prison affairs and an excellent record in lower positions" were considered for wardens' positions.[101] Earlier that year, on 11 January, the assistant director of military-educational institutes asked Maksimovskii to find a position as "assistant warden or something else" for a young man who had dropped out of "infantry cadet school . . . as a result of unsuitability for military service." Maksimovskii underlined the part of the letter that read "the emperor is interested in the fate of this young man as a former student of a military academy." He took more care with this case than with most others. He did not want to offend this man by rejecting his request; nonetheless, he refused. He replied on 7 February that

> service in prison administration requires . . . not only specialized knowledge, firm character, and energy but also sound health. . . . [A boy who had to leave school] could hardly be suited for extremely difficult and responsible service in the prison system, especially in contemporary conditions. . . . Apart from this I consider it my duty to inform you that I am taking all measures to raise the level of the staff in the department entrusted to me . . . and consequently I pay special attention to the educational qualifications of candidates.

The GTU, he added, frequently hired ex-officers, but he could not offer any position to the failed cadet.[102] The men who were hired that year were educated and experienced but not obviously well connected.[103]

A greater number of good candidates were rejected in the following years as ever more qualified men applied for positions with the GTU. Some candidates not so desirable as others were easy to eliminate: a medical doctor who had been released from service in the Main Medical Inspection Administration; a former land captain who had not been "sufficiently scrupulous" in handling money; a railroad inspector who, background investigation revealed, had once been an assistant warden in a Moscow prison until he had been fired for incompetence. Others who had no blots on their records but who did not have suitable training or experience were also quickly rejected. One poor fellow who had been trained as an historian at St. Petersburg University and was currently an assistant secretary in the Kurland Province Midwifery Administration was turned down before he had a chance to submit further credentials. A provincial-board secretary who came highly recommended by Vologda's governor was rejected because he lacked the requisite education.[104]

Some candidates with excellent credentials and experience seem to have been turned down only because of their age. Captain Leonid Liudovigovich Lemmerman, a military veteran, ex-peace arbitrator, and a county police captain, applied for an inspector's post in December 1908. The provincial prison inspector from Ekaterinoslav forwarded Lemmerman's application with a glowing recommendation. Lemmerman was "an excellent, knowledgeable worker" and a "brave man." He wanted to change jobs so that he could move to a provincial capital, where he could educate his son and find medical care for his sick wife. The GTU was impressed enough to write the Ekaterinoslav governor, who also supplied an excellent reference, adding that he "would be sorry to lose such a good worker." After some consideration the GTU rejected Lemmerman's application; it offered only its standard reply that there were no openings. The only apparent negative information in all of Lemmerman's service record was his birth date, 1882, which was underlined in red by the GTU evaluators.[105]

Evgenii Ivanovich Troianovskii came recommended just as highly. Former Kaluga Governor and Senator A. A. Ofrosimov wrote to GTU Director S. S. Khrulev in April 1909 to support the candidacy of Troianovskii, who had been "diligent, efficient and tireless" as police chief in Kaluga. He enclosed a copy of the 1905 annual report of Kaluga's Workhouse Aid Society, of which he and Troianovskii had both been members, to emphasize Troianovskii's experience in prison affairs. Troianovskii had also been a director of the Kaluga POoT Committee and had helped to organize prisoner labor. The only notations made by the GTU on the forty-three sheets of his credentials were a blue-penciled underlining of his birth date, 1854, and a marginal note beside it, "55 years old!" Khrulev responded to the senator three weeks after he had written. Out of respect for Ofrosimov and his excellent recommendation, he was willing to offer Troianovskii a post as inspector;

> however, I must tell [you] that the number of candidates for posts in provincial prison inspectorates is quite large right now, and among them are people who have long been on the candidate list and have the complete right to hold the indicated posts both by education and by the posts they now hold; some of them have already been formally promised appointment to the next vacancies.

Khrulev "did not want to hide" from Ofrosimov that "despite his wish" he could not offer Troianovskii a position "for quite a while." Another former governor of Kaluga, A. Bulygin, and N. D. Golitsyn also wrote for Troianovskii, but the GTU never did offer him a job.[106]

Candidates for wardens' positions were also numerous and well qualified by

1909. Many more were refused than were hired. Twenty years earlier the GTU had been glad to find officers with good records who wished to retire early from the military and enter prison service, but by 1909 this was not always so. When Captain K. I. Tsakoni applied to be warden of the Ekaterinburg prison, the governor sent a strong letter of support to the GTU. He also sent a petition to the emperor and a copy of that to the GTU. Still, the GTU responded that it would not hire "an inexperienced man for such a responsible position."[107] They had more than enough better candidates.

As the number of qualified candidates increased, this became increasingly true for more distant, less desirable appointments and, to a lesser extent, for lower-ranking wardens and assistants in smaller prisons, whose appointment was not legally controlled by the GTU. Governors had the authority to appoint prison personnel in the lower seven ranks of the "table of ranks." Sometimes they hired assistant wardens, and even wardens, without consulting the GTU, but over time this practice decreased. By 1909 most governors consulted the administration or, where they were established, the provincial prison inspectorates when they needed to fill a vacancy. The GTU had developed lists of superior candidates, whom it would recommend. When, for example, the ataman of the Don Cossacks wrote late in 1909 to ask the GTU to appoint a county prison warden, it supplied him with several names but noted it could not always do this for "lower ranks." As far as the fifth and sixth ranks were concerned, the GTU had a "huge list." Wardens of larger prisons and more modern prisons were appointed at these higher ranks.[108]

In some cases, when governors acted without consulting the GTU to appoint an unsuitable warden, the GTU would later act to correct the "mistake." In 1909, for example, the Kovno governor hired an assistant warden for the Kovno provincial prison while the provincial prison inspector was absent in St. Petersburg. He appointed him without checking up on him, he later told the inspector, "because he had received his education in the Corps of Pages and has an influential relative." The inspector discovered that the new assistant warden had been released from both military and civilian service because of financial "irregularities" and soon found a similar problem in Kovno.[109]

It would appear that with each passing year applications became more numerous and qualifications higher. Many men with excellent records and recommendations failed to receive the appointments they desired. A land captain with thirteen years of experience and the highest recommendations from the Land Office and the St. Petersburg governor applied in 1912 to be made a provincial inspector. He had applied, the governor wrote, because "the salary he receives as a land captain, for hard responsible work demanding constant effort and frequent traveling . . . does not supply him with even a decent existence." The most the GTU could offer him, however, was an assistant inspector's job, which paid little more than he had been making.[110] An army colonel with high recommendations from his superiors applied for an inspector's job in 1912. The GTU told him the job was "large and complex" and took a while to master. He would need to spend some time "under the guidance of an experienced specialist, namely a provincial prison inspector." He was offered an assistant inspector's slot—and he accepted.[111] Others hired that year as assistant inspectors had wide experience, usually including previous experience in prison affairs, and excellent service records.[112]

The search for wardens was made more systematic in 1912. On 1 September the GTU sent a confidential circular to all provincial inspectors asking their help in compiling "a list of candidates for warden sixth class." They hoped "to encourage excellent service . . . in the lower ranks" by promoting the GTU assistant wardens and wardens of lower rank to more responsible positions. It sent its inspectors forms to fill out on any "fully worthy candidates," forms with spaces for all basic personal information and for a short history of service. At the bottom was a space for "detailed comments on service and moral qualities."[113] The inspectors' replies did help to stimulate promotion from within, and consequently the number of other applicants who were rejected rose rapidly.[114]

World War I complicated many aspects of Russian life. Huge conscriptions made it harder to find good workers in many fields, but the GTU continued to have many more applicants than openings and to find qualified men. Men with long years of experience as land captains, police, procurators, and court investigators, among others, were told that because they had no experience in prison administration, they could be offered at best assistant warden or assistant inspector positions. GTU Director P. K. Gran' continued, as his predecessors had, to parry applications with influential supporters. V. A. Teliakovskii, director of the imperial theaters of St. Petersburg, wrote to MIu I. G. Shcheglovitov to support the candidacy of his relative N. N. Teliakovskii in 1914. The candidate had been a land captain for eighteen years and had excellent references from the Land Office and the governor of Iaroslavl province. The GTU entered his name on the list of candidates for assistant inspector in June, but in December he received a letter that it would not be able to offer him a position "before the end of the war." A court investigator from Saratov, whose father had served with Gran', reminded him of that when he applied to be an assistant inspector. Gran' did not reply personally. His assistants warned the applicant when they put him on the candidates' list that there were no openings and none were expected in the near future. They added that a special trip to St. Petersburg "would not be necessary."[115]

By the time of World War I and the February Revolution, the staff of the GTU, both in St. Petersburg and in the provinces, had become significantly professionalized. Like men in many other professions, they looked more to the ideals and rules of their profession for guidance and identity than to anachronistic values associated with the autocracy. When Nicholas II abdicated in March 1917, men of the GTU overwhelmingly welcomed his fall and what seemed to be the dawn of a new "liberal" era.[116]

Inspectorates

The Zubov Committee had insisted in 1875 that the reformed administration of Russian prisons include local organs of administration. These were to be called provincial prison inspectorates and, according to a majority of the committee, would operate as a department of provincial boards. The suggestion immediately sparked hot debate about the structure, administrative placement, and cost of the inspectorates. A minority within the committee urged that it be allowed to operate independently of the provincial boards, some to remove it from MVD influence, others to put it more directly under the governors. The MF from the first wanted to know how much any of these variations might cost. Too much, it turned out. The Grot Commission, reacting to the MF's objections, limited its discussions to central administration, temporarily making moot all of that debate, but actually only postponing it.

From the beginning the GTU's central administration wanted to establish some sort of local organ that might keep it informed of conditions in the provinces and help to implement the reforms and other improvements devised in St. Petersburg. In the West, as the Russian reformers perceived it, prison reform had begun at the bottom, with the reform of individual prisons and their staffs through experimentation by inspired individual wardens. Central administration came later and remained secondary.

> But such an approach to prison reform in the West is explained by the relatively small number of places of imprisonment, the insignificance of distances and ease of communication, and the always sufficient contingent of people qualified for and ready to dedicate themselves to prison service. These conditions are completely absent here.[117]

Russia could not rely on inspired individuals in isolated, distant places. Russia needed to gather together its inspired men to organize a general, uniform reform and then send them out to teach the many others. They would have to be tied to the center so they would not lose the source of their inspiration, but they would need to remain in the provinces so they could continuously exhort, uplift, and inspire the locals. GTU officials believed that if it were only to issue orders and circulars to the provinces and did not check regularly to see that they were obeyed, they would be largely ignored. Establishment of the inspectorates was central to its effort to implement reform. As N. F. Luchinskii put it in his semi-official history of the GTU, "real reform" of the system did not begin until the inspectorate system was established.[118]

As with other reforms, establishment of the inspectorate system was delayed by the crises of financing and overcrowding and by political maneuvering. Executive-level discussion of the problem did not begin until 1882, when M. S. Kakhanov, chairman of the Special Commission for the Compilation of Projects of Local Administration, wrote to the MVD for information about administration at the local level of various MVD departments. The MVD informed Galkin-Vraskii, who responded to Kakhanov on 24 November.[119] He explained that the question of local prison administration had been discussed by several commissions but had been left undecided when the GTU was established. Since then it had continually concerned the GTU, "for the separation of powers and responsibilities among many offices for running prisons has been a problem."

Galkin-Vraskii rehearsed the standard complaint about too many chiefs in local prison administration. The POoT had many responsibilities for various types of prisons, ranging from housekeeping concerns (provisioning, clothing, bedding), through administrative obligations (proper separation of categories of prisoners, maintenance of prison buildings, the appointment of wardens and guards), to philanthropic duties (to reform "prisoners' morality"). At the same time, provincial boards had unclear and overlapping responsibility for policing and supplying prisons. Within provincial boards there were also special organizations *(popechitel'stva)* responsible for similar functions in correctional arrest units. On paper these groups were united in the office of the governor, but in reality neither they nor the governors had the time to concentrate on prison affairs or the training to be "specialists in all of the fine points of prison administration." None carried out its work particularly enthusiastically or effectively, and wardens were hamstrung by their dependence on these many separate offices. The GTU was certain that "until some provincial office, which can be part of the provincial administration and under the governor, unites all of the duties spread among the offices described above, all of the GTU's efforts to improve prisons will meet with unavoidable difficulties."[120]

The GTU wanted to do away with prisons' reliance on volunteers and amateurs. Penology had become something of a science and was becoming a profession. Prisons could no longer be properly administered by men who joined the POoT "mostly in hope of being decorated" and by clerks who were arbitrarily assigned to prison affairs in provincial boards:

> It is necessary to replace today's many-headed and powerless [system of administration] with one that is firm, independent, and responsible . . . , removing from direct administration all of those elements whose activities are determined not by service responsibilities but by voluntary or obligatory labor, springing from either a feeling of charity or the expectations of medals.[121]

The GTU's solution was to create prison inspectorates that would inherit all of the duties and the staff of provincial boards connected with prison affairs. The inspectors would still meet with the provincial boards when a collegial decision was required but would otherwise work independently of them. They would be directly subordinate to the governors. Each inspector would also be made an obligatory member and chief clerk *(deloproizvoditel')* of the provincial POoT and would direct all administrative duties belonging to it. To help him he would need an assistant (just as the provincial medical inspector, surveyor, and architect had assistants) and a chancellery, which would include a chief clerk, his assistant, and junior clerks. Altogether, each inspectorate would cost between 4,600 and 5,500 rubles a year, which, Galkin-Vraskii hastened to add, could be found by decreasing the budget of each provincial board according to the duties and staff removed from it and assumed by the inspectorate.[122]

The GTU had already once sent a circular to the governors asking for information on the amount of money spent on personnel working on prison affairs, but the responses had been somewhat ambiguous. Because the various councilors and clerks involved in prison work also handled other functions, it was "impossible to closely estimate" how much money could be released from the boards' budgets. It seemed that at least a chief clerk, an assistant, and a junior clerk could be freed from each board. Galkin-Vraskii hoped that one councilor might also be freed and that experienced people and their salaries could be transferred into the new inspectorates. If some additional money were needed, the GTU would ask the MF.[123]

The Kakhanov Commission apparently did not discuss local prison administration before it disbanded in 1883, but the Council on Prison Affairs took up the discussion. In 1884 Kakhanov appeared before the council to offer expert advice, and the result was a decision to send another circular to the governors. The GTU circular, dated 6 July 1884, asked the governors to explain as precisely as they could what prison affairs were handled by how many clerks in provincial boards. The GTU wanted to determine what percentage of the paperwork and man-hours of the boards' work was devoted to prisons in order to document its claim to that percentage of the boards' budgets and manpower.[124]

The GTU could not have been especially pleased with the replies it received that summer and fall. Some governors welcomed the idea of centralizing prison affairs; others were clearly hostile. In some boards, prison affairs made up a major part of daily work, but in others it was almost insignificant. In a few boards, a councilor and clerk, occupied almost wholly with prison work, could probably be freed for transfer to a new inspectorate, but in most boards councilors could not. In others, governors foresaw difficulty even in releasing a clerk or two. Like the several commissions that had discussed inspectorates, the governors also disagreed about whether they ought to be part of the boards.[125] The only inspectorate the GTU was permitted to establish in 1884 was in the province of St. Petersburg, and this was subordinated directly to the GTU, with no increase of staff or budget.[126]

The GTU drafted a proposal to establish inspectorates in all fifty provinces, which passed through the MVD to the MF and the State Council in 1885. The GTU had been unwilling to significantly reduce the provincial boards' budgets, so the plan carried a hefty price tag. The MF balked at putting up the 220,000–230,000 rubles per year and entered into negotiations with the MVD. The MVD then proposed a compromise: to introduce the reform gradually, beginning with ten provincial inspectorates in the second half of 1886. MF N. K. Bunge agreed that the inspectorates were desirable but asked that the experiment begin with only five provinces. The State Council asked that expenses be cut further by eliminating assistant inspectors.[127]

On the basis of these objections, the GTU wrote a new project in 1887 for five provinces, in which the inspectors would serve directly under governors and would command staffs that varied in size according to the workload anticipated in each province. This was vigorously debated within the GTU and the MVD and was not sent to the State Council until 5 April 1889. By then, MVD D. A. Tolstoi had vetoed Galkin-Vraskii's plan for independent inspectorates and had put them back in the provincial boards. To remove them from "the highest administrative organ in the province" would destroy the purpose of the boards, he contended. MIu N. A. Manasein objected that he thought the inspectorates should be independent of the boards; otherwise he approved the project on 11 March 1889. The MF approved also, but only with the condition that assistant inspectors, who had been put back into the project, serve also as chief clerks, thereby eliminating that position. The State Controller supported the MF's response of 12 June with his response of 14 October, adding that the assistant inspector/chief clerk must be found among the councilors serving in the provincial board. The State Council looked over the project and comments on 11 November and approved them with minor changes to effect further savings in the chancellery. In that form the project became law on 21 March 1890. It established prison inspectorates in Vilna, Kiev, Perm, Saratov, and Kharkov provinces.[128]

Before the GTU was transferred from the Ministry of Internal Affairs to the Ministry of Justice in 1895, inspectorates were established in twenty-five provinces. Then, because of financial and political complications arising from the transfer, no more were established until 1909. Between 1909 and 1914 thirty-five more provincial and regional inspectorates were formed. All of them were made independent of provincial boards after 1896, as the MIu had always preferred.[129]

The new inspectorates experienced various minor start-up difficulties. Usually there was nowhere to house their offices but in the rooms already occupied by the provincial board, which meant that an extra worker or two had to be squeezed into already overcrowded office space. In Kharkov, "because of a lack of room" at the provincial board's offices, part of the inspectorate staff was put up at the governor's house, which was "a considerable distance away." Immediately the GTU began to receive requests for additional funds to rent rooms or expand buildings. No money was available for these extras, however, so the inspectorate's staffs had to do their best until their governors could find additional space for them.[130]

Once they were established, the inspectorates quickly met the GTU's hopes for them. The inspectors immediately began tours of the prisons in their provinces, discovered shortcomings, and ordered them corrected before the next inspection. In Saratov, for example, the inspector agreed informally with the governor that he would visit any prison whenever he chose rather than ask for permission on each occasion, as the GTU had foreseen. He visited the correctional arrest unit and the prison in the city of Saratov almost weekly and at "various times of day and night," without warning. The nine county prisons, fifteen arrest facilities, and the single juvenile shelter, which were spread throughout the province, he visited an average of three times a year.[131] When the inspector in Voronezh had completed his prison inspections, he sent wardens letters of commendation or warning. He informed one warden "that in case of repetition of the disorder noticed during the inspection" he would be fired. Others were warned about faulty record keeping, improper handling of food supplies, and the organization of prison labor.[132] The same pattern was followed wherever inspectorates were established. The GTU received more comprehensive reports on a regular basis on all of the facilities under its control. On the basis of these reports and theoretical considerations that guided decisions in St. Petersburg, the

GTU could issue orders to improve the prison system and with increasing confidence expect that they would be carried out.

Materials from the only regional archive I have been able to examine strongly support this conclusion. One of the first five prison inspectors was assigned to Perm. Not only did Perm have a regular complement of county prisons, city lockups, and a large central prison, it also had a large transfer prison to handle exiles as they were transported from European Russia to points east. The new prison inspector seems to have made rapid improvements in the administration of all of these.

Record keeping improved considerably. After 1890 the GTU knew precisely how many prisoners were kept in or passed through Perm's prisons. It was kept informed of the condition of the prisons, the cost of recommended repairs, the health of the prisoners, the cost of their maintenance, and the income they earned from internal and external labor. The cost of maintaining the prisons and the prisoners dropped, apparently as the inspector discovered and ended corrupt billing and purchasing. The amount of labor accomplished by prisoners within the prisons, for the city of Perm and for local businesses, increased considerably, as did the money returned to the prisons and the prisoners.[133]

Perhaps most interesting and impressive are the records of the inspector's inquiries into prisoners' complaints against administrators. I do not know what the procedure was before the establishment of the inspectorate, and it is impossible to know what abuses and complaints were left uninvestigated, but it seems clear that the inspector took seriously any complaints made by prisoners, even those of a fairly petty nature. Prisoners complained that clothing, money, writing paper and postage stamps, and other articles taken from them upon sentencing were not returned when they were released. They complained that money they had earned on work details had not been paid to them. Some complained of mistreatment in prison: poor food, unfairly assessed fines, and beatings by guards and other prisoners. In two cases that seemed particularly petty, one prisoner complained that a deck of cards had been stolen from him, and another that a guard had sworn at him. All of these charges were investigated, often over several months. Lengthy correspondence involved the prisoners, the administrators against whom the complaints were lodged, witnesses, local police who were asked to get involved, and the inspector's office. In the majority of cases the prisoners' complaints were not satisfied, but in many others they were. Money was returned; administrators were reprimanded and, in at least one case, fired. It seems clear from the growing number of complaints that prisoners knew they had rights and a new champion to protect them and that prison administrators had been put on notice to run their facilities by the book.[134]

When MVD I. N. Durnovo wrote to the State Council on 19 February 1894 to ask that five new inspectorates be opened, he praised the experience of the first ten inspectorates, which had been operating for three or four years by then. Provinces with inspectorates, he said, had a much better record than those without in holding down the cost of construction, in carrying out repairs more cheaply, and, apparently, in hiring superior lower-level personnel. They survived the crisis years of 1891 and 1892, when a severe famine caused widespread suffering in Russia, much better than did other provinces, by organizing the wholesale purchase of foodstuffs and by enforcing special measures of hygiene and health care. The mortality rate in Russian prisons was lower than in the population as a whole in most of the provinces with inspectorates. Similar economies were realized in purchasing shoes, clothing, and bedding for prisoners. The inspectors had put an end to sweetheart deals between POoT committeemen and suppliers it seemed. In the five inspectorates opened in 1890, the cost of such supplies quickly fell by 47 percent; in the five established the following year, prices dropped by 34 percent. Similarly, the earned income from prisoner labor increased rapidly in these provinces.[135] Members of the Tagantsev Commission, meeting in 1895–1896 to discuss the transfer of the GTU to the MIu, agreed that the inspectorates had been very successful and ought, in one form or another, to be introduced into the rest of the provinces.[136] M. M. Isaev, a critic of the GTU and later a leading Soviet criminologist, criticized other aspects of the GTU's performance but had only high praise for the inspectorate system.[137]

TRANSFER TO THE MINISTRY OF JUSTICE

Several major political events significantly disrupted the operation of the GTU between its establishment in 1879 and its demise in November 1917. The revolutionary terrorism of 1878–1881 and the autocracy's response to it affected the very creation of the GTU and probably its administrative attachment to the MVD. The displacement of M. N. Galkin-Vraskii and the appointment of K. K. Grot to his extraordinary position at the head of prison affairs were part of the turmoil of those years. After order was restored by Alexander III, who directed a firm policy of repression against the terrorists after his father's assassination in 1881, the GTU was able to sail a relatively smooth course until 1894. Early in the reign of Nicholas II another major change once again required the GTU's executives to pay more attention to high-level politics and less to prison reform. In 1895 the GTU was transferred from the MVD to the MIu.

Precisely why the transfer occurred when it did and why the MVD seems to have acquiesced at the time and resisted so vigorously after the fact will probably remain a mystery. The participants in the events of 1895–1896 did not leave diaries or memoirs that explain the transfer, and the official documents, though apparently clear, leave unsaid much that might have contributed to an understanding of the process. The official explanation closely resembles the arguments used by Zubov when he unsuccessfully recommended attaching the GTU to the MIu twenty years earlier. The MIu and MVD "agreed" in their joint "most humble report," which Nicholas II signed into law on 13 December 1895, that imprisonment had become the "primary weapon in the struggle against crime." Prisons, said the report, were used in every step of the modern process of criminal justice: for preliminary arrest to allow the procuracy to properly investigate criminal acts and the courts to provide just trials of accused persons, and then to carry out punishments assigned by the courts. In them was placed the hope that convicts could be reformed and discharged "to honorable and respectable lives." Because of the close connection between the work of courts and prisons and because the modern conception of justice was so closely linked with corrections, it was thought best to have one ministry administer both courts and prisons. Prison administration, the report concluded, was drawn "by its very essence to the interests of criminal justice." On these points the report cited the conclusions of international congresses as if they supplied irrefutable proof of the report's assertions.[138]

Nothing in the documents explains why the set of arguments that had failed to win the GTU for the Ministry of Justice in the 1870s should have succeeded in the 1890s. The transfer seems to have occurred when it did for two main reasons. In 1878–1879, when the Grot Commission was completing its work, the tsarist government was under heavy attack by terroristic revolutionaries. It flirted with the idea of placating liberals, and maybe some radicals, with political reforms (or by displaying a willingness to discuss reforms) but decided instead, after Alexander II was assassinated, to crush rebellion by force. The court system and proponents of legal order were unpopular with those who wished to preserve the autocracy and order by whatever means necessary, and the Ministry of Justice lost out in 1879. Sixteen years later, however, Russia had enjoyed a long period of peace, domestic tranquillity, and prosperity. In such times people tend to be more generous in their assessment of human nature and in their support of benevolent programs such as corrections. This may have helped to create the atmosphere in which the transfer occurred.

Probably more important were personnel changes at the top of the government. The transfer does not seem to have been considered under Alexander III, who for most of his reign had as MVDs the strong, conservative D. A. Tolstoi and the compliant, conservative I. N. Durnovo. They probably would not have countenanced the change had it been suggested. Nicholas II inherited a relatively new but strong MIu in N. V. Murav'ev, and in 1895, for reasons that are not clear, he replaced Durnovo with the weaker I. L. Goremykin. When Nicholas succeeded his father on 20 October 1894, he was young, not eager to be emperor, and not particularly strong willed or decisive.[139] His training for the position was poor, and it is quite possible that he was not certain what direction to take. His intentions were so unclear that V. A. Maklakov and P. N. Miliukov thought the country could be on the verge of new reforms.[140] That Nicholas permitted or encouraged the transfer, which appears on the surface to be part of the "liberal" program and was strongly supported by proponents of legal order, is less surprising early in his reign than it would have been later on.

N. V. Murav'ev had become MIu on 1 January 1894. A graduate of the law faculty of Moscow University when it was led by liberals such as S. A. Muromtsev, Murav'ev had been both a procurator and a professor of law before gaining wider notice as the prosecutor of Alexander II's assassins. According to his contemporaries—even those, like A. F. Koni, who did not like him—he was a bright and capable man.[141] They also agree that Murav'ev underwent a personal change at about the time he became MIu. Having been, in V. I. Gurko's words, "a liberal defender of the courts and justice," as minister he became much more conservative. S. Iu. Vitte, who considered Murav'ev an "outstanding minister," regretted that during his tenure he "somewhat lowered the flag of independence of justice." Samuel Kucherov subscribed to a similar view.[142] Koni lumped him with the archconservative procurator of the Holy Synod K. P. Pobedonostsev and despised him for his failure to defend the independence of the courts. Two recent Soviet historians have also linked him with the influential conservative journalist M. N. Katkov and charged him with consciously planning "judicial counter-reforms."[143]

What caused Murav'ev to modify his philosophy, and did it have anything to do with the transfer of the GTU to his ministry? Kucherov dated the change to Murav'ev's first year in office, while Alexander III was still alive.[144] Gurko, Vitte, and, according to Vitte, V. K. Pleve would put it a little later. They believed that the change was opportunistic and associated with Murav'ev's desire while MIu to become Nicholas II's MVD.[145] Murav'ev apparently tried to appear as he thought Nicholas would expect or want an MVD to be. According to Koni, in the first months of Nicholas's reign Murav'ev was careful not to be too strongly identified with any policy, but when he thought he knew which way the wind blew, "in the spring of 1895 he removed his mask and acted sincerely the defender of traditions and the legal views of the tsar-peacemaker. . . . [He] took upon himself the role of Paladin of the great reforms of Alexander II."[146] Murav'ev failed to be appointed MVD and was apparently disappointed, but he obviously did not displease Nicholas. He remained his MIu until 1905.

It is possible that Murav'ev overplayed his hand. Vitte recalls that Nicholas considered for the post both Assistant MVD D. S. Sipiagin and V. K. Pleve, who had also served as assistant MVD, but he rejected both of them on Vitte's and Pobedonostsev's advice. Pobedonostsev told Nicholas that Pleve was a "scoundrel," and Vitte called him a "chameleon." But whereas Pobedonostsev thought Sipiagin a "fool," Vitte told Nicholas that Sipiagin was experienced in provincial affairs from his service as a vice governor and governor and was a man of "good common sense." His weakness was that his convictions were "narrow," belonging to the camp of the gentry and the autocracy! Pobedonostsev recommended Vitte for the position, but he apparently did not want it.[147] On 15 October 1895 Nicholas appointed I. L. Goremykin, who had been an assistant MVD and was Murav'ev's assistant MIu. According to Gurko, when he was appointed, Goremykin was considered a "liberal . . . even a disciple, platonic of course, of [L. N.] Tolstoi's gospel." Vitte agrees that Goremykin had "liberal tendencies" and had to be careful later to follow a "rather reactionary policy" in order to safeguard his career.[148]

If this résumé is correct, after October both of the powerful ministries involved in the transfer were headed by men of "liberal tendencies" who, for the sake of their careers, were careful not to appear so liberal as to displease the emperor. From a philosophical standpoint, both might be expected to prefer having the GTU in the MIu, or at least to have no strong objection to the move. The interests and personalities of the two ministers may also help to explain the transfer. Murav'ev had long been interested in prison affairs. He had spoken out for prison reform at least as early as 1878, when he was at Moscow University, and he continued to do so.[149] Since December 1882 he had served on the MVD's Council on Prison Affairs. Moreover, he was a highly energetic man who liked to take on additional responsibilities.[150] Goremykin, on the other hand, seems never to have had a personal interest in prisons and tended to avoid issues that might cause him problems. According to Gurko, his outstanding characteristic, "which became more pronounced as the years went by, was an imperturbable calm which approached indifference. . . . Goremykin's course of action was also influenced by the fact that he was incurably lazy."[151]

If Murav'ev already had Nicholas's support for the transfer of the GTU when Goremykin became MVD—and this seems to have been the case—Goremykin would have been slow to raise objections. It is clear that the transfer project was produced in Murav'ev's ministry before or immediately after Goremykin's appointment and was sent to the MVD only perfunctorily for approval. Just a month after Goremykin had been appointed, Murav'ev sent him the completed "joint" "most humble report" and the personal imperial *ukaz* to the Senate that would become the law of 13 December 1895. On 8 December, less than two weeks after first inviting his comments—an extraordinarily short time in Russian bureaucratic practice—he sent Goremykin the same report, with the request that he sign it before the thirteenth, when Murav'ev was scheduled to present it to the emperor.[152]

The MVD had powerful institutional interests in the GTU's operations, however, and soon made itself felt. When the GTU was established in 1879, it was the product of years of debate, wrangling, and compromise. Many details of its operation had been worked out slowly in the Department of Executive Police within the MVD from which it had grown, and others were appended by the series of prison-reform commissions over more than a decade. Many of its responsibilities had been thrust upon it by other departments and ministries, which were often more than willing to part with them. The transfer of the GTU to the MIu, on the contrary, was more of a coup, accomplished suddenly and, it would seem, hastily. By the law of 13 December 1895, almost all of the duties and powers of the MVD pertaining to the operations of the GTU passed with the GTU to the MIu. In theory, so should the budget lines and personnel, but those and other "details" had not been worked out beforehand. They became the source of a great deal of friction.

To work out the details—particularly of the local administration of prisons, then centered in the MVD-dominated provincial boards—Murav'ev organized a Special Commission for Compiling Legislative Proposals on the Organization of the Prison Administration in the Ministry of Justice, which was authorized by imperial permission on 20 December, 1895.[153] He chose as chairman Senator N. S. Tagantsev, an erudite and much-published criminalist then serving in the Criminal Cassational Department of the Senate, who, according to Koni, was Murav'ev's "own man" in the Senate.[154] Before inviting other ministries and departments to appoint representatives, he appointed numerous MIu department heads and officials and three top officials of the GTU, including Director Galkin-Vraskii, who were now, of course, also MIu staff. On 23 December he invited participation by representatives of the MVD, the MF, and the State Chancellery.[155] Interestingly, one of the two MVD representatives, acting Tobolsk Governor N. M. Bogdanovich, became the GTU's next director, after Galkin-Vraskii resigned on 28 February 1896.

Tagantsev began his commission's first meeting on 15 January 1896 with a speech on the history of prison administration in Russia, the point of it being that prison administration properly belonged in the MIu. After explaining the commission's tasks, he invited comments.[156] V. N. Kokovtsov, who for many years had worked in the GTU but was now representing the State Chancellery, immediately took the floor to ask the current cost of various operations and to warn that many of the changes the commission would consider might be unacceptably costly. The MF's representative, S. F. Veber, seconded Kokovtsov's warnings.[157] Their comments and questions set the tone for much of the commission's work.

At fifteen meetings that stretched over the whole of 1896, the Tagantsev Commission thoroughly reviewed the functions of officials and organizations involved in prison administration and their relationships to one another and to other government offices. The commission prepared projects that revised relationships at the top, abolishing, for example, the MVD's Council on Prison Affairs and transferring its functions to the MIu's *Konsultatsiia*. But it spent the bulk of its time, as had several of the commissions in the 1870s, debating again the composition, cost, and placement of the provincial inspectorates.

When the earlier commissions had met, they were primarily concerned with deciding whether provincial inspectorates should be directly subordinate to governors or made part of provincial boards. Now the question became one of how to reorganize inspectorates in order to bring them under MIu control. As always, both effectiveness and cost were important considerations. Two commission members recommended that the procuracy could handle the inspectorates' duties. Even if the procuracy staff had to be increased, it would cost less than separate inspectorates would.[158] D. A. Dril', the MIu's legal counsel, believed that no special organs were needed. He would give greater responsibility to individual prison wardens and their staffs and would have the staffs of the largest central prisons provide guidance, assistance, and coordination—particularly in matters of economy and provisioning—to smaller prisons in their province or region. In his plan the procuracy would receive some additional powers, and local public institutions would also participate in "special supervisory committees."[159] As Russia's most prominent criminologist of the anthropological (Lombrosian) school, Dril' believed strongly in the participation of "social forces" in matters concerning crime. He was himself active in the *patronat* movement and in volunteer philanthropical organizations that aided juvenile delinquents.

Neither of these opinions received serious attention. They were apparently put forward at the commission's second meeting on 23 January and were quickly rejected. At the third meeting, a week later, the overwhelming majority (twelve of fifteen commissioners) agreed that, although the procuracy was the most suitable of the MIu's offices, "to assign the procuracy administration of the prison system is decisively impossible." Not only was it already overburdened, it was not experienced in prison affairs, which were "complex" and required "specialists" and "undivided attention." Being legalists, the commissioners were also concerned that having an office that helped to prosecute criminal acts and carry out the courts' sentences would constitute a conflict of interest. They also raised again the sad fact, or opinion, that everything was more difficult in Russia because of the incompetence and untrustworthiness of the people. The majority concluded that inspectorates must be retained "as special organs of local administration."[160] They also agreed to cut governors out of the chain of command, making the inspectorates more directly subordinate to the MIu through the GTU.[161]

The next question, which occupied most of the rest of the meetings, concerned the number and size of the inspectorates. The majority preferred to have an inspectorate in each province. Prison inspection "could not be carried out successfully by written, bureaucratic relations," they insisted, "but required personal executive action." Increasing the area covered by an inspectorate would necessarily reduce the inspectors' "quality of performance." Moreover, the provincial system had grown out of and fit into the usual system of tsarist administration. A regional system would require a wholesale reorganization and would probably turn out to be temporary, as finances made a provincial system possible and as a growing workload made it necessary. They acknowledged that a provincial system would be much more expensive, but the majority believed that "in such an important large-scale reform" financial considerations must not be primary.[162]

Kokovtsov and Veber insisted nonetheless that finances be considered. Only twenty-four provinces in addition to St. Petersburg had inspectorates before 1895, and the GTU hoped to spread the institution throughout the empire. But removing the existing inspectorates from the provincial councils already entailed substantial new expenses. At a meeting on 2 April 1896, four members submitted separate reports with detailed estimates for a variety of inspectorate systems. The most detailed reports came from Kokovtsov and Bogdanovich, whose plans were remarkably similar. Bogdanovich, who had replaced Galkin-Vraskii as GTU director on 8 March 1896, may have been presenting the GTU's own compromise. Both allowed that some provinces were large and populous enough to warrant their own inspectorates. Other provinces they incorporated into existing inspectorates or combined in a modified regional system. Kokovtsov worked out appropriate staffs for each combination; Bogdanovich drew up three tables of organization to suit units of different sizes.[163]

The plan that was finally adopted by the commission resembled these systems. Prison inspectors were to be called "chief of provincial [or regional *(oblast')*, as appropriate] prison administration." With his staff, the "chief" carried the burden of executive responsibility in his territory. In each area there would also be established a "board *[prisutstvie]* of prison affairs," headed by the chairman of the local *okrug* court and including the vice governor, procurator, and two POoT directors.[164] In discussion that followed the commission's work, the GTU resisted the inclusion of POoT directors, tried to limit the powers of the procurator, and in general tried to protect the autonomy of its inspectors and their direct association with the MIu.[165]

On 3 December 1896, almost a year after the GTU was made part of the MIu, the Tagantsev Commission wound up its work and soon thereafter submitted its several hundred pages of reports.[166] After reworking these materials in the GTU, on 9 October 1897 the MIu sent a project of approximately sixty pages to the necessary ministries and departments for study and comment.[167] This became the focus of further interministerial wrangling that would delay for another five years projects the GTU hoped to carry out. Galkin-Vraskii and others who found fault with the project were given a chance to respond to it,[168] but the most damaging reactions came, as might be expected, from the MVD and the MF.

MVD Goremykin began the protracted process of his response with a circular letter to Russia's governors on 26 December 1897, soliciting their reaction to the project as a whole and asking specifically that they determine how much money had been spent by the MVD's provincial offices on prison affairs.[169] The Tagantsev project had estimated the costs of the GTU and its components to the MVD, which now presumably wanted the governors to return lower estimates. Most of the governors viewed the transfer as a fait accompli and responded directly but laconically to the MVD's request. A few, like Kharkov's governor, defended some of the governors' prerogatives in prison administration but for the most part accepted or welcomed the proposed changes.[170] The Irkutsk governor general applauded the transfer of the GTU to the MIu except for the exile system, in which, he cogently explained, local administrators and the police were more important than the courts.[171]

Most of those who responded at greater length expressed hostility to the project, primarily because it undercut their powers as governors. Moscow, whose response was among the quickest and most negative, believed that "the whole project, without a doubt, has the goal of completely removing governors from prison affairs." The governor feared that the GTU's inspectors would be "paralyzed." Subordinate to the highly centralized GTU, they would be hamstrung; independent of other provincial agencies, they would be isolated. Although the governor was in charge of prison administration in his province, all agencies whose cooperation was needed (the police, medical inspector, architect, POoT directors, controller, and others) were subordinate to him. All of these men would not be subordinate to the GTU. "Where formerly a single word of the governor would suffice, a whole correspondence is required, which often despite the goodwill of both sides cannot be successfully concluded."[172]

On 23 January 1898 MIu Murav'ev and the new GTU director (since 11 November 1896) A. P. Salomon reminded Goremykin that they needed his response as soon as possible. Before the last of the replies came in from the provinces almost a year later, Goremykin replied to the MIu on 30 September, summarizing the governors' misgivings and expressing his unwillingness "to transfer to the budget of the prison department in the [MIu] money now expended under the budget of the Ministry of Internal Affairs on the needs of local prison administration." A later report to the MF, on 20 May 1899, made clear that the MVD meant to transfer none of its budget lines if it could be avoided. It specifically refused to reduce the personnel or budgets of provincial boards, saying that, even with prison affairs removed, those institutions would be heavily burdened.[173] The MIu had already complained to the MF that, "as Your Honor will permit yourself to see," the MVD was avoiding its responsibilities under the law of 13 December 1895. Vitte agreed, and on 10 June 1899 he wrote the MVD that freeing the provincial boards from prison affairs "must lead directly to a reduction of [their] staff . . . and to the offer of freed funds to the Ministry of Justice." Vitte was able to cite an earlier MVD report that had said prison administration was the main, if not exclusive, concern of one councilor in many provincial boards, and it entirely occupied two councilors in large provinces, such as Moscow. He suggested that at least one-third of the funds expended on provincial boards could be released to the MIu.[174]

A revised MIu project of 24 December 1899 made some concessions to the governors' complaints,[175] but it did not loosen the MVD's purse strings. D. S. Sipiagin, who had become acting MVD on 20 October 1899 and MVD early in 1900, responded to this project on 4 March 1901. He agreed in principle that money freed by the transfer process should be given to the MIu but insisted that none had been freed. He claimed that, despite the transfer of some responsibilities, the bulk of work in prison affairs that had been in the provincial boards remained there and that, moreover, the law of 12 June 1900, which largely abolished criminal exile, made more work for the police and the boards. Neither argument has much merit, but Sipiagin concluded, "Like the previous minister of internal affairs, I cannot allow the transfer of any part of the credits allocated now for the business of the provincial boards."[176]

Sipiagin found many other problems with the revised project. In addition to the regional inspectorates recommended in the original project, the MIu now also offered to establish simplified inspectorates, to be run by procurators in less populous areas. The compromises were designed to produce economies and make the inspectorate system financially palatable, but Sipiagin rejected both as insufficient to their task. Rehashing objections that had been raised to those plans in the Tagantsev Commission, he asserted that only provincial inspectorates could handle the workload. But, he took the opportunity to remind the MF, according to the law of 13 December 1895, the transfer was not to require new expenditures from the treasury. Sipiagin also demanded that all powers previously held by the governors in prison affairs be restored to them.[177]

The MVD's response must have caused hair pulling and teeth gnashing at the MIu. Not only had Sipiagin refused to relinquish the money that had long been due the MIu, but he disapproved their plans to save money, approved the parts of the project that would cost more, and reminded the MF that the law enjoined them not to spend additional sums. This may have been a first salvo in an MVD counteroffensive to regain the GTU. Sipiagin explained in detail his doubt that the MIu's projects conformed to the "imperial will" as expressed in the 1895 law. The aims of that law were to unify the work of courts and prisons, both at the center and at the local level; to improve prisons and their administration; to reduce the cost of administration; and to relieve the MVD of part of its heavy burden. Concerning the first point, Sipiagin showed that judicial personnel were not directly involved in prison affairs and that prison administrators were not active in the court's work; nor did he think they should be. On the second point he suggested that neither prisons nor administration were likely to be improved by the new arrangements: "I cannot foresee that the Main Prison Administration and its organs could act more beneficially in the future than they do now, and on the contrary fear that its activities will meet with many problems." Disingenuously, he added that their greatest problem would be lack of money. As to reducing expenses, Sipiagin repeated his disapproval of the MIu's plans to cut costs, saying that they would harm prison administration, and concluded that total costs would have to rise. Having everywhere else emphasized the complexity and scope of prison administration, his conclusion comes somewhat as a surprise. On the final point he asserted that the transfer did not significantly reduce the MVD's burden. On the contrary, it constituted a responsibility that the MIu could not bear without doing harm to the procuracy and/or the courts. He recommended that the project be entirely rewritten "along different principles."[178]

What became of the MVD's objections is difficult to say. The GTU remained in the MIu until the end of the tsarist regime, and when new inspectorates were finally established in 1909, they were organized according to the GTU's preference for independent, provincial inspectorates. The major result of the MVD's resistance was a long delay in the GTU's plans for improvements and reform. Shortly before his retirement on 29 June 1900, GTU Director Salomon reported that numerous projects to introduce uniform methods of management, reporting, and accounting had been canceled or stalled because they were based on the spread of the inspectorate system. Because of the interministerial dispute,

> an indefinite, transitional situation has arisen for the prison administration. In twenty-four provinces, provincial prison inspectorates are established. In all other regions the former order of prison administration remains. The Ministry of Justice must act in these localities through organs outside its control.[179]

Although many new expenses were added to the GTU's responsibilities, little new money came its way.[180] As a consequence the building program, along with many reforms, suffered from severe shortages and long delays.

FURTHER EFFORTS

AT REFORM

AND THE

DENOUEMENT

THE CONTINUING STRUGGLE WITH THE POoT

After the Prison Aid Society was made part of the MVD in 1841, prison-aid committees seemed to lose what little remained of their original enthusiasm. In the era of the Great Reforms, when corporal punishment was curtailed, and in all of the prison-reform commissions that followed they were assailed as outmoded and useless. V. A. Sollogub, who chaired the first of the commissions, attacked the POoT in his correspondence and in his commission's project. Believing, as he did, that a most important ingredient in successful reforms would have to be enlightened and enthusiastic administrators, he deplored the dampening of the POoT's early volunteerism by the government's interference. "All that remains," he wrote in 1866, "is superficial bureaucratic formality that retards movement toward improvement."[1] Konstantin Karlovich Grot, chairman of the last of the commissions from which the GTU emerged, was himself a highly regarded philanthropist, known particularly for his work with the blind, but he distrusted the volunteer nonspecialists in prison administration:

> We need most of all for prison affairs to stop being an amateur occupation for the volunteers who become directors of prison committees. They have no desire for real, profound philanthropy. People join the Prison Aid Society for ranks and medals and lord it over the prison inspectors and provincial administrators.[2]

Grot believed that prisons could reform criminals, but being up-to-date with modern theory, he saw discipline and labor as the keys to reformation and had little regard either for the do-nothing reputation the POoT enjoyed or for the religious emphasis in the little work they did.

In the late 1870s Russia's jurists, its professors of law, and officials of the new Main Prison Administration agreed that the most effective weapon in the struggle against crime was modern, professionally run prisons. Like Grot, many of them engaged in philanthropy, working with the blind, with juvenile offenders, and with the poor, but they were not philanthropists from the same mold as the founders of the POoT. As practical and learned men, they had little patience with older views of criminality and reformation through penitence. They had seen and studied the prison systems of the West and were eager to build and administer such a system in Russia. The amateurs of the POoT, because they had been given control of important funds and authority in the prisons, now stood in the way of their desire to make prison administration efficient and effective.

But because the prison-aid societies had so many responsibilities and so much authority, the GTU had to work with them. One of the first official contacts was made by the GTU in a disdainful circular on 27 March 1880,[3] which asked that POoT committees submit monthly reports on their finances, as they were supposed to do. Neither the MVD nor the GTU, since its recent establishment, had been receiving the reports, and "judging from available information," the GTU surmised "that prison committees almost everywhere either do not meet or meet only rarely" and that some do not even keep track of their finances let alone report them. No wonder, the circular went on, directors and members "lose all interest in their work." In a confidential letter written about this time, GTU Director Galkin-Vraskii expressed his concern to Archpastor Varlaam, bishop of Vyborg, who was chairman of a committee, that the POoT could not be made to function as it was currently complected.[4] Because most committee directors who were dues-paying volunteers "belong to that class of people who cannot devote much time to public activities," they cannot do the work expected of them. He would like to require that they at least meet regularly, but if they were asked to meet even twice a month, they would find it "a distraction from their own affairs," and many would quit. "The committees, deprived of the dues from these people, would suffer a material loss."

In June the GTU had special forms distributed to the POoT committees for their monthly reports. By October the "flood of paper" coming in from the provinces had become so great that the GTU had to reconsider. They now asked that the committees continue to meet twice a month but report to St. Petersburg only every fourth month.[5] These reports give a revealing look at the state of the POoT committees in the 1880s. Written by the people who would most likely want to put the POoT's activities in the best light, the reports show, instead, that they were in most places inactive and in many others, ineffective and corrupt. In Arkhangelsk province, for example, the county committees rarely met, often because they existed only on paper; where they had members, they had little money with which to operate. The provincial committee, on the other hand, had 11,000 rubles in cash and notes, but it apparently did little with the funds.[6]

An important topic of discussion at a committee meeting in Ekaterinoslav was the need to select directors who were "known for their charity toward prisoners." One such director singled out for praise had donated money for a bell for a prison church,[7] an expenditure that may not have advanced the purposes of modern corrections as the GTU officials understood them. At Blagoveshchensk, in Amur *oblast'*, there was still no POoT committee in 1881. As a matter of fact, the prison had only one warden, "who because of extreme need takes into his prison administration as warders the prisoners themselves." A POoT committee was eventually established there in December 1882.[8] A report from the procurator of the *okrug* court at Izium claimed that the local POoT met only four times in 1882.[9] Reports from Orel and Sevastopol complained of inactivity and of peculation of government funds by committee chairmen.[10]

Reports from some of the larger POoT committees indicate that they may have been run more honestly and relatively effectively. Moscow's and St. Petersburg's committees had by far the most money to work with, and although they held surprisingly large sums in reserve, they did raise and spend thousands of rubles beyond the government's allotments.[11] Among the provinces, Samara and Saratov stand out in the thoroughness of their reports and their apparent concern for fulfilling their responsibilities.[12] Still, they give the impression more of thoughtfulness than of effectiveness. At Saratov, for example, the committee discussed establishing a prison bakery and garden in 1883. Both of these relatively simple projects had been carried out elsewhere and might have been completed at Saratov decades earlier, but a year later they were still not even begun.

The GTU remained antipathetic to the POoT, and as it could, it gradually stripped the society of its functions. In a report to the State Council on 9 March 1883, which asked that the GTU be allowed to assume some of the powers of the POoT, the MVD claimed that the committees had not become more active and continued to fail to carry out their responsibilities.[13] The official history of the GTU's first ten years leveled the same charge.[14] Where the committees were active, particularly in the capital cities, they were permitted to be useful, but elsewhere other departments of the MVD began to take over some of their functions. In most places they were too weak or apathetic to resist. Laws of 15 June 1887 and 21 March 1890 severely curtailed the committees' authority. The latter law, by which the first prison inspectorates were established, ended the subordination of prison wardens to local POoT committees, making them finally, as their title claimed, "chief of the prison."[15] Because of political opposition and, probably more important, because of financial restraints, however, these and other changes came piecemeal and slowly.

The story of the GTU's effort to bring to heel the powerful and well-connected St. Petersburg men's and women's committees of the POoT illustrates some of the problems they encountered. The MVD's report of March 1883 eventually resulted in an imperially confirmed opinion of the State Council, dated 30 May 1884, that gave the GTU direct control of St. Petersburg's prisons, which were meant to be models of modernity.[16] This was six years before the first inspectorates were established in five other provinces and constituted the first experiment in that direction. The difficulties in St. Petersburg may help to explain why inspectorates were not established until 1890. In response to the State Council's opinion, the GTU appointed a special internal committee that produced a "Project Charter of the St. Petersburg Society of Prison *Patronat.*" The *patronat*, which was meant to replace the POoT committees, would be an entirely philanthropical organization with no authority to operate inside prisons. Galkin-Vraskii sent copies of the charter to the heads of the men's and women's committees on 27 April 1885.[17]

The ladies responded quickly, on 25 June, that they did not object to the proposed changes. When the men had still not replied by 23 August, Galkin-Vraskii wrote again to ask for their reaction. On 27 August one of the committee's vice presidents, Sergei, bishop of Vyborg, replied that the matter could not be presented to the committee during the summer months because most of its officers and directors were absent from the city. That must have prompted knowing nods in the GTU's inner sanctum. Sergei promised that the matter would receive the "careful and serious examination" it deserved at the first directors' meeting, on 11 September. On 10 October Vice President G. I. Shleifer wrote Galkin-Vraskii that the directors had studied the project, elected a committee that had worked out emendations and comments to it, and accepted their committee's work at a meeting on 2 October.[18]

The more important product of that meeting was a "special opinion" by committee member G. I. Andreev, who launched a counteroffensive against the GTU's assault. Andreev defended what he called the glorious activities of the St. Petersburg Prison Committee during the sixty-three years of its operation. The POoT, he said, was a "noble," "worthy," and "truly Christian idea." If it had not been as active as it should for the last ten years (this was not a man in a hurry!), that could be explained by unfortunate, but temporary, circumstances, some bad choices of directors, and a leadership that lacked initiative. What it needed was reorganization, not dissolution. Moreover, he charged, the GTU had gone beyond its competence and the intention of the State Council's opinion and did not have the authority to recommend the dissolution of the prison committees.[19]

The ladies may have been emboldened by the men's resistance. Their charter allowed up to one-third of their membership to be men, and the two committees did have some members in common. At a meeting on 25 February 1887 they too began to fight back. Taking up Andreev's point, they claimed the GTU was not empowered by the State Council's opinion to limit the committee's rights and responsibilities. A. F. Koni, who was a member of the women's committee, wrote a separate note to emphasize the point and to insist that the charter be completely rethought. Princess E. M. Ol'denburg, patroness of the committee, expressed her agreement. All of these notes accompanied the GTU's project, which was rejected and returned.[20]

For almost four years the uncomfortable status quo was maintained. Apparently the GTU did not rest easy, however. Its file concerning this confrontation contains several heavily marked up copies of the *patronat* project, which were probably worked over in the next few years.[21] Finally, on 7 December 1890, the

GTU sent a revised project charter to the committees,[22] and on 27 March 1891 Galkin-Vraskii attended a meeting of the St. Petersburg Ladies Prison Committee to discuss it.[23] Also present were six directresses, including a princess and two countesses, and eight titled and high-ranking directors. Galkin-Vraskii naturally defended the new project, which once again relegated to the committees purely philanthropical tasks. The committee responded by recounting the fruits of its work over the last six years while it worked "under the cloud of 1884." No longer did the committee members challenge the GTU's authority to limit their powers, so that question had apparently been settled. Instead, they tried to persuade Galkin-Vraskii that even if they were to be transformed into a *patronat*-like body, they would need most of the powers and support they had had in the past. They were concerned that "moral regeneration and corrections" remain part of a *patronat*'s work and insisted that this must begin in the prisons, not after a convict's release. Among the minimal changes they wanted in the project, they asked to retain the right of visitation and the annual subsidy the government had provided to them.

On 24 December 1891 the GTU sent yet another revision of the charter to the State Council.[24] The project was scheduled for discussion on 9 May 1892 but had to be postponed because several ministries had not yet responded to it. The MIu did not forward its comments to the State Council until 8 November, and the imperial court had still not done so when MVD I. N. Durnovo inquired on 30 January 1893. Apparently a large part of this struggle was being carried on outside the view of the surviving documents, and in this invisible struggle the high-ranking directors and directresses may have called on favors and pulled strings not available to Galkin-Vraskii. When the charter finally emerged from the State Chancellery's Department of Laws, "imperially confirmed," on 12 May 1893, the prison committees had been reined in by the GTU. Between 1893 and 1895 the St. Petersburg and Moscow men's and women's POoT committees were reorganized, mostly along the lines the GTU had established, and were renamed charitable-prison committees. At the same time, however, they were taken "under imperial protection,"[25] and, by a State Council opinion of 16 July 1893, they were allowed to retain some of the powers they had asked for. Even in their diminished condition they remained an annoying thorn in the side of the GTU.[26]

Two years later, when the GTU was transferred into the MIu, the Tagantsev Commission again looked into the role of the POoT committees. At its meeting of 5 March 1896 the commission agreed that "in the majority of cases the activity of the committees and branches in all the time they have existed has been very weak." The members accepted the common complaint that the major stimulus for participation in the committees was not a desire to serve prisoners' needs but to acquire contracts and awards. They believed that the committees served little purpose other than as a pipeline for government money and had done "practically nothing" toward accomplishing their larger purposes of reeducation and reformation. The commission concluded that it was not worth radically reorganizing the POoT to try to make it work and recommended that it be transferred into the MIu as it was.[27]

A further report of the Tagantsev Commission called for the complete reform of the POoT. It recommended stripping the committees of most of their responsibilities and leaving them purely charitable functions, as the GTU had long wanted. Among the duties to be taken from POoT were the supplying of clothing, bedding, and footwear, the punishment of recalcitrant prisoners by fines and solitary confinement, and general responsibility for maintaining good conditions and carrying out all orders of law in prisons. The commission would confer the committees' powers on the wardens of individual prisons and the inspectorates that had been established in almost half of Russia's provinces by this time.[28] Over the next decade most of these recommendations were enacted into law.

And so, quietly and slowly, the POoT faded away. Although the Prison Aid Society did not attract wide support for its work or for its struggle to survive, there were many Russians of a philanthropical bent who nonetheless felt strongly that the public had an important role to play in the struggle against crime. They expressed this belief most clearly in the *patronat* movement.

PATRONATSTVO

As I have shown, Russia undertook to build a modern prison system almost a century after the first penitentiaries were built in the United States and Europe. An irony of the Russian effort is that, even before it was begun, confidence in the efficacy of imprisonment had been considerably eroded in the West. The most modern prisons were being called "cradles of vice" and "schools of crime," some alternatives to imprisonment had already been introduced, and others were under discussion. Parole and probation, for example, were being used in Europe and the United States in efforts to shorten potentially harmful imprisonment or to avoid it altogether. Consequently, the Russian experience was telescoped. Even as the GTU built new prisons, reformers among the criminalists discussed ways to minimize their use. One of the alternatives, which they brought back along with parole and probation from the international associations to which they belonged, was the idea of patronage.

Patronatstvo embodied the idea that prisons alone could not prepare criminals to live in "normal" society but that, working in concert with the prisons, society itself could. Like the POoT committees, *patronaty* (patrons) would work with prisoners and ex-convicts, but most of the work would take place after a prisoner's release and would be practical, rather than moral. *Patronaty* might find housing or work for an ex-con, they might provide counseling of a sort to "reconcile" him with his family, they might provide clothing, food, a loan or a grant, or a ticket back home. Their job was to keep the newly freed individual from the need to commit a crime to support himself.

In *patronatstvo*, as in other penal reforms, the Russian reformers found their models in the West. Every argument about their establishment, their relationship to the government, their work, and their financing was shaped by what was being done in Europe and the United States. From 1878 on, Russians attended the international prison congresses, where *patronatstvo* was discussed, and later also attended *patronat* congresses, which were begun in Antwerp in 1890. After 1896 they belonged to the *Union des Sociétés de Patronage*. Their articles on Russian *patronatstvo* are filled with discussions of and comparisons with European and American *patronatstvo* and with quotations from the resolutions of the international congresses. Their assumptions about what might be effective in Russia were clearly based on what seemed to work abroad.[29]

The early history of patronage societies is identical to the early history of the POoT. Russia's prison-aid societies, as I have demonstrated, had been inspired by the same charitable impulse and by some of the same individuals who led movements for correctional prisons and prison-aid societies in the West. They began with the same avowed purposes as did organizations that became the Volunteer Prison League in the United States, the Reformatory and Refuge Union in England, and the *sociétés de patronage* in France, but because of the nature of Russia's government the POoT evolved differently. As one of the Russian advocates of *patronatstvo* understood it, governments in western nations, particularly in the United States, were "not very different from society." They therefore not only permitted the activities of unofficial and volunteer organizations but encouraged them, sometimes with government funds.[30] The Russian government, on the other hand, either closely controlled or forbade unofficial activity. Russian reformers found in that difference the explanation for the failure of the POoT and hope for the future success of *patronatstvo*.

In *patronatstvo* Russian officialdom and public activists found an institution they could all support. First, it allied them in hostility to the POoT. GTU officials wanted to destroy the POoT because it was in their way. Reformers wanted to dismantle the POoT because it did not work and because they wanted to replace it with its western cousin. As they conceived it, *patronaty* would differ from the POoT in two important ways. First, although their work would begin with sitting prisoners, *patronaty* would have no authority in the prisons. They would work with prisoners only in preparation to help them after their release. Second, they would be independent organizations, free to do their philanthropical work without government interference.

The assumptions that guided the prison officials and the advocates of *patronatstvo* are somewhat contradictory. The men who ran the GTU long struggled to persuade lawmakers and budget planners that their work was complex and difficult and could be carried out only by trained specialists. Those officials came to accept that although prisons were expensive, their effectiveness justified their great expense. Slowly they gave the GTU funds to build new prisons and authority to ease the old prison-aid societies out of the prisons so they could do their work without interference from amateurs and volunteers. On the other hand, largely outside the government, another group of men insisted that prisons did not accomplish correction, at least not fully, and that "society" must complete that task. And they insisted, pointing to the failure of the earlier quasi-governmental POoT committees, that "society" must be permitted to do that on its own, without interference from the bureaucrats, who of course included the trained specialists. And they, too, would slowly prevail.

Life is full of contradictions, and most people involved in prison work were able to tolerate these. Prisons, they told themselves, had one task, which required authority and discipline; and the *patronaty* had another—the final reintegration of ex-convicts into society, which required informality, flexibility, and charity. As P. I. Liublinskii, one of the most prolific writers among the criminologists at the turn of the century and an ardent supporter of *patronatstvo,* put it: salaried prison workers could only be expected to have a sense of "duty to a job," whereas volunteers would bring to the *patronaty* "social and moral duty," that is, "love and devotion to the work, humane sympathy and . . . tact."[31]

Not everyone was so optimistic or tolerant, however, especially in the early years of the effort to establish *patronaty*. In 1878, for example, while Konstantin Grot was chairman of the last major prison-reform commission that established the GTU, he had also been Russia's delegate to an international prison congress. In his report on the congress to Alexander II he stated with apparent approval that the congress had resolved that *patronaty* "are a necessary addition to correctional discipline and must be widely spread by private initiative . . . without giving [them] an official character." The emperor, apparently without irony, wrote in the margin, "Yes, but under the control of the government."[32]

The *patronat* movement grew slowly and was a great disappointment to criminalists who believed in the power of "social forces." It is difficult to say just what kept the movement small, but it would seem that the most likely explanation would be lack of interest. Russia was not yet ready to develop professionalized social services, but once they could no longer win contracts or be awarded honorary medals for POoT activities or condescend and preach to prisoners, many "philanthropists" seem to have lost interest in prison-aid activities.

Advocates of *patronatstvo,* who saw its failure to take deeper roots in Russia as a failure of public activism, found a variety of ways to explain it. In 1899, for example, when the MIu was preparing to end the system of exile, the ministry circularized Russia's governors to ask whether they felt their populations would be sufficiently protected from discharged prisoners who would no longer be sent to Siberia. Many, it turned out, feared the added danger of ex-convicts in their midst and did not see that much was likely to be done to minimize this additional danger. The difficulty governors most frequently mentioned was the lack of funds to deal with new problems. Of eighty-two replies, twenty-three also mentioned *patronaty,* which they thought might be useful or even necessary for dealing with this new problem, but all of these went on to lament the lack of *patronaty* in their territories. Among the reasons they gave for the absence of *patronaty,* most prominent were the "weak development of social independence" and the "insufficiency of intelligentsia forces free and able to devote themselves to so lofty a cause."[33] Although the governors did not go on to explain the causes of "weak development of social independence," it seems clear they believed, as did many academics and other intellectuals at this time, that it was the nature of Russia's government and history that rendered Russians unable to think and act independently. One does not have to stretch such thoughts far to think that these governors would welcome change in Russia's psyche and government.

The Russian Group of the International Union of Criminalists took up the struggle to establish *patronatstvo* at its second and third congresses, in 1900 and 1901. Members apparently agreed unanimously that *patronaty* would be valuable and disagreed only on how to encourage their establishment.[34] Their debates focused once again on the difficulty of balancing volunteerism and the power of the government. Maybe thinking of the recent history of the GTU and of their own close and useful ties to the government, some members believed that having a central administration of *patronaty,* particularly one with governmental ties, would help to hasten their spread. But a majority, still more concerned with the failure of the POoT and intent on harnessing the strength of "social forces," feared the government's damping effect in that area. A different majority was mustered, however, who thought that it would be helpful at least to write a normative charter, which could provide guidance to inexperienced enthusiasts, ensure the uniformity of their activities, and at the same time allay the government's suspicions of private initiative. More radical proponents of "social forces" objected that a model charter, which suggested rather than required certain structures and activities, would be more suitable than would a normative charter, but they were outvoted. The group appointed a committee, headed by Chairwoman Princess Liven of the Moscow Women's Charitable Prison Committee (as the Moscow Women's POoT Committee was renamed in 1893), to write a normative charter, which the group quickly approved. After further work by the committee, the charter was sent through the GTU in November 1901 and on to the MIu. Minister Murav'ev noted with approval that "social independence and private initiative" must be relied on and developed to make *patronatstvo* work, but he did not immediately endorse the charter.

The experience of the St. Petersburg Patronage Society in these years illustrates well the hopes and frustrations of *patronat* activists.[35] It was begun in 1901, not long after the third congress of the Russian Group, and included among its founders officers of the group and lawyers and judges of the St. Petersburg *okrug* court. I. Ia. Foinitskii, chairman of the group, became chairman of the Patronage Society as well. Meeting in October, November, and December and basing their work on the group's draft charter, the society's members wrote a charter for their new organization. As required, they sent the charter to the MIu, where the GTU found objections to it. Rewriting and the process of approval continued over the next three and a half years, during which time the society could not be active. By the time the charter was confirmed, on 18 May 1905, Russia was in the midst of revolution, and the society's busy and politically active organizers were unable to give time to it. Only in 1908, with the revolution behind them and the Third Duma sitting, did Foinitskii pull the society together again. In their first full year of operation, the society's 171 members made about 600 visits to prisons, received 300 appeals for help from the prisoners they visited, and extended them a variety of aid. They managed to find jobs for 30 of the 46 people who asked about employment, successfully intervened with the authorities in 13 of 15 cases to allow discharged prisoners to remain in St. Petersburg, and placed 3 children of prisoners in shelters. They gave 150 rubles to

99 needy ex-convicts, loaned 27 rubles to another 16, loaned 22 rubles to 5 prisoners' families for housing, gave out 161 rubles' worth of clothing to 49 people, and spent 36 rubles on tickets to send 9 home. Assuming that there is some double counting in these numbers (that some of the people who were permitted to stay in the capital were also among those who found work, that some who were given money had also been given clothes), the society managed to help about as many discharged prisoners as it had members and helped them to less than 2 rubles each.

It took seven years to guide the Russian Group's normative charter through the bureaucracy. Even the Revolution of 1905 and the new constitutional structure of Russian government, which did a great deal to set "social forces" free and to energize them, did not spring the charter loose or immediately hasten the development of *patronaty*. Instead, it reopened debate in professional and official journals about whether a normative charter was needed in Russia's new political circumstances.[36] Some who had earlier supported the charter now found it superfluous. Meanwhile, the *patronat* movement languished. According to how one counted the variously named prison-aid societies outside the POoT, there were between seventeen and twenty-one of them in the whole country in 1907, and most of these were small, poor, and largely inactive.[37] Only in St. Petersburg, Moscow, and a few other cities were there active *patronaty* by 1908, and I have shown how little the largest of them did.[38]

Several legislative acts between 1908 and 1912 eventually created the conditions in which *patronatstvo* began to flourish. On 10 September 1908 the MIu finally confirmed the normative charter.[39] The timing of the confirmation was clearly tied to the passage of a new law on parole that was then moving through the Duma. Soon after it was introduced to the penal system in June 1909, parole began to produce a large clientele for the *patronaty*. At this point the GTU, the academic criminalists, and *patronat* activists cooperated to encourage their establishment throughout the country. Several acts of the GTU make it clear how important they now considered the *patronaty* to be. On 11 September 1908, the day after the confirmation of the normative charter, the GTU sent multiple copies of the charter with a circular to Russia's governors, asking them to encourage the establishment of *patronaty* "at all places of imprisonment" in their territories. In May of the following year, a month before the enactment of parole, it sent another circular, whose language made clear the strength of the GTU's support. It told governors that "until *patronaty* are opened throughout Russia even the most perfect prisons will not help in the struggle against crime and especially with recidivism" and asked them to convene meetings personally with interested individuals to encourage the founding of *patronaty*.[40] In order to encourage membership in and donations to *patronaty*, the GTU also asked a commission on uniforms and insignia in the emperor's chancellery to establish a special medal for outstanding members. It was exactly this sort of medal that they had belittled when it was awarded to POoT members a decade or so earlier. MIu I. G. Shcheglovitov gave his personal support to the request for the medal and also to an effort begun by private advocates of *patronatstvo* to find government subsidies for *patronaty*. The medal was soon approved.[41] Not surprisingly, it took a little longer to pry money out of the treasury. What is somewhat surprising is that it took so few years to persuade the government to fund the largely independent *patronaty*. The law of 24 December 1912 was modeled on the English system, which provided government subsidies to prison-aid societies according to a complicated formula involving the number of people assisted, the type of aid offered, and the amount of money taken in from donations.[42]

This flurry of activity was successful in establishing many new *patronaty*. A 1913 study counted 117 *patronaty* and another 38 similar organizations.[43] According to their own reports, they gave much-needed aid to those with whom they worked.[44] On the other hand, statistics make it clear that they were able to offer help to only a small proportion of parolees and ex-convicts each year.[45]

World War I and revolution burst on Russia too soon after these events to give *patronaty* much of a chance to develop under favorable conditions. Their few short years of rapid growth in these strained circumstances do not allow me to judge clearly how well they functioned or might have functioned. I can make one important observation about their growth and operation, however. By 1908–1914, bureaucrats, professionals, and amateurs had arrived at similar views of criminality and corrections. There is every good reason to think that they could have continued to work together.

THE LEGISLATIVE EFFORT TO INTRODUCE PAROLE

Parole was established and, in theory at least, worked to enhance both of the major purposes of punishment: for prisoners, it provided a strong incentive to rehabilitation or correction; for parolees, it maintained a strong deterrent, if only for the term of their parole. Prisoners who were eligible for parole had to earn their early release by behaving as penologists and administrators wanted them to. Similarly, parolees had to behave well in freedom to avoid returning to prison.

These theoretical considerations were perhaps paramount in the adoption of parole in various western nations and remained prominent in the debates over its use in Russia. Another important and practical consideration was that early release reduced the prison population and, thereby, the costs of prison administration. In addition, and as usual in Russian penology, an important justification for the use of parole was the observation that it seemed to work well in Europe and the United States.

The effort to introduce parole in Russia began shortly after the GTU was established. The penal code already contained a form of parole, though it was not called that. Convicts sent to penal servitude in exile had the opportunity to progress with time and with good behavior from the initial category of that punishment, called "probationary," to the "improving" or "correcting" category. After a specified time in the latter group, they could be released and receive permission to build their own homes, to marry, and to engage in business. Commission of a new crime or other unsatisfactory behavior could result in their return to penal servitude. Another form of parole had been available to juvenile offenders since 1866 in some of the few facilities Russia had for juveniles. Although no statistics were ever compiled to attest to its efficacy, the administrators of the juvenile facilities and several criminologists thought highly of the program.[46] Reformers wished to apply so useful a tool to the greater part of prison inmates.

The first attempt to write parole for regular adult prisoners into Russian penal law was made in 1882, when a government commission began what turned out to be a twenty-year project to rewrite Russia's criminal code. The commission recommended continuing the use of parole in penal servitude and trying it experimentally in houses of correction for prisoners sentenced to at least three years.[47] Most Russian criminologists and jurists applauded the addition, both in the press and in official comments they were invited to make by the commission,[48] but even before the project reached the State Council the new application of parole was excised from it.[49] Arguments against the innovation were still strong.

The most common and persuasive argument against parole in 1882 was that the prison administrative system and the police were not yet capable of handling parole and parolees. Prison administrators, wardens, priests, and others wrote the commission that the power to grant or withhold parole was more likely to lead to abuse and corruption in the prisons than to good.[50] The fear of theorists and top-level administrators that not enough trained, competent, and honest men could be found to administer reforms was an impediment to this and other penal reforms, as I have demonstrated. A minority of jurists found another reason to object. They complained that parole boards would undermine the authority of judges by tampering with court sentences. The Russian courts, and particularly the jury system, had come under strenuous attack in recent years. Since the recent campaign of terror, which included Vera Zasulich's acquittal and Alexander II's assassination, some of their powers and independence had been curtailed, and many in the system were sensitive to any suggestion that might seem to further reduce their authority.[51] Also, although they were few by 1880 and their attitudes were derided by academic criminologists, there were still powerful men in the government who were unpersuaded by modern corrections. The whole concept of corrections, of which parole was a much too kind and gentle part, contradicted their belief that the best deterrent to crime was swift and fearful punishment.

Parole was not included in the draft law-code revision in 1882. The versions of 1885, 1895, and 1897 also excluded parole, although the editing commission continued to express its opinion that parole is "a necessary addition to a rationally structured prison system." In several articles the commissioners recommended, instead, that unconditional early release be adopted because of "the condition of our prisons and the absence here of properly organized police supervision."[52] They meant that Russian prisons were as likely to further corrupt offenders and make them better criminals as they were to reform them. The sooner as-yet-unhardened criminals could be removed from them, the better. Parole, they thought, would be a better way to handle their reintegration into society, but because neither the prison system nor the police could be trusted to handle that process, it would be preferable to release the prisoners unconditionally. The thought that prisons might "infect" or "harden" prisoners became a stronger argument for parole as time went on and was used side by side with the contradictory argument that parole was a reward for prisoners who had been re-habilitated by their stay in prison. None of the arguments was strong enough to overcome the many objections still raised at the turn of the century, however. When parts of the new criminal code were adopted in 1903, neither conditional nor unconditional early release had been extended to parts of the system where it was not already in use.

Two other factors had to enter into the debate before parole could be adopted. Both were indirect results of the revolutionary turmoil of 1905–1906. First, as I have shown, the government's suppression of the revolt filled Russia's prisons far beyond their legal capacity. The GTU had inherited prisons severely overcrowded because of the radical activity of 1878–1881 but had overcome that problem by 1890 and, consequently, felt little pressure to adopt parole as a means of reducing prison population until the Revolution of 1905 created the problem again. Between 1906 and 1916 (the problem was especially severe until 1912) the number of prisoners exceeded the legal capacity of Russia's prisons as defined by the Main Prison Administration itself, and proponents of parole adopted the additional argument that parole would reduce the number of pris-oners and the costs of maintaining them.

The second factor was the political awakening brought about by the revolu-tion and the opportunities created by the new "constitutional" government. Practical, liberal men in the government could now ally themselves with, or make use of, liberals in the Duma to attain what they had not been able to attain from the prerevolutionary government. Duma liberals were overwhelmingly hos-tile to the Russian prison system. They did not believe that the tsar's over-crowded prisons could reform offenders completely, if at all. Some were certain that prisons did more harm than good. If they held out hope that criminal of-fenders could be reformed, they believed that "society" was the force that might accomplish or complete that reform. The successes of the revolution reinforced enthusiasm for such thinking. As postrevolutionary proponents saw it, parole would protect prisoners from prison and society from recidivism and would en-courage the development of "social forces" to combat crime, which was increas-ingly seen as an environmental and social problem, rather than as a moral one.[53] When it was finally introduced into the Russian criminal-justice system by the law of 22 June 1909, parole was specifically tied to the development of *patronaty* as nongovernmental, voluntary, public organizations that would act as a parole-officer corps.[54]

The Duma, which is usually seen as an antagonist or, at best, a loyal opposi-tion to the government, on this issue provided an opportunity for those in the government who wanted to adopt "progressive" reform in prison administration. After twenty-five years of failure to push parole, or probation, through the com-mission on law-code reform, the MIu was apparently eager to make the most of the opportunity. It prepared legislation that proposed the introduction of parole, obtained approval of the project from the Council of Ministers, and had it ready for the opening of the Second Duma.[55] When the Second Duma was unable to take up the issue before it was dismissed by Nicholas II, the MIu sent it right back to the Third Duma.[56]

In the Third Duma the MIu's project was sent to the Commission on Judicial Reforms, which quickly recommended passage of the project.[57] Its spokesman, Count E. P. Bennigsen, presented the project to the Duma for consideration on 27 February 1908.[58] Two days of stormy debate ensued, and parts of another three days were given to details, before an only slightly amended version passed the Duma on 4 June. All of the standard arguments for and against the use of parole, and a few not heard in academic circles, were thoroughly aired.

Bennigsen led off with a rather dry and academic presentation, which gave no hint of the storm to follow. Saying nothing of the problem of overcrowding or of the opportunity to reduce prison expenses, he recommended parole as an enlightened, supplementary incentive to correction, which had proved its value in many western nations. Although he did not touch on all of the expected benefits, Bennigsen was apparently familiar with the objections that would be raised. He anticipated and dismissed several, claiming that Russia's prison system was much improved and would be able to administer parole as well as did other European nations, "whose prisons are no better than Russia's."[59] Moving from general to specific remarks, Bennigsen expressed the commission's support for most of the details of the project. The only problem he admitted to was the shortage of *patronaty* needed to supervise parolees. But, he insisted, Russia could not wait for them to appear before beginning so important a reform, and he expressed confidence that they could grow quickly to meet the challenge. To assist their rapid growth, the commission suggested that a normative charter be adopted and that the government subsidize the operation of *patronaty*, as was already done in several European countries. MIu I. G. Shcheglovitov, who followed Bennigsen to the rostrum, also emphasized the corrective influence of parole and cited European experience and expertise in support of its adoption in Russia. He seconded Bennigsen's concern for *patronaty* and announced that the MIu was already at work on a plan to subsidize them, which it would soon bring to the Duma.[60] As I pointed out, a normative charter was adopted in September of that year, and a program of subsidies began in 1912.

The debate that occupied most of the next two meetings was, like many Duma debates, a fascinating exercise in Russian democracy. Viewpoints ranged from scholarly to redneck, from pedantic to impassioned. The debate involved representatives of most of the Duma factions and from much of the Russian Empire. Speakers' opinions usually suited their party affiliation, but not always.

S. P. Maksudov, a representative of the Moslem Group from Kazan, welcomed the work of the MIu and the Duma commission. Citing "with reverence" the work of eighteenth-century criminal-law and prison reformers and displaying familiarity with modern criminological thought and the experience of parole and patronage in Europe, he praised parole as penal law suited to "cultured humankind of the twentieth century."[61] Kadets (Constitutional Democrats) and Octobrists agreed with this view, although some of them displayed more enthusiasm than knowledge.[62] Kadet A. F. Babianskii, for example, had rather quaint ideas about criminal offenders and prisons. Russian criminality, he was persuaded, was different from that of cold and calculating Europe; it was an impulsive and unpremeditated kind that needed little in the way of correction. Where other speakers cited native and foreign criminological and penological experts, Babianskii seems to have formed his impressions of prisons from reading Dostoevskii's *House of the Dead,* published in 1860, and Tolstoi's *Resurrection,* which was at least more recent (1899). However odd his sources may have been, his conclusion coincided with that of the experts: parole was needed to move people out of prison.

The most impressive of the speakers in favor of parole was L. G. Liuts, an Octobrist from Kherson. The gist of Liuts's speech was that parole was a proven commodity; it was not theory but long experience in Europe and the United States that demonstrated its utility. His speech displayed wide knowledge of the history of prisons, parole, and patronage in the West and familiarity with the POoT and *patronaty* in Russia.[63]

Most of the opposition came from the right, which raised a variety of objections. N. E. Markov from Kursk, the most thorough of these speakers, offered sarcastic and damaging comments on the whole process, from the granting of parole to the supervision of parolees. Hardened but cunning prisoners, he explained, would quickly learn how parole worked and would win their release with false displays of contrition for the naive volunteers who visited and observed them. Alternatively, prisoners or their friends (or enemies) on the outside could influence members of the parole board with power or money. Opportunities and temptation for corruption and injustice were great. The *patronaty,* which were supposed to supervise parolees, said Markov, were not worth speaking about "until there are some." And the freedom of parole (in Russian, literally "conditional early liberation") was actually, as a consequence, unconditional. He concluded that the project was particularly untimely. Russia had just experienced a revolution, and the country was still unsettled. It was no time to return more lawbreakers to freedom. "Our people," he said, meaning his constituents in Kursk province, "the majority of them, want increased severity, increased criminal repression, and not only for political crimes but for all crimes from the pettiest theft."[64]

Another point made by the rightists was more surprising. Although many of them thought of themselves as nationalists and would soon be calling themselves Nationalists, it is clear that they thought less of the abilities and character of the Russian people than did the liberals. As Markov put it: "The fact of the matter is, in addition to ideas, to theory, to that abstract science that the minister of justice recites, there is real life; in addition to Belgium and France, there is that country called Russia"—where, apparently, he thought criminals were less corrigible, prisons and their personnel less able, and the charitable impulse more misguided.[65] F. F. Timoshkin, a rightist from the Transcaucasus, seconded this opinion at the following meeting. Russia was not France, with well-developed patronage societies, or England, whose prisons were few and well run. Russia was huge, disorderly Russia. "Let Petrov out of jail," he warned, "and three rubles later he has a false passport and has become Ivanov and won't be found." Offering parole to Russian prisoners, he complained, would be like "dressing Russian peasants in Brussels lace."[66]

The rightists were not united in their opposition, however. Two priests who belonged to the moderate right and one from the far right spoke for parole as an act of redemption and mercy.[67] Count A. A. Bobrinskii, who often acted as spokesman for the bloc, announced its official stance. Although they could see merits in the theory of parole, the lack of *patronaty* and the lawlessness of the time would require them to vote against the project.[68]

Only the rightists voted against parole, but for different reasons the Social Democrats also opposed the project. E. P. Gegechkori explained their position. For the Marxists, parole was a meaningless addition to an unjust penal system built on mistaken notions about the causes of crime. They could not support any part of the system of repression that had been erected by contemporary "bourgeois classes and governments" and a whole school of jurists who were "foaming at the mouth." "Punishing and persecuting, contemporary governments, especially our own, are not concerned with correcting and raising criminals up. I am not talking about raising up on the gallows, of course. That we do with particular pleasure." Instead of refining the means of repression—which Gegechkori characterized as a page from "the archives of criminal science," old, ineffective, and obsolete—the Duma should solve the social and political problems that cause crime: land hunger, working conditions, unemployment. In the face of really important problems, parole was meaningless. Therefore, he concluded, "the Social Democratic fraction . . . abstains from voting on the present project."[69] Another Social Democrat, G. S. Kuznetsov, later added his suspicion that the reform was meant to clear jails of criminals only to make room for additional political prisoners and reiterated the party's intention to abstain.[70]

At the end of the first day's debate, MIu Shcheglovitov spoke in response to some of the objections that had been raised. Although it must have been clear he did not need their vote to assure passage of the project, he seems to have been most concerned about conciliating the rightists. He assured them that serious offenders, like murderers, usually wound up in *katorga* prisons and would not be eligible for parole. Was not conditional early release preferable to the unconditional early release already in use in some parts of the penal system, including *katorga*? And, for the first time, he raised the issue of overcrowding in the prisons.[71] Speaking at the end of the second day, Count Bennigsen followed the same line. He insisted that *patronaty* had not flourished previously only because they had nothing to do and that they would develop in response to the challenge of parole. Rather than increase the opportunity for bribery, the creation of parole boards would bring "social forces" into the penal system and reduce illegal activity. Echoing Shcheglovitov, he reminded the delegates of the heavy expenses involved in imprisonment that would be reduced by parole. And, clearly ignoring the Social Democrats and speaking to the rightists, he insisted that the coercion to behave that was the heart of parole increased repression rather than reduced it.[72]

At the end of the second day the Duma voted to proceed to an article-by-article discussion, and at the next session it took up that work. Only two issues provoked lengthy discussion. The first was wording in the project that "instructed" the MIu to submit a project on subsidizing the *patronaty*. The assistant MIu objected that the Duma was not empowered to instruct the ministries and suggested that they "request" instead. He was supported by Counts Bennigsen and Bobrinskii. P. N. Miliukov, chairman of the Kadets, argued for the power of the Duma, but by vote the wording was changed to "request."[73] The second issue was the problem of horse thieves. After representatives of several parties had spoken of the special seriousness of horse theft in peasant society and no one had spoken for the thieves, a clause that specifically exempted them from parole was easily adopted.[74]

The project was given a second reading, on 26 March 1908, and passed after its third reading, on 4 June.[75] From the Duma the project followed the normal legislative path to the State Council, where it was not acted on until the fall. On 23 October, the State Council sent the project to its Committee on Legislative Proposals, where it was discussed at four meetings in November and December. The committee's report to the council was similar in its details and its arguments to the Duma commission's report and unanimous in its support for parole, but it was not as enthusiastic. In essence it said, despite the real and obvious difficulties in implementing parole in Russia, that it ought to be tried.[76]

The council finally returned to the issue in February 1909. Not surprisingly, debate there focused on the same points that had dominated the issue for several decades, but this debate was at once more scholarly, more thorough, and more bitter than in the Duma. On both sides the protagonists were men of wider experience and greater reputations. Several of the country's best-known criminologists and jurists, including N. S. Tagantsev and A. F. Koni, spoke for parole. Against it stood, among others, P. N. Durnovo, the previous MVD, who was well if not fondly remembered for his determined suppression of the Revolution of 1905. Since 1906 Durnovo had been the leader of a group of conservative monarchists in the State Council, "the nucleus of a solid conservative bloc which formed a nearly permanent majority in that chamber."[77]

Procedure in the council was the same as in the Duma. V. F. Deitrikh spoke first, as reporter for the Committee on Legislative Proposals, followed by Shcheglovitov for the MIu. Deitrikh described parole as a useful addition to conventional repressive or correctional measures, a powerful carrot and stick that had been successful in "all European experience." He reviewed objections to its adoption that had been discussed by the committee—that parole reduces the authority of judges, encourages arbitrary authority in prisons, and decreases repression while crime is increasing and that the observation needed to determine who deserved parole was impossible in Russia's overcrowded prisons—but he dismissed these objections as invalid or not as compelling as the arguments for parole. As to the supervision of parolees, he suggested that the remaining POoT committees could be called on to assist *patronaty*. A majority of the committee held that view; a minority preferred courts to play that role in the absence of *patronaty*.[78]

Shcheglovitov explained the benefits of parole to the state councilors at much greater length and at a much higher level of discourse than he had to the Duma. He began in the realm of legal philosophy, citing the great European scholars, and worked toward parole through a history of the idea of individualization in punishment. In this telling, parole stood at the end of a long evolution of Europe's best thinking and experience.

Turning to the Russian case, for which he cited Russian experts, Shcheglovitov explained the particular needs and benefits that made the case for parole urgent there. Overcrowding caused by the revolution topped his list of domestic problems. Some prisons had been destroyed by explosion and fire in those years, while thousands of additional arrests had been made. He added the little-known fact that the peace treaty signed with Japan in 1905 required Russia to relocate penal-labor-colony inmates, who were numerous and usually serious offenders, from Sakhalin to prisons on the mainland. As a consequence, discipline and prison work programs, whose importance he emphasized, suffered in severely crowded conditions. He recalled that one of the reasons parole had not been adopted early on in the criminal-code reform (1882–1903) was the experts' assumption that only an orderly prison system could administer parole. But since then, he explained, the experts had changed their minds. Now they thought that parole was especially important in overburdened and disordered prisons, to help both the paroled individuals and those who remained behind in improved circumstances.

Shcheglovitov finally addressed the issue of money, the last of the reasons he adduced for the adoption of parole, as if it were least important. I do not believe that it was least important, in general or in the minister's mind, and it would be raised again in this debate more forcefully and with supporting details, but at the outset the minister seems to have wanted to occupy the theoretical and moral high ground. The only problem he admitted to was the shortage of *patronaty*, and here he repeated the familiar assertion that "social forces" would rise to the challenge and responsibility of supervising parolees.[79]

Before the council moved on to an article-by-article discussion of the project, two councilors rose to oppose it in its entirety, two spoke in its defense, and Deitrikh and Shcheglovitov were given an opportunity to respond and sum up. Between them, I. O. Kovrin-Milevskii and P. N. Durnovo covered a wide range of objections to parole. Some arose from mistaken assumptions about how the prison system worked and how parole would fit into it; others were better-founded, familiar apprehensions.

Kovrin-Milevskii had interpreted the legislation to say that offenders in crimes of passion and political crimes (groups that were sometimes sentenced to a fortress rather than a prison) would be ineligible for parole, and he was upset that the law would benefit only "true scoundrels." He also asserted that Russian prison sentences were already shorter than were those in any European nation and that shortening them further by parole was unnecessary.[80] Shcheglovitov was able to show that both assumptions were mistaken. In describing the length of prison sentences, for example, Kovrin-Milevskii had cited only maximum sentences for various offenses, which were lower in Russia than in the rest of

Europe. On the other hand, as Shcheglovitov showed, Russian minimum sentences were longer. Judicial discretion in sentencing was greater abroad, but actual sentences were similar.[81]

Kovrin-Milevskii's other objections were similar to those heard in the Duma and in the press, and they were more difficult to rebut: prison conditions and personnel weaknesses made it impossible to make necessary observations; one could not know that a prisoner was truly reformed; the power to grant or withhold parole created opportunities for corruption; and *patronaty* did not exist to supervise parolees. A. F. Koni and Shcheglovitov could only reassert that the potential benefits outweighed the risks and that the *patronaty* would come into being.

One last suggestion made by Kovrin-Milevskii and rebutted by Koni spoke profoundly to the changing nature of Russian government. If overcrowding were the primary problem addressed by parole, Kovrin-Milevskii would prefer that the MIu present a long list of prisoners to the tsar for pardoning. Koni explained, as his listeners surely knew, that pardon was the granting of the tsar's mercy and had nothing to do with the prisoners' behavior. Parole, on the other hand, was the prisoner's right, earned by his good behavior. That prisoners had rights was an important claim—an assistant minister of justice would later specifically deny that parole was a right, calling it a privilege[82]—but what was left unsaid in Koni's explanation was more important. Modern Russians preferred the rational exercise of authority by professional administrators to the arbitrary exercise of power by the tsar. That this issue was not raised again shows how far that preference had progressed.

Durnovo's objections were of a different nature. He believed that sentences were already too lenient and, apparently, that modern corrections were misguided in general. Once, when he had been robbed, he explained, he did not think of the etiology of the crime or the criminal; nor did he think about the purposes of punishment and corrections. All he wanted was for the criminal to be punished. He was certain that the average Russian felt the same. Like him, they would welcome laws that reduced crime, but parole could only encourage and increase criminality. Nor was Durnovo persuaded that it was necessary to reduce overcrowding in prisons. Even in current conditions, prisoners were no more crowded than were most peasants in their homes or soldiers in their barracks, he claimed. If crowding actually existed, it could be tolerated, or it could be corrected by arranging for more prison space, but it should not be an excuse for releasing criminals.[83]

Koni responded to Durnovo that the average man should not act as a measure of Russia's needs and aspirations. In Russia, as elsewhere, the average man usually stands for old ways. He asked rhetorically whether the French government should respond to the bloodthirstiness of crowds that watched executions by devising more imaginative and entertaining ways to execute criminals. Concerning overcrowding, Koni did not refute what Durnovo had said about peasants and soldiers. Durnovo may have been correct. Rather, he declared that Russian prisoners should be treated more kindly than should the more fortunate western European prisoners, because they had already had more difficult, hungrier, less healthy lives. The stenographer did not record what Durnovo might have said under his breath.

At the end of this discussion the chairman asked for a vote on Durnovo's motion to reject the legislation as a whole. A written vote was requested. The motion failed, seventy-two to fifty-eight, and the legislation progressed to an article-by-article discussion.[84] The project received extensive further discussion at three meetings in February and March 1909.[85] At a fourth meeting, on 15 April, the State Council voted for the project and passed it to a conference committee of six Duma delegates and six state councilors. This committee met several times in May, ironed out minor differences, and returned the project to the Duma, which voted for it on 2 June. The State Council passed this final version on 12 June 1909, and it became law ten days later.[86]

The GTU anticipated the passage of the law and was ready to carry out its obligations. On 4 July, less than two weeks after its passage, GTU officials distributed to their wardens a copy of the law and an intricate printed form on which wardens were to report how many of their prisoners were eligible for parole, how many were paroled by the special conferences the law instructed them to form, and to whom they were entrusted.[87] Summer vacation seems to have slowed the formation of the special conferences, and when they did meet they were less than certain about how to proceed with their work. At the first meeting of a new "parole board" in Moscow, for example, the members began by agreeing that they did not have enough information about the prisoners whose cases were presented to them to make an informed decision. They spent most of the meeting drawing up a list of questions they wanted answered about each prisoner, including biographical data; his attitude to labor, school, and daily life in prison; his habit of saving; and his contacts outside prison. When they realized that they could not obtain such complete information for many prisoners, they decided to hold their next meetings in the prisons and to interview each candidate directly. Meanwhile, they paroled one prisoner.[88]

As wardens, special conferences, and others encountered difficulties in interpreting the law and administering aspects of parole, reports and queries streamed into the GTU.[89] The MIu and GTU responded with circulars explaining various points, until in January 1910 they formed an internal commission to study all of the problems that had been brought to their attention. A GTU circular of 22 May 1910 reported the commission's decisions and advice.[90]

The special conferences' decisions became easier as their work became more familiar and as the number of parolees grew. Too few years were left, however, before the collapse of the tsarist government for good statistical evidence to have been gathered on parole's efficacy. What evidence there is suggests that, although parole may have helped individual parolees, it benefited Russian society little if at all. The GTU's inquiries revealed that most parolees simply disappeared after their release. They did not have the means to determine how many of those who disappeared were later rearrested elsewhere. One semiannual report, which was not atypical, reported that, of 171 prisoners paroled in a province, 1 had died, 2 had been returned to prison, 14 were free and behaving properly; the other 154 had fled the area or had otherwise disappeared.[91] Professional penologists and criminologists and advocates of *patronatstvo* continued to praise the "progressive" advance of adopting parole, but in the last years of the tsarist regime many others increasingly condemned the practice.

THE LEGISLATIVE EFFORT TO INTRODUCE PROBATION

The effort to introduce probation presents an interesting parallel with the struggle over parole. Probation is, after all, a logical extension of parole, a next step in the movement away from the use of prisons in corrections and further evidence of growing doubt that prisons could reform criminals. Rather than sending an offender to prison at all, probation frees him, after sentencing, under the threat of carrying out his sentence should he commit a subsequent offence (in addition to any sentence occasioned by the subsequent offence). The Russian phrase for probation means literally "conditional sentencing." In theory, the purpose of probation was more repressive than correctional. It was meant to frighten first-time and minor offenders without subjecting them to prison, which, theory now held, might do them more harm than good. The primary justification for probation was the idea that imprisonment for less than a year could not reform prisoners. The shortness of time to work on prisoners' minds and habits was compounded by the absence of labor in many short-term facilities. An important practical consideration was that, by reducing the prison population, probation also reduced the cost of prison administration.

Probation was used first in Boston in 1878, from where it spread slowly through Massachusetts, being systematized in state law only at the turn of the nineteenth century. It was applied initially to juveniles, then to other first-time and minor offenders who would otherwise have received short sentences. But because it seemed to many observers that probation allowed criminals to avoid punishment altogether, it caught on more slowly than parole had. The public and its elected representatives were not enthusiastic about further "lenience," and even some experts who had advocated parole had their doubts about probation. International prison congresses either tabled or rejected motions to urge the use of probation until 1895.[92] Illinois, the second state to use it, did not begin until 1899. Thereafter it spread more rapidly. By 1911 forty-one of the forty-seven states had adopted its use, twenty-three of them for adults, all forty-one of them for juveniles.[93] Meanwhile, many European nations had also begun to probate offenders. England began in 1887; Belgium in 1888. Before 1900 France, Norway, Portugal, and Italy had also adopted its use.[94]

Because probation was devised and adopted in western penal systems and earned the approval of international associations so much later than parole, Russian specialists did not promote its adoption until late in the lengthy process of developing Russia's new criminal code. S. K. Gogel' seems to have raised the question first in September 1897. In an article in the MIu's official journal he asked why, when other western innovations in penology had been adopted in

Russia, a tool as useful as probation had not. In its support he emphasized its widespread use in the United States and Europe and cited claims that it was extremely effective everywhere it was used. Gogel' asserted that probation was at least 90 percent successful, that is, that fewer than 10 percent of probationers were rearrested during their probation. This compared favorably with the approximately 30 percent recidivism of first-time offenders who had served prison terms. It was "high time," he wrote, for Russia to catch on and catch up, "for Russia will soon be the only civilized country that does not use probation."[95]

Probation's proponents liked to say that the practice had come not from academics but from men who were engaged "in the practical struggle against crime" and that it had spread rapidly because of its "practical success." This allowed them, among other things, to minimize the reluctance of academic criminalists to see its value. When the matter had first been raised at an international prison congress in Rome in 1885, it had been left undecided. At Paris, in 1888, a majority of the delegates had voted against the use of probation. And two years later, in St. Petersburg, they had tabled the question pending additional data. Theorists were reluctant to embrace probation, despite its apparent efficacy, because it seemed to violate the principle that crime must be punished. Whereas parole offered conditional early freedom to convicts in prison, probation provided a way to avoid imprisonment altogether. Only slowly did theorists come to accept that probation did provide punishment as well as deterrence. In 1895 a congress finally endorsed its use.[96]

Gogel'—who was better known for his philanthropic work among juvenile offenders, discharged prisoners, and the blind than for his academic work—may have taken the lead because he was less of an ideologue or theoretician than were most of his colleagues and had less of an intellectual stake in the reforms of the previous decades. He did not need to feel as defensive about probation, which implied the failure of those reforms. He was saying, less than two decades after Russia had given official recognition to the reforming potential of modern prisons, that probation was needed precisely because those prisons had failed. Crime rates were growing more rapidly than was population everywhere that prisons were in general use, including Russia, and recidivism was increasing "to frightening proportions." Moreover, he added, modern prisons were enormously expensive.[97]

He was correct on all counts, of course. Parole, probation, prison-aid societies, and other reforms undertaken in the West in recent years had been designed to reduce or avoid the use of prisons, to complete the process of correction that prisons could only begin, or to undo the harm they were now thought to cause. Even in Russia, reformers were calling prisons "cradles of vice." But the irony and the difficulty of the Russian situation (noted above in the discussion of *patronatstvo* and parole) were that Russia had begun to build its system only after the experts had begun to doubt the reforming powers of prisons. In a short time the Russians had caught both the enthusiasms and the doubts of their more experienced western colleagues. On the one hand, particularly in academia, the Russians were up-to-date and therefore aware of the statistics and doubts; on the other hand, they had just accomplished a great deal of catching up at great expense by building modern prisons. Many of the criminalists and administrators had a heavy stake in the new prisons.[98] It would therefore be especially difficult in Russia to promote the use of probation by proving the "failure" of prisons.

The immediate result of Gogel's essay was that the St. Petersburg Juridical Society, of which he was a member, unanimously voted to approve the introduction of probation. In the following few years practically every other important organization and many prominent individuals in Russian criminal affairs added their support. In 1899 the first Congress of the Russian Group of the International Union of Criminalists approved a resolution urging the adoption of probation. In 1902 the Congress of the International Union, meeting in St. Petersburg, adopted a similar resolution. Finally, in 1903, at the tail end of the process of developing a new criminal code, Russia's MIu produced a draft of a law on probation that became the basis for discussion of the matter in the government.[99] In May 1904 the special commission that was working on adopting the new code, led by its chairman, MIu N. V. Murav'ev, decided to send copies of that project to experts throughout the government and academia.[100] This was not an unusual procedure, but it seems to have been unusually thorough in this case. I suspect that Murav'ev, who favored the use of probation, knew that he faced strong opposition on the commission and elsewhere in the government and wished to gather as much additional support for the project as he could.

In this he was successful. The responses overwhelmingly supported the project. Six of eight assistants to the ober-procurator of the Criminal Cassational Department of the Senate "did not perceive barriers to the introduction in our law of the institution of probation." The other two assistants who responded "expressed doubts concerning the desirability and possibility" of probation in Russia. The two problems they discussed were those most commonly raised against probation. First, Russia was a huge country with a large number of minor offenders who might be released on probation. It would be impossible, they said, to keep track of them all, and they might repeatedly commit minor crimes in different places, be repeatedly probated, and never be punished. Second, despite what the supporters of probation said, these two assistants believed the hope of escaping punishment through probation might seduce many, who would otherwise be deterred, into petty crime. They referred to Belgian statistics that showed that the number of petty offenses had risen since probation was introduced there in 1884.[101]

All eleven court chambers replied positively, nine of them unanimously. All eighty-six *okrug* courts supported probation, as did fifty-nine of sixty-two justice-of-the-peace congresses.[102] Two repeated the fear that probation might seem like no punishment at all, while one raised the less popular objection that what worked in Europe might not work in Russia because Russia was not as cultured as Europe. Procurators of court chambers and *okrug* courts overwhelmingly approved. So did military *okrug* courts and military procurators. The bar associations of St. Petersburg and Moscow and the juridical societies of five cities also lent their eloquent and well-documented support.[103]

A spate of articles in support of the project appeared in professional journals and legal newspapers in the next year or so,[104] but in 1905 revolution interrupted its progress toward enactment. When the MIu turned its attention back to the project in February 1907, it forwarded it to the Council of Ministers. The Council of Ministers raised no objections to sending the project through the "usual legislative process," which by then meant the radical Second State Duma,[105] where it was once again delayed by Russian politics. The tsar dismissed the Second Duma before it took up the project, and the Third Duma was slow to consider this relatively minor matter. When it eventually did, in the fall of 1909, just a few months after the legal enactment of parole, the project provoked heated discussion in the Duma and a vicious response in the conservative press.

M. S. Adzhemov, a Kadet, reported the project out of the Duma's Commission on Judicial Reform to the whole Duma on 24 October 1909. Like Bennigsen, introducing the parole project a year and a half earlier, Adzhemov tried to place probation in the long history of western penology and to support its passage by citing its successful use abroad. His concluding remark that probation was "a ray of light in our dark, gloomy penal system" drew applause and a few bravos from the left and the center.[106]

Immediately, however, G. G. Zamyslovskii, a rightist in the Duma and a Black Hundreder outside it,[107] took the floor to oppose the project. Zamyslovskii complained that the Duma had been inundated with law projects whose purpose was to make life easier for criminal offenders and whose result was, or would be, to put the law-abiding public at risk and to cost them money, presumably because of repeated offenses. Of "all these privileges and guarantees for robbers and thieves," probation was the "most dangerous." He claimed to admire the humanity of the project and said that he would not object to it if it applied only to poor people who were caught stealing food to allay hunger. But he did object that it would extend to attempted murder, arson, attempted robbery, and some political crimes. While he was enumerating the political offenses, voices from the left heckled "Union of the Russian People" and "incitement to pogroms." Zamyslovskii rose quickly to the bait, responding that he understood why the leftists found that part of the project attractive. Obviously, much more than practical penology was involved in the delegates' debates and decision.

After the chairman admonished both sides of this exchange, Zamyslovskii continued to develop his objections. By inventing cases, he tried to show the unfairness and danger inherent in the project. One presented a "harmless," "accidental" *(sluchainyi)* offender—he had murdered his wife's lover—who was ineligible for probation and contrasted him with dangerous, professional criminals who might be freed. Another focused on a peasant victim who was left confused and angry when the man who had robbed and beaten him was freed on probation. The right cheered Zamyslovskii's comment that such mistrust of authority was just what revolutionaries needed in these unstable times. His remaining objection I presented before in the debate on parole. Conceding that probation might work in some "exotic" places (he mentioned New Zealand and Massachusetts) that had specially trained police, probation agents, *patronatstvo,* registration of their population, and money, he did not see how it could work in Russia, which had none of those things. Once again, he concluded, the law-abiding would be made to pay for concessions to lawbreakers.[108]

MIu Shcheglovitov spoke next, in defense of the project. Those who are familiar with Shcheglovitov only as a conservative and anti-Semitic minister, or perhaps through his shameful involvement in the Beilis case, may be surprised to find him here eloquently defending a "liberal" project. But that is because they do not know the whole man. Shcheglovitov was an anti-Semite and a careerist, who apparently did become more conservative as he tried to keep the tsar's favor from 1906 to 1917, but he was also an extremely capable, practical, and up-to-date lawyer and minister.[109] In all likelihood he presented and defended the projects on parole, and now probation, because he was convinced by the best of modern penological theory and experience that they were effective means for combating criminality. And certainly, as he did in the discussions of parole, he must have also thought of the expense of prisons, which had been in the MIu's keeping—and budget—since 1895. His long speech—explaining probation's place in the history of modern prisons and his responses to Zamyslovskii's and other, anticipated objections—was intelligent, temperate, and conciliatory. He was loudly applauded by the center.[110]

The last speaker on that first day of debate was V. A. Maklakov, of the Kadets. Maklakov agreed that probation was needed and would be beneficial, but he was not about to thank the government for initiating the project. Although he apparently agreed with what the MIu had to say and aggressively countered Zamyslovskii's views on repression, he also used his opportunity to speak to condemn the government as a primary cause of criminality. He urged that probation be applied more widely than the project envisioned, especially to political offenders.[111]

While the project was being prepared for the Duma and being deliberated by it, the popular press was conducting its own discussion, which was even less decorous than the Duma's. The liberal press was, predictably, for its adoption. The conservative press was shrilly opposed. St. Petersburg's *Russkoe Znamia* and Moscow's *Moskovskiia Vedomosti*, for example, claimed in similar articles that probation caused disrespect for the law. Because it gave hope for impunity, it led to a rise in crime. Nor was probation nearly as effective as had been claimed; statistics had been made to lie. The St. Petersburg *Zemshchina* and the Moscow *Veche* warned in identical articles of the coming "golden age of criminals," which the "kike-Kadets" were preparing.[112]

When the Duma reconvened two days later, nineteen more speakers addressed the project as a whole before the Duma advanced to an article-by-article consideration of it, but they had little new to say. Several simply seconded previous speakers; others presented arguments that had been heard in the earlier, similar debate over parole. A priest who had spoken for parole as an act of Christian mercy made the same point about probation. A bishop who was attached to the rightists could not go quite that far. The bishop approved of mercy, of course, but he did not think that political offenders, for example, merited quite as much mercy.[113] Most of the later speakers added more heat than light to the discussion. E. P. Gegechkori, who had performed the same function in the vote on parole, announced that the Social Democrats would abstain because "until new relations of social forces are established, it is premature to think of a rational way to fight crime." He took advantage of his time at the podium to savage speakers from the right.[114] V. M. Purishkevich, at the opposite end of the political spectrum, called the project "a long, continuous amnesty for criminals that holds the whole Russian people under a knife." When delegates on the left—all men— laughed at his evident belief in an anthropological view of criminality, which had only a small following among professional criminologists in the West and Russia, Purishkevich remarked on their resemblance to the murderesses in P. N. Tarnovskaia's recent book, *Women Murderers*.[115] The vote to move on to an article-by-article discussion was taken among insults hurled from right and left.[116]

Vituperative exchanges began again immediately with consideration of the first article. Members debated which offenses might be probated and clashed bitterly over political offenses and horse theft. Their longest debate concerned which courts would have the power to assign probation. The left wanted to extend the power, which the project gave to judges, to juries as well. In the end the amendment failed, and the article stood as originally presented by the MIu.[117] With the passage of this last article the project as a whole was adopted and forwarded to the State Council.

While the project awaited action in the State Council, the tone of newspaper articles became even more shrill. In December 1909 *Russkoe Znamia* described a particularly gruesome beating and murder as a lead-in to an attack on probation. The murder had nothing to do with probation, because the project did not foresee probating the sentences of convicted murderers, but pretending there was a connection allowed the newspaper to construct the following soliloquy for the MIu: "Did you steal only once? Please, do it again. How many murders did you commit? Only one? That's not much, go kill again." In a second article in the same issue the newspaper accused the Duma of blaspheming against Christ and the Holy Ghost and called probation "that godless reform."[118]

When the project was taken up at the State Council a few months later, it was given an unfriendly reception. N. S. Tagantsev, who had spoken forcefully for parole less than a year before, introduced the Duma's project on 11 January 1910. This time he immediately pointed to what he called "difficulties" in the project and asked that it be sent to the council's Committee on Legislative Proposals before it came to the whole council. One of his problems seems minor, a matter of carelessness or inconsequence, easily fixed or maybe safely ignored. (He was concerned by the inconsistency that hunters who were guilty of poaching would be fined, whereas fishermen could be probated.) But his other objection was a matter of great importance and was not overcome in the debate that eventually followed. On this first day, Tagantsev's motion to commit the project to committee carried.[119]

Tagantsev was of two minds about probation. He had spoken and written favorably about it in the past but had apparently changed his mind. It may be that he did not want to say that directly, so he said, instead, that the project was flawed. I believe there was more to it than that, however. I think that, like many other Russians, especially of the upper class, Tagantsev had been alarmed by the revolution that had just ended and by the restlessness that still prevailed. Judging from his later comments, it also seems that he was losing confidence in the efficacy of corrections and was finding the idea of simple punishment more acceptable—although he did not say this directly, either. What is clear is that Tagantsev was anxious about the impact that probation might have in Russia in 1910. I believe he gained what he wanted from his motion to commit when the committee returned the project to the council on 7 April with a negative recommendation.

S. F. Platonov reported for the committee that although it unanimously approved the idea of probation, a majority found the project premature. All thirteen members accepted the usual arguments for probation, but ten agreed that its implementation faced insurmountable difficulties in contemporary Russia. One major obstacle was the current condition of the lower-level courts that handled most petty crime. Volost' courts had not been given the power to probate by the project, but urban local (mestnye) courts had. Platonov opined that this was a mistake, because rural people were less "depraved" than urban dwellers. On the other hand, the majority believed that the local courts were in poor condition and did not want to give them the authority to grant probation, either. Furthermore, they were undergoing reform, and it was not yet known how they would emerge from that process. The majority found an even greater problem in the lack of records. It feared that judges would be unlikely to know whether the convicts they were about to sentence were already repeat offenders who should not be probated or, indeed, whether they were probationers whose offense should revoke their current probation.[120] This was the larger difficulty that Tagantsev had foreseen in January. By a ten-to-three margin the committee recommended the project be rejected.

MIu Shcheglovitov rose to defend the project. In an extraordinarily long and impressively well-crafted speech he marshaled evidence and opinions from many different fields to respond to the committee's concerns and to urge the project's passage. His speech to the council was considerably different from his earlier speech to the Duma—as had been the case with his advocacy of parole—obviously playing to both the higher education and the greater conservatism of the state councilors. Although he argued in vain, Shcheglovitov apparently knew his audience well and chose his arguments and emphases to appeal to blocs of state councilors of varying backgrounds and attitudes.[121]

He began by calling probation "desirable, necessary, and timely" and reminded his listeners that it had ancient roots in Russia, in the practice of poruchitel'stvo, a pledge of personal surety. As usual, he listed the many, mostly European, countries that already used probation, but he was careful to sandwich this information with disclaimers that it was neither the experience of Europe nor the theoretical support of experts by themselves that persuaded him of the usefulness of probation. Probation recommended itself, he insisted, by "purely practical" considerations. He then tried to show "in practical terms" that probation was "necessary, timely and in complete accord with Russian popular legal consciousness."

Probation was needed, he claimed, because criminality was on the rise. The incidence of serious crime and recidivism was up. At the same time, the cost of prisons continued to grow, and confidence in their use had been shaken. Judges in lower courts were responding by passing more "acquittals against convictions" in minor cases, that is, acquitting offenders they knew to be guilty rather than sending them to prison. In lower courts, from 30 to 35 percent of criminal cases then ended in such acquittals.

Timeliness, he recognized, was a matter of opinion, but he urged on the councilors his opinion that the introduction of probation should precede the reform of local courts, which should then be remodeled in light of that change. *Volost'* courts, he pointed out, already were using probation of a sort in the form of reprimand, which could replace either fines or short-term imprisonment. He argued further that it was common and useful for penal reforms to precede and lead court reforms. The law of 17 April 1863 on corporal punishment, for example, had properly preceded the major court reform of 20 November 1864. Recently, despite similar arguments, probation had been introduced into German law in advance of a major court reform. The related objection about insufficient statistics on recidivism he found even easier to dismiss. The only major law that specifically addressed recidivism—the law of 3 February 1892, which provided stricter punishment for a second offense—had preceded such statistics and had begun the collection of data. "First we need the law," he said, "and then improvement of statistics." Although Shcheglovitov did not say it here, the fact that not so long ago the council had passed the project on parole before the establishment of a sufficient number of *patronaty,* and with the expectation that parole would produce *patronaty,* must have occurred to them as a logical parallel.

Returning to the issue of popular legal consciousness, he raised again the ancient practice of *poruchitel'stvo.* Not only were the peasants long used to this form of probation (it was formally imposed with a "reproof prior to a subsequent offense") but two major government commissions that had studied laws governing the peasants had recommended maintaining its use.[122] There was no reason to expect that probation would be an unsettling innovation. Through reprimands and surety bonds many peasants had already experienced kinds of probation, and most were familiar with their use.

Shcheglovitov then tried to overcome the perception that probation was an extreme extension of recent penal reforms and tried to frame it, rather, as a middle ground between more drastic alternatives. Responding to the objection that lower-court judges were too incompetent to grant probation, he asked why, if the judges were empowered to convict or to acquit, they should not also be empowered to probate? Probation was more severe than acquittal but less severe than a prison sentence. In closing, he asked the councilors to remember that practicing Russian jurists had strongly supported probation since at least 1902 and that, because it worked, none of the many countries that used probation were currently discussing its repeal. He strongly urged passage of the project.

When the council reconvened after a short break, only six members found more to say, and of them only M. Ia. Govorukho-Otrok said anything the councilors had not already heard. The most conservative of the speakers, Govorukho-Otrok presented himself as something of a cracker-barrel philosopher. He would not dare address the judicial, theoretical, or international arguments about probation, about which he confessed to know nothing, but he would present the "provincial" point of view, with which he must have presumed superior familiarity. Disorder was growing in the countryside, he claimed, theft and hooliganism were on the rise, and anarchy was looming. Everyone talked about possible solutions, including increasing repression, using more corporal punishment, or reforming education, but no one in the countryside ever mentioned probation, because the people saw it as amnesty, not punishment. Nor was Govorukho-Otrok impressed by the argument that prisons corrupted inmates. Make prisons, he suggested, so they "destroy the desire of criminals to commit a second crime," and they would be doing their jobs. Despite disclaiming knowledge of the international aspects of the arguments he concluded, without elucidation, that probation might be fine for Americans, Spaniards, and Belgians, but it would not be fine for Russians.[123]

The vote that soon followed suggests that many of the state councilors shared these views, yet none of them chose to say so. Their silence may tell us something about the temper of the time. It seems probable that the preceding discussion or private talks had made it clear to the councilors that the project would be defeated. They did not need to speak against it before the vote. It may be as simple as their not wanting to waste time beating a dead horse or not wanting to offend the MIu or colleagues on the other side of the fence. But I wonder whether it was not at least partly a matter of not wanting to appear ignorant or reactionary by opposing what the professionals and specialists advocated. What was all right for Purishkevich or Zamyslovskii in the Duma was beneath the dignity of a state councilor. They might think those thoughts and silently, without explanation, vote against probation.

The speaker who followed Govorukho-Otrok also spoke against the project, but in a more refined and tentative way. N. S. Tagantsev, the well-known criminalist who had recommended consigning the project to the committee three months earlier, now assailed the logic behind probation. Before probation was available elsewhere and in Russia, still, the percentage of minor offenders who were fined rather than imprisoned had risen. Tagantsev raised doubts about this reasoning and about the next step, which substituted probation for imprisonment or fines. First, he was not convinced, he said, of the harmfulness of prisons. But even if they were bad, he thought other short-term facilities, like *arestnye doma*, were not. Moreover, justifying probation by the harmfulness of prisons did not explain why probation should be preferred to fines. The bottom line, which he did finally say, was that he feared probation would create the belief that first offenses were not punished and would give rise to more petty crime. Tagantsev was also concerned that an uneven application of probation would damage respect for courts and the law. He cited French and Belgian experiences: from county to county the percentage of eligible offenders probated ranged from 10 to 40 percent. Tagantsev concluded that although probation might be useful later, "it might be dangerous now."[124]

The last speaker, M. O. Kovrin-Milevskii, tried to save the project from immediate defeat by suggesting alternatives to the committee's motion to reject it as a whole. He believed it could be made acceptable by amendment. He would, for example, narrow the scope of sentences that would be eligible for probation and would give fewer courts the authority to grant probation, but he would not have probation replace fines. If that were not acceptable, he hoped the council might find in an article-by-article discussion of the project elements that "might be useful in another form." As a final alternative, he recommended the project be returned to another committee for further consideration. None of his suggestions found fertile ground. When no one else chose to speak to the project, the chairman put the motion to vote. It carried, and the project was killed.[125]

Unlike the movement to establish parole, which had succeeded in 1909, and unlike the many other innovations that in recent decades had been introduced into the Russian criminal-justice system, the movement to introduce probation would never succeed in imperial Russia. Despite the support of criminologists, judges, lawyers, procurators, the people's elected representatives in the Duma, and others, the State Council rejected the concept. Why? Several factors combined in 1910 to doom passage of probation. First, modern penology had made grandiose promises for more than a century in the West, and for half a century in Russia. Russia had spent millions of rubles on its experiments, and still the crime rate continued to rise. The councilors had reason to doubt the experts. This, of course, had been true also in 1909 and had contributed to the opposition to parole, which they had approved by a rather narrow margin. Also contributing to their opposition may have been an increased sense of social danger. The councilors were clearly distressed by the recent revolution and by the continuing social and political unrest. This too had been true in 1909, but their fear may have been slightly greater in 1910. There were a few more references in 1910 to revolutionary unrest in Duma and council debates than there had been in 1909, and other observers have commented on a growing fear of a new revolution in 1910.[126] Any concession to lawbreakers might have been more difficult to approve in 1910. Probably the most important factor, however, was the very nature of probation. Probation seemed to go that one unacceptable step farther than did parole in its diminution of punishment, on the one hand, and its rejection of correctional imprisonment, on the other. Paroled ex-convicts had at least had a taste of prison, which might serve to deter them from repeat offenses, if not to correct them. Probationers could seem to have emerged scot-free. Under the circumstances, that was too much. Despite what the experts might say, at least for a while, in 1910, it was all right to reject the experience of Europe and the advice of the experts and to choose not to change yet again.

THE FALL OF THE GTU

The revolutions of 1905 and 1917 seriously disrupted the operation of the GTU. As I have noted, the events of 1905–1906 delayed many reform programs by filling Russian prisons beyond their legal capacity. Many regulations about separating prisoners into categories, permitting them room for exercise, and providing work could not be observed. Money intended for building new model prisons and improving the operation of other prisons was absorbed in the effort to maintain the thousands of new inmates.

The 1917 revolutions immediately disrupted prison administration more seriously than the Revolution of 1905, and they soon destroyed the GTU. During the February Revolution many prisons were "liberated" by revolutionaries, and many prison workers were relieved of their positions because of their association with "the old order." Many others fled, fearing revolutionaries and unruly prisoners. Ad hoc revolutionary groups had to step in to administer the abandoned facilities in some cases, and in others they asserted their right to do so.

The Kineshma Revolutionary Committee, for example, telegraphed the new MIu A. F. Kerenskii on 6 March 1917, "Criminal prisoners demand immediate release. Kineshma Revolutionary Committee of public security did not think possible given time to free. Criminal prisoners threaten to destroy prison. We await your orders . . . telegraph . . . urgent." That same day Kerenskii replied that the committee should tell the prisoners "violence is impermissible." If they rioted, they would not be eligible for the amnesties and paroles the government was considering. A telegram arrived from Revel the same day: "There is nothing for the prison staff and guard to do. In reopened prisons new personnel must be appointed due to extreme hostility against old order. How shall we proceed?" From Iaroslavl came a more reassuring telegram: "All disorders headed off by timely measures. . . . Political and religious prisoners all unconditionally freed. . . . Acts of the inspector and his subordinates fully answer demands of moment." Only eleven days after that first telegram, however, a second followed from Iaroslavl to say that "serious unrest is appearing among criminal prisoners" and that a "greater part of prison staff at all levels [is] trying to leave the service." Staff members feared that they would soon be fired by more liberal administrators or killed by rioting prisoners. What they were paid could not hold them to such fearful work; salaries had been eroded by several years of wartime inflation.[127]

Changes made at the top of the GTU at first heartened the more progressive prison workers, but others quickly abandoned their jobs. P. K. Gran', who had been director since 1913, stepped down under pressure on 28 February 1917. Gran' had made his career in the police and prison bureaucracies and was deemed unsuitable in the new order. He was replaced by a liberal professor of criminal law, A. A. Zhizhilenko, who had no experience in administration. For a brief time, while professors and lawyers tried to steer the provisional government through the morass of war and shortages, Russia ran on enthusiasm and euphoria. Telegrams poured in from prison administrators around the country to laud the passing of the old and the victory of the new. The Kherson provincial inspector saw the "transition to a better, brighter future." A Simbirsk committee praised the new government and asked permission to fire its inspector, Shtriker, for being a German and "a supporter of the old order." A warden in Blagoveshchensk congratulated Kerenskii and swore his fealty to "renewed Russia." Samara's inspector rejoiced that "Russia is freed from the fetters of slavery." On 6 March the GTU staff in St. Petersburg signed the following document.

> Freed by the blessed heroism of the people from the chains of the old bloody regime that bound thought and will, all workers of lower ranks of the Main Prison Administration with a feeling of deep relief and boundless joy, gathered together, are in full readiness to unanimously give all our strength to long-needed work based on new thought for the good of the Motherland and under the leadership of the people's power.
>
> May the unenlightened nightmarish night of many centuries never return.[128]

Hope was briefly raised high in some breasts that such change could be made quickly. In his first day in office, April Fools' Day, Professor Zhizhilenko issued an order intended to begin the transformation. Former prison personnel, he wrote, had been raised "in an atmosphere of lawlessness and disrespect for the individual and with the habits of the old order." With the rebirth of Russia, "such people are not considered fit for prison service."[129] Zhizhilenko and his staff laid plans to begin courses to train contemporary, humane administrators. Before they were driven out of public life in October, they managed to graduate twenty students.[130] To signal how different it was from the old GTU, the administration changed its name on 4 May 1917 to the Main Administration of Places of Incarceration (*Glavnoe Upravlenie Mest Zakliucheniia,* or GUMZ). Even the fearsome word "prisons" might be done away with in the new world. The GTU–GUMZ found, however, as did the provisional government, that change ran ahead of it and out of control. Workers continued to leave their posts. Soviets and other local provisional committees continued to fire inspectors and wardens who did not fit their conception of the new order. Revolutionaries and prisoners from time to time liberated and sacked more prisons. The administration's headquarters were ransacked in March.[131] New and remaining prison workers began to unionize in May and quickly outstripped the GUMZ in their demands for reforms and raises. By the time the provisional government and the GUMZ were toppled in October they barely retained nominal control of Russia's prisons.

CONCLUSION

It has never been accurate and has long been unfashionable to explain the course of history by describing the changing ideas of societies' intellectuals. Ideas alone do not move history. The writing of history has been significantly enriched since materialism displaced idealism as the primary philosophical mode of the western world a century and a half ago. Exploring the forces that stand behind and give rise to climates of opinion provides a much more profound explanation for historical change. However, in our search for history's primum mobile we sometimes undervalue the contributions made by spiritual and idealistic forces.

For example, Marxist historians—Soviet historians, in particular—long had to argue that economic causation and class struggle were primary. In Soviet historiography the emancipation of Russia's peasants usually comes as a reluctant concession by the ruling classes. The bureaucracy's fear of the consequences of economic backwardness and the gentry's fear of a peasant jacquerie compelled them to free the serfs and the state peasants. Recent American scholarship, on the other hand, suggests that Russia's defeat in the Crimean War—that is, the Russians' perception of their industrial and economic backwardness—was an important but not the most important factor in emancipation and that fear of peasant rebellion was at most a minor contributing factor. Statesmen who discussed the emancipation mentioned these factors little. Much more frequently they talked about how uncivilized serfdom was, how inappropriate and shameful it was in a modern, European nation. Explanations tied tightly to economics and class have insufficient room for *raznochintsy* and "repentant noblemen."

The same is true in the history of punishment. Workhouses were first established in the wealthiest mercantile nations of western Europe. Historians who try to explain them have usually concluded that they were created to make money for the men who operated them. These men are said to have devised a new form of punishment as just another, and reprehensible, way to make more money. Historians of this school do not sufficiently appreciate that a society that had become wealthy and powerful by demanding orderly, sedulous labor of itself might naturally think that a dose of the same could do the unemployed and vagrant more good than could whipping or idle incarceration. In their attempts to reach the deepest roots of men's behavior, such writers unfairly underestimate the strength of more purely intellectual and psychological motivations. A presentist view will likely see greed and injustice in the operation of workhouses, but a more generous understanding of their contemporary values might rather see a sensible altruism. Altruism and the desire of people to make the world conform to their ideals have been powerful forces in history.

Altruism and well-meant reformism can be both misguided and unwanted, however. They can cause resentment and disenchantment and often achieve ends far removed from reformers' intentions. Personal or governmental benevolence may deeply disturb the objects of that benevolence, who do not wish to be "improved." Reformers then think that their efforts have "failed" and variously blame themselves, the ungrateful objects of their efforts, or other forces in society, which, they think, somehow perverted their work. Movements that begin with altruism and idealism quickly become enmeshed in traditions, institutions, and the will of influential people, all more powerful than the movement's initiators. They are deflected to ends that then seem to be the product of these other forces. It is important, however, to remember how such movements are conceived.

A good example of this in Russian history is the well-known story of the populist movement of the 1870s. Young people of a fairly wide range of political views reached out to the peasants, whom they hoped to embrace as brothers and to help, and they were repeatedly rebuffed. By the end of the 1870s, after a series of failures and tribulations, many of these young people reviled the peasants, whom they then assumed would not and could not be helped. Some dropped out of the movement; others turned violently against the government, which, in their view, had made the peasants the ignorant, stubborn creatures they had found them to be. What began as an effort to forge closer ties between urban intellectuals and peasants became a war between urban intellectuals and officialdom and somewhat later a movement that directed its efforts toward helping urban industrial workers.

The movement for prison reform in Russia had a similar genesis and went about as far astray. It began with the effort to abolish corporal punishment, a movement that at first had nothing to say about prison reform. Corporal punishment had to be abolished in Russia, said the reform's proponents, because it had been in Europe, where enlightened thinkers had explained that violent physical behavior was "barbaric," "uncivilized," and "Asiatic." Russian reformers, happily but mistakenly, discovered that original or natural Russian law did not include corporal punishments, which were indeed a barbaric Asiatic accretion imposed on Russia by the Tatar invaders and made to seem traditional only by the unfortunately long duration of the "Tatar yoke." Barbarism, of course, suits only a barbaric people. In the 1860s, Russians vigorously affirmed their civilization and their place as a European nation with the Great Reforms. The partial abolition of corporal punishment was part and parcel of these. Barbaric punishment was beneath the dignity of civilized men, who now included Russia's emancipated serfs. Like serfdom, corporal punishment was an anachronistic remnant of the feudal past. So, despite real fears among the statesmen who discussed the reform's merits and dangers, corporal punishment was largely abolished.

Toward the end of their discussions, the men who wrote the corporal-punishment reform acknowledged that Russia did not have a suitable replacement for the punishment they outlawed. They recommended that the responsible government ministries look into doing something about Russia's prisons. Prisons, too, were disgraceful in the 1860s. They did not have as their purpose the worthy, optimistic goal of rehabilitating prisoners that the penitentiaries of Europe and the United States professed. And soon after corporal punishment was curtailed, offenders who could no longer be whipped began to overcrowd Russia's old prisons, which consequently became even more disgraceful. Reformers therefore strove to find the means and the money to make prisons serve the corrective purposes that they believed prisons might but corporal punishment never could.

At this point the reform effort fell into the hands of institutions and powerful men. The MVD began to centralize prison administration in one of its departments and carried out a few changes where other institutions were willing to cede their operations to the MVD. However, as soon as the MVD proposed more far-reaching change—reform that would involve, among other things, a change in the philosophy of punishment—other institutions joined battle with them to demand their say in the process. Four commissions then debated the course that prison reform would take. Because millions of rubles, a bureaucratic empire, and the Russian state's operating definition of human nature were at stake, they wrangled for a dozen years.

Once their horns were locked, the institutions and individuals lost control of any chance to make a coherent and comprehensive statement. They had to compromise. The framework within which they could compromise was their agreement that European penal systems, like most things European, were better than their own. The hopes they expressed were those of the European Enlightenment, which proclaimed the perfectibility of man, and of mid-nineteenth-century European thought, which explained the environmental causes of behavior. The cures they proposed for criminal offenders were those that were already in use in

Europe and the United States. Each time they reached agreement to produce a plan of reform, however, the MF rejected their plan as too expensive. This hard fact of Russian reality repeatedly delayed and altered plans for prison reform, causing the reformers much frustration. On the other hand, it may have saved the state from wasting millions of rubles.

Systematic prison reform began in 1879, when the Main Prison Administration was established in the MVD. Limited by niggardly finances and hampered by political disputes and revolutionary events, the GTU slowly reformed Russia's prison system. It planned and oversaw the construction of modern correctional facilities; it wrote projects for correctional prison regimes and saw them implemented; it attracted increasingly well-trained men to serve in prisons. Considering the obstacles in the way of their work, the GTU's achievements were impressive. The GTU modernized Russia's prisons and made them into a coherent system, which was what they had set out to do. They did not, however, achieve the correction of Russia's prisoners: crime and recidivism rates rose between 1879 and 1917. The GTU's success was that it permitted the Russian government to hold its head up while failing in a modern and professional way. And that is all any European government was able to do in its struggle against crime.

INTRODUCTION

1. J. Soley, "British Russophobia during the Crimean War," in *War and Society in the Nineteenth Century Russian Empire,* ed. J. G. Purves and D. A. West (Toronto: New Review Books, 1972), 106–21.

2. See Donald Senese, *S. M. Stepniak-Kravchinskii: The London Years* (Newtonville, Mass.: Oriental Research Partners, 1987).

3. Ibid., 48.

4. Peter Kropotkin, *In Russian and French Prisons,* introduction by Paul Avrich (New York: Schocken Books, 1971), 259, 263, 271, 273–74, 283, 294–95, 299, 300–301.

5. V. Burtsev, *Bor'ba za svobodnuiu Rossiiu: Moi vospominaniia* (Berlin, 1923), vol. 1, 134–42; and Senese, *Kravchinskii,* 101–3.

6. George Kennan, *Siberia and the Exile System,* 2 vols. (New York: Century Company, 1891).

7. Senese, *Kravchinskii,* 93.

8. Much of my discussion depends on ibid., 91–109.

9. Harry deWindt, *From Pekin to Calais by Land* (London, 1889).

10. Harry deWindt, *Siberia as It Is* (London, 1892).

11. Senese, *Kravchinskii,* 94–95.

12. M. N. Gernet, *Istoriia tsarskoi tiur'my,* 5 vols. (Moscow: Iuridicheskoe izdatel'stvo Narodnogo komissariata iustitsii, 1951–1956).

13. M. N. Gernet, *Obshchestvennyia prichiny prestupnosti: Sotsialisticheskoe napravlenie v nauke ugolovnago prava* (Moscow: S. Skirmunt, 1906); and M. N. Gernet, *Prestuplenie i bor'ba s nim v sviazi s evoliutsiei obshchestva* (Moscow, 1914).

14. Gernet, *Istoriia,* vol. 1, 57. On Peter and Paul and Shlissel'burg, see pp. 90–157.

15. A. D. Margolis, "Sistema sibirskoi ssylki i zakon ot 12 iiunia 1900 goda," in *Ssylka i obshchestvenno-politicheskaia zhizn' v Sibiri, xviii–nachalo xx v.* (Novosibirsk: Nauka, 1978), 126–40.

16. According to M. P. Chubinskii, "Sudebnaia reforma," in *Istoriia Rossii v xix veke,* vol. 3 (St. Petersburg, 1910), 247, 12.5 percent of trials ended in acquittals. About 75 percent left the accused neither convicted nor acquitted but free "under suspicion," in accordance with *Svod zakonov Rossiiskoi Imperii,* vol. 15 (1857), sec. 4, art. 313. Only the remaining approximately 12 percent resulted in convictions. In a survey of the annual *Otchet Ministerstva Iustitsii,* Richard Wortman found a higher rate of convictions. They declined, he writes, from 36 percent in 1840 to 27 percent in 1854, whereas verdicts of "remains under suspicion" varied between 10 percent and 13 percent. See his *The Development of a Russian Legal Consciousness* (Chicago: University of Chicago Press, 1976),

239, 316. He mentions the other figures but does not explain the difference.

17. *Ob otmene telesnykh nakazanii* (n.p. [1863]), 34.

18. *Ulozhenie o nakazaniiakh ugolovnykh i ispravitel'nykh* (St. Petersburg, 1845). See, for example, arts. 84–88.

19. *Ministerstvo vnutrennykh del, 1802–1902: Istoricheskii ocherk,* vol. 1 (St. Petersburg, 1902), 66.

20. On the difficulties not overcome by would-be reformers in the 1840s, see G. S. Fel'dshtein, *Glavnyia techeniia v istorii nauki ugolovnago prava v Rossii* (Iaroslavl: Tipografiia gubernskago pravleniia, 1909), 552–58, 649–64; Samuel Kucherov, *Courts, Lawyers, and Trials under the Last Three Tsars* (New York: Frederick A. Praeger, 1953), 22–25; and Wortman, *Legal Consciousness,* passim.

21. This is a major point of Wortman's book, *Legal Consciousness,* 198–234, 244–67. Fel'dshtein also discusses the great outpouring of legal writing in a few established and many new journals at this time, including the Ministry of Justice's own *Zhurnal.* See Fel'dshtein, *Glavnyia techeniia,* 660–68.

CHAPTER 1: THE MOVEMENT TO ABOLISH CORPORAL PUNISHMENT

1. Carl Ludwig von Bar, *A History of Continental Criminal Law,* trans. Thomas S. Bell (Boston: Little, Brown, 1916; reprint, New York: Augustus M. Kelley, 1968), 35, 96–97, 103, 273.

2. The philosophes were not the first to attack torture, capital, and corporal punishments. A few Roman and medieval European writers had found many of the same faults earlier. John H. Langbein believes that torture, for example, survived not because its failures were not known but because until the eighteenth century no alternative existed. He calls the historiography that attributes most penal reform in the eighteenth and nineteenth centuries to the writers of the Enlightenment the "fairy tale" of the reforms. See his *Torture and the Law of Proof: Europe and England in the Ancien Régime* (Chicago: University of Chicago Press, 1977), 8–10, 64–69. And Richard Mowery Andrews has made it clear that the more grisly corporal and capital punishments were being applied less frequently, at least in France, well before the French Revolution. See his *Law, Magistracy, and Crime in Old Regime Paris, 1735–1789,* vol. 1, *The System of Criminal Justice* (Cambridge: Cambridge University Press, 1994), esp. 283–84, 383–93. My argument is not that the philosophes' writing led to the end of "barbarous" punishments in Europe. Their writing was a reflection of what was already beginning to occur in their countries as well as a program for further reform. What is important in this study is that their writing was available in Russia, where those changes were not so advanced, and helped to spur them on. Following Langbein, I agree that the existence of an alternative to corporal punishments was important for their abolition, but I argue that other causes for reform cited by Langbein and others were absent in Russia (and in some cases in Europe, where they saw them).

3. Cesare Beccaria, *On Crimes and Punishments,* trans. Henry Paolucci (Indianapolis: Bobbs-Merrill, 1963), 42.

4. See Nicholas V. Riasanovsky, *A Parting of the Ways: Government and the Educated Public in Russia, 1801–1855* (Oxford: Clarendon Press, 1976), 3–53.

5. Beccaria, *On Crimes and Punishments,* 43.

6. John Locke, *Of Civil Government: Two Treatises* (London: J. M. Dent and Sons, 1940), 122.

7. On Catherine's *Nakaz,* see chap. 8, esp. art. 82, in W. F. Reddaway, ed., *Documents of Catherine the Great* (Cambridge, England: Cambridge University Press, 1931), 225–27.

8. Beccaria, *On Crimes and Punishments,* 43–44.

9. Charles-Louis de Secondat Montesquieu, *The Spirit of the Laws,* ed. David Wallace Carrithers (Berkeley: University of California Press, 1977), 159.

10. Paul Dukes, *Catherine the Great and the Russian Nobility: A Study Based on the Materials of the Legislative Commission of 1767* (Cambridge, England: Cambridge University Press, 1967), 6.

11. N. D. Chechulin, ed., *Nakaz Imperatritsy Ekateriny II* (St. Petersburg, 1907), passim; and Robert V. Allen, "The Great Legislative Commission of Catherine II of 1767" (Ph.D. diss., Yale University, 1950), esp. 103–50.

12. Mikhail Stupin, *Istoriia telesnykh nakazanii v Rossii ot sudebnikov do nastoiashchago vremeni* (Vladikavkaz, 1887), 41–43; and Coleman Phillipson, *Three Criminal Law Reformers: Beccaria, Bentham, Romilly* (Montclair, N.J.: Patterson Smith, 1970), 21.

13. Dukes, *Catherine the Great,* 221. On the success of this effort, see A. Lortholary, *Le Mirage russe en France au XVIIIe siècle* (Paris, n.d.), cited in Riasanovsky, *A Parting of the Ways,* 20–22, 22n.

14. Allen, "Great Legislative Commission," 91–92, 129, cites the *nakazy* that were published in the *Sbornik Imperatorskogo russkogo istoricheskogo obshchestva (SIRIO).* Torture was curbed by *Polnoe Sobranie Zakonov Rossiiskoi Imperii,* Seriia pervaia (hereafter *1PSZ*) (St. Petersburg, 1830), 10 February 1763, 11527.

15. *SIRIO* 4: 148–49, 152, 288, 302, 462–63, 468; 36: 18–19; 68: 7, 657–58. See also Dukes, *Catherine the Great,* 160–61.

16. *SIRIO* 4: 148–49, 152; 36: 18–19; 68: 7, 657–58.

17. Beccaria, who borrowed a great deal, conceivably adopted his attitude from Montesquieu, to whom, he told another philosophe, he owed his "conversion to Philosophy." Peter Gay, *The Enlightenment, an Interpretation: The Rise of Modern Paganism* (New York: Alfred A. Knopf, 1975), 10.

18. Cited in Henry J. Merry, *Montesquieu's System of Natural Government* (West Lafayette, Ind.: Purdue University Studies, 1970), 264.

19. The best treatment of the eighteenth-century gentry's intellectual development is Marc Raeff, *Origins of the Russian Intelligentsia: The Eighteenth-Century Nobility* (New York: Harcourt, Brace, Jovanovich, 1966).

20. A few historians have argued that the end of the Pugachev uprising marked the beginning of a new ambivalence toward the peasant, who was seen not only as an "uncouth half-beast" but also as "a child who has to be carefully protected against himself and guided into the new 'civilization.'" See Marc Raeff, "Pugachev's Rebellion," in *Preconditions of Revolution in Early Modern Europe,* ed. Robert Forster and Jack P. Greene (Baltimore: Johns Hopkins University Press, 1970), 199–201. A few sensitive souls may have felt this way when Pushkin wrote *The Captain's Daughter* sixty-three years after Pugachev's death, but it does not seem to me that many did at any time in the eighteenth century.

21. Jeremy Bentham, *The Rationale of Punishment* (London: Robert Howard, 1830), 84. Not everyone was always impressed with Catherine in this regard. When the New York State legislature debated the abolition of capital punishment in the 1840s, one legislator put Catherine forward as an example to be emulated. J. S. Van Rensselaer responded, "And if we are to be influenced by imitation, if 'patterns of noble clemency' are to be sought, we shall go somewhere else than to an Empress who was twice, at least, a murderer of the foulest degree, and always a loathsome adulteress." Cited in David Brion Davis, "The Movement to Abolish Capital Punishment in America, 1787–1861," *American Historical Review* 63 (October 1957): 39.

22. *1PSZ,* 17916.

23. *1PSZ,* 19856, 19885, 19920.

24. *1PSZ*, 29362, 29125.

25. *1PSZ*, 27197.

26. *1PSZ*, 20115, 23274. See also Stupin, *Istoriia telesnykh nakazanii*, 54–56.

27. *1PSZ*, 25211, 27 November 1801.

28. See, for example, V. Korolenko, "Russkaia pytka," *Russkoe Bogatstvo* 1 (1912): 75, 84.

29. A. G. Timofeev, *Istoriia telesnykh nakazanii v russkom prave* (St. Petersburg, 1904), 104.

30. "Rozgi doloi!" *Kolokol* 75 (1 July 1860), 1. See also I. Gol'denberg, *Reforma telesnykh nakazanii* (St. Petersburg, n.d.), 44. Judging from its contents, I would estimate that this book was written between 1900 and 1917.

31. Timofeev, *Istoriia telesnykh nakazanii*, 157–58.

32. G. A. Dzhanshiev, *Epokha velikikh reform* (St. Petersburg, 1907), 233.

33. Gol'denberg, *Reforma*, 46.

34. Ibid., 48–49.

35. Dzhanshiev, *Epokha*, 233, cites art. 25 of the *Obshchee polozhenie o krest'ianakh*.

36. V. Spasovich, *Uchebnik ugolovnogo prava*, vol. 1 (St. Petersburg, 1863), 195–98.

37. *Kolokol* 127 (1 April 1862), 1–2.

38. Gol'denberg, *Reforma*, 49. Orlov's letter is included in *Ob otmene telesnykh nakazanii*, 1–8, which appears to be a collection made by the committee that produced the law of 17 April 1863. It has no further bibliographical information. All citations are to this edition, which I read at the Library of Congress.

39. E. M. Feoktistov, *Vospominaniia za kulisami politiki i literatury, 1848–1896*, ed. Iu. G. Oksman (Leningrad, 1929), 47–59, 73n; and P. A. Valuev, *Dnevnik*, ed. P. A. Zaionchkovskii (Moscow, 1961), vol. 1, 272.

40. N. M. Karamzin, *Istoriia gosudarstva rossisskago*, vol. 4 (Moscow, 1818), 217.

41. N. D. Sergeevskii, *Russkoe ugolovnoe pravo* (St. Petersburg, 1900), 141; N. S. Tagantsev, *Russkoe ugolovnoe pravo* (St. Petersburg, 1902), vol. 2, 1134–41; and N. Evreinov, *Istoriia telesnykh nakazanii v Rossii* (St. Petersburg, 1906; reprint New York: Chalidze Publications, 1979).

42. I. Ia. Foinitskii, *Uchenie o nakazanii v sviazi s tiur'movedeniem* (St. Petersburg, 1889), 155–62. The Russians were not the only people to blame foreigners for aspects of their penal systems they no longer admired. Propagandizing against the continued use of torture, Jardine, Coke, Blackstone, and other Englishmen spread the idea that it was an un-English practice borrowed from the Continent and Roman law. See Langbein, *Torture and the Law of Proof*, 131–32.

43. *Ob otmene telesnykh nakazanii*, 1.

44. Ibid., 12.

45. Feoktistov, *Vospominaniia*, 121–22n.

46. *Ob otmene telesnykh nakazanii*, 12–14.

47. Their replies are in ibid., 28–94.

48. Valuev's comments are in ibid., 28–37.

49. These replies are in ibid., 41, 68–69, 38, and 50–68, respectively. The quotation from Konstantin Nikolaevich's reply is on p. 50.

50. Ibid., 39–40. Pieter Spierenburg argues that a major cause of the abolition of particularly grisly punishments and the disappearance of other punishments from public view to behind prison walls was a growing sensitivity, especially among the upper classes,

to pain and suffering. Because they considered the execution of such punishments repugnant, they ended some and moved others out of their sight. See *The Spectacle of Suffering: Executions and the Evolution of Repression: From a Preindustrial Metropolis to the European Experience* (Cambridge, England: Cambridge University Press, 1984), 183–89. Murav'ev, who would soon gain an unpleasant reputation as the "hangman of Vilna" for his brutal suppression of the Polish uprising of 1863, seems not to have shared this repugnance, but he may have been willing to recognize it in his colleagues.

51. *Ob otmene telesnykh nakazanii,* 44.

52. Ibid., 69–71.

53. Ibid., 45–50. He may have been careless, or he may have counted on his secular colleagues not to check up on him. What the passages do say is that the apostles considered such punishment dishonorable but that they were proud to suffer dishonor for Jesus: "When they had called in the apostles, they beat them and charged them not to speak in the name of Jesus and let them go. Then they left the presence of the council, rejoicing that they were counted worthy to suffer dishonor for the name" (Acts 5: 40–41). Uncharitably interpreted, Filaret's lesson also draws an analogy between evangelizing and committing crime, which he certainly would not have wanted to draw. Note how much Filaret sounds like the bishops of Kiev who advised Prince Vladimir in 994–996 "that he was appointed of God for the chastisement of malefaction and for the practice of mercy toward the righteous, so that it was entirely fitting for him to punish a robber condignly" (*The Russian Primary Chronicle, Laurentian Text,* trans. and ed. Samuel Hazzard Cross and Olgerd P. Sherbowitz-Wetzor [Cambridge, Mass.: The Mediaeval Academy of America, 1973], 122).

54. *Ob otmene telesnykh nakazanii,* 71–92.

55. The word I have been translating—"deter"—is *ustrashat',* which also means to terrify. The etymological link is equally clear in English. *Ustrashat'* was the only word used for this meaning in nineteenth-century works on crime and punishment. It is still used, along with *uderzhivat'* (to restrain).

56. *Ob otmene telesnykh nakazanii,* 74.

57. Ibid., 129–37.

58. Ibid., 75, 72.

59. Ibid., 43, 44.

60. Ibid., 38–39.

61. Ibid., 34, 31–32, 36–37.

62. Ibid., 98–120.

63. Ibid., 154–99.

64. Timofeev, *Istoriia telesnykh nakazanii,* 169.

65. See Evreinov, *Istoriia telesnykh nakazanii,* 130–31.

66. Myra Glenn, *Campaigns against Corporal Punishment: Prisoners, Sailors, Women, and Children in Antebellum America* (Albany: State University of New York Press, 1984), 14–17, 113–14.

67. David D. Cooper, *The Lesson of the Scaffold: The Public Execution Controversy in Victorian England* (Athens: Ohio University Press, 1974), 54.

68. Spierenburg, *Spectacle of Suffering,* 203–7.

69. See William Walter Adams Jr., "Capital Punishment and the Russian Revolution" (Ph.D. diss., Columbia University, 1968), 252–424.

70. Langbein, *Torture and the Law of Proof,* 4, 8–10.

71. See Janet Tavrov, *The Russian Noble Family: Structure and Change* (New York: Garland Publishing, 1987); Patrick P. Dunn, "'That Enemy Is the Baby': Childhood in

Imperial Russia," in *The History of Childhood: The Untold Story of Child Abuse* (New York: Peter Bedrick Books, 1988); and Andrew Baruch Wachtel, *The Battle for Childhood: Creation of a Russian Myth* (Stanford, Calif.: Stanford University Press, 1990). I thank James Downey for directing me to these sources.

72. Spierenburg, *Spectacle of Suffering*, 183–89; James Turner, *Reckoning with the Beast: Animals, Pain, and Humanity in the Victorian Mind* (Baltimore: Johns Hopkins University Press, 1980), 25, 28, 34.

73. Laura Engelstein notes a similar chasing after "modernity" by Russians who found their model of modernity in the West in her book, *The Keys to Happiness: Sex and the Search for Modernity in Fin-de-Siècle Russia* (Ithaca, N.Y.: Cornell University Press, 1992), esp. 9, 17.

74. Adams, "Capital Punishment," 73–78, 100–138.

75. Timofeev, *Istoriia telesnykh nakazanii*, 2. See also pp. 47–58. The emphasis is mine.

76. Ibid., 41–44.

77. TsGIA SSSR, f. 1286, o. 28, d. 801, ll. 123–24.

78. Cited in Peter Czap Jr., "Peasant-Class Courts and Peasant Customary Justice in Russia, 1861–1912," *Journal of Social History* 2 (1967): 170. The translations in the quotations are Czap's.

79. "Khronika-vnutrennee obozrenie," *Vestnik Evropy* (November 1872): 342.

80. *2PSZ*, 27722.

81. *Ob otmene telesnykh nakazanii*, 85–86.

82. Vysochaishe uchrezhdenaia Osobaia Komissiia dlia razrabotki meropriiatii, vyzyvaemykh izdaniem novago ugolovnago ulozheniia. Otdel tiuremnykh voprosov. *Tiuremnoe preobrazovanie*, vol. 1, *Ispravitel'nyi dom, zakliuchenie v kreposti, i tiur'ma* (St. Petersburg, 1905), 4–5.

83. *Ob otmene telesnykh nakazanii*, 198.

CHAPTER 2: PRISON ADMINISTRATION IN THE MINISTRY OF INTERNAL AFFAIRS

1. Matt. 25: 36, 40.

2. Harry Elmer Barnes, *The Evolution of Penology in Pennsylvania* (Indianapolis: Bobbs-Merrill, 1927), 80–86.

3. John Aiken, *A View of the Life, Travels, and Philanthropic Labors of the Late John Howard* (Philadelphia, 1794).

4. *A Memoir of Daniel Wheeler with an Account of His Gospel Labours in the Islands of the Pacific* (Philadelphia, 1866), 57–65; and Janet Whitney, *Elizabeth Fry: Quaker Heroine* (New York: Benjamin Blom, 1972), 175–82.

5. Richard Knill, *Memoir of the Life and Character of Walter Venning* (London, 1822).

6. Ibid., 18–22; Whitney, *Elizabeth Fry*, 196–99.

7. Knill, *Memoir*, 27–34; *2PSZ*, 27895, 19 July 1819; D. Krainskii, *Materialy k izsledovaniiu istorii russkikh tiurem v sviazi s istoriei uchrezhdeniia Obshchestva Popechitel'stva o Tiur'makh* (Chernigov, 1912), 66–67.

8. Krainskii, *Materialy*, 68. Like John Howard, Venning died in Russia. He is buried in St. Petersburg, where the Prison Aid Society raised a monument to his memory. On one side a bas relief shows Venning entering a prison with a Bible in his hand. The other bears the inscription: "The St. Petersburg Prison Aid Society has raised this monu-

ment to the memory of their beloved co-worker, Walter Venning, compatriot of Howard and founder of the Prison Institutions of this country." See Knill, *Memoir*, 101–2.

9. Knill, *Memoir*, 41–42.

10. Krainskii, *Materialy*, 68–71.

11. A. F. Koni, "Fedor Petrovich Gaaz," in *Sobranie sochinenii*, vol. 5 (Moscow: Iuridicheskaia literatura, 1969), 301–2.

12. Ibid., 303–4, 314–15.

13. Ibid., 317–33.

14. A. F. Koni, "Dmitrii Aleksandrovich Rovinskii," in *Sobranie sochinenii*, vol. 5, 13–14.

15. Krainskii, *Materialy*, 80–81.

16. Ibid., 71–77.

17. See, for example, V. A. Sollogub, *Ob organizatsii v russkoi tiur'me truda* (Moscow, 1866), 10–11, who wrote, "All that remains is superficial bureaucratic formality, braking movement toward improvement....Prisons remain in their deplorable, sometimes even disgraceful state." Sollogub would soon become chairman of a commission that investigated ways of improving Russia's prisons.

18. Krainskii, *Materialy*, 85–86.

19. F. N. Malinin, "Tiuremnyi patronat (Po povodu razrabotki proekta normal'-nago ustava obshchestv pokrovitel'stva litsam, osvobozhdennym iz mest zakliucheniia Rossiiskoi Imperii)," *Tiuremnyi Vestnik* 8 (1905): 608–12; and S. K. Gogel', "O razvitii i pravilnoi postanovke patronata v Rossii," in *Voprosy ugolovnago prava, protsessa i tiur'-movedeniia* (St. Petersburg: Obshchestvennaia Pol'za, 1906), 612–13.

20. Krainskii, *Materialy*, 87–104.

21. Ibid., 105–10.

22. See especially Malinin, "Tiuremnyi patronat," 612. See also Gogel', *Voprosy*, 612; and Krainskii, *Materialy*, 110–19.

23. I translate the Russian word *smotritel'* as "keeper" to distinguish it from *nachal'nik tiur'my*, which I translate as "warden"; *Materialy po voprosu o preobrazovanii tiuremnoi chasti v Rossii, izdannye Ministerstvom vnutrennykh del po svedeniiam dostavlen-nym ot Nachal'nikov Gubernii* (St. Petersburg, 1865), i–ii.

24. Ibid.

25. Ibid.

26. Ibid., ii.

27. Ibid., 239–90.

28. The Moscow report is in ibid., 232–318. Most of the summary comments are on pp. 314–17.

29. Ibid., 237.

30. Ibid., 243.

31. Ibid., 318.

32. Ibid., iv–v. I have no better source of information on this group than this introduction to *Materialy po voprosu*. They apparently produced no published papers and only a vague memory of their existence even among men interested in prison reform. Another commission, writing up its conclusions only fifteen years later, referred to previous committees and commissions that had studied the same question. They named and dated the other groups correctly but associated no names with this group and dated their activity in 1865. See *Materialy o preobrazovanii tiuremnoi chasti* (St. Petersburg, 1878), journal 6, 3–4. Journal 7, 8–12, which contains a more detailed history of the commissions on prison reform, does not mention this one at all. These are the journals of the

Grot Commission. The volume contains journals, appendices, and memoranda, all individually paginated. The MVD's official centennial history recorded that "the first Commission on the prison problem was appointed in 1864." *Ministerstvo vnutrennykh del, 1802–1902: Istoricheskii ocherk* (St. Petersburg, 1902), vol. 1, 134.

33. *Materialy po voprosu,* v. One of these men is identified here as Galkin. This is almost certainly Galkin-Vraskii (sometimes spelled Galkin-Vraskoi), who later became the first director of the Main Prison Administration. See M. N. Galkin, "Mesta zakliucheniia vo Frantsii," *Russkii Vestnik* 12 (1864): 487–542; and Galkin-Vraskoi's introduction in "Materialy k istorii tiuremnoi reformy v Rossii: Pis'ma grafa V. A. Solloguba i K. K. Grota k M. N. Galkinu-Vraskomu," *Zhurnal Ministerstva Iustitsii* 9–10 (1901): 250–51. The other young man was A. Passek.

34. *Materialy po voprosu,* vi–viii. The MVD print shop ran off four hundred copies of *Materialy po voprosu* and distributed three copies to each POoT around the country.

35. TsGAOR, f. 109, o. 3, ed. khr. 866, ll. 1–2. This is a file of the Third Department of the Imperial Chancellery, Russia's secret police. It is titled "Sekretnyi Arkhiv. Obzor Deiatel'nosti i reorganizatsii uchrezhdenii politsii ispolnitel'noi s 1862, po noiabr' 1880."

36. Ibid., ll. 1–3.

37. *Ministerstvo vnutrennykh del, 1802–1902,* vol. 1, 136.

38. For a general account, see ibid., 137–38.

39. TsGIA SSSR, f. 1149, o. 9, d. 9, 329–62, contains a historical essay on exile and the prison system written by I. Ia. Foinitskii, who was then a Master of Laws and docent at the Imperial St. Petersburg University. It is part of the records of the Zubov Committee.

40. TsGIA SSSR, f. 1282, o. 1, ed. khr. 1048, ll. 175–76; TsGIA SSSR, f. 1149, o. 9, d. 3, ll. 40–41.

41. TsGIA SSSR, f. 1149, o. 9, d. 3, ll. 331–33.

42. TsGIA SSSR, f. 1282, o. 1, ed. khr. 1048, l. 175.

43. This is apparently a rare book. I found it in TsGIA SSSR, f. 908, o. 1, d. 278, "Proekt preobrazovaniia tiurem." I have been unable to locate any other copies.

44. Ibid., l. 2.

45. Ibid., ll. 3–18. The principles following are from l. 18.

46. Many works discuss the American and European experience. Two of the better are David J. Rothman, *The Discovery of the Asylum: Social Order and Disorder in the New Republic* (Boston: Little, Brown, 1971); and Michael Ignatieff, *A Just Measure of Pain: The Penitentiary in the Industrial Revolution, 1780–1850* (New York: Pantheon Books, 1978).

47. These additional comments are in TsGIA SSSR, f. 908, o. 1, d. 278, ll. 45–48.

48. TsGIA SSSR, f. 1286, o. 28, d. 798, l. 1.

49. Ibid., ll. 2–4.

50. Ibid., ll. 15–16, 21. The project *(Proekt polozheniia ispravitel'nykh tiurem)* is in ll. 26–29, with appendices and an explanation *(obiasnenie)* in ll. 30–79.

51. This discussion of the project is taken from ibid., ll. 26–29.

52. The appendices, which include rank, title, and salary, are in ibid., ll. 30–32.

53. Ibid., ll. 22–24, 80–87.

54. Ibid., l. 94, dated 30 June 1869.

55. Ibid., ll. 128–35.

56. For example, ibid., ll. 137, to Prince S. N. Urusov.

57. Ibid., ll. 140, 149.

58. Ibid., o. 29, d. 871, ll. 1–2.

59. Ibid., o. 28, d. 798, ll. 105–6, 107–20.

60. Ibid., ll. 121–25.

61. Ibid., ll. 153–58.

62. Ibid., ll. 160–64.

63. Ibid., ll. 165–84.

64. Ibid., ll. 185–86, 187–88, 207–8, 209–13.

65. Ibid., d. 799, l. 304.

66. Ibid., d. 801, ll. 104.

67. Ibid., d. 799, l. 202.

68. Ibid., l. 208.

69. Ibid., ll. 77–78.

70. Ibid., l. 45.

71. Ibid., d. 801, l. 15.

72. Ibid., l. 128.

73. Ibid., d. 799, ll. 1–2.

74. Ibid., d. 801, ll. 123–27. We met this priest earlier when he argued that corporal punishment might still have a role in prisons.

75. Ibid., d. 799, l. 40.

76. Ibid., l. 199.

77. Ibid., l. 43.

78. Ibid., ll. 208–34.

79. Ibid., l. 340.

80. Ibid., d. 801, ll. 104–5.

81. Ibid., d. 800, l. 47.

82. Ibid., d. 801, l. 1.

83. Ibid., d. 800, ll. 7–11.

84. Ibid., d. 801, ll. 15–22.

85. Ibid., d. 798, ll. 147–48.

86. Ibid., d. 799, ll. 3–4.

87. Ibid., l. 340.

88. Ibid., d. 801, l. 2.

89. Ibid., d. 800, ll. 24–25.

90. Ibid., d. 798, l. 203.

91. Ibid., d. 799, ll. 3–7.

92. Ibid., l. 44.

93. Ibid., ll. 78–79.

94. Ibid., ll. 189–210.

CHAPTER 3: THE COMMISSIONS DISCUSS PRISON REFORM

1. I. Ia. Foinitskii, *Na dosuge: Sbornik iuridicheskikh statei i izsledovanii s 1870 goda,* vol. 1 (St. Petersburg, 1898), 428. See also TsGAOR, f. 109, o. 3, ed. khr. 810, ll. 2–3. V. A. Sollogub's book was *Ob organizatsii v russkoi tiur'me truda* (Moscow, 1866).

2. This discussion is taken from the letter that is partially preserved in TsGAOR, f. 109, o. 3, ed. khr. 810, ll. 1–5. The letter, dated 11 August 1866, is addressed to Mikhail Nikolaevich Pokhvisnev in St. Petersburg and is from Sollogub, who had arrived in Moscow the day before.

3. Ibid., l. 2.

4. "Materialy k istorii tiuremnoi reformy v Rossii: Pis'ma grafa V. A. Solloguba i K. K. Grota k M. N. Galkinu-Vraskomu," *Zhurnal Ministerstva Iustitsii* 9–10 (1901): 252–82.

5. TsGIA SSSR, f. 1286, o. 28, d. 799, l. 342. The reply is in ibid., d. 801, ll. 235–304.

6. TsGIA SSSR, f. 1286, o. 28, d. 801, ll. 236–37.

7. Ibid., ll. 240–45.

8. Ibid., ll. 255–58, 262.

9. Ibid., ll. 250–62.

10. Ibid., ll. 262–67.

11. Ibid., ll. 265–66.

12. Ibid., ll. 246–47.

13. Ibid.

14. Ibid., ll. 2–3. This was not entirely true. Many military officers in early or pensioned retirement served as wardens.

15. Ibid., l. 282.

16. Ibid., ll. 282, 268–70.

17. Ibid., ll. 247–49.

18. Ibid., l. 302.

19. Ibid., ll. 280, 283–93.

20. E. C. Wines, *Report on the International Penitentiary Congress of London, Held July 3–13, 1872* (Washington, D.C.: Government Printing Office, 1873), 100.

21. TsGIA SSSR, f. 1286, o. 28, d. 801, ll. 297–302.

22. K. Golovin, *Moi vospominaniia,* vol. 1 (St. Petersburg: Kolokol, 1908), 227.

23. This discussion and that of the Sollogub Commission are derived from V. L. Binshtok, "Materialy dlia istorii russkoi tiur'my," *Sbornik pravovedeniia i obshchestvennykh znanii* 3 (1894): 151–90; and I. Ia. Foinitskii, "Proekt osnovnykh polozhenii tiuremnago preobrazovaniia v Rossii," in *Na dosuge,* vol. 1 (St. Petersburg, 1898), 206–60. The title of Foinitskii's article, which first appeared in nine issues of *Sudebnyi Vestnik* in 1872, is the title of the commission's first project.

24. My discussion of the planning session derives mainly from Binshtok, "Materialy," 152–54.

25. TsGIA SSSR, f. 1286, o. 28, d. 802, ll. 1–2, 15–24.

26. Ibid., l. 14.

27. Ibid., ll. 27–30.

28. Ibid., ll. 3–13.

29. Binshtok, "Materialy," 155; and Foinitskii, "Proekt," 211.

30. TsGIA SSSR, f. 1286, o. 28, d. 798, l. 36.

31. TsGAOR, f. 122, o. 3, ed. khr. 294, l. 22. I have concluded that the notes are in Sollogub's handwriting because the document is accompanied by the original letter from Shidlovskii and Iuferov addressed to Sollogub and from the nature of the comments.

32. Binshtok, "Materialy," 154–58.

33. Ibid., 175–85.

34. TsGAOR, f. 122, o. 3, ed. khr. 294, ll. 23–24.

35. Binshtok, "Materialy," 172–74.

36. Ibid., 169–70.

37. Ibid., 171–72, 160.

38. Ibid., 164–67.

39. TsGIA SSSR, f. 1286, o. 28, d. 798, ll. 41–47.

40. Binshtok, "Materialy," 185–86.

41. TsGAOR, f. 122, o. 3, ed. khr. 294, l. 33.

42. Binshtok, "Materialy," 186; and Foinitskii, "Proekt," 258.

43. TsGIA SSSR, f. 1286, o. 28, d. 871, l. 5.

44. On his work at the Congress, see Wines, *International Penitentiary Congress,* 20–21, 32–33. In the fall of 1872 Sollogub used the staff of the commission to distribute copies of the congress's reports to ministries and libraries throughout the country. TsGAOR, f. 122, o. 3, ed. khr. 300.

45. Golovin, *Moi vospominaniia,* vol. 1, 231–32.

46. TsGIA SSSR, f. 1149, o. 9, d. 3, l. 4; and Binshtok, "Materialy," 186. I do not know where Sollogub's projects now rest. I suspect they are in TsGAOR, where I found, or rather was brought, a few documents relating to his commission's work. Requests for more produced no more. It is less likely they are in TsGIA SSSR, where I received wonderful cooperation and saw materials of most of the other commissions and committees discussed in this chapter.

47. TsGAOR, f. 122, o. 3, ed. khr. 294, l. 19.

48. K, "Deiatel'nost' Konstantina Karlovicha Grota po tiuremnoi reforme," in *Konstantin Karlovich Grot kak gosudarstvennyi i obshchestvennyi deiatel',* vol. 1 (Petrograd, 1915), 247–48.

49. Foinitskii, "Russkaia karatel'naia sistema," in *Na dosuge,* vol. 2 (St. Petersburg, 1900), 1–2. This article was originally published in 1874.

50. K, "Deiatel'nost' Konstantina Karlovicha Grota," 148–49, cites journal 107 of the Joint Departments of the State Council, 30 November 1874.

51. TsGIA SSSR, f. 1286, o. 28, d. 801, ll. 249–50; and Binshtok, "Materialy," 187.

52. TsGIA SSSR, f. 1282, o. 1, d. 1048, l. 1.

53. TsGIA SSSR, f. 1149, o. 9, d. 3, ll. 1–2, 4, and 363–558 passim. This *delo* contains the committee reports and journals and official responses to the reports.

54. Ibid., ll. 4–6. This is part of the committee's first official report, sent to the State Council on 28 February 1874. The report and appendices are contained in ll. 4–28.

55. Ibid., l. 5.

56. Ibid.

57. Ibid.

58. See Daniel T. Orlovsky, *Limits of Reform: The Ministry of Internal Affairs in Imperial Russia, 1802–1881* (Cambridge, Mass.: Harvard University Press, 1981), 123–96.

59. TsGIA SSSR, f. 1149, o. 9, d. 3, ll. 6–7.

60. Ibid., ll. 11–13.

61. Ibid., ll. 16–18.

62. Ibid., ll. 3, 29–31.

63. Ibid., ll. 32, 37–42.

64. Ibid., ll. 42–46, 52–53.

65. Ibid., ll. 55–58. The *okrug* was much larger than a province *(guberniia).* The Moscow Court Chamber, for example (for which Sollogub's second "experimental" project was designed), encompassed ten provinces.

66. Ibid., ll. 59–68.

67. Ibid., ll. 101, 102–21.

68. Ibid., ll. 43, 106.

69. Ibid., ll. 106–9.

70. Ibid., ll. 110–12.

71. Ibid., ll. 113–24.

72. Ibid., l. 121.

73. Ibid., ll. 70–94.

74. Ibid., ll. 98–99, 124, 140, 141, 165.

75. Ibid., ll. 124–39.

76. Ibid., ll. 140, 141–64; the response of the Ministry of War is dated 3 December 1874.

77. Ibid., ll. 165–78.

78. Ibid., ll. 238–558. The committee project, "Proekt polozheniia o mestakh zakliucheniia grazhdanskago vedomstva," is in ll. 309–22. Its explanatory notes, "Po proektu polozheniia...," occupy ll. 239–308. Zubov's paper, "Proekt tiuremnago upravleniia," runs only four sheets, ll. 327–31.

79. M. S. [M. I. Semevskii], *Petr Alekseevich Zubov, 1819–1880* (St. Petersburg, 1880). This pamphlet is a eulogy to Zubov, who died on 26 June 1880. It was also published in *Golos* on 12 July 1880 and in *Russkaia Starina* 28 (August 1880).

80. Utin's letter is in TsGIA SSSR, f. 1149, o. 9, d. 3, l. 238. The commissioned article by I. Ia. Foinitskii, "Istoricheskii ocherk i sovremennoe sostoianie ssylki i tiuremnago zakliucheniia," is in ll. 329–62. The thirty-eight journals take up ll. 363–558. List 559 is the file copy of the letter from the secretary of state to the MVD, dated 27 May 1875, that accompanied the documents. It bears the penciled notation that identical packets were sent to the other offices.

81. Ibid., l. 726.

82. Ibid., ll. 560–61. The letter from Palen to the secretary of state is dated 29 November 1875.

83. Ibid., ll. 562–67.

84. Ibid., ll. 568–69.

85. TsGAOR, f. 102, o. 136, d. 7, l. 1. "Instruktsiia po upravleniiu S. Peterburgskim Domom Predvaritel'nago Zakliucheniia," 9 June 1875.

86. Ibid., ll. 570–71.

87. Ibid., ll. 572–74.

88. Ibid., ll. 575–671 and an appendix, ll. 632–34.

89. Ibid., ll. 576–85.

90. TsGAOR, f. 102, o. 136, d. 7, ll. 586–93.

91. Ibid., ll. 597–600.

92. Ibid., ll. 607–11.

93. Ibid., ll. 611–22. The article referred to is art. 64.

94. Ibid., ll. 626–31.

95. Ibid., ll. 632–34.

96. The Second Department reply is in ibid., ll. 689–724; the "Svod zamechanii na proekt polozheniia o mestakh zakliucheniia grazhdanskago vedomstva" is in ll. 635–88.

97. Ibid., ll. 728–29.

98. Ibid., ll. 730–32; ll. 733–43 contain the address of the secretary of state to Grand Prince Konstantin, the chairman of the State Council, asking him to make the request to the emperor.

99. Ibid., l. 744.

100. This early association is suggested by the anonymous author K in

"Deiatel'nost' Konstantina Karlovicha Grota," 244. It is possible that K is A. F. Koni, a friend of Grot who mentioned his work with prisoners and the blind in a eulogy for Grot, which is now stored in TsGAOR, f. 564, o. 1, ed. khr. 75, l. 3.

101. This discussion comes from an untitled autobiographical note in *Konstantin Karlovich Grot* (Petrograd, 1915), vol. 1, 20–21; and from the biographical article by K, "Deiatel'nost' Konstantina Karlovicha Grota," 246.

102. TsGIA SSSR, f. 1149, o. 9, d. 3, l. 744.

103. The commission's journals are bound as *Materialy o preobrazovanii tiuremnoi chasti* (St. Petersburg, 1878). This volume in the collection of the Lenin Library in Moscow includes the journals and appendices, each separately paginated with consecutive page numbers penciled in. Because this is the source of my information, my notes to them will appear as, for example, *Materialy,* journal 2, 57–59/115–17. The journals and appendixes are also in TsGIA SSSR, f. 1149, o. 9, d. 3, ll. 748–891; and in TsGAOR, f. 122, o. 1, chast' 1, ed. khr. 176, ll. 57–180.

104. K, "Deiatel'nost' Konstantina Karlovicha Grota," 257, 277–79.

105. *Materialy,* journal 1, 1–3/33–36.

106. Ibid., 4–6/31–39.

107. Ibid., 10–18/42–50.

108. Ibid., 18–20/50–52.

109. Ibid., journal 2, 47/105, 57–59/115–17.

110. Ibid., journal 3, 5–6/123–24.

111. The summary was gleaned from several sources. Ibid., 6–8/24–26 has a skeleton summary with references to the *Ulozhenie o nakazaniiakh, PSZ,* and other sources from which the skeleton was slightly fleshed out.

112. The proposal of the Ministry of Justice from which my discussion is derived appears in *Materialy,* journal 3, 8–9/126–27.

113. Second Department and MVD objections are in ibid., 9–10/127–28.

114. Ibid., 11/129.

115. Ibid., 13/31.

116. Ibid., 8/26,12/30.

117. Facts about the debate on isolation are derived from ibid., 17–21/25–29.

118. The commissioners were surely aware of this from previous reading and previous debate. If not, they could read appendix 1 to their own journals, a paper prepared for the commission entitled "0 sostoianii odinochnago zakliucheniia na Zapade," which emphasizes the dangers and shortcomings of isolation. Ibid., appendix 1, 1–18/295–312.

119. Ibid., journal 3, 21–23/139–41.

120. Ibid., 23–24/141–42.

121. Ibid., 24–25/142–43.

122. Ibid., 31–32/149–50.

123. Ibid., 32–33/150–51.

124. Ibid., 33–34/151–52.

125. Ibid., 34/152, 36/154.

126. Ibid., journal 6, 3–4/198–99, 11–16/251–56.

127. My discussion is derived largely from ibid., journal 7, 1–39/253–91.

128. Ibid., 1–14/253–66.

129. Ibid., 14–18/266–70.

130. Ibid., 18/270 and 18n.

131. Ibid., 17/269.

132. Ibid., 16–17/268–69.

133. Ibid., 17–18/269–70.

134. "Vsepoddanneishii doklad Stats-Sekretaria Grota po uchastiiu ego v tiurem-nom kongresse v Stokgol'me (1878g.)," in *Konstantin Karlovich Grot,* vol. 1, 55–62.

135. Ibid., 56.

136. Ibid.

137. Ibid., 56–57.

138. K, "Deiatel'nost' Konstantina Karlovicha Grota," 280.

139. *Materialy,* journal 7, 20/272.

140. TsGIA SSSR, f. 1149, o. 9, d. 3, l. 892.

141. Orlovsky, *Limits of Reform,* 93–100. See also P. A. Zaionchkovskii, *Krizis samoderzhaviia na rubezhe 1870–1880-kh godov* (Moscow: Nauka, 1964), 84–95.

142. E. A. Peretts, *Dnevnik E. A. Perettsa, gosudarstvennogo sekretaria (1880–1885)* (Moscow, 1927), 10, 15.

143. *Materialy,* journal 7, 21–22/273–74.

144. Ibid., 34/286, 39/291.

145. Ibid., 37/289.

146. Ibid.

147. TsGIA SSSR, f. 1149, o. 9, d. 3, ll. 897–98.

148. *Materialy,* journal 7, 35–36/287–88.

149. Ibid., 26–27/ 278–79.

150. Ibid., 35/287.

151. *Materialy,* 1–3. This is the last document in the bound volume and does not have the additional penciled pagination.

152. *2PSZ,* 59360.

CHAPTER 4: THE MAIN PRISON ADMINISTRATION

1. K, "Deiatel'nost' Konstantina Karlovicha Grota," 280–81.

2. Ibid., 281–82.

3. Ibid., 266.

4. Ibid., 281–82.

5. N. F. Luchinskii, *Kratkii ocherk deiatel'nosti Glavnogo Tiuremnago Upravleniia za pervyia xxxv let ego sushchestvovaniia (1879–1914)* (St. Petersburg: Tipo-litografiia S.Peterburgskoi odinochnoi tiur'my, 1914), 16. Luchinskii records the director's surname as Galkin-Vraskoi. So do many other sources, including Grot's biographer, K. In other secondary sources it appears as Galkin-Vraskii, as it does in GTU documents bearing his signature. I have assumed the latter to be correct.

6. Ibid., 16, 107.

7. TsGIA SSSR, f. 1286, o. 28, d. 798, ll. 1, 5, 10, 15.

8. Ibid., d. 802, l. 3.

9. Luchinskii, *Kratkii ocherk,* 16.

10. TsGAOR, f. 122, o. 1, chast' 1, ed. khr. 176, ll. 8–17; *2PSZ,* 60268, 31 December 1879.

11. TsGAOR, f. 122, o. 1, chast' 1, ed. khr. 610, ll. 232–33.

12. Luchinskii, *Kratkii ocherk,* 16–17.

13. TsGAOR, f. 122, o. 1, chast' 1, ed. khr. 176, ll. 190, 193, 196, 197.

14. The circular is in Glavnoe tiuremnoe upravlenie, *Sbornik tsirkuliarov izdan-nykh po Glavnomu Tiuremnomu Upravleniiu v 1879–1910* (St. Petersburg, 1911), 5. It required that each prisoner have two cubic *sazhen* of space, which approximately equals

19.4 cubic meters. GTU officials were concerned about prisoner hygiene and contagious diseases. With proper ventilation they believed that volume of air would suffice for an individual. This standard was high: the Soviet government never met the goal it set for itself of giving each free citizen nine square meters of living space. If an eight-foot ceiling is assumed, this yields only 21.9 cubic meters. In 1977 each Soviet citizen had on the average only eight square meters of space or, assuming an eight-foot ceiling, 19.5 cubic meters. Prisoners in tsarist isolation cells had more room than that. See James H. Bater, *The Soviet City: Ideal and Reality* (Beverly Hills, Calif.: Sage Publications, 1980), 106.

The statistics are from Luchinskii, *Kratkii ocherk,* 17–18. More precise totals are offered in Vysochaishe uchrezhdenaia Osobaia Komissiia dlia razrabotki meropriiatii, vyzyvaemykh izdaniem novago ugolovnago ulozheniia, *Tiuremnoe preobrazovanie,* vol. 1, *Ispravitel'nyi dom, zakliuchenie v kreposti, i tiur'ma* (St. Petersburg, 1905), 36, which says that as of 11 December 1879 there were 96,796 prisoners in 76,090 spaces. *Obzor desiatiletnei deiatel'nosti Glavnago Tiuremnago Upravleniia, 1879–1889* (St. Petersburg, 1890), 6–7, claims that figures were unavailable for 1879, which is incorrect, and that statistics for 1881 showed 94,796 prisoners in 76,090 spaces.

15. *Obzor desiatiletnei deiatel'nosti,* 7.

16. Ibid., 8.

17. *2PSZ,* 58466, 4 May 1879; *2PSZ,* 59073, 29 November 1879; *2PSZ,* 59553, 11 April 1880.

18. *Obzor desiatiletnei deiatel'nosti,* 7, 18–19.

19. TsGAOR, f. 122, o. 1, ed. khr. 610, ll. 108–9.

20. Ibid., o. 2, ed. khr. 100, ll. 3–5, 6, 7–8, 12–13, 19–20, 22–23, 26.

21. Ibid., o. 1, ed. khr. 610.

22. Ibid., ll. 157–62.

23. Ibid., ll. 125–28.

24. Ibid., ll. 146–49.

25. Ibid., ll. 129–32.

26. Ibid., o. 1, chast' 1, ed. khr. 180, ll. 2, 6, 7, 8.

27. Ibid., ed. khr. 148, ll. 1–2, 4–9, 13–15, 26.

28. Luchinskii, *Kratkii ocherk,* 21.

29. I. Ia. Foinitskii, "Kak my proveli 1878 god?" in *Na dosuge,* vol. 2 (St. Petersburg, 1900), 337–38.

30. TsGIA SSSR, f. 1284, o. 51, d. 112, l. 61.

31. E. A. Peretts, *Dnevnik E. A. Perettsa gosudarstvennogo sekretaria, 1880–1885,* Introduction by A. E. Presniakov (Moscow, 1927), 10, 15.

32. TsGIA SSSR, f. 1263, o. 1, ed. khr. 4162, microroll 27, ll. 241–46.

33. Ibid., ed. khr. 4161, microroll 25, ll. 373–79.

34. Ibid., l. 375.

35. Daniel T. Orlovsky, *Limits of Reform,* 176.

36. TsGIA SSSR, f. 1263, o. 1, ed. khr. 4161, no. 366, microroll 25, ll. 378–79.

37. Ibid., ll. 373–74; *2PSZ,* 61814.

38. K, "Deiatel'nost' Konstantina Karlovicha Grota," 285.

39. Luchinskii, *Kratkii ocherk,* 23.

40. K, "Deiatel'nost' Konstantina Karlovicha Grota," 285. Apparently Galkin-Vraskii and Grot enjoyed good relations at least until September 1879. See the four letters from Grot to Galkin-Vraskii in "Materialy k istorii tiuremnoi reformy v Rossii," 283–88.

41. This and the following information derives from the draft of a letter from

Loris-Melikov to D. N. Nabokov, minister of justice, in TsGIA SSSR, f. 1284, o. 51, d. 112, ll. 78–81. It is undated, unsigned, and marked "confidential." Because of several acts that the writer attributes to himself (for example, "I sent to the Committee of Ministers..."), it can definitely be attributed to Loris-Melikov. I place its writing in March or April 1881 because it mentions Alexander III, who succeeded his father to the throne in March, and because by 29 April Loris-Melikov had resigned.

42. The best account of Loris-Melikov's fall is in P. A. Zaionchkovskii, *Krizis samoderzhaviia na rubezhe* (Moscow: Nauka, 1964), 300–378.

43. Luchinskii, *Kratkii ocherk*, 23.

44. K. K. Grot, untitled autobiographical notes in *Konstantin Karlovich Grot*, vol. 1, 22.

45. K, "Deiatel'nost' Konstantina Karlovicha Grota," 288–89.

46. Foinitskii, "Kak my proveli 1878 god?" 336.

47. Foinitskii, "Tiuremnaia reforma i tiur'movedenie," in *Na dosuge*, vol. 1, 426–27.

48. K, "Deiatel'nost' Konstantina Karlovicha Grota," 289–90.

49. Ibid., 290.

50. Ibid., 284; and Peretts, *Dnevnik*, 10, 236.

51. Zaionchkovskii, *Krizis samoderzhaviia*, 382–84.

52. K, "Deiatel'nost' Konstantina Karlovicha Grota," 290.

53. Peretts, *Dnevnik*, 117.

54. TsGIA SSSR, f. 1284, o. 51, d. 112, ll. 100–101.

55. Luchinskii, *Kratkii ocherk*, 23.

56. *Tiuremnoe preobrazovanie*, 37–39.

57. Ibid., 40–42.

58. Ibid., 42–45.

59. Ibid., 46–47.

60. Luchinskii, *Kratkii ocherk*, 53; *Tiuremnoe preobrazovanie*, 47, states that the St. Petersburg Isolation Prison had 895 isolation spaces and 180 general spaces and that the prison in Odessa had 408 isolation spaces and 263 general spaces.

61. Luchinskii, *Kratkii ocherk*, 53; and *Tiuremnoe preobrazovanie*, 47–50.

62. These statistics are from Gernet, *Istoriia tsarskoi tiur'my*, vol. 4, 23; and S. T. Gavrilov, "Russkie tiur'my po otchetam Glavnago Tiuremnago Upravleniia za 1903–1909 gody," *Iuridicheskii Vestnik* 2 (1913): 246.

63. *Tiuremnoe preobrazovanie*, 60.

64. Ibid., 61–63.

65. Ibid., 52.

66. "Kratkii ocherk tiuremnago ustroistva i meropriiatii v oblasti tiuremnago dela v Rossii za 1905–1910 gg," *Zhurnal Ministerstva Iustitsii* 7 (1910): 208.

67. Two of the best studies of this question are A. D. Margolis, "Sistema sibirskoi ssylki i zakon ot 12 iiunia 1900 goda," in *Ssylka i obshchestvenno-politicheskaia zhizn' v Sibiri, xviii–nachalo xx v.* (Novosibirsk: Nauka, 1978), 126–40; and N. A. Minenko, "0 vliianii ssylki na semeinuiu zhizn' russkikh krest'ian Zapadnoi Sibiri v xviii–pervoi polovine xix veka," in *Ssylka i obshchestvenno-politicheskaia*, 282–93.

68. See, for example, I. Ia. Foinitskii, *K voprosu o ssylke v Sibir'* (Moscow, 1879); I. Ia. Foinitskii, *Ssylka ili tiur'ma?* (Moscow, 1881); and Sergei V. Maksimov, *Sibir' i katorga* (St. Petersburg, 1871).

69. N. V. Murav'ev, *Poslednie Rechi, 1900–1902 gg.* (St. Petersburg, 1903), 11, 13–17, 37. The speech was delivered on 24 April 1900.

70. The law that almost ended exile was passed on 12 June 1900. *3PSZ*, 18839. See also *3PSZ*, 18777. See Margolis, "Sistema sibirskoi ssylki," 126–40. See also *Tiuremnoe preobrazovanie*, 63–68.

71. Ibid., 72–75.

72. Ibid., 75–76, 81.

73. V. A. Sollogub, *Ob organizatsii v russkoi tiur'me truda* (Moscow, 1866), 1–6, 12–14.

74. Ibid., 6n.

75. Luchinskii, *Kratkii ocherk*, 26–27.

76. *3PSZ*, 3447

77. Luchinskii, *Kratkii ocherk*, 26, 124–25.

78. Ibid., 135.

79. TsGAOR, f. 122, o. 1, ed. khr. 1059, ll. 7–8, 27. The phrase I translate as "housekeeping" is *khoziaistvennaia rabota*.

80. Ibid., ed. khr. 2593, ll. 1–10, 13–15.

81. Ibid., ed. khr. 2520, ll. 2–15.

82. Ibid., d. 2557, ll. 24–27.

83. Ibid., d. 2928, 2938, 2935, passim.

84. S. K. Gogel', "Arestantskii trud v russkikh i inostrannykh tiur'makh," *Voprosy ugolovnago prava, protsessa i tiur'movedeniia* (St. Petersburg, 1906): 498–500. The article first appeared as a monograph and in *Zhurnal Ministerstva Iustitsii* in 1897 under the title "Arestantskii trud v russkikh tiur'makh."

85. See F. N. Malinin, *Postanovleniia shesti mezhdunarodnykh tiuremnykh kongressov: Sistematicheskii ukazatel' k nim* (St. Petersburg, 1904), passim.

86. Gogel', *Voprosy*, 502–5, 582.

87. Murav'ev, *Poslednie rechi*, 40–48.

88. N. F. Luchinskii, *Osnovy tiuremnago dela* (St. Petersburg, 1904), 5–6, 87–89.

89. Luchinskii, *Kratkii ocherk*, 78–93, passim. On war work, see, for example, "Arestantskii trud i ego primenenie po obstoiatel'stvam voennago vremeni," *Tiuremnyi Vestnik* 10 (1915): 1807–12.

90. Gogel', *Voprosy*, 536, 547, 549–79.

91. Gogel', "Arestantskii trud," *Tiuremnyi Vestnik* 2 (1913): 297–333.

92. TsGAOR, f. 122, o. 1, chast' 1, ed. khr. 180.

93. Luchinskii, *Kratkii ocherk*, 23; *3PSZ*, 668.

94. TsGAOR, f. 122, o. 1, ed. khr. 925, ll. 1–2, 5, 100–150, passim.

95. Luchinskii, *Osnovy tiuremnago dela*, 16–18.

96. TsGAOR, f. 122, o. 1, chast' 2, ed. khr. 5121, ll. 72–78.

97. Ibid., ll. 28, 92, 95–97.

98. Ibid., ll. 34, 51–53, 64.

99. Ibid., ed. khr. 5122, l. 66.

100. Ibid., ll. 4–10.

101. Ibid., ll. 13–15.

102. Ibid., ll. 1–3.

103. See, for example, ibid., ll. 65–69.

104. Ibid., d. 5779, ll. 1–7, 9–17, 40–57, 207–8, 210–25.

105. Ibid., ll. 19–38.

106. Ibid., ll. 97–150.

107. Ibid., d. 5780, ll. 34–39.

108. Ibid., ll. 87–89.

109. Ibid., ll. 268–71.

110. Ibid., d. 6531, ll. 2–16.

111. Ibid., ll. 112–27.

112. Ibid., ll. 18–33, 35–52.

113. Ibid., d. 6533, ll. 3–4.

114. Ibid., d. 6532, is a file of rejected applications, mostly for assistant warden positions, for 1912. It is 580 pages long.

115. Ibid., d. 6899, ll. 2–21, 30, 81, 96–97.

116. Ibid., d. 7332.

117. TsGAOR, f. 122, o. 1, ed. khr. 3090, l. 61.

118. Luchinskii, *Kratkii ocherk,* 28.

119. This discussion derives from TsGAOR, f. 122, o. 1, ed. khr. 806, ll. 2–5, 14–16. On the Kakhanov Commission, see George L. Yaney, *The Systematization of Russian Government: Social Evolution in the Domestic Administration of Imperial Russia, 1711–1905* (Urbana: University of Illinois Press, 1973), 346–51.

120. TsGAOR, f. 122, o. 1, ed. khr. 806, ll. 16–18.

121. Ibid., ll. 36, 44. This is part of a document dated July 1882, which seems to be a draft for the shorter paper sent to Kakhanov in November. This material was not included in the later paper.

122. Ibid., ll. 18–21.

123. Ibid., ll. 21–23.

124. Ibid., ed. khr. 3090, l. 61.

125. The governors' replies are in ibid., ed. khr. 1072.

126. *3PSZ,* 2267, 30 May 1884.

127. TsGAOR, f. 122, o. 1, ed. khr. 3090, ll. 62–63.

128. Ibid., ll. 62–65; *3PSZ,* 6653. This history of the prison inspectorates also appears in TsGIA SSSR, f. 1405, o. 542, d. 739, ll. 151–59. It is an appendix to the journals of the Tagantsev Commission, which sat to discuss the transfer of prison affairs to the MIu in 1895–1896.

129. *3PSZ,* 7844, 14 June 1891; 19568, 2 May 1894; 19597, 9 May 1894; 11742, 29 May 1895; 11757, 1 June 1895; 32,006, 7 June 1909; 33,693, 10 June 1910; 41,233, 28 June 1912.

130. Information on these initial difficulties comes from reports by a GTU central inspector who traveled to inspect each new inspectorate, help set it up, standardize its practices, and intercede with governors to obtain needed cooperation and assistance. See, for example, TsGAOR, f. 122, o. 1, ed. khr. 1839, ed. khr. 1840, and ed. khr. 2837. This last ed. khr. is obviously mislabeled, misnumbered, and misfiled. It refers to the new inspectorate in Kiev.

131. Ibid., ed. khr. 1840, l. 91.

132. Ibid., d. 2932, ll. 12–37.

133. Gosudarstvennyi arkhiv permskoi oblasti (GAPO), f. 164. On numbers, conditions, and costs, see, for example, o. 1, ed. khr. 17, and o. 9, ed. khr. 7 and 9. On prisoner labor, see, for example, f. 164, o. 1, ed. khr. 52, 56, and 76.

134. GAPO, f. 164, o. 1, ed. khr. 27, 31, 93. My brief article, "Istoriia russkikh tiurem tsarskogo rezhima v dokumentakh gosudarstvennogo arkhiva permskoi oblasti," in *Vystupleniia i tezisi dokladov nauchno-prakticheskoi konferentsii "Arkhivy vchera, segodnia, zavtra"* (Perm, 1994), 49–52, provides a few more details.

135. TsGAOR., ed. khr. 3090, ll. 21–24.

136. Ibid., l. 117.

137. M. M. Isaev, "Obzor deiatel'nosti tiuremnago vedomstva pri novykh zakono-datel'nykh uchrezhdeniiakh," *Trudy iuridicheskago obshchestva pri Imperatorskom S-Peter-burgskom Universitete* 7 (1913): 46–47.

138. TsGIA SSSR, f. 1405, o. 542, d. 736, ll. 5–12. This document is also in TsGAOR, f. 122, o. 1, ed. khr. 3090, ll. 2–6.

139. S. S. Oldenburg, *Last Tsar: Nicholas II, His Reign and His Russia*, trans. Leonid I. Mihalap and Patrick J. Rollins, ed. Patrick J. Rollins (Gulf Breeze, Fla.: Academic International, 1975–1978), vol. 1, 35–47.

140. Hans Rogger, *Russia in the Age of Modernisation and Revolution, 1881–1917* (London: Longman, 1983), 18, 26.

141. S. Iu. Vitte, *Vospominaniia* (Moscow, 1960), vol. 1, 320–21; and V. I. Gurko, *Features and Figures of the Past: Government and Opinion in the Reign of Nicholas II* (Stanford, Calif.: Stanford University Press, 1939), 90; A. F. Koni, "Triumviry," in *Sobranie sochinenii*, vol. 2 (Moscow: Iuridicheskaia literatura, 1966), 321, 328.

142. Samuel Kucherov, *Courts, Lawyers and Trials under the Last Three Tsars* (New York: Frederick A. Praeger, 1953), 99–100.

143. V. A. Tvardovskaia, *Ideologiia poreformennogo samoderzhaviia: M. N. Katkov i ego izdaniia* (Moscow: Nauka, 1978), 251; P. A. Zaionchkovskii, *Rossiiskoe samoderzhavie v kontse deviatnadtsatogo stoletiia* (Moscow: Nauka, 1970), 258–61.

144. Kucherov, *Courts,* 99.

145. Gurko, *Features,* 90; and Vitte, *Vospominaniia,* vol. 1, 163–67.

146. Koni, "Triumviry," 321.

147. Vitte, *Vospominaniia,* vol. 2, 33–36, 508.

148. Ibid., 37–39; and Gurko, *Features,* 75–76, 80.

149. N. V. Murav'ev, "Nashi tiur'my i tiuremnyi vopros," in *Iz proshloi deiatel'nosti: Stat'i po sudebnym voprosam* (St. Petersburg: M. M. Stasiulevich, 1900), vol. 1, 107–46. See the various speeches in Murav'ev, *Poslednie rechi,* for example, 142–43, 156; and N. V. Murav'ev, "Vsepoddanneishii doklad Ministra Iustitsii Stats-Sekretaria Murav'eva o deiatel'nosti Ministerstva Iustitsii za istekshee desiatiletie, 1894–1904," *Zhurnal Ministerstva Iustitsii* 2 (1904): 33–76.

150. Zaionchkovskii, *Krizis samoderzhaviia,* 260.

151. Gurko, *Features,* 75–76.

152. TsGIA SSSR, f. 1405, o. 542, d. 736, ll. 2–15. Nicholas II signed this document in the presence of Murav'ev and A. P. Salomon, who would become director of the GTU less than a year later. Goremykin was not present. TsGIA SSSR, f. 1284, o. 185, d. 93, chast' 2.

153. TsGIA SSSR, f. 1405, o. 542, d. 736, l. 38. See also TsGIA SSSR, f. 1284, o. 185, d. 93, ll. 1–2; and TsGAOR, f. 122, o. 1, ed. khr. 3090, ll. 98–100.

154. Koni, "Triumviry," 328.

155. TsGIA SSSR, f. 1405, o. 542, d. 736, ll. 40–43, 55.

156. Ibid., d. 739, ll. 3–5. Information on the establishment and journals of the meetings of the Tagantsev Commission is also in TsGAOR, f. 122, o. 1, ed. khr. 3090.

157. TsGIA SSSR, f. 1405, o. 542, d. 739, ll. 6, 8–9. See also ll. 37–38.

158. Ibid., ll. 17–19.

159. Ibid., l. 19.

160. Ibid., ll. 12–17.

161. Ibid., l. 25.

162. Ibid., ll. 35–37.

163. Ibid., ll. 37–74.

164. Ibid., ll. 109–14.

165. TsGAOR, f. 122, o. 1, ed. khr. 3090, ll. 205–10.

166. TsGIA SSSR, f. 1405, o. 542, d. 739, ll. 109–226.

167. Ibid., f. 1284, o. 185, d. 93, l. 80; f. 565, o. 5, d. 20148, l. 1.

168. Ibid., ll. 62–76.

169. Ibid., l. 64.

170. The governors' responses are in ibid., ll. 81–524. On Kharkov, see ll. 103–8.

171. Ibid., ll. 127–44.

172. Ibid., ll. 81–82.

173. Ibid, d. 93, chast' 2, ll. 1–3.

174. Ibid., ll. 2–6.

175. Ibid., ll. 21–79, and "explanatory notes" in ll. 80–94.

176. Ibid., ll. 167–69.

177. Ibid., ll. 176–81.

178. Ibid., ll. 181–93.

179. TsGAOR, f. 122, o. 1, ed. khr. 3511, ll. 2–3.

180. TsGIA SSSR, f. 1405, o. 543, d. 497, l. 13.

CHAPTER 5: FURTHER EFFORTS AT REFORM AND THE DENOUEMENT

1. V. A. Sollogub, *Ob organizatsii v russkoi tiur'me truda* (Moscow, 1866), 10–11.

2. K, "Deiatel'nost' Konstantina Karlovicha Grota," 273–74.

3. TsGAOR, f. 122, 1880, o. 1, chast' 1, ed. khr. 512, ll. 3–4. Circular 2680.

4. Ibid., ll. 5–8.

5. Ibid., ll. 14, 19–20. Circulars 5594 of 24 June 1880 and 9119 of 12 October 1880.

6. Ibid., ed. khr. 514, l. 16.

7. Ibid., 1881, o. 1, chast' 1, ed. khr. 526, ll. 1–2.

8. Ibid., ed. khr. 721, ll. 2–4, 9.

9. Ibid., 1880, o. 1, chast' 1, ed. khr. 512, ll. 21–22.

10. Ibid., ll. 23–26, 27.

11. For Moscow, see ibid., ed. khr. 541; for St. Petersburg, ibid., ed. khr. 550.

12. For Samara, see ibid., 1883–1884, o. 1, ed. khr. 934; for Saratov, ibid., 1880–1881, o. 1, chast' 1, ed. khr. 557.

13. TsGAOR, f. 122, o. 1, ed. khr. 3090, l. 56.

14. *Obzor desiatiletnei deiatel'nosti Glavnago Tiuremnago Upravleniia, 1879–1889* (St. Petersburg, 1890), 9.

15. D. Krainskii, *Materialy k izsledovaniiu istorii russkikh tiurem v sviazi s istoriei uchrezhdeniia Obshchestva Popechitel'stva o Tiur'makh* (Chernigov, 1912), 122–26.

16. The information concerning this confrontation comes entirely from the GTU's file of correspondence on the matter in TsGAOR, f. 122, 1885–1895, ed. khr. 1228, which comprises 299 *listy*. On the State Council's opinion, see ll. 8–9. The project is in ll. 28–54.

17. Ibid., ll. 1, 6–9.

18. Ibid., ll. 10–13.

19. Ibid., ll. 14–22.

20. Ibid., ll. 60–75.

21. Ibid., ll. 76–117.

22. Ibid., l. 119.

23. The journal of this meeting is filed in ibid., ll. 118–27.

24. Ibid., l. 130. The new charter is in ll. 131–48.

25. Ibid., ll. 149–51.

26. Ibid., ll. 161–62. See also ll. 272–80.

27. TsGAOR, f. 122, o. 1, ed. khr. 3090, ll. 133–35. On the Tagantsev Commission, see above chapter 4.

28. TsGIA SSSR, f. 1284, o. 185, d. 93, ll. 18–21.

29. See F. Malinin, "Tiuremnyi patronat (Po povodu razrabotki proektu normal'-nago ustava obshchestv pokrovitel'stva litsam, osvobozhdennym iz mest zakliucheniia Rossiiskoi Imperii)," *Tiuremnyi Vestnik* 8 (1905): 596–604, and 9 (1905): 822–23; N. F. Luchinskii, "Tiuremnyi patronat," *Tiuremnyi Vestnik* 1 (1913): 1656, 1662–1680; P. I. Liublinskii, "Sovremennoe sostoianie i zadachi obshchestv patronata," in his *Na smenu starago prava: Sbornik statei po voprosam tekushchei pravovoi zhizni* (Petrograd, 1915), 300–306, 311–19; and Liublinskii, "Gosudarstvennaia pomoshch' obshchestvam patronata," in his *Na smenu,* 331–57, 361–62.

30. Liublinskii, "Sovremennoe sostoianie," 300–306.

31. Liublinskii, "Gosudarstvennaia pomoshch'," 328–29.

32. K. K. Grot, "Vsepoddanneishii doklad Stat's-Sekretaria Grota po uchastiiu ego v tiuremnom kongresse v Stokgol'me," in *Konstantin Karlovich Grot,* vol. 1, appendix, 59, 62.

33. Malinin, "Tiuremnyi patronat," 622–25.

34. Most of the discussion that follows is derived from A. Khristianovich, "O merakh k razvitiiu patronata v Rossii (Tretii s'ezd russkikh kriminalistov)," *Tiuremnyi Vestnik* 4–5 (1902): 255–62; and Malinin, "Tiuremnyi patronat," 628–30.

35. This paragraph is derived from Liublinskii, "S-Peterburgskoe Obshchestvo Patronata," in his *Na smenu,* 321–27, which in turn is based on the society's 181-page *otchet,* dated 1 January 1909, and on the memory of Liublinskii, who was a member of the society.

36. Malinin, "Tiuremnyi patronat," 8 (1905): 628–29 and 9: 811.

37. See Liublinskii, "Sovremennoe sostoianie," 306; and Malinin, "Tiuremnyi patronat," 620.

38. Luchinskii, "Tiuremnyi patronat," 1648, 1657, 1675–80.

39. Ibid., 1648. The *normal'nyi ustav* is in D. A. Koptev, ed., *Zakon ob uslovnom dosrochnom osvobozhdenii s izlozheniem razsuzhdenii, na koikh on osnovan* (St. Petersburg: Gosudarstvennaia tipografiia, 1909), 363–74.

40. The circulars, Shcheglovitov's letter of 24 May 1909, and other documents supporting these points are in a folder concerned with the special medals. For the circulars, see TsGAOR, f. 122, o. 1, chast' 2, ed. khr. 5795, ll. 3–5.

41. Ibid., ll. 1–2, 6–14.

42. Liublinskii, "Gosudarstvennaia pomoshch'," 338, 363–66.

43. Liublinskii, "Sovremennoe sostoianie," 308.

44. N. A. Okunev, "Iz praktiki zakona ob uslovnom dosrochnom osvobozhdenii," *Trudy iuridicheskogo obshchestva pri Imperatorskom S.-Peterburgskom Universitete* 3 (1910), 244–63; and TsGAOR, f. 122, o. 1, chast' 2, ed. khr. 5795.

45. Liublinskii, "Sovremennoe sostoianie," 308.

46. A. A. Piontkovskii, *Uslovnoe osvobozhdenie: Ugolovno-politicheskoe izsledovanie* (Kazan, 1900), 84–86.

47. Ibid., 87–91.

48. *Svod zamechanii na proekt obshchei chasti ulozheniia o nakazaniiakh, obrabotannyi redaktsionnoi kommissiei* (St. Petersburg, 1884), 193, 503, 517, 519, 528, 572–75.

49. Piontkovskii, *Uslovnoe osvobozhdenie,* 93.

50. Ibid., 96–101, 167–69, 171–73.

51. Ibid., 92.

52. Ibid., 93.

53. Koptev, *Zakon*, 33–105, 117–362.

54. *Zakonoproekt ob uslovnom dosrochnom osvobozhdenii* (St. Petersburg, 1909), 33–39.

55. Minister of Justice I. G. Shcheglovitov sent the project to Prime Minister Stolypin on 1 February 1907. The Council of Ministers approved it on 9 February. Shcheglovitov sent this project, along with ten other projects (including probation), to the state secretary for the Duma's consideration on 17 February, three days before its opening session. TsGIA SSSR, f. 1405, o. 543, d. 517, ll. 2, 108, 72, in that order. The project itself is in ll. 3–6, with explanations in ll. 7–31.

56. Ibid., l. 116, a letter from Shcheglovitov to the chairman of the Duma dated 1 November 1907, the opening day of the first session of the Third Duma.

57. This report is in ibid., ll. 152–63; or Koptev, *Zakon*, 21–27.

58. For Bennigsen's speech, see Koptev, *Zakon*, 106–11. This volume includes the complete stenographic records of the discussion concerning the parole law in the State Duma (pp. 106–217) and the State Council (pp. 217–357).

59. Ibid., 107–8.

60. Ibid., 112–14.

61. Ibid., 114–16.

62. See ibid., 127–30, 134–35.

63. Ibid., 124–27.

64. Ibid., 116–21.

65. Ibid., 117.

66. Ibid., 146–49.

67. See the speeches of Fathers M. N. Dmitriev (ibid., 150–51), K. P. Roznatovskii (pp. 151–53), and N. E. Gepetskii (pp. 153–54).

68. Ibid., 143–46.

69. Ibid., 130–33.

70. Ibid., 158–59.

71. Ibid., 139–43.

72. Ibid., 166–68.

73. Ibid., 169–70.

74. Ibid., 179–84.

75. Ibid., 204–13 and 213–17.

76. Ibid., 27–33, 217.

77. Patrick J. Rollins, "Petr Nikolaevich Durnovo," in *Modern Encyclopedia of Russian and Soviet History,* vol. 10 (Gulf Breeze, Fla.: Academic International Press, 1982), 58–61.

78. Koptev, *Zakon*, 218–22.

79. Ibid., 222–31.

80. Kovrin-Milevskii's speech appears in ibid., 231–38.

81. Shcheglovitov's speech is in ibid., 256–61.

82. Koni's speech is in ibid., 244–49.

83. Durnovo's speech is in ibid., 238–43.

84. Ibid., 262.

85. Ibid., 262–357.

86. Ibid., 357–62.

87. TsGIA SSSR, f. 1405, o. 543, d. 517, ll. 183–86.

88. From an article in "Russkiia Vedomosti," dated 12 September 1909 and filed in ibid., l. 190.

89. See, for example, the long list of questions in ibid., ll. 214–18.

90. The commission's journals are in ibid., ll, 223–51; the circular is in l. 220.

91. TsGIA SSSR, f. 1405, o. 543, ed. khr. 520, l. 304.

92. S. K. Gogel', *O zhelatel'nosti i vozmozhnosti vvedeniia v Rossii instituta uslovnago osuzhdeniia* (St. Petersburg: Tipografiia Praviushchago Senata, 1897), 7–8.

93. P. I. Liublinskii, "Uslovnoe osuzhdenie," *Zhurnal Ministerstva Iustitsii* 9 (1912): 105–7.

94. Gogel', *O zhelatel'nosti,* 5.

95. Ibid., 3–6, 12.

96. Ibid., 6–9. See also P. I. Liublinskii, "Poniatie nakazaniia," *Iuridicheskii Vestnik* 3–4 (1914): 78–109.

97. Gogel', *O zhelatel'nosti,* 10–21. See also Liublinskii, "Uslovnoe osuzhdenie," 81–84.

98. David Rothman argues that prisons remained the dominant mode of punishment in the United States long after their flaws were understood for precisely these reasons. See his excellent monograph, *Conscience and Convenience: The Asylum and Its Alternatives in Progressive America* (Boston: Little, Brown, 1980).

99. Gogel', "Rech' v zasedanii Peterburgskago iuridicheskago obshchestva v noiabre 1904 goda pri obsuzhdenii proekta ministerstva iustitsii ob uslovnom osuzhdenii," in *Voprosy ugolovnago prava, protsessa i tiur'movedenii* (St. Petersburg: Obshchestvennaia Pol'za, 1906), 201–2. See also TsGIA SSSR, f. 1405, o. 543, d. 497, ll. 35–36.

100. TsGIA SSSR, f. 1405, o. 543, d. 484, ll. 127–36.

101. Ibid., ll. 279–84.

102. Ibid., ll. 285–98, 298–312, 313–18.

103. Ibid., ll. 318–27, 335–36, 328–31, 337–43.

104. Ibid., d. 516, l. 11.

105. Ibid., ll. 2, 30, 32, 61.

106. Gosudarstvennaia Duma, *Stenograficheskie otchety* (St. Petersburg: Gosudarstvennaia Tipografiia, 1910), columns (cc.) 681–92.

107. The Black Hundreds were loosely organized groups of conservative, anti-Semitic nationalists. Zamyslovskii had a well-deserved reputation as an archconservative and an anti-Semite. O. O. Gruzenberg, one of the lawyers who defended Mendel Beilis in a celebrated case of "ritual murder," called Zamyslovskii "a man of great ability, but exceptionally vile." See Gruzenberg, *Yesterday: Memoirs of a Russian-Jewish Lawyer,* ed. and with an introduction by Don C. Rawson (Berkeley: University of California Press, 1981), 113, 222.

108. Gosudarstvennaia Duma, *Stenograficheskie otchety,* cc. 692–705.

109. For the testimony of a fellow lawyer who saw both sides of Shcheglovitov, see Gruzenberg, *Yesterday,* 78–81.

110. Gosudarstvennaia Duma, *Stenograficheskie otchety,* cc. 707–21.

111. Ibid., cc. 723–34.

112. Clippings are included in TsGIA SSSR, f. 1405, o. 543, d. 516, ll. 212–19.

113. Father Gepetskii's remarks are in Gosudarstvennaia Duma, *Stenograficheskie otchety,* cc. 791–96. Bishop Mitrofan's are in cc. 763–70.

114. Ibid., cc. 779–83.

115. Ibid., cc. 745–54. Tarnovskaia's book was published in St. Petersburg by Khudozhestvennaia Pechat' in 1902.

116. Ibid., c. 830.

117. Ibid., cc. 831–943.

118. TsGIA SSSR, f. 1405, o. 543, d. 516, ll. 212–19.

119. Gosudarstvennyi Sovet, *Stenograficheskii Otchet* (St. Petersburg: Gosudarstvennaia tipografiia, 1911), cc. 594–600.

120. Ibid., cc. 2101–6.

121. His entire speech is in ibid., cc. 2108–30.

122. Shcheglovitov was referring to the commissions headed by M. N. Liuboshinskii on the reform of the *volost'* courts (1872–74) and by A. S. Stishinskii on the legal administration of peasant society (1902–04).

123. Gosudarstvennyi Sovet, *Stenograficheskii Otchet,* cc. 2143–46.

124. Ibid., cc. 2146–57.

125. Ibid., cc. 2163–68.

126. See, for example, A. Ia. Avrekh, *Tsarizm i tret'eiun'skaia sistema* (Moscow: Nauka, 1966), 137–45.

127. TsGAOR, f. 122, o. 1, chast' 2, ed. khr. 7239, ll. 16–17, 46, 97–98, 105–7, 140–41.

128. Ibid., ed. khr. 7332, ll. 1–2, 8–9, 19, 26.

129. Ibid., ed. khr. 7329, l. 211.

130. Ibid., o. 13, ed. khr. l.

131. Ibid., o. 1, chast' 2, ed. khr. 7329, ll. 193–94, 212–14, 218–24, 320–29, 406–7, 437. One result of the attack on the GUMZ's headquarters in March was the destruction of "most of the documents of the Main Administration." Its historical record has many lacunae.

ARCHIVAL SOURCES

Gosudarstvennyi Arkhiv Permskoi Oblasti (GAPO), fond 164, Tiuremnaia inspektsiia.
Tsentral'nyi Gosudarstvennyi Arkhiv Oktiabr'skoi Revoliutsii (TsGAOR), fond 63, Ot-delenie po okhraneniiu obshchestvennoi bezopasnosti i poriadka v gorode Moskve.
TsGAOR, fond 102, Departament Politsii.
TsGAOR, fond 109, Osobennaia Kantseliariia Ministerstva Vnutrennykh Del.
TsGAOR, fond 122, Glavnoe Tiuremnoe Otdelenie.
Tsentral'nyi Gosudarstvennyi Istoricheskii Arkhiv (TsGIA), fond 908, P. A. Valuev, lichnyi arkhiv.
TsGIA, fond 1149, Departament Zakonov Gosudarstvennogo Soveta.
TsGIA, fond 1263, Komitet Ministrov.
TsGIA, fond 1282, Kantseliariia Ministerstva Vnutrennykh Del.
TsGIA, fond 1284, Departament Obshchikh Del, Ministerstvo Vnutrennykh Del.
TsGIA, fond 1286, Departament Politsii Ispolnitel'noi, Ministerstvo Vnutrennykh Del.
TsGIA, fond 1405, Ministerstvo Iustitsii.

PERIODICALS

American Historical Review.
Golos.
Iuridicheskii Vestnik.
Kolokol.
Russkaia Starina.
Russkoe bogatstvo.
Sbornik Imperatorskogo russkogo istoricheskogo obshchestva.
Sbornik pravovedeniia i obshchestvennykh znanii.
Sudebnyi Vestnik.
Tiuremnyi Vestnik.
Trudy iuridicheskago obshchestva pri Imperatorskom S-Peterburgskom Universitete.
Vestnik prava.
Zhurnal grazhdanskago i ugolovnago prava.
Zhurnal Ministerstva Iustitsii.

OFFICIAL PUBLICATIONS

Glavnoe tiuremnoe upravlenie. *Otchety.* 1884–1915.
———. *Sbornik tsirkuliarnykh rasporiazhenii i instruktsii po tiuremnoi chasti, 1859–1879.* St. Petersburg, 1880.

———. *Sbornik tsirkuliarov izdannykh po Glavnomu Tiuremnomu Upravleniiu v 1879–1910.* St. Petersburg, 1911.

Gosudarstvennaia Duma. *Stenograficheskie Otchety.* St. Petersburg: Gosudarstvennaia tipografiia, 1906–1916.

Gosudarstvennyi Sovet. *Stenograficheskii Otchet.* 13 vols. St. Petersburg: Gosudarstvennaia tipografiia, 1906–1917.

Kokovtsev, V. N., and S. V. Rukhlov, comps. *Sistematicheskii sbornik uzakonenii i rasporiazhenii po tiuremnoi chasti.* St. Petersburg, 1890.

Lopato, T. M., comp. *Zakony i pravitel'stvennyia rasporiazhenii po tiuremnoi chasti: Spravochnaia kniga dlia tiuremnykh inspektorov, tiuremnykh komitetov i ikh otdelenii, nachal'nikov tiurem.* Poltava, 1898.

Malinin, F. N. *Postanovleniia shesti mezhdunarodnykh tiuremnykh kongressov i sistematicheskii ukazatel' k nim.* St. Petersburg, 1904.

Materialy o preobrazovanii tiuremnoi chasti. St. Petersburg, 1878.

Materialy po voprosu o preobrazovanii tiuremnoi chasti v Rossii, izdannye Ministerstvom vnutrennykh del po svedeniiam dostavlennym ot Nachal'nikov Gubernii. St. Petersburg, 1865.

Ministerstvo iustitsii za sto let, 1802–1902: Istoricheskii ocherk. St. Petersburg, 1902.

Ministerstvo vnutrennykh del, 1802–1902: Istoricheskii ocherk. 3 vols. St. Petersburg, 1902.

Murav'ev, N. V., "Vsepoddanneishii doklad Ministra Iustitsii Stats-Sekretaria Murav'eva o deiatel'nosti Ministerstva Iustitsii za istekshee desiatiletie, 1894–1904." *Zhurnal Ministerstva Iustitsii* 2 (1904): 33–76.

———. "Vsepoddanneishii doklad Ministra Iustitsii Stats-Sekretaria N. V. Murav'eva ob obrazovanii osoboi Kommissii dlia razrabotki meropriiatii, vyzyvaemykh izdaniem novago ugolovnago ulozhenii." *Zhurnal Ministerstva Iustitsii* 6 (1903): 35–43.

Ob otmene telesnykh nakazanii. N.p., [1863].

Obshchaia Tiuremnaia Instruktsiia. Petrograd, 1916.

Obzor desiatiletnei deiatel'nosti Glavnago Tiuremnago Upravleniia, 1879-1889. St. Petersburg, 1890.

Polnoe Sobranie Zakonov Rossiiskoi Imperii.

Svod zakonov Rossiiskoi Imperii. 16 vols. St. Petersburg, 1892.

Svod zamechanii na proekt obshchei chasti ulozheniia o nakazaniiakh, obrabotannyi redaktsionnoi kommissiei. St. Petersburg, 1884.

Ulozhenie o nakazaniiakh ugolovnykh i ispravitel'nykh. St. Petersburg, 1845.

Ulozhenie o nakazaniiakh ugolovnykh i ispravitel'nykh. Petrograd, 1916.

Vysochaishe uchrezhdenaia Osobaia Komissiia dlia razrabotki meropriiatii, vyzyvaemykh izdaniem novago ugolovnago ulozheniia. *Tiuremnoe preobrazovanie.* Vol. 1, *Ispravitel'nyi dom, zakliuchenie v kreposti, i tiur'ma.* St. Petersburg, 1905.

Zakonoproekt ob uslovnom dosrochnom osvobozhdenii. St. Petersburg, 1909.

BOOKS, DISSERTATIONS, AND ARTICLES

Adams, Bruce F. [Adams, Brius]. "Istoriia russkikh tiurem tsarskogo rezhima v dokumentakh gosudarstvennogo arkhiva permskoi oblasti." In *Vystupleniia i tezisi dokladov nauchno-prakticheskoi konferentsii "Arkhivy vchera, segodnia, zavtra,"* 49–52. Perm: GAPO, 1994.

Adams, William Walter, Jr. "Capital Punishment and the Russian Revolution." Ph.D. diss., Columbia University, 1968.

Aiken, John. *A View of the Life, Travels, and Philanthropic Labors of the Late John Howard.* Philadelphia, 1794.

Allen, Robert V. "The Great Legislative Commission of Catherine II of 1767." Ph.D. diss., Yale University, 1950.

Andrews, Richard Mowery. *Law, Magistracy, and Crime in Old Regime Paris, 1735–1789.* Vol. 1, *The System of Criminal Justice.* Cambridge, England: Cambridge University Press, 1994.

"Arestantskiia raboty pri sooruzhenii Amurskoi zheleznoi dorogi v techenie 1910–1911g." *Tiuremnyi Vestnik* 4 (1912): 686–846.

"Arestantskii trud i ego primenenie po obstoiatel'stvam voennago vremeni." *Tiuremnyi Vestnik* 10 (1915): 1807–12.

Avrekh, A. Ia. *Tsarizm i tret'eiun'skaia sistema.* Moscow: Nauka, 1966.

Barnes, Harry Elmer. *The Evolution of Penology in Pennsylvania.* Indianapolis: Bobbs-Merrill, 1927.

Bater, James H. *The Soviet City: Ideal and Reality.* Beverly Hills, Calif.: Sage Publications, 1980.

Beccaria, Cesare. *On Crimes and Punishments.* Translated with an Introduction by Henry Paolucci. Indianapolis: Bobbs-Merrill, 1963.

Bentham, Jeremy. *The Rationale of Punishment.* London: Robert Howard, 1830.

Binshtok, V. L. "Materialy dlia istorii otmeny telesnykh nakazanii v Rossii." *Iuridicheskii Vestnik* 7, 8 (1892): 400–444.

———. "Materialy dlia istorii russkoi tiur'my." *Sbornik pravovedeniia i obshchestvennykh znanii* 3 (1894): 151–90.

Burtsev, V. *Bor'ba za svobodnuiu Rossiiu: Moi vospominaniia.* 2 vols. Berlin, 1923.

Chechulin, N. D., ed. *Nakaz Imperatritsy Ekateriny II.* St. Petersburg, 1907.

Chekhov, Anton. *The Island: A Journey to Sakhalin.* Translated by Luba Terpak and Michael Terpak. Introduction by Robert Payne. New York: Washington Square Press, 1967.

Chubinskii, M. P. "Sudebnaia reforma." In *Istoriia Rossii v xix veke,* vol. 3, 231–68. St. Petersburg, 1907–1912.

Cooper, David D. *The Lesson of the Scaffold: The Public Execution Controversy in Victorian England.* Athens: Ohio University Press, 1974.

Czap, Peter, Jr. "Peasant-Class Courts and Peasant Customary Justice in Russia, 1861–1912." *Journal of Social History* 2 (1967): 149–78.

Davis, David Brion. "The Movement to Abolish Capital Punishment in America, 1787–1861." *American Historical Review* 63 (October 1957): 23–46.

DeWindt, Harry. *From Pekin to Calais by Land.* London, 1889.

———. *Siberia as It Is.* London, 1892.

Dostoevsky, Fyodor. *The House of the Dead.* Translated by Constance Garnett. New York: Macmillan, 1931.

Dukes, Paul. *Catherine the Great and the Russian Nobility: A Study Based on the Materials of the Legislative Commission of 1767.* Cambridge, England: Cambridge University Press, 1967.

Dunn, Patrick P. "'That Enemy Is the Baby': Childhood in Imperial Russia." In *The History of Childhood: The Untold Story of Child Abuse,* edited by Lloyd De Mause, 383–405. New York: Peter Bedrick Books, 1988.

Dzhanshiev, G. A. *Epokha velikikh reform.* St. Petersburg, 1907.

Engelstein, Laura. *The Keys to Happiness: Sex and the Search for Modernity in Fin-de-Siècle Russia.* Ithaca, N.Y.: Cornell University Press, 1992.

Evreinov, N. *Istoriia telesnykh nakazanii v Rossii.* St. Petersburg, 1906. Reprint. New York: Chalidze Publications, 1979.

Fel'dshtein, G. S. *Glavniia techeniia v istorii nauki ugolovnago prava v Rossii.* Iaroslavl: Tipografiia gubernskago pravleniia, 1909.

Feoktistov, E. M. *Vospominaniia za kulisami politiki i literatury, 1848–1896.* Edited by Iu. G. Oksman. Leningrad, 1929.

Foinitskii, I. Ia. *Kurs ugolovnago prava.* St. Petersburg, 1890.

———. *K voprosu o ssylke v Sibir'.* Moscow, 1879.

———. *Na dosuge: sbornik iuridicheskikh statei i izsledovanii s 1870 goda.* 2 vols. St. Petersburg, 1898–1900.

———. *Ssylka ili tiur'ma?* Moscow, 1881.

———. *Uchenie o nakazanii v sviazi s tiur'movedeniem.* St. Petersburg, 1889.

Foucault, Michel. *Discipline and Punish: The Birth of the Prison.* Translated by Alan Sheridan. New York: Vintage Books, 1979.

Galkin, M. N. "Mesta zakliucheniia vo Frantsii." *Russkii Vestnik* 12 (1864): 487–542.

Gavrilov, S. T. "Russkie tiur'my po otchetam Glavnago Tiuremnago Upravleniia za 1903–1909 gody." *Iuridicheskii Vestnik* 2 (1913): 241–55.

Gay, Peter. *The Enlightenment, An Interpretation: The Rise of Modern Paganism.* New York: Alfred A. Knopf, 1975.

Gernet, M. N. *Istoriia tsarskoi tiur'my.* 5 vols. Moscow: Iuridicheskoe izdatel'stvo Narodnogo komissariata iustitsii, 1951–1956. Reprint. Moscow: Gosudarstvennoe izdatel'stvo iuridicheskoi literatury, 1961–1963.

———. *Obshchestvennyia prichiny prestupnosti: sotsialisticheskoe napravlenie v nauke ugolovnago prava.* Moscow: S. Skirmunt, 1906.

———. *Prestuplenie i bor'ba s nim v sviazi s evoliutsiei obshchestva.* Moscow, 1914.

Glenn, Myra. *Campaigns against Corporal Punishment: Prisoners, Sailors, Women, and Children in Antebellum America.* Albany: State University of New York Press, 1984.

Gogel', S. K. "Arestantskii trud." *Tiuremnyi Vestnik* 2 (1913): 297–333.

———. *Arestantskii trud v russkikh tiur'makh.* St. Petersburg, 1897.

———. *O zhelatel'nosti i vozmozhnosti vvedeniia v Rossii instituta uslovnago osuzhdeniia.* St. Petersburg: Tipografiia Pravuiushchago Senata, 1897.

———. *Voprosy ugolovnago prava, protsessa i tiur'movedenii.* St. Petersburg: Obshchestvennaia Pol'za, 1906.

Gol'denberg, I. *Reforma telesnykh nakazanii.* St. Petersburg, n.d.

Golovin, K. *Moi vospominaniia.* 2 vols. St. Petersburg: Kolokol, 1908–1910.

Grot, K. K. "Vsepoddanneishii doklad Stat's-Sekretaria Grota po uchastiiu ego v tiuremnom kongresse v Stokgol'me." In *Konstantin Karlovich Grot kak gosudarstvennyi i obshchestvennyi deiatel',* vol. 1, appendix, 55–62. Petrograd, 1915.

Grünhut, Max. *Penal Reform: A Comparative Study.* Oxford: Clarendon Press, 1948.

Gruzenberg, O. O. *Yesterday: Memoirs of a Russian-Jewish Lawyer.* Edited and with an Introduction by Don C. Rawson. Berkeley: University of California Press, 1981.

Gurko, V. I. *Features and Figures of the Past: Government and Opinion in the Reign of Nicholas II.* Stanford, Calif.: Stanford University Press, 1939.

Howard, Benjamin. *Prisoners of Russia: A Personal Study of Convict Life in Sakhalin and Siberia.* New York: D. Appleton and Company, 1902.

Ignatieff, Michael. *A Just Measure of Pain: The Penitentiary in the Industrial Revolution, 1750–1850.* New York: Pantheon Books, 1978.

Isaev, M. M. "Obzor deiatel'nosti tiuremnago vedomstva pri novykh zakonodatel'nykh uchrezhdeniiakh." *Trudy iuridicheskago obshchestva pri Imperatorskom S-Peterburgskom Universitete* 7 (1913): 41–58.

K. "Deiatel'nost' Konstantina Karlovicha Grota po tiuremnoi reforme." In *Konstantin Karlovich Grot kak gosudarstvennyi i obshchestvennyi deiatel',* vol. 1, 241–92. Petrograd, 1915.

Karamzin, N. M. *Istoriia gosudarstva rossisskago.* 12 vols. Moscow, 1816–1826.

Kennan, George. *Siberia and the Exile System.* 2 vols. New York: Century Company, 1891.

Khristianovich, A. "O merakh k razvitiiu patronata v Rossii (Tretii s"ezd russkikh kriminalistov)." *Tiuremnyi Vestnik* 4–5 (1902): 255–62

"Khronika-vnutrennee obozrenie." *Vestnik Evropy,* November 1872, 342.

Knill, Richard. *Memoir of the Life and Character of Walter Venning.* London, 1822.

Knutson, G. D. "Peter Valuev: A Conservative Approach and Reactions to the Reforms of Alexander II." Ph.D. diss., University of Kansas, 1970.

Kokovtsev, V. N. *Out of My Past: The Memoirs of Count Kokovtsev.* Edited by H. H. Fisher. Translated by Laura Matveev. Stanford, Calif.: Stanford University Press, 1935.

Koni, A. F. *Sobranie sochinenii.* 8 vols. Moscow: Iuridicheskaia literatura, 1966–1969.

Konstantin Karlovich Grot kak gosudarstvennyi i obshchestvennyi deiatel' (12 January 1815– 30 October 1897). 3 vols. Petrograd, 1915.

Koptev, D. A., ed. *Zakon ob uslovnom dosrochnom osvobozhdenii s izlozheniem razsuzhdenii, na koikh on osnovan.* St. Petersburg, 1909.

Korolenko, V. "Russkaia pytka." *Russkoe bogatstvo* 1 (1912): 127–46.

Krainskii, D. *Materialy k izsledovaniiu istorii russkikh tiurem v sviazi s istoriei uchrezhdeniia Obshchestva Popechitel'stva o Tiur'makh.* Chernigov, 1912.

"Kratkii ocherk tiuremnago ustroistva i meropriiatii v oblasti tiuremnago dela v Rossii za 1905–1910 gg." *Zhurnal Ministerstva Iustitsii* 7 (1910): 175–242.

Kropotkin, Peter. *In Russian and French Prisons.* Introduction by Paul Avrich. New York: Schocken Books, 1971.

Kucherov, S. *Courts, Lawyers and Trials under the Last Three Tsars.* New York: Frederick A. Praeger, 1953.

Langbein, John H. *Torture and the Law of Proof: Europe and England in the Ancien Régime.* Chicago: University of Chicago Press, 1977.

Leroy-Beaulieu, Anatole. *The Empire of the Tsars and the Russians.* Translated by Zinaide A. Ragozin. 3 vols. New York: G. P. Putnam's Sons, 1903.

Liublinskii. P. I. *Na smenu starago prava: Sbornik statei po voprosam tekushchei pravovoi zhizni.* Petrograd, 1915.

———. *Pamiati trekh russkikh kriminalistov: I. Ia. Foinitskago, D. A. Drilia, N. D. Sergeevskago.* St. Petersburg, 1914.

———. "Poniatie nakazaniia." *Iuridicheskii Vestnik* 3–4 (1914): 78–109.

———. "Uslovnoe osuzhdenie." *Zhurnal Ministerstva Iustitsii* 9 (1912):102–50; 10 (1912): 68–84.

Locke, John. *Of Civil Government: Two Treatises.* London: J. M. Dent and Sons, 1940.

Luchinskii, N. F. *Kratkii ocherk deiatel'nosti Glavnago Tiuremnago Upravlenii za perviia xxxv let ego sushchestvovaniia (1879–1914).* St. Petersburg: Tipo-litografiia S.Peterburgskoi odinochnoi tiur'my, 1914.

———. "Kurs prakticheskago tiur'movedeniia." *Tiuremnyi Vestnik* 12 (1912): appendix, 1–144.

———. "Ocherednye voprosy tiuremnoi zhizni." *Tiuremnyi Vestnik* 3 (1903): 259–72; 8 (1903): 636–54; 1 (1904): 50–70; 4 (1904): 280–87; 5 (1904): 355–78.

———. *Osnovy tiuremnago dela.* St. Petersburg, 1904.

———. "Reforma tiuremnago upravlenii." *Tiuremnyi Vestnik* 2 (1905): 137–46.

———. "Tiuremnyi patronat." *Tiuremnyi Vestnik* 1 (1913): 1648–80.

Maksimov, Sergei V. *Sibir' i katorga.* St. Petersburg, 1871.

Malinin, F. N. *Postanovleniia shesti mezhdunarodnykh tiuremnykh kongressov: Sistematicheskii ukazatel' k nim.* St. Petersburg, 1904.

———. "Tiuremnyi patronat (Po povodu razrabotki proekta normal'nago ustava obshchestv pokrovitel'stva litsam, osvobozhdennym iz mest zakliucheniia Rossiiskoi Imperii)." *Tiuremnyi Vestnik* 8 (1905): 578–630; 9 (1905): 783–823.

Margolis, A. D. "Sistema sibirskoi ssylki i zakon ot 12 iiunia 1900 goda." In *Ssylka i obshchestvenno-politicheskaia zhizn' v Sibiri, xviii–nachalo xx v.,* 126–40. Novosibirsk: Nauka, 1978.

"Materialy k istorii tiuremnoi reformy v Rossii: Pis'ma grafa V. A. Solloguba i K. K. Grota k M. N. Galkinu-Vraskomu." *Zhurnal Ministerstva Iustitsii* 9–10 (1901): 252–88.

A Memoir of Daniel Wheeler with an Account of His Gospel Labours in the Islands of the Pacific. Philadelphia, 1866.

Merry, Henry J. *Montesquieu's System of Natural Government.* West Lafayette, Ind.: Purdue University Studies, 1970.

Minenko, N. A. "O vliianii ssylki na semeinuiu zhizn' russkikh krest'ian Zapadnoi Sibiri v xviii–pervoi polovine xix veka." In *Ssylka i obshchestvenno-politicheskaia zhizn' v Sibiri (xviii–nachalo xx v.),* 282–93. Novosibirsk: Nauka, 1978.

Montesquieu (Charles-Louis de Secondat). *The Spirit of the Laws.* Edited with an Introduction, Notes, and Appendixes by David Wallace Carrithers. Berkeley: University of California Press, 1972.

Murav'ev, N. V. *Iz proshloi deiatel'nosti: stat'i po sudebnym voprosam.* 2 vols. St. Petersburg: M. M. Stasiulevich, 1900.

———. *Poslednie rechi, 1900–1902 gg.* St. Petersburg, 1903.

———. "Vsepoddanneishii doklad Ministra Iustitsii Stats-Sekretaria Murav'eva o deiatel'nosti Ministerstva Iustitsii za istekshee desiatiletie, 1894–1904." *Zhurnal Ministerstva Iustitsii* 2 (1904): 33–76.

O'Brien, Patricia. *The Promise of Punishment: Prisons in Nineteenth-Century France.* Princeton, N.J.: Princeton University Press, 1982.

Okunev, N. A. "Iz praktiki zakona ob uslovnom dosrochnom osvobozhdenii." *Trudy iuridicheskogo obshchestva pri Imperatorskom s-peterburgskom universitete* 3 (1910): 244–63.

Oldenburg, S. S. *Last Tsar: Nicholas II, His Reign and His Russia.* Translated by Leonid I. Mihalap and Patrick J. Rollins. Edited by Patrick J. Rollins. 4 vols. Gulf Breeze, Fla.: Academic International Press, 1975–1978.

Orlovsky, Daniel T. *Limits of Reform: The Ministry of Internal Affairs, 1802–1881.* Cambridge, Mass.: Harvard University Press, 1981.

Osherovich, B. S. *Ocherki po istorii russkoi ugolovno-pravovoi mysli (vtoraia polovina xviii veka–pervaia chetvert xix veka).* Moscow, 1946.

Ostroumov, S. S. *Ocherki po istorii ugolovnoi statistiki dorevoliutsionnoi Rossii.* Moscow, 1961.

———. *Prestupnost' i ee prichiny v dorevoliutsionnoi Rossii.* Moscow, 1960.

Peretts, E. A. *Dnevnik E. A. Perettsa, gosudarstvennogo sekretaria, 1880–1885.* Moscow, 1927.

Phillipson, Coleman. *Three Criminal Law Reformers: Beccaria, Bentham, Romilly.* Montclair, N.J.: Patterson Smith, 1970.

Piontkovskii, A. A. *Uslovnoe osvobozhdenie: Ugolovno-politicheskoe izsledovanie.* Kazan, 1900.

Raeff, Marc. *Origins of the Russian Intelligentsia: The Eighteenth-Century Nobility.* New York: Harcourt, Brace, Jovanovich, 1966.

———. "Pugachev's Rebellion." In *Preconditions of Revolution in Early Modern Europe*, edited by Robert Forster and Jack P. Greene, 161–202. Baltimore: Johns Hopkins University Press, 1970.

Reddaway, W. F., ed. *Documents of Catherine the Great.* Cambridge, England: Cambridge University Press, 1931.

Riasanovsky, Nicholas V. *A Parting of the Ways: Government and the Educated Public in Russia, 1801–1855.* Oxford: Clarendon Press, 1976.

Rogger, Hans. *Russia in the Age of Modernisation and Revolution, 1881–1917.* London: Longman, 1983.

Rollins, Patrick J. "Petr Nikolaevich Durnovo." In *Modern Encyclopedia of Russian and Soviet History,* vol. 10. Gulf Breeze, Fla.: Academic International Press, 1982.

Rothman, David J. *Conscience and Convenience: The Asylum and Its Alternatives in Progressive America.* Boston: Little, Brown, 1980.

———. *The Discovery of the Asylum: Social Order and Disorder in the New Republic.* Boston: Little, Brown, 1971.

"Rozgi doloi!" *Kolokol* 75 (1 July 1860): 1.

The Russian Primary Chronicle, Laurentian Text. Edited by Samuel Hazzard Cross and Olgerd P. Sherbowitz-Wetzor. Cambridge, Mass.: Mediaeval Academy of America, 1973.

S., M. [M. I. Semevskii]. *Petr Alekseevich Zubov, 1819–1880.* St. Petersburg, 1880.

Salomon, A. P. *Tiuremnoe delo v Rossii: Lektsiia.* St. Petersburg, 1898.

Senese, Donald. *S. M. Stepniak-Kravchinskii: The London Years.* Newtonville, Mass.: Oriental Research Partners, 1987.

Sergeevskii, N. D. *Russkoe ugolovnoe pravo.* St. Petersburg, 1900.

Soley, J. "British Russophobia during the Crimean War." In *War and Society in the Nineteenth Century Russian Empire,* edited by J. G. Purves and D. A. West, 106–21. Toronto: New Review Books, 1972.

Sollogub, V. A. *Ob organizatsii v russkoi tiur'me truda.* Moscow, 1866.

Spasovich, V. *Uchebnik ugolovnogo prava.* 2 vols. St. Petersburg, 1863.

Spierenburg, Pieter. *The Spectacle of Suffering: Executions and the Evolution of Repression: From a Preindustrial Metropolis to the European Experience.* Cambridge, England: Cambridge University Press, 1984.

Ssylka i Katorga v Sibiri (xviii–nachalo xx v.). Novosibirsk: Nauka, 1975.

Ssylka i obshchestvenno-politicheskaia zhizn' v Sibiri, xviii–nachalo xx v. Novosibirsk: Nauka, 1978.

Stupin, Mikhail. *Istoriia telesnykh nakazanii v Rossii ot sudebnikov do nastoiashchago vremeni.* Vladikavkaz, 1887.

Sutton, Richard C. "Crime and Social Change in Russia after the Great Reforms: Laws, Courts, and Criminals, 1874–1894." Ph.D. diss., Indiana University, 1984.

Tagantsev, N. S. *Russkoe ugolovnoe pravo.* 2 vols. St. Petersburg, 1902.

Tarnovskaia, P. N. *Zhenshchiny-ubiitsy.* St. Petersburg: Khudozhestvennaia pechat', 1902.

Tavrov, Janet. *The Russian Noble Family: Structure and Change.* New York: Garland Publishing, 1987.

Timofeev, A. G. *Istoriia telesnykh nakazanii v russkom prave.* St. Petersburg, 1904.

Tolstoy, Leo. *Resurrection.* Translated by Louise Maude. New York: Norton, 1966.

"Trud zakliuchennykh na nuzhdy armii." *Tiuremnyi Vestnik* 10 (1910): 1229–59.

Turner, James. *Reckoning with the Beast: Animals, Pain, and Humanity in the Victorian Mind.* Baltimore: Johns Hopkins University Press, 1980.

Tvardovskaia, V. A. *Ideologiia poreformennogo samoderzhaviia: M. N. Katkov i ego izdaniia.* Moscow: Nauka, 1978.

Valuev, P. A. *Dnevnik*. Edited by P. A. Zaionchkovskii. 2 vols. Moscow, 1961.

Verner, Andrew M. *The Crisis of Russian Autocracy: Nicholas II and the 1905 Revolution*. Princeton, N.J.: Princeton University Press, 1990.

Vitte, S. Iu. *Vospominaniia*. 3 vols. Moscow, 1960.

Von Bar, Carl Ludvig. *A History of Continental Criminal Law*. Translated by Thomas S. Bell. Boston: Little, Brown, 1916. Reprint. New York: Augustus M. Kelley, 1968.

Wachtel, Andrew Baruch. *The Battle for Childhood: Creation of a Russian Myth*. Stanford, Calif.: Stanford University Press, 1990.

Whelan, Heidi W. *Alexander III and the State Council: Bureaucracy and Counter Reform in Late Imperial Russia*. New Brunswick, N.J.: Rutgers University Press, 1982.

Whitney, Janet. *Elizabeth Fry: Quaker Heroine*. New York: Benjamin Blom, 1972.

Wines, E. C. *Report on the International Penitentiary Congress of London, Held July 3–13, 1872*. Washington, D.C.: Government Printing Office, 1873.

Wortman, Richard S. *The Development of a Russian Legal Consciousness*. Chicago: University of Chicago Press, 1976.

Yaney, George L. *The Systematization of Russian Government: Social Evolution in the Domestic Administration of Imperial Russia, 1711–1905*. Urbana: University of Illinois Press, 1973.

Zaionchkovskii, P. A. *Krizis samoderzhaviia na rubezhe 1870–1880-kh godov*. Moscow: Nauka, 1964.

———. *Rossiiskoe samoderzhavie v kontse deviatnadtsatogo stoletiia*. Moscow: Nauka, 1970.

Filaret, Metropolitan, 29, 43, 44
Foinitskii, I. Ia., 23, 65, 99, 127, 129, 172
Fon-der-Palen. *See* Palen, K. I.
Frish, E. V., 60, 70–72, 77–79, 91, 96, 97, 115; Frish Commission, 77–78
Frolenko, Mikhail, 4
Fry, Elizabeth, 41

Gaaz, F. P., 43, 44
Galkin-Vraskii, M. N., 8, 66, 67, 72, 121–23, 125–30, 132, 136, 144, 150–52, 155, 159–61, 165, 167, 168
Gegechkori, E. P., 179, 189
Gernet, M. N., 7–9
Gogel', S. K., 140–43, 184, 185
Golitsyn, A. N., 41–43
Golitsyn, D. V., 43
Golitsyn, N. D., 147
Golovin, K. F., 76
Goremykin, I. L., 156–58, 161
Govorukho-Otrok, M. Ia., 192
Gran', P. K., 149, 194
Grellet, Stephen, 41
Grot, K. K., 8, 97–99, 115–18, 120–22, 127–30, 144, 150, 155, 156, 164, 165, 171; Grot Commission, 97–120
Gurko, V. I., 157, 158

Herzen, Alexander, 4, 20, 22
Holy Synod, 29, 58, 157
Howard, John, 41

Ignat'ev, N. P., 130
Imperial Chancellery, 79; Second Department of, 25, 32, 54, 58, 60, 64, 70, 72, 77, 79, 91, 95, 99, 107; Third Department of, 25, 28, 31, 58, 59, 70, 76, 77, 89, 91, 95
Imperial Court, 20, 28, 41, 168
Isaev, M. M., 155
Iuferov, 73, 79
Ivan IV, 4

Kadets, 177, 180, 187, 188
Kakhanov, M. S., 127, 150, 152, 127
Kampengauzen, Baltazar, 43
Kaptsevich, P. M., 43
Karamzin, N. M., 23
Katkov, M. N., 157

Katorga. *See* Ladder of punishments
Kennan, George, 5–9
Kerenskii, A. F., 194, 195
Kholodkovskii, K. G., 54
Khrulev, S. S., 147
Kokovtsov, V. N., 8, 121, 122, 137, 144, 159, 160
Koni, A. F., 43, 156–58, 167, 180, 182
Korf, M. A., 32, 38, 39, 46, 48, 49
Kovrin-Milevskii, I. O., 181, 182, 193
Krainskii, Dmitrii, 44
Kravchinskii, Sergei, 4–6, 9
Kropotkin, Petr, 4, 5
Kuznetsov, G. S., 179

Ladder of punishments, 30, 67, 68, 71, 72, 77, 78, 91, 97–99, 102–9, 112, 115, 122, 132, 134, 137 (*see also* Prisons); arrest (brief incarceration) 24, 31, 37, 105, 107–9, 114, 122; capital punishment, 4, 6, 14, 15, 17, 22, 30, 34, 36, 101–3, 130, 182; correctional arrest companies, 10, 39, 55, 59, 104; correctional arrest units, 71, 103–6, 109–10, 112, 123, 124, 126, 134, 139, 142, 143, 151, 153; exile, 3–7, 9, 26, 27, 29, 30, 33, 43, 49–51, 68, 71–73, 77, 91, 92, 95, 99–104, 106, 109, 110, 112, 122–23, 129, 135, 136, 142–43, 154, 161, 162, 171, 174; fines, 9, 13, 18, 25–27, 31, 37, 38, 105, 107, 108, 114, 154, 169, 189, 191, 192, 193; houses of correction, 4, 10, 65, 74, 90, 92–94, 95, 104–14, 116, 122, 125, 175, 178; penal servitute (*katorga*), 26, 43, 50, 51, 68, 72–73, 76, 77, 90, 92, 93, 99–103, 106, 109–10, 112, 122, 123, 129, 136, 174–75, 179; reprimands, 105, 107, 191; strait houses 10, 39, 46, 55, 67, 71, 75, 77, 90, 92, 94–97, 105–7, 109, 112, 122; workhouses, 10, 39, 46, 55, 71, 77, 96, 97, 104, 105, 107, 112, 122, 144, 147, 197
Leg irons, 43
Leroy-Beaulieu, Anatole, 12
Liublinskii, P. I., 171
Liuts, L. G., 178

www.ingramcontent.com/pod-product-compliance
Lightning Source LLC
Chambersburg PA
CBHW030406270326
41926CB00009B/1295